Hidden in Plain Sight
Protestants and the Apocrypha

Hidden in Plain Sight
Protestants and the Apocrypha

1ˢᵗ Edition

Kristofer Carlson

Dormition Publishing
Norfolk, Virginia

Copyright

Dormition Press, Norfolk, Virginia 23503
Copyright © 2016 by Dormition Press
All rights reserved. You may not use or reproduce this book in any manner except as defined by the Fair Use provision of U.S. copyright law, without written permission from Dormition Press: whymarymatters@gmail.com.

ISBN-13: 978-0692747919
ISBN-10: 0692747915

Scripture quotations, unless otherwise noted, are from the Authorized King James Version.

Cover Art: Peacock in the Woods
Thayer, Thayer, and Handerson, 1907. Concealing-coloration in the animal kingdom; an exposition of the laws of disguise through color and pattern: being a summary of Abbott H. Thayer's discoveries. New York: The Macmillan Co. (Plate 1, Frontispiece)
Public Domain

Dedication

This book is dedicated to Archpriest Michael Koblosh, under whose tutelage I entered the Orthodox Church.

Epigraph

Conclusions are ambiguous without the argument which leads to them.

Eric Osborn[1]

---

[1] (Osborn 1997, 6)

Table of Contents

Copyright	ii
Dedication	iii
Epigraph	iv
Tables	vii
Figures	vii
Prologue	viii
INTRODUCTION	VIII
CONSPECTUS	X
Part I: The Development of the Canon	**1**
1: WHICH BIBLE? WHICH CANON?	2
2: THE JUDAIC OLD TESTAMENT CANON	9
3: CANON AND CANONICITY	23
4: SEPTUAGINT HISTORY & PURPOSE	37
5: THE EVOLUTIONARY HISTORY OF THE HEBREW TEXT	44
6: TRANSLATION STYLES AND THE AUTHORITATIVE TEXT	50
7: THE SEPTUAGINT & ITS MANUSCRIPTS	54
8: FLAVIUS JOSEPHUS AND THE CANON	59
9: THE CHRISTIAN OLD TESTAMENT	64
10: PEOPLE OF THE BOOK	71
11: LITERACY AND THE CANON	75
12: SCRIBAL CULTURE	82
13: THE CURIOUS CASE OF JEREMIAH	92
14: THE DEVELOPMENT OF THE NT CANON	96
Part II: Inspiration and Authentication	**107**
15: THE SELF-AUTHENTICATING SCRIPTURES	108
16: THE COMMUNITY-CANON APPROACH	119
17: OBJECTIONS TO THE COMMUNITY-CANON APPROACH	127
18: CANONICITY AND THE GREAT APOSTASY	135
19: CANONICAL STANDARDS AND THE NEW TESTAMENT	137
20: THE NT USE OF THE OT SCRIPTURES	141
21: THE INTRINSIC-CANON APPROACH	145
22: OBJECTIONS TO THE INTRINSIC-CANON APPROACH	147

23: THE VERBAL ICON AND THE HOLY SPIRIT	152
24: THE NEW TESTAMENT WITNESS	170
25: JOHN CALVIN, THE CHURCH, AND THE CANON	172
26: CANONICITY AND THE HOLY SPIRIT	176

Part III: Inspiration and Inerrancy   179

27: THE RECENT INVENTION OF VERBAL INERRANCY	180
28: INERRANCY: A PROTESTANT SHIBBOLETH	185
29: ON THE SEEMING ERRANCY OF SACRED SCRIPTURE	193
30: INERRANCY AND THE AUTOGRAPHS	195
31: INERRANCY AND THE NATURE OF GOD	201
32: INERRANCY AND THE HEBREW AUTOGRAPH OF MATTHEW	205
33: INERRANCY AND THE LOSS OF FAITH	210
34: INERRANCY VS. INFALLIBILITY	212
35: INSPIRATION, DOCTRINE, TEXT	214
36: INERRANCY AND LUTHERAN ORTHODOXY	220
37: ON THE DOCTRINE OF INSPIRATION	228

Part IV: Inerrancy, Canonicity, and the Dead Sea Scrolls   231

38: THE NEED FOR THE DEAD SEA SCROLLS	232
39: VOWEL POINTS AND TEXTUAL INTERPRETATION	238
40: TEXTUAL ALTERATIONS	247
41: CANONICAL DIFFERENCES	250
42: THEOLOGY AND THE APOCRYPHA	258

Part V: References to the Apocrypha in the Scriptures   263

43: THE NEW TESTAMENT WITNESS	264
44: CITATIONS	266
45: QUOTATIONS	268
46: ALLUSIONS	297
47: DOCTRINAL SOURCES AND EXPLANATIONS	347

Conclusion	371
Appendix A: Arguments Against the Apocrypha	373
1: JOHANN GERHARD AND THE APOCRYPHA	374
2: MERRILL UNGER AND THE APOCRYPHA	396

Appendix B: Second Temple Writings and the Bible	403
1: The Apocrypha and Other Second Temple Writings	404
2: The Apocalypse and Second Temple Judaism	411
3: The Place of Enoch within Judaism	414
4: Enoch and the Book of Revelation	426
5: The Place of Enoch in the New Testament	429
6: Enoch and the Ancient Church	447
7: Jubilees	452
8: Melchizedek	456
9: Eschatological & Messianic Titles	460
10: Second Temple Writings and the Canon	476
Glossary	478
Bibliography	Error! Bookmark not defined.
Index	516

Tables

Table 1: The American KJV and the Septuagint 40
Table 2 Chiastic Structure of 1 Esdras 48
Table 3: Jeremiah in the LXX and MT Versions 93
Table 4: Books Referenced in the Old Testament 149
Table 5: The Number of the Beast 397
Table 6: Literary Types 400
Table 7: 1 Enoch and the Gospels 430
Table 8: 1 Enoch and the Apostolic Writings 435

Figures

Figure 1 The Prophetic Cycle 160

Prologue

Introduction

For much of my life, I accepted a Bible consisted of 66 books; while growing up, I concerned myself mainly with the 27 books of the New Testament.[2] Eventually, I began reading the Bible from cover to cover when someone asked me: "How could I know I believed the Bible if I had not read it?" However, although I found the Old Testament fascinating, it remained something of a mystery to me. The Old Testament is a collection of unusual stories, strange customs, and dark sayings. After a brief flirtation with Eastern Orthodoxy, I became Lutheran. I continued to use the same Bible throughout, as well as the same arguments about canon, authority, and inspiration.

While serving on the staff of a Lutheran seminary, I took on some special projects requiring research into ancient Christian sources. These readings led me to an appreciation of the church fathers, provided a deeper understanding of the faith, and eventually led to my questioning the Protestant canon of scripture. Among other things, I discovered the early church nearly always used the Septuagint (LXX), which explains why the NT quotations often do not match their OT counterparts.[3]

English language translations usually use the Masoretic Hebrew text instead of the Greek Septuagint. The Septuagint, the early Greek translation of the Old Testament, contains more books than do the Hebrew Scriptures. Protestants call these extra books the Apocrypha while Roman Catholics call these the Deuterocanonical books. As we shall see, the

---

[2] The neglect of the Old Testament is a manifestation of pseudo-Marcionite theology, with its *de facto* separation of the God who created from the God who redeems. (Palphrey 2013, Kindle Locations 4530-4531)

[3] Curiously, the difference between the New Testament quotations with the Old Testament originals is rarely an issue when discussing verbal inerrancy.

apostles and church fathers used the Septuagint (and the Apocrypha) as scripture.

Were the apostles wrong to use the larger canon? Were the church fathers wrong? Did the reformers know something the church fathers did not? Did the reformers change the canon, or recover an earlier canon? What criteria did the reformers use, and what was the basis for their authority? Questions like these led me to examine the standards used to decide the canon of scripture — what theologians call "canonicity."

I gradually realized Protestants were using a truncated canon, and that Protestant's treatment of the Apocrypha changed over the years. [4] The early reformers believed the Apocrypha to be useful reading, but not inspired. Modern Protestants don't read the Apocrypha, do not include the Apocrypha in their bibles, nor do they use the Apocrypha as background material for interpreting the New Testament. I intend to show the Apocrypha deserve to be part of the scriptural canon or, at a minimum, they could be "recognized as having a case for inspiration."[5] I intend to show the arguments for rejecting these books are ill-conceived and misleading.

Martin Luther decided the Apocrypha were not scripture mainly because they did not support his doctrinal positions. His secondary argument was that Hebrew was a sacred language, so anything not originally written in Hebrew must not be inspired.[6] While translating the Sacred Scriptures into German, Luther separated the Hebrew Scriptures from the Apocrypha and placed them into a separate section between the Old and New Testaments. This decision by Martin Luther became the standard manner of printing Protestant Bible

---

[4] If using a truncated canon, does the Gospel suffer? Yes and no. No sensible person would say that a person cannot be "saved" using only the Protestant canon. The issue is more about the fullness of the faith, not the faith itself.

[5] (Freeman, Has Your Bible Become a Quran? 2014)

[6] A misguided assertion, as demonstrated by the Dead Sea Scrolls.

translations. Eventually, American publishers removed the Apocrypha altogether.

In essence, one man decided for all Protestants that the Apocrypha were not scripture. You must decide if this one man was correct. You will have to step outside your comfort zone, read things you might normally avoid, and take the arguments of your theological opponents seriously (which means. In the words of Samuel Taylor Coleridge, this requires a "willing suspension of disbelief," something that doesn't come naturally to we fallen creatures.

The evidence and argumentation contained in this book are no match for the still, small voice of the Holy Spirit — and may be a distraction. If this book should cause you to question your faith, stop reading it. Do not let your intellect distract you from a life of prayer, for God is beyond all understanding and cannot be contained by the human mind.

> Oh Lord, forgive me my presumption.
> Teach me to pray.
> And, yourself, pray in me.
> Amen.

Conspectus

In the Christian East, a theologian is one who prays truly, and one who prays truly is a theologian. Or, as St. Silouan the Athonite says: "If you are a theologian, your prayer is pure. If your prayer is pure, you are a theologian."[7] Vladimir Lossky explains it this way: "Theology is an expression, for the profit of all, of that which can be experienced by everyone."[8] Elder Sophrony describes theology as: "[Being] replete with knowledge of the mystery of God and of the ways of God. ...Theology is therefore a gift of the Holy Spirit. It is a

---

[7] (Archimandrite Sophrony 1991, 138)

[8] (Lossky 1958, 9)

spiritual condition."⁹ In the Christian East, theology is dogmatic and experiential, intellectual and practical.

In the Christian West, however, theology is an academic pursuit, and a theologian is a scholar, whether by profession or by avocation. Theology is the domain of preachers and professors who analyze, systematize, and categorize the subject. I am the product of the Western tradition, and I am most comfortable in that environment. My academic training reinforced my natural tendencies. This book does theology in a western manner; may God forgive me.

Cognitive scientist George Lakoff says our physical, neural circuitry constrains our conscious thoughts. He writes:

Our fixed worldviews are made up of complex ideas carried out by relatively fixed neural circuitry. Our worldviews determine how we think the world operates, as well as how we think it should operate. ...Here is the crucial fact about worldview differences: **We can only understand what our brain circuitry allows us to understand.** *If facts don't fit the worldviews in our brains, the facts may not even be noticed — or they may be puzzling, or ignored, or rejected outright, or if threatening, attacked. [Emphasis in the original.]* ¹⁰

Much of this book is concerned with laying down a cognitive framework within which to discuss the arguments concerning canonicity. Without a grasp of that framework, the rationale for the Apocrypha will be confusing at best. I begin with a systematic description of the "concepts, assumptions, expectations, beliefs, and theories"¹¹ used by those who either support or dismiss the Apocrypha. The same material may be repeated in multiple places and different contexts. Like a person who cannot discern the phonemes in a foreign language, you may not notice the

---

⁹ (Archimandrite Zacharias Zacharou 2015, 73)

¹⁰ (Lakoff 2016)

¹¹ (Maxwell 2013, 39)

argument the first time you read it. Subsequent readings may be ignored, may puzzle you, or may make you angry. If you push through, you may eventually realize why others believe differently, whether you agree with them or not.

Part I of this book provides information on the development of the Canon of Scripture. Part II covers Inspiration and Authentication, or how we know a text is inspired. Part III provides some background on Inspiration and Inerrancy. Part IV provides some background on Scriptural Inerrancy, the nature of Canonicity, and the Dead Sea Scrolls. In Part V we provide the New Testament witness to the Apocrypha in the form of Citations, Quotations, and Allusions. Appendix A covers some Protestant arguments against the inspiration of the Apocrypha. Finally, Appendix B discusses the influences other Second Temple writings had upon the New Testament and explain the reason why the Apocrypha have a claim to inspiration while other Second Temple writings do not.

As to format, I have striven to use the Chicago Manual of Style. However, I do not alter quoted material to make it conformant. I also do not enforce modern spelling, punctuation, and grammar upon material that has been translated, or material from another country or era. I prefer to use "ibid" to refer back to the previous source, but not to use 'op. cit' to refer back to a previously sourced work, a practice I find distracting.

Part I: The Development of the Canon

1: Which Bible? Which Canon?

Protestant say the Bible contains 66 books: the 39 books of the Old Testament (OT) and the 27 books of the New Testament (NT). They might even be able to name them. Roman Catholics say the Sacred Scripture consisted of 77 books while the Eastern Orthodox say there are 81. The Ethiopian Orthodox Church has an even larger canon. There are other groups, like the Syriac and the Coptic churches which have different canonical criteria.[12] Rev. Dr. Wil Gafney writes:

The Protestant Bible is the shortest and newest of Christian bibles and used by the fewest number of Christians around the world, yet its adherents — particularly in the American context – are the loudest. Catholic, Orthodox, Anglican and Episcopal bibles like the original 1611 King James Version of the bible, Martin Luther's revolutionary translation and the earliest manuscript with both testaments, Codex Sinaticus [sic], have 72 to 80 books or more and are read by the vast majority of Christians on the planet, more than a billion and a half people. There is perhaps the most diversity among the Orthodox with Ethiopian Orthodox including Jubilees and the Books of Enoch and some Slav churches including all four Esdrases.[13]

The books which Protestants do not accept they call the Apocrypha. F.F. Bruce uses the term Apocrypha to mean 'spurious works';[14] however, the etymology of the term suggests it means 'hidden books.' Robert Henry Charles writes concerning the development of the term Apocrypha.

How the term 'Apocryphal Books' (ἀπόκρυφα βιβλία) arose has not yet been determined. It did not, as Zahn (Gesch, des Neutestamentlichen Kanons I. i. 123 sq.), Schurer, Porter, N.

---

[12] (Halnon n.d.)

[13] (Gafney 2013)

[14] (Bruce, The Canon of Scripture 2010, 77)

Schmidt, and others maintain, originate in the Late Hebrew phrase, ספרים נסתרים, 'hidden books.' But Talmudic literature knows nothing of such a class. The Hebrew word ganas (גנז) does not mean to hide', but 'to store away' things in themselves precious. Indeed, so far is it from being a technical term in reference to non-Canonical writings, that it is most frequently used in reference to the Canonical Scriptures themselves. When writings were wholly without the pale of the Sacred books—such as those of the heretics or Samaritans—they were usually designated hisonim, i.e. ' outside.'[15]

The ancients did not use the term 'Apocryphal' in the way we use it today; indeed, Apocryphal never referred to what Protestants today call the Apocrypha. There were books in the Hebrew Scriptures (such as the Song of Solomon) which were considered to have hidden meanings; these books come closer to the idea contained in the ancient term 'Apocryphal.'

As far as the canon goes, the group Islamic Awareness provides an interesting look into the canonical problem. They list eight different canons of Christian scripture: the Anglican Church, the Armenian Church, the Coptic Church, the Ethiopian (Abyssinian) Church, the Greek Orthodox Church, the Protestant Church, the Roman Catholic Church, and the Syriac Church.[16] How curious that it takes the Muslims to tell us the canon of Christian Scriptures is not as settled as we like to think.

We often think of the Bible as a fixed collection of books. However, canonical history is complicated. In our discussions of inspiration and the canon of scripture, we forget about the human factor. The Scriptures did not just fall from the sky in finished form; instead, the writings and collections were a human effort. Karl Barth reminds us of

---

[15] (Charles, The Apocrypha and Pseudepigrapha of the Old Testament in English Vol 1 1913, vii)

[16] (Islamic Awareness n.d.) They neglected the canon of the Orthodox Tewahedo Church, which is perhaps the largest of all the canonical collections.

this when he speaks of "the two humanly composed and selected collections which we call the Bible."[17] Christians rightly credit inspiration to the Holy Spirit, but sometimes forget holy men of God mediated this inspiration. (2Pe 1:21) Just as with inspiration of individual books, so too with the canon as a whole; the Holy Spirit works through human beings. Like all human endeavors, the canon of Scripture is messy.

Some people credit Emperor Constantine with the creation of the Bible as we know it, but this is historically inaccurate.[18] The church fathers were less interested in defining what was in the canon as what was most definitely outside the canon. In Jesus day, the Old Testament canon was not well-defined. Hershel Shanks, writing for the Biblical Archaeology Society, writes of the canonical status of Jesus' day: "At this point in history there was no fixed canon, no authoritative list of sacred books."[19] Karlfried Froehlich writes:

At the time of Jesus, therefore, the later Pharisaic canon was by no means standard. If one considers that for the Sadducees scriptural authority rested in the five books of Moses only, while the canon of the Qumran sect or the Septuagint (the Greek Bible) included additional books often apocalyptic in nature, the Pharisaic canon appears as a compromise endorsing as normative neither a minimum nor a maximum of the available literature in use among Jews. It does reveal a bias against the newer apocalyptic and pseudepigraphic[20]

---

[17] (Barth, Church Dogmatics I.2 2004, 468)

[18] This position is expressed in Dan Brown's "The Da Vinci Code", for example.

[19] (Shanks 2007, 19)

[20] Pseudepigrapha are falsely-attributed works. The attribution may be intentionally misleading, or may mean the work is following in the tradition of an earlier authority.

literature and its use in sectarian circles, perhaps including the Christians.[21]

Canonically speaking, the most conservative group within Judaism was the Samaritan sect who, it is often stated, considered only the five books of Moses to be Scripture. Some scholars (like Karlfried Froehlich) think the Sadducees only accepted the Pentateuch as Scripture, which would explain why Jesus answered the Sadducees' question on resurrection using the Pentateuch. (Matt 22:23-32) Most modern scholars think the Sadducees and Pharisees used roughly the same authoritative writings, although they by no means considered them all to be Scripture.[22] The Pharisees considered the Law, the Prophets, and other writings[23] as Scripture; then also added oral traditions and interpretations as authoritative.

According to the popular view (based on the supposed association of the Dead Sea Scrolls with the Essenes), the Essenes had an even larger group of inspired and authoritative texts. The Dead Sea Scrolls include different versions of the same text, implying the text of certain Old Testament books were not yet standardized.[24] The Septuagint

---

[21] (Froehlich 1984, Kindle Locations 67-70)

[22] (McDonald 2007, 139-141) There is a difference between writings considered authoritative and writings considered to be scripture. For example, most Lutherans consider the Book of Concord to be an authoritative interpretation of Scripture, but not itself a Scripture.

[23] The phrase 'other writings' refers to an amorphous group. The three-fold division of the Hebrew scriptures was created by later Rabbinic Judaism in response to the fall of Jerusalem and the rise of Christianity. It is only by reading this later development into earlier history that some find evidence for a closed canon.

[24] (Shanks 2007, 19) The association of Qumran with the Essenes is based on archeological digs by a Dominican monk named Roland de Vaux, as interpreted through the translation (by a Polish scholar named Jozef Milik) of a scroll called "The Rule of the Community". Roland de Vaux's views were widely accepted in the academic community in the 1970s and fired the popular imagination. More

was the Greek translation of the Hebrew Scriptures used by the Jewish diaspora,[25] the contents of which had not yet been settled by the Jews. The Septuagint contains additional historical and wisdom literature as well as alternate versions of some other books. Some synagogues even used the Septuagint in Jerusalem.[26]

The typical Protestant understanding of the Old Testament canon assumes a closed catalog of books was established well before Jesus' day. F. F. Bruce provides a succinct description of the Protestant view in his book, *The Canon of Scripture* when he writes about the Scriptures used by both Jews and Christians in the time of Christ.

Our Lord and his apostles might differ from the religious leaders of Israel about the meaning of the Scriptures; there is no suggestion that they differed about the limits of the Scriptures. 'The Scriptures' on whose meaning they differed were not an amorphous collection: when they spoke of 'the Scriptures' they knew which writings they had in mind and could distinguish them from other writings which were not included in 'the Scriptures.'[27]

---

recent archeology has cast doubt upon the identification of the Qumran community with the Essenes, and suggests that the texts hidden away in the caves of Qumran were deposited by the Jews of Jerusalem in anticipation of the Roman's capture of Jerusalem. This view is bolstered by the inclusion of a copper scroll comprising a list of possible second temple treasures hidden away in anticipation of the Roman advance. (Lawler 2010) However, Dennis Mizzi shows that this view, popularized by Norman Golb, has its own problems — chiefly that there are plenty of caves in the vicinity of Jerusalem, such that no one would have had to make the journey to Qumran to hide their libraries. (Mizzi 2017, pp. 23-25)

[25] The Jewish Diaspora consists of the Jews spread throughout the Greco-Roman world and beyond.

[26] (Lawler 2010)

[27] (Bruce, The Canon of Scripture 2010, 28-29)

I am using F. F. Bruce as a foil — as someone whose views are emblematic of and stand in for an entire movement. Many think of F. F. Bruce as one of the shapers of the modern Evangelical movement, and his writings on the Canon are still source material for today's Evangelical scholars.[28]

F. F. Bruce argues the Canon of the Old Testament was closed before Jesus' day. He supports his premise with specious arguments from Scripture. His arguments are not consistent with the historical evidence, which suggests the canon of the Hebrew Scriptures took shape around 300 years after the destruction of Jerusalem in 70 A.D. Bruce also fails to mention how the Apocrypha heavily influenced the New Testament documents.

As we shall see, the Apocrypha are consistent with the New Testament. Sometimes the authors of the New Testament quote the Apocrypha, paraphrase it, or simply condense the Apocryphal material. In still more cases the authors merely alluded to the Apocrypha, assuming their reader would be familiar with the source material.[29] And finally, as we shall see, the New Testament fulfills prophecies found in the Apocrypha.

None of this necessarily means the Apocrypha are scripture. Different groups of Christians hold different views regarding the authority and value of the Apocrypha. For some the Apocrypha are of no value and should not be read; for others, the Apocrypha are worth reading, but not authoritative; a few claim the Apocrypha to be authoritative, yet not on the same level as Sacred Scripture. The arguments for why the Apocrypha are not part of Sacred Scripture are weak. I hope you, dear reader, will appreciate the value of

---

[28] (Grass 2012, 39)

[29] Jesus often used a single comment as a means of bringing an entire passage to his hearer's minds. For example, while on the cross, Jesus cried out: "My God, my God, why hast thou forsaken me?" His hearers should have been aware he was quoting the first phrase from Psalm 22, and eventually some understood the entire Psalm was a depiction of what they had seen taking place on the cross.

the Apocrypha to the authors of the New Testament. I also hope you will find the Apocrypha of value to you as well, even if you do not accept them as scripture.

2: The Judaic Old Testament Canon

The idea of the canon as a list of authoritative books would have been strange to Jews of the Second Temple period. For them, the Temple was the center of their religion. Lester L. Grabbe, Emeritus Professor of Hebrew Bible and Early Judaism at the University of Hull, England, writes:

It is natural that people often assume that Judaism in the Second Temple period was more or less like contemporary Judaism, in which people meet weekly or even more frequently in synagogues to pray, worship, and hear the Bible read. The written scripture and its reading and study are assumed to be the focus of Judaism at all times. …Yet the Judaism of pre-70 times was formally structured in a quite different way from the Judaism of later times. The main religious institution was the Jerusalem temple, and temple worship went back many centuries in Jewish and Israelite history. …The main activity in the temple was blood sacrifice.[30]

Lester L. Grabbe goes on to discuss the issue of the supposed canon during Second Temple Judaism.

When and how the present canon became finalized is still not known, despite a number of studies on the subject. Some Jewish groups seem to have accepted a different set of books as authoritative compared to other groups.[31]

Jaroslav Pelikan agrees with Grabbe, and writes:

Not only is the use of the word canon as a designation for an authoritative list of sacred books a rather late phenomenon within the history of the Jewish community, but even the idea of a fixed and final list came about only after a long evolution.[32]

---

[30] (Grabbe 2010, Kindle Locations 536-538; 540-541)

[31] (Ibid, Kindle Locations 561-562)

[32] (Pelikan 2005, 39)

Julio Trebolle Barrera notes the idea of a canon was foreign to the Jewish mind. He notes the word canon is a term connected to "New Testament studies," and Jews did not use it until "the 4th cent. CE." He writes:

To apply the term «canon» to the Hebrew Bible, therefore, is quite unsuitable. Hebrew has no term which corresponds to Greek «canon.» Rabbinic discussions concerning the canonical or apocryphal character of certain biblical books such as Song of Songs and Qoheleth, turn on the expression «defiles the hands.» The supposition is that books of which it is said that «they defile the hands» were considered as canonical, whereas books to which this expression was not applied were excluded from the biblical canon. However, the expression «defile the hands» may have no more significance than to refer to ritual purification to be performed after having used such books and before starting any other secular activity.[33]

Saying Hebrew has no term corresponding to the Greek word 'canon' is not precisely true. The Greek word 'canon' is itself a loan word from the Semitic languages. In Hebrew, the word is קָנֶה (*qaneh*) meaning 'tube' or 'reed'. The Hebrew word *qaneh is* related to the Assyrian word *qanu* and the Arabic word *qanah*, meaning 'hollow stick' or 'reed'. From Greek philosophy came the idea of canon in the sense of a rule or measuring stick, an idea expanded upon by the ancient church to mean the rule of faith, which rule measured truth from error.

The concept of canon as the rule of faith is a Christian idea that developed rather late. The Jews eventually adopted the idea of a canon as the rule of faith and applied it to the Hebrew Scriptures, but such an idea was unknown in Jesus' day. There were different Jewish groups with competing ideas as to the extent of their Scriptures. More importantly, the concept of a canon was a gentile concept; as such it is unreasonable to think the term would have been used in

---

[33] (Barrera 1998, 148)

Second Temple Judaism to limit their Scriptures to a specific set of books.

The Swiss Protestant theologian Robert Hanhart, writing in the introduction to Martin Hengel's "The Septuagint as Christian Scripture," says the introduction to Sirach (aka Ecclesiasticus) "assumes the three divisions transmitted by the Masoretes." Hanhart draws a distinction between the material described by these divisions and that of his translation of his grandfather's commentary on Scripture.[34] He, therefore, concludes Second Temple Judaism distinguished between canon and Apocrypha. By stating this, Robert Hanhart is reading the medieval Masoretic traditions back into the Second Temple period, two periods separated by nearly a millennium. Lutheran professor and theologian Emil Schürer differs with Robert Hanhart: "The most ancient testimony to the collocation of both collections with the Thorah [sic] is the prologue to the Book of Wisdom. ...We cannot, however, determine from it that the third collection was then already concluded."[35]

The disagreement between Robert Hanhart and Emil Schürer illustrates the manner in which scholars disagree regarding the boundaries of the Old Testament canon in the second temple period and reflects the wide range of perspectives among Jews of the second temple period. The Baptist Professor Jeff S. Anderson writes about the diversity existing within Second Temple Judaism.

What flourished in the Second Temple Period was not a single, fixed, "normative" Judaism, but a developing, evolving religion... No straight evolutionary line of the Jewish faith emerges. Consequently, it is preferable to speak of multiple Judaisms rather than a monolithic ideology that views one brand of Judaism as orthodox and the rest as "sects." All

---

[34] (Hengel, The Septuagint as Christian Scripture 2002, 2-3)

[35] (Schürer, A History of the Jewish People, Second Division, Volume 1 1890, 308)

Judaisms, consequently, competed for an audience and for the authority that accompanies broad-based acceptance.[36]

Epiphanius of Salamis (c. 310–320 – 403 CE) describes twelve specific sects of the Jews: the Samaritans, the Essenes, the Sebuaeans, the Gorothenes, the Dositheans, the Sadducees, the Scribes, the Pharisees, the Hemerobaptists, the Nasaraeans, the Ossaeans, and the Herodians.[37] The Jerusalem Talmud (c. 200 – 400 CE) quotes Rabbi Johanan as saying there were twenty-four heretical sects of Judaism in the time of Ezekiel.[38] With different Judaisms competing for acceptance, it is no wonder there was no consensus on the limits of the Hebrew Scriptures.[39] The Protestant scholar of Second Temple Judaism, Martin Hengel, writes:

We cannot prove the existence of a genuine Jewish, pre-Christian collection of canonical value, unambiguously and clearly delimited, distinguishable through its greater scope from the canon of the Hebrew Bible in the realm of the historical books and wisdom writings and written in Greek. Nor, especially, can it be shown that such a 'canon' was already formed in pre-Christian Alexandria. One can only proceed from the fact that the five books of Moses' Torah, the so-called Pentateuch, were translated into Greek under Ptolemy II Philadelphus (282-246), at the latest toward the middle of the third century [BC].[40]

---

[36] (Anderson 2002, 5-6)

[37] (Epiphanius of Salamis 2012, Book 1, Section 1, Parts 9-20)

[38] (Bowker 1973, 161) The Jerusalem Talmud was written well into the Christian era, in a period after many of the competing Judaisms had died out. Thus, the reference to them as 'heretical sects.'

[39] The scholar April D. DeConick writes: "Judaism and Christianity are companion expressions of Second Temple Judaism, sibling religions that developed simultaneously within comparable historical contexts." (DeConick 2006, 3)

[40] (Hengel, The Septuagint as Christian Scripture 2002, 19)

The picture of Second Temple Judaism is much more complex than is commonly thought. There was the temple cult centered in Jerusalem, and there was the law which Jews agreed was scripture. Most Jews accepted the Prophets as well. Beyond that, we know different branches of Judaism accepted a varying list of writings as authoritative, and possibly as scripture. Dr. Brennan Breed, writing in Ancient Jew Review, notes multiple canons used in ancient Judaism.

From the start of the canonization process, there have, always been multiple Jewish canons: there is the rabbinic canon listed in the Babylonian Talmud (b. Baba Bat. 14a), which disagrees with the Masoretic order in the Leningrad and Aleppo codices – neither of which agree with any Christian canonical ordering. Some communities, such as the Beta Israel Jews of Ethiopia, include in their distinct canon diverse texts such as the Testament of Abraham, a Jewish text from the early centuries of the Common Era. Then there is the particular canon held by the Samaritans, a community closely related to Judaism that still lives on today.[41]

The canon of the Hebrew Scriptures was open until well into the Christian era, something described by Margaret Barker as follows:

There were many possible books, and yet only 24 became Scripture. The others were not just set aside; they were firmly forbidden. Rabbi Akiba, teaching some 50 years after the destruction of Jerusalem in 70 CE, said that anyone who read the excluded books had no part in the world to come. The context of this teaching was the second Jewish revolt against Rome, but also the decision about the Hebrew canon. Since the non-canonical Jewish books surviving from that period have been preserved by Christian scribes, R. Akiba's firm prohibition must have concerned the distinction between Jews and Christians. A few years later, Justin was claiming that the Jews

---

[41] (Breed 2015)

had even altered their Hebrew texts in order to remove material important to Christian claims,[42] and this 'altered' text is the one now used for translations of the Old Testament.[43]

The early church adopted the broadest possible set of Jewish writings as their Scriptures. As John Barton writes:

The formation of the Christian Bible is a story with neither beginning nor end. The first Christians already had a scripture, inherited from Judaism, whose origins time has concealed; while still today the edges of the biblical canon are blurred, with old disputes about the 'deuterocanonical' books asleep perhaps, but by no means dead.[44]

The idea of a biblical canon whose edges are blurred should come as a surprise to most Western Christians. Since the Reformation, the idea of a fixed canon has been an article of faith for both Roman Catholics and Protestants.[45] When the Protestants drew up their truncated list of approved Scriptures, the Latins responded by dogmatically defining a

---

[42] Justin Martyr's list is too extensive to list here; you can find it in the Ante-Nicene Fathers, Volume 1, Chapters LXXI - LXXIII

[43] (Barker, The Mother of the Lord, Volume 1 2012, Kindle Locations 697-704)

[44] (Barton 1997, 1) The term 'deuterocanonical' is used by Roman Catholics, and means 'second canon.' This does not mean it is less authoritative. The books of the first canon are contained in the Hebrew Scriptures, a collection finalized well after the time of Christ. The second canon are those books which were not included in the Hebrew Scriptures.

[45] The idea of the "fixed canon," meaning a catalog of authoritative, inspired books, had originally developed in response to heresy. However, the Protestant idea of the Old Testament consisting only of those books found in the Hebrew Scriptures is a recent development, one that cannot be supported in light of recent archeological discoveries — to say nothing of the church fathers (Jerome excepted) and (as we shall see) the witness of the New Testament.

list of Scriptures and approved texts. The Eastern Orthodox, having never experienced a Reformation, have never felt the need to define the canon dogmatically. For them, the common consensus is enough.[46]

The 20th-century discoveries of the Dead Sea Scrolls and the Nag Hammadi Library have prompted a reexamination of the issues of canon and canonicity among Protestants. Lee McDonald provides the following list of assumptions which were once widely accepted and taught in Protestant seminaries, but which are now questionable.

Recent scholarly research has challenged some of the most widely held views on the origins and formation of the Bible, including the following: (1) the Hebrew Scriptures reached their canonical acceptance among the Jews in a three-stage development beginning around 400 B.C.E. for the Pentateuch, around 200 B.C.E. for the Prophets, and around 90– 100 C.E. for the Writings; (2) the early Christians received from Jesus a closed or fixed collection of OT Scriptures; (3) most of the collection of NT Scriptures was fixed by the end of the second century C.E.; and (4) evidence of the latter is provided by a late second-century canonical list called the Muratorian Fragment.[47]

Despite the 20th-century discoveries, a significant number of evangelicals and fundamentalist still hold to a pre-20th-century view of canonical development. Among Protestants

---

[46] Protestants often misunderstand which books the east considers to be Scripture. For example, Philip Schaff writes: *"[O]pinion in the Orient was mostly against making any books not in the Hebrew canon of canonical authority, and from the fourth century the Eastern Fathers used them less and less. They were, however, officially recognized as a part of the canon by numerous medieval and modern synods until 1839, when the larger Catechism of the Orthodox Catholic Eastern Church, the most authoritative standard of the Graeco-Russian Church, expressly excluded them."* This is incorrect, as the Church lectionary in the East makes extensive use of the so-called Apocrypha. (Schaff, NPNF2-01 1890, 244)

[47] (McDonald 2007, Kindle Locations 987-992)

F. F. Bruce's book, *The Canon of Scripture* is a widely-cited source even though his methods and conclusions cannot withstand scholarly examination. Much of Bruce's argument is based on outdated assumptions; when Bruce writes of the canon of Sacred Scripture as closed, we need to examine the premise more closely.

The words 'to which nothing can be added ... and from which nothing can be taken away', whatever they precisely meant in this context, seem certainly to imply the principle of a closed canon. There are some scholars who maintain that the word 'canon' should be used only where the list of specially authoritative books has been closed; and there is much to be said in favour of this restrictive use of the word (a more flexible word might be used for the collection in process of formation), although it would be pedantic to insist on it invariably.[48]

F. F. Bruce also tries to have it both ways, to argue for the sanctity of the canon while arguing that it is the contents of the canon that matter, not the text itself.

It is from the contents, the message, of the book that it derives its value, whether we think of the gospel in particular or the Bible as a whole. It is therefore important to know what its contents are, and how they have come to be marked off from other writings— even holy and inspired writings. That is the point of examining the growth of the canon of holy scripture.[49]

F.F. Bruce claims support for his idea of the canon from various sources but fails to note the ancients did not think of a canon as a list, but as a rule or guide. Bruce cites from the Old Testament, (Deut 4:2; cf 12:32) the New Testament, (Re 22:18 ff) the Didache, and Josephus. Of all these citations, Bruce says: "This language can scarcely signify anything other than a closed canon."[50] F. F. Bruce misstates the

---

[48] (Bruce, The Canon of Scripture 2010, 22)

[49] (Bruce, The Canon of Scripture 2010, 24)

[50] (Ibid, 23)

evidence. Only Josephus supports the idea of a closed canon and, as he was writing after the fall of Jerusalem, was reading the newfound importance of the texts back into Jewish history. F. F. Bruce's other citations are even more problematic.[51]

In F. F. Bruce's Deuteronomy citation we read: "Ye shall not add unto the word which I command you, neither shall ye diminish ought from it, that ye may keep the commandments of the LORD your God which I command you." (Deut 4:2) If God intended this statement to close the canon, how are we to account for the rest of Deuteronomy, to say nothing of the remainder of the Old Testament? Apart from the book of Job and the Torah, none of the Old Testament existed. Moreover, if the Deuteronomy text implies a closed canon, how do we account for the New Testament?

The Christian Church accepted the canon of the Old Testament (including the Apocrypha) until the time of the Reformation. The Anglican Henry Wace, in his commentary on the King James Version, admits as much when he writes:

When the Reformers denied the inspired authority of the books of the Apocrypha, it was by no means their intention to exclude them from use either in public or in private reading. The Articles of the Church of England quote with approbation the ruling of St. Jerome, that though the Church does not use these books for establishment of doctrine, it reads them for example of life and instruction of manners.[52]

Having already truncated their canon, some Protestants look back to the ancient church for support, citing various church fathers who seemingly support their position. The 'ruling of

---

[51] Aaron Milavec notes the Didache "is older than the canonical gospels." (Milavec, The Didache 2003, Kindle Location 41)

[52] (Wace 1811, xxxvi) The ruling of St. Jerome was his private theological opinion, was contrary to the practice of the wider Christian Church, and was not accepted as dogma anywhere.

St. Jerome' falls into this category. St. Jerome was not a bishop, and his opinion was not authoritative. St. Jerome ultimately accepted the ruling of his bishop, something noted by the scholar Martin Hengel: "Jerome himself, who was not only a great and combative scholar but also a smooth diplomat, largely abandoned any effort to defend the Hebrew original in the Apocrypha question."[53]

Bishops devised lists of books approved for use in the church. These lists were authoritative within the Bishop's jurisdiction. These lists are occasionally similar to the canon used by Protestants today, but these individual lists were not authoritative in the wider church. Even where the lists of Old Testament books matched those of the Protestant canon, these lists wouldn't match the New Testament books — and vice versa. (We will provide more detail on this later).

St. Athanasius (c. 296-373) is widely cited as having provided the first complete listing of the 27 books of the New Testament. Matt Slick, the President and Founder of the Christian Apologetics and Research Ministry (CARM), cites Festal Letter 39 (c. 367 AD) as proof that Athanasius condemns the Apocrypha, which is incorrect.[54] First, St. Athanasius was speaking for his own diocese, not the entire Church. Second, alternate lists were created for centuries afterward. While St. Athanasius did not approve of all the so-called Apocrypha, his festal letter approved several of them. For example, his list contains "the first and second of the Chronicles are reckoned as one book"; "Jeremiah with Baruch"; "Lamentations, and the epistle, one book"; Esther; and Daniel. Baruch is one of the so-called Apocrypha, as is the Epistle of Jeremiah. The versions of 2 Chronicles, Esther, and Daniel judged by St. Athanasius as genuine contain material Protestants judge to be Apocryphal.[55] In the unabridged King

---

[53] (Hengel, The Septuagint as Christian Scripture 2002, 49-50)

[54] (Slick 2014)

[55] The Masoretic text favored by many conservative Protestant scholars did not exist at this time. The favored text in the Church was the Septuagint (see chap. 4).

James Version, these are called "The Prayer of Manassas" (placed at the end of 2 Chronicles); "The rest of Esther" (material found throughout Esther in the Septuagint); "The History of Susanna" (comes before Daniel chapter 1); "The Song of the Three Holy Children" (comes in the middle of Daniel chap. 3); and "Bel and the Dragon" (comes after Daniel chap. 12). If Protestants want to claim Festal Letter 39 of St. Athanasius as sealing the canon of the New Testament, they should also be prepared to accept all the Old Testament Apocrypha cited by Athanasius.

In his book *The Divine Names*, the author known today as Pseudo-Dionysius (late 5th to early 6th century) quotes from the Wisdom of Solomon, describing it as "introductory Scriptures."[56] Some might think this supports the general Protestant view. However, Paul Rorem and John Lamoreaux say the term "introductory Scripture" merely means that the Old Testament was an introduction to the New; in other words, the entire Old Testament could be termed "introductory Scripture."[57] The question, then, is how extensive that introduction is.

Among early Protestants, there was substantial disagreement and confusion as to the extent of the Old Testament. For example, John Wycliffe's Bible translation, first hand-printed in 1382 AD, contains 48 Old Testament books, as opposed to the 39 contained in the Protestant Old Testament.[58] We should note the Bibles printed *following* the

---

[56] (Pseudo-Dionysius, the Areopagite 1987, 81)

[57] (Rorem and Lamoreaux 1998, 48)

[58] The various eBooks and online sources like Bible Gateway only reproduce the part of Wycliffe's translation that are acceptable to the Protestants. Wycliffe's complete Old Testament contained the following books considered unacceptable after the Reformation: 1 Esdras, 2 Esdras, 3 Esdras, Tobit, Judith, Wisdom (Wisdom of Solomon), Syrach (Sirach, a.k.a. Ecclesiasticus), Preier of Jeremiah (Epistle of Jeremiah), Baruk (Baruch), along with 1 Machabeis & 2 Machabeis (1st and 2nd Maccabees). John Wycliffe's New Testament also contains Paul's letter to the Laodiceans, a contested document

Protestant Reformation also include what Protestants call the Apocrypha.[59] For example, Martin Luther's German translation of 1522 contained the Apocrypha. The English Language Matthew-Tyndale Bible, published by John Rogers in 1537, contained the Apocrypha.[60] Both the Geneva Bible of 1560 and the original King James Version (KJV) of 1611 contained the Apocrypha. Unabridged editions of the KJV with the Apocrypha are still available today, although printed versions are rare in the United States.[61]

Abridged Bibles without the Apocrypha are an American invention. The Continental Congress approved and funded the printing of Bibles without the Apocrypha. Rev. Dr. Will Gafney writes:

---

found in no generally accepted version or translation. (Wycliffe 2008)

[59] When asked if The Online Bible (www.onlinebible.net) would be providing a copy of the original King James Version with the Apocrypha, Larry Pierce, (the founder) responded: "We have no intention of mixing Jewish fables with the infallible Word of God." (Pierce 2014) Pierce is quoting Titus 1:14 here, equating Paul's reference to 'Jewish fables' with the Apocrypha, an interpretation that cannot be found in the text. Pierce chooses to use an abridged version of the King James Version rather than provide it as originally printed. In an email to Pastor EJ Hill, Larry Pierce admitted to redacting and editing other people's work when they do not agree with his theology (such as Thayer's 1889 Greek-English Lexicon). (Hill 2012)

[60] The Matthew-Tyndale Bible, generally known as the Matthew Bible, contains the following books not found in the Protestant Bible: 1 Esdras, 2 Esdras, Tobit, Judith, Rest of Esther, Wisdom of Solomon, Ecclesiasticus, Baruch, 3 Holy Children, Suzanna, Bel & the Dragon, Prayer of Mannesah, 1 Maccabees, and 2 Maccabees. (Rogers and Coverdale 1537)

[61] An excellent resource is the Official King James version online which contains the American truncation of the King James Version, the Apocrypha, and the original 1611 version with the apocrypha. http://www.kingjamesbibleonline.org/Apocrypha-Books/

Many are unaware that the shorter Protestant bible was created in the new America, during the revolutionary war when a printer took it upon himself without the authority of a church council to print a bible whose contents he chose. That bible, The Aitken Bible[62] is also significant for having been printed with the authority of the Continental Congress.[63]

F. F. Bruce raises the issue of the Liturgical Relevance of the Sacred Scriptures. In Liturgical services, the priest, pastor, or rabbi raises the Scriptures before the congregation before being read. Bruce describes the special treatment accorded to the Scriptures among the Jews, the Eastern Orthodox, the Catholics, the Anglicans, and the Reformed. (He omits the Lutherans, some of whom also have this practice). In his description of the Eastern Orthodox tradition, F. F. Bruce does a good job of describing the difference between venerating the Scriptures as text vs. the venerating the content of the Sacred Scriptures.

In the liturgy of the Orthodox Church the gospel book is carried in procession, and the reading from it is preceded by the call: 'Wisdom! All stand; let us hear the holy gospel.' The veneration thus paid to the gospel book is not paid to the materials of which it is composed nor to the ink with which it is inscribed, but to the Holy Wisdom which finds expression in the words that are read.[64]

The place of the Sacred Scriptures as part of worship is complicated by lectionary history. Lectionaries are the scripture readings appointed for a particular day of the Church year, and (as David Parker notes) date back as early as the 4th century.[65] The "formal Byzantine lectionary system" appears to have been standardized by the "late

---

[62] http://www.theworldsgreatbooks.com/Aitken Bible.htm

[63] (Gafney 2013)

[64] (Bruce, The Canon of Scripture 2010, 23)

[65] (Osburn 2013, 94)

seventh or early eighth Century."[66] Complicating things further, "patristic citations" often treat lectionary readings as biblical citations, meaning they treat the lectionaries as biblical manuscripts.[67]

Since the ancient lectionary readings include the Apocrypha, the removal of the Apocrypha from Protestant lectionaries is troubling. The *King James Bible with Commentary by Henry Wace* describes the gradual elimination of the Apocrypha from the Anglican Lectionary.[68] Henry Wace notes:

So small a portion of the apocryphal books has been retained in the present [Anglican] Lectionary that the retention of any would seem intended for little more than an assertion of the Church's right to use these books if she pleases in public reading. This [diminution] is still more true of the American Church, which entirely discontinued the use of lessons from the Apocrypha on ordinary week-days; but still uses such lessons on two or three holy days. The Irish Church on its last revision of the Lectionary has not even retained so much as this.[69]

The complete elimination of the Apocrypha from the Protestant Church turns out to be a recent innovation. As such, it deserves a second look.

---

[66] (Ibid, 97)

[67] (Parker 2012, 53)

[68] The Anglican Lectionary did not include readings from Maccabees.

[69] (Wace 1811, xxxviii)

3: Canon and Canonicity

The Greek word canon (κανών) contains shades of meaning lacking in English. In his *Excursus on the Meaning of the Word "Canon,"* Fr. Vasile Mihai writes:

The word was originally a Semitic word (qanneh) borrowed into the Greek language and understood as a "straight rod," "line" or "yardstick" used in mundane activities as carpentry, tailoring and construction. Then a metaphorical use of the word in ancient Greek philosophy and science brought to it the sense of "criterion" or "norm", and eventually it was used in Hellenistic thought with notions close to "order" and "discipline." The Roman equivalent stressed mostly those notions of order and discipline through the use of the terms «norma» and «regula».[70]

As we discussed in chapter 2, the early Church used the term canon to mean the *regula fidei* (rule of faith). The apostle Paul captures this idea when he says of the Scriptures: they are "profitable for doctrine, for reproof, for correction, for instruction in righteousness: That the man of God may be perfect, throughly furnished unto all good works." (2Ti 3:16-17) This idea of a canon as the *regula fidei*, the rule of faith, does not include a list of authoritative writings.

However, the idea of a canon as the rule of faith could lead to the canon being thought of solely as a means of separating truth from error. William J. Abraham writes:

Construing the canon of Scripture as a criterion may drastically diminish what it means to perceive Scripture as canonical. The impression given in this interpretation is that the provision of the canon of Scripture is the provision of a criterion to settle contested questions.[71]

---

[70] (Mihai 2014, 449)

[71] (Abraham 1998, 6)

William J. Abraham says viewing the canon solely as a criterion diminishes the revelation, and must also be viewed as "a sophisticated means of grace which is related to formation in holy living."[72] This "formation in holy living" is the meaning the Apostle Paul provides Timothy when describing all the ways the Scriptures profit us.

When we think of the canon today, we think about a comprehensive list. However, the idea of a canon as a list is a fairly recent development; the ancients used a different term (*pinakes* or *katalogos*) for a catalog of writings. Stephen Voorwinde, writing for Vox Reformata, explains the use of the word canon from the early church through the Reformation, and into the time of the Enlightenment.

While the Greek word «kanon» does occur in the New Testament it cannot be translated by 'canon' in English. In each case it is more suitably translated 'rule' or 'standard' (2 Cor.10:13,15,16; Gal.6:16; Phil.3:16). It will be noted that all the occurrences of the word are in Paul's writings, and in none of these instances is he referring to the canon of Scripture. That was to be a much later development. Movement in this direction occurred when 'in the second century in the Christian church «kanon» came to stand for revealed truth, rule of faith.' It was not until the fourth century that the church began to refer to the Scriptures of the Old and New Testaments as «ho kanon» ('the canon'). ...The term 'canon' as we use it when referring to the canon of Scripture is therefore not a use of the term in its biblical sense, but conforms to ecclesiastical usage from the fourth century onwards. This is also the way the word was used at the time of the Reformation. Particularly in the Reformed confessions the term is used almost exclusively of the 'rule,' 'norm' or 'established list' of the Scriptures. In these doctrinal statements it is closely conjoined to such concepts as 'inspiration,' 'authority' and 'the regulation, foundation and

---

[72] (Ibid, 6)

confirmation of our faith.' The idea of normativity comes very much to the forefront.[73]

Martin Hengel notes that Christians of the second century began to explore the breadth of material which might have a claim to inspiration. In doing so, they began to decide which books were not useful, and perhaps not inspired.

The uncertainty with respect to the delineation of the 'Scriptures of the Old Covenant' ...which is perceptible throughout the second century may be related to the fact that Christian theologians (including the Gnostics) in this period attempted for the first time to work carefully through the rich Jewish literature which was originally Greek or had been translated into Greek and to investigate its usefulness for church doctrine and practice and theological speculation.[74]

Fr. John Behr says by the end of the second century the term "canon" referred to the inspired Scriptures *as well as the writings of the church fathers.*[75] It should be noted, however, that the inclusion of the writings of the church fathers means the ancients used the term canon in the sense of the rule of faith. That a canon did not mean a list is demonstrated by Martin Hengel, who notes there was still no commonly agreed upon list of the inspired Scriptures in the third century.[76] Even into the fifth century we see the canon used in the sense of a rule of faith rather than a catalog of texts, meaning Athanasius' Festal Letter 39 (c. 367) did not decide the issue. As evidence, consider the Acts of the Fourth Ecumenical Council (451 A.D) which contains the following statement:

---

[73] (Voorwinde 1995)

[74] (Hengel, The Septuagint as Christian Scripture 2002, 55)

[75] (Behr 2001, 73)

[76] (Ibid, 74)

Let each one of the most reverend bishops of the present synod, hasten to set forth how he believes, writing without any fear, but placing the fear of God before his eyes; knowing that our most divine and pious lord believes according to the «ecthesis»[77] of the three hundred and eighteen holy fathers at Nice, and according to the «ecthesis» of the one hundred and fifty after them, and according to the Canonical epistles and «ectheses» of the holy fathers Gregory, Basil, Athanasius, Hilary, Ambrose, and according to the two canonical epistles of Cyril, which were confirmed and published in the first Council of Ephesus, nor does he in any point depart from the faith of the same. [Extracts from the Acts, Session I][78]

The Council of Chalcedon did not use the term 'canon' to mean a list of Sacred Scriptures. The council referred to councils, authors, and writings which were in accord with the apostolic faith as 'canon.' This meaning of 'canon' can be demonstrated by 1) the failure to expressly list the canonical works, and 2) the description of two epistles of Cyril as canonical.

If the word "canon" originally referred to the rule of faith and indicated normative truth, how then did our modern understanding of the term develop? In his book *The Conservative Reformation and its Theology*, Charles Porterfield Krauth draws a distinction between the rule of faith of the Apostles (before the closing of the Canon) and the rule of faith of the Church (following the closing of the canon). He writes:

While the Apostles lived the Word was both a rule of faith, and in a certain sense, a confession of it; when by direct inspiration a holy man utters certain words, they are to him both a role of faith, and a confession of faith — they at once express both what he is to believe and what he does believe; but when the Canon was complete, when its authors were gone, when the

---

[77] Ecthesis is the use of a thesis to state a belief.
[78] (Schaff, NPNF2-14 2005, 370)

living teacher was no longer at hand to correct the errorist who distorted his word, the Church entered on her normal and abiding relation to the Word and the Creed which is involved in these words: the Bible is the rule of faith, but not the confession of it; the Creed is not the rule of faith, but is the confession of it.[79]

Charles Porterfield Krauth is drawing a false distinction. The early church recognized no such division between the *regula fidei* of the Apostles and the *regula fidei* of the Church. There was no official (or ecumenical) Creed for the first three hundred years of the Church. His distinction between the Apostolic and the post-Apostolic church does not stand up to historical scrutiny.

Interestingly, by the time Charles Porterfield Krauth published his work on the Conservative Reformation (c. 1875 A.D.), the idea of a Canon as a "closed collection of writings" was barely one hundred years old. Its use in a theological context was younger than that. Lee McDonald writes:

The word canon was not regularly used in reference to a closed collection of writings until David Ruhnken used it this way in 1768. In his treatise entitled «Historia critica oratorum Graecorum», he employed the term canon for a selective list of literary writings. ...In antiquity [the Greek word] «pinakes» is more commonly used of catalogues or lists.[80]

When we consider the use of the term canon to mean a closed list, we are giving the word a meaning it did not originally have in the ancient church. Fr. Stephen Freeman writes: "The creation of a 'canon' of Scripture was never more than a declaration of what a general consensus of the Church treated as authoritative."[81] Fr. Freeman furthers his

---

[79] (Krauth 1875, 184-185)

[80] (McDonald 2007, 51)

[81] (Freeman, There Is No "Bible" in the Bible 2014) For the Orthodox, Holy Tradition is the general consensus of the Church.

argument by noting that even the term "Bible," meaning a book, would have been foreign. The early church used the term "Holy Scriptures" and St. John Chrysostom (c. 347-407 AD) sometimes referred to "the books," [82] but never did they consider these sacred writings to be a single book.[83]

More importantly, the ancient church did not have our obsession with New Testament manuscripts. As mentioned previously, patristic citations sometimes quote the lectionaries, treating them as scripture. David Parker writes:

The modern concept of a New Testament manuscript is based upon the theological model of canonicity. As is well known, the idea of a canon emerged over the course of many years, and the list with which we are familiar was first given by Athanasius in his Thirty-Ninth Festal Letter, written in 367. Until then there evidently could not be any manuscript whose contents intentionally corresponded to this list, and in fact there is precious little evidence that many copies did so for centuries thereafter, and rarely then until the advent of printing. Even when Greek-speaking Christianity came to agree [upon] a canon, it did not really occur to anyone that such a canon should be the basis for the contents of a manuscript.[84]

Dr. Brennan Breed observes that within a particular canon their exist a 'pluriformity[85] of texts,' such that books contained within the canon come in multiple forms.

The text of the book of Daniel, for example, is remarkably different in several Qumran scrolls that preserve it. The text of the Septuagint version of Daniel, canonical for the Eastern Orthodox churches, preserves one of these ancient versions that diverges from the Masoretic Text, and also includes

---

[82] (Schaff, NPNF1-11 2002, 865)

[83] (Constantinou, Introduction to the Bible Lesson 9 2008)

[84] (Parker 2012, 61)

[85] Pluriformity has to do with diversity or variety of forms

additional stories such as Susannah and the Elders. The canons of religious communities generally do not regulate the textual tradition of the books included; Jews and Christians in Late Antiquity used a wide variety of textual types and did not seem to think that the differing texts were un-biblical.[86]

Early on the church began cutting scrolls into sheets and binding them into a codex, the predecessor of today's books.[87] The first codex consisted of the Gospels and was used during Christian worship.[88] Later the rest of the New Testament (except Revelation), was collected into a second codex. The Church used the codex in liturgical worship. Our conception of the Bible as a single book is an outgrowth of the printing press.[89] The printing press not only created the conditions for Protestant ideas to spread, but it also created the first bibles as we know them today. The idea of a canon as something akin to a table of contents is a modern innovation.

When modern theologians conceive of canon as a list, they speak solely of the text; when ancient theologians speak of the rule of faith, they speak of the revelation contained within the pluriformity of texts. The two thoughts are not in opposition. A book becomes part of a list of Scriptures texts because of the revelation it contains. However, when we conceive of canon solely as a list, we wind up arguing over the side issues of canon and canonicity. Arguments over the canon keep us from focusing on the revelation of Jesus Christ

---

[86] (Breed 2015)

[87] Martin Hengel writes: "The thorough Christian appropriation of the LXX also manifests itself in the external form of the documents. Long before there was a 'New Testament', the Christian LXX was distinguished by the use of the *codex* rather than the Jewish *scroll*." (Hengel, The Septuagint as Christian Scripture 2002, 41)

[88] The Gospels were usually kept by the reader, and were brought in during the service and set upon the altar; later the priest would read a passage from these gospels. This same pattern is followed today in the Orthodox liturgy.

[89] (Freeman, There Is No "Bible" in the Bible 2014)

— which is the whole point of the Sacred Scriptures. F. F. Bruce writes:

The Christian church started its existence with a book, but it was not to the book that it owed its existence. It shared the book with the Jewish people; indeed, the first members of the church were without exception Jews. The church owed its distinctive existence to a person — to Jesus of Nazareth, crucified, dead and buried, but 'designated Son of God in power ... by his resurrection from the dead' (Rom. 1: 4). This Jesus, it was believed, had been exalted by God to be universal Lord; he had sent his Spirit to be present with his followers, to unite them and animate them as his body on earth. The function of the book was to bear witness to him.[90]

The Christian church owes its existence to Christ. The Christian church interprets the Old Testament Scriptures by reading Christ into the Old Testament. The Christian Church began its normative functioning with the descent of the Holy Spirit on the day of Pentecost — to the descent of the Comforter, who guides us into all truth. Moreover, the Holy Spirit guided the Church for several decades before the apostles wrote a single book of the New Testament. Fr. Stephen Freeman draws our attention to the importance of this latter point.

The Christian community predates its own texts (the New Testament) and is not described as in any way having a foundation on the Scriptures – the Apostles and Prophets are described as the foundation of the Church. And though the Tradition does not describe the Scriptures as somehow inferior to the Church, neither do they consider the Scriptures to exist apart from the Church. They are the Church's book.[91]

Alexis Stepanovich Khomiakoff (Khomyakov), from his *Essay on the Church (c. 1850)* continues this point for us.

---

[90] (Bruce, The Canon of Scripture 2010, 27)
[91] (Freeman, Has Your Bible Become a Quran? 2014)

The Spirit of God, who lives in the Church, ruling her and making her wise, manifests Himself within her in divers manners; in Scripture, in Tradition, and in Works; for the Church, which does the works of God, is the same Church which preserves tradition and which has written the Scriptures. Neither individuals, nor a multitude of individuals within the Church, preserve tradition or write the Scriptures; but the Spirit of God, which lives in the whole body of the Church. Therefore [sic] it is neither right nor possible to look for the grounds of tradition in the Scripture, nor for the proof of Scripture in tradition, nor for the warrant of Scripture or tradition in works. To a man living outside the Church neither her scripture nor her tradition nor her works are comprehensible. But to the man who lives within the Church and is united to the spirit of the Church, their unity is manifest by the grace which lives within her.[92]

Fr. Boris Bobrinskoy, former Dean and Professor at St Sergius Institute in Paris, writes:

A living theology cannot be severed from the living environment that forms the body of the Church, where the Spirit of knowledge and truth breathes. A theological reading of Scripture cannot be made outside the great Tradition which, generation after generation, searches the Bible in order to discover within it the presence of Christ, and, in Him, the face of the Father. Thus, we will be led to read Scripture on different levels: that of a historical, literal reading — but also that of the typological or prophetic reading (the "type" being the "figure" of Christ, or the Spirit, or the Church, or the Mother of God, symbolized, prophesied by the Old Testament). The typological dimension discloses the quintessence of the Old Testament; it detects its correspondence with the new, which forms its fulfillment and its key.[93]

---

[92] (Palmer 1895, 198)
[93] (Bobrinskoy 1999, 7)

Given that "tradition" is a loaded word for Protestants, it is time for a brief discussion of the subject. Tradition does not stand apart from Scripture but is necessary for the proper understanding of Scripture.[94] Historically, both the Church and the heretics appeal to scripture in support of their views. To defeat the heretics, the Church appealed to the apostolic tradition over against the interpretations of the heretics. For example, Georges Florovsky writes regarding Marcion:

In the Second century the term "Scriptures" denoted primarily the Old Testament and, on the other hand, the authority of these "Scriptures" was sharply challenged, and actually repudiated, by the teaching of Marcion. The Unity of the Bible had to be proved and vindicated. What was the basis, and the warrant, of Christian, and Christological, understanding of "Prophesy," that is — of the Old Testament? It was in this historical situation that the authority of Tradition was first invoked. Scripture belonged to the Church, and it was only in the Church, within the community of right faith, that Scripture could be adequately understood and correctly interpreted.[95]

The Russian theologian and philosopher Aleksei Khomyakov provides an Orthodox understanding of the relationship between Scripture and Tradition.

The whole Church wrote the Holy Scriptures and then gave life to them in Tradition. To put it more accurately, Scripture and Tradition, as two manifestations of one and the same Spirit, are a single manifestation. Scripture is nothing but written Tradition, and Tradition is nothing but living Scripture. [96]

---

[94] Each Protestant denomination (or sect) has its own interpretive tradition, and each sect uses that tradition as the framework for understanding Scripture. Each sect believes its tradition to have been handed down by means of the Holy Spirit, and believes the Holy Spirit has guided it unto all truth.

[95] (Florovsky 1972, 75)

[96] (Khomyakov 1977, 53)

The role of Scripture is to reveal Jesus Christ. The revelation of Jesus Christ exists within His Church. Scripture describes the Church as both Christ's body and the pillar and ground of the truth. Given all this, it is odd that the idea of canon has shifted away from the rule of faith to a simple catalog of inspired books.

The modern understanding is of canon as a list of authoritative and inspired books, and canonicity as the process by which an individual text became part of a said collection of books. As we mentioned previously, these understandings have come into question following the discovery of the Dead Sea Scrolls and the Gnostic writings contained in the Nag Hammadi library. These discoveries have fueled the imagination of biblical scholars and have added detail to the background of our Sacred Scriptures — all of which have sparked a renewed interest in the subject of canon and canonicity.

The debates over canon and canonicity are taking place between the Protestant and Roman Catholic Churches as opposite poles of modern Christianity. This phenomenon is recent and does not involve the Eastern Orthodox, as it raises questions and uses methods that are foreign to the Eastern Orthodox Church.[97]

In the 16th century, theological conversations took place between the Protestants and the Orthodox. In the discussions, the issues of canon and canonicity didn't come up at all — in part because the Lutherans never mentioned their use of a different canon.[98] Instead, the Lutherans

---

[97] For the Eastern Orthodox, the fall of Constantinople in 1453 A.D. is recent history.

[98] In the late 17th century, a group of Lutheran theologians sent a Greek translation of the Augsburg Confession to Patriarch Jeremiah II of Constantinople. What followed is an intriguing correspondence which took place over a period of years. While this theological correspondence is well known among the Orthodox, surprisingly few Lutherans and Protestants know anything about it, and fewer still have read the actual texts. It is unclear what the Lutherans were

argued for the authority of Scripture, an issue then Ecumenical Patriarch Jeremiah II accepted without comment. The discussion between the Lutherans and the Orthodox involved matters of faith and practice. The Lutherans kept bringing up Scripture as the authority, and the Patriarch accepted their position but included Holy Tradition as part of that discussion. In a sense, neither of them understood the other's position, and they simply talked past one another.[99]

Among Protestant commentaries and introductions to the Scriptures, the issues of canon and canonicity are common and are often of first importance. The Orthodox, by way of contrast, largely ignore the issue. For example, the two-volume *Introduction to the Old Testament* by the Very Rev. Paul Nadim Tarazi, Professor of Old Testament at St Vladimir's Orthodox Theological Seminary, does not discuss the issues of canon and canonicity at all.[100] Dumitru Staniloae's *Orthodox Dogmatic Theology* discusses the nature

---

trying to do. Some think the Lutherans were trying to convert the Ecumenical Patriarch (unlikely). Some think the Lutherans were trying to become part of the Orthodox Church (also unlikely). The text seems to indicate that the Lutherans merely wanted the Ecumenical Patriarch to accept that the Lutheran doctrine was consistent with that of the Orthodox Church; the position of the Ecumenical Patriarch was that Lutherans were heterodox.

[99] (Mastrantonis 1982, passim) Another excursus on the meaning of tradition is in order. Georges Florovsky writes:

Tradition [is] ...an hermeneutical principle and method. Scripture could be rightly and fully assessed and understood only in the light and in the context of the living Apostolic Tradition, which was an integral factor of Christian existence. It was so, or course, not because Tradition could add anything to what has been manifested in the Scripture, but because it provided that living context, the comprehensive perspective, in which only the true "intention" and the total "design" of the Holy Writ, of Divine Revelation itself, could be detected and grasped. (Florovsky 1972, 79)

[100] The Very Rev. Paul Nadim Tarazi is a controversial and polarizing figure, so perhaps we should not read too much into his failure to deal with the issue of canonicity.

of revelation and its relationship with the world, the Church, and Holy Tradition. However, Staniloae's books do not deal in any substantive manner with canonicity. Fr. John Breck's book *Scripture in Tradition* avoids the subject of the canon altogether, instead focusing on the person and work of the Holy Spirit. Georges Florovsky's book *Bible, Church, Tradition*, which covers these issues, has been out of print for many years. John Behr's book *The Way to Nicaea* discusses the issues of canon and canonicity but from a different point of view than that of Protestant and Catholic scholars. Metropolitan Hilarion Alfeyev's book *Orthodox Christianity: Doctrine and Teaching of the Orthodox Church* only briefly discusses the issue of scriptural canon. How do we account for the difference between these approaches? What impact do these issues have on the *regula fidei*, the faith once delivered to the saints?

While the use of canon to mean a catalog of inspired Scriptures is modern, the issues of canon and canonicity have their roots in Roman Catholic medieval scholasticism. Fr. John Breck writes:

Scripture determines what constitutes genuine Tradition, yet Tradition gives birth to and determines the limits of Scripture. To many people's minds, this way of envisioning the circular relationship between Scripture and Tradition appears untenable. The Protestant Reformers attempted to break this form of the hermeneutic circle by advancing the teaching known as sola scriptura [Scripture alone], holding that Scripture alone determines faith and morality... This was to a large extent in reaction to medieval Roman Catholicism which had separated Scripture and Tradition into separate domains, giving priority to the latter.[101]

It is helpful to discuss the canon and canonicity of the Old and New Testaments separately, as they each took different paths in their development. The authors of the New Testament called the Old Testament scripture. There is little

---

[101] (Breck 2001, 11)

evidence the New Testament's authors or the apostolic church considered the New Testament to be scripture. Two passages suggest some parts of the New Testament were scripture (1 Tim 5:18 and 2 Pet 3:15-16), but these are by no means convincing. The apostle Paul did not refer to his writings as scripture, but instead classed his teachings as "traditions," and referred to his books as letters. (2Th 2:15) The Revelation of St. John describes itself as scripture but has a contentious canonical history. Nowhere in the New Testament do we have a catalog of canonical books — neither of the Old Testament books (which are explicitly called scripture) nor of the writings of the New Testament. Therefore, it behooves us to examine the development of the Christian Old and New Testament separately.

4: Septuagint History & Purpose

The Septuagint is generally thought of as a translation of the Hebrew Scriptures into Greek. As professor Peter Gentry writes, this is imprecise.

What is meant by the term Septuagint? A lack of precision is common in both popular and scholarly use of the word. Mainly responsible for this lack of precision are uncertainties about the history of the process of translation of the Hebrew Scriptures into Greek.[102]

The Pentateuch (also known as the five books of Moses), was translated sometime between 285-240 BC. Alfred Edersheim says the Septuagint contained only the Pentateuch,[103] but scholars differ on this point. The Letter of Aristeas describes the supposed miraculous origins of the Septuagint, but only mentions the Pentateuch.[104] We do not know whether translating the Pentateuch alone was the original intent, but the translation work continued. Alfred Edersheim cites evidence from the prologue to the Wisdom of Solomon and argues the Septuagint was completed by 221 BC. In 2009, Peter J. Gentry claims the Septuagint was completed by 130 B.C.E.; just five years later he claims it was completed by 100

---

[102] (Gentry, The Great Code: Greek Bible and the Humanities 2014, 51)

[103] Edersheim 1993, 17-18. Martin Hengel describes Septuagint studies as a "realm [for] Old Testament and Patristics scholars." He also says it is "one of the most exclusive — because it is so complicated — specialties of theology of *philologia sacra*." (Hengel, The Septuagint as Christian Scripture 2002, 19) We will not be delving that deeply into the subject.

[104] (Hengel, The Septuagint as Christian Scripture 2002, 76) Although a number of church fathers from Justin Martyr held to the miraculous origins of the Septuagint, the historical evidence suggests the translation of the obscure Hebrew text into Greek was a product of the Jewish diaspora.

B.C.E.[105] Scholars differ in their assumptions about where the task of translation ends, and recension begins — in part due to differing assumptions about the extent of the canon. Alfred Edersheim, for example, is arguing for the truncated Protestant canon and therefore claims an earlier date.

There are differences of opinion as to the origin of the Septuagint. As described by Peter Gentry, there are five reasons given for the translation.

Five major hypotheses have been advanced: (1) a generation of Greek-speaking Jews in the Hellenistic period begun by the conquest of Alexander the Great (333-323 B.C.E.) required Greek scriptures for their liturgy, or (2) for the education of their young; (3) the translation was required as a legal document or (4) as cultural heritage for the royal library being assembled in Alexandria; (5) Aristarchus' new edition of Homer around 150 B.C.E. employed textual criticism to produce an authoritative text and served as a model to produce an authoritative text of the Bible for Alexandrian Jews (hence early revisions and The Letter of Aristeas).[106]

It should be clear that these five reasons are not mutually exclusive. Like all human endeavors, there were likely many reasons for the translation. What is clear is that the Jewish diaspora needed the translation, as many of them no longer spoke Hebrew. Even in Palestine, where Hebrew was the

---

[105] (Gentry, The Text of the Old Testament 2009, 24) (Gentry, The Great Code: Greek Bible and the Humanities 2014, 51)

[106] (Gentry, The Great Code: Greek Bible and the Humanities 2014, 52)

sacred language,[107] the "diaspora synagogues"[108] used the Septuagint and considered it authoritative.[109] One side effect of the Septuagint was that Jewish religion and culture became part of the mainstream and available to anyone who spoke Greek. Of the period before the existence of the Septuagint, the scholar Jaroslav Pelikan writes:

The Jewish religion was enshrined, but therefore was also locked, in a sacred book, in a code of conduct, and in a liturgical ritual that were purposely being kept hidden from the outside world in one of the most esoteric of all those exotic languages and therefore virtually unavailable, except in bits and pieces, to anyone who did not know Hebrew.[110]

From an obscure religion of a backwater country, Judaism became well known and respected, even gaining a special legal status in the Roman Empire.[111] This rise to respectability came about because the Septuagint made the Jewish faith accessible to the Gentiles. Jaroslav Pelikan observed:

---

[107] The scriptures clearly state that Jesus spoke Hebrew (Acts 26:14), and Paul spoke Hebrew (Acts 21:40). The charge against Jesus, which Pilate had affixed to Jesus' cross, was written in Greek, Latin, and Hebrew (Lu 23:38). While Aramaic was the language spoken immediately after the Jews returned from Babylon, the Hasmonean dynasty appear to have changed the language back to Hebrew. (Bivin and Blizzard Jr. 1994, Chapter 2) Alfred Edersheim explicitly states of Jesus: "He spoke Hebrew, and used and quoted the Scriptures in the original." (Edersheim 1993, 175)

[108] (Hengel, The 'Hellenization' of Judea in the First Century after Christ 1989, 13)

[109] (Edersheim 1993, 20)

[110] (Pelikan 2005, 46)

[111]The term *religio licita* is a term attributed to Tertullian, but is not a term derived from Roman law. The equivalent Roman term is *collegia licita*, which designated religious groups authorized to organize and hold services. The Jews were *collegia licita*, and Christians were not. (Askowith 1915, 173)

It had long been part of the hope of Israel, voiced by the prophets, that peoples "far and remote" would finally come to Mount Zion and learn the Torah, which was intended and revealed by the One True God for all peoples, not only for the people of Israel. Yet without their learning to read Hebrew, that hope was largely beyond realization. But when we read the account of Pentecost in the New Testament, we hear of "devout Jews drawn from every nation under heaven, Parthians, Medes, Elamites; inhabitants of Mesopotamia, of Judaea and Cappadocia, of Pontus and Asia, of Phrygia and Pamphylia, of Egypt and the districts of Lybia around Cyrene; visitors from Rome, both Jews and proselytes, Cretans and Arabs." Many of the "Jews" in this mouth-filling catalog must have been Gentiles by birth but were now converted Jews, "proselytes," by faith and observance. From an obscure sect turned inward, huddled around its Torah and reciting its Shema, Judaism had now become a world religion, a significant force in the civilization of the Mediterranean world.[112]

Table 1: The American KJV and the Septuagint

King James Bible	Septuagint
Genesis	Genesis
Exodus	Exodus
Leviticus	Leviticus
Numbers	Numbers
Deuteronomy	Deuteronomy
Joshua	Joshua
Judges	Judges
Ruth	Ruth
1 Samuel	1st Kingdoms
2 Samuel	2nd Kingdoms
1 Kings	3rd Kingdoms
2 Kings	4th Kingdoms
1 Chronicles	1 Chronicles
2 Chronicles	2 Chronicles

---

[112] (Pelikan 2005, 54)

King James Bible	Septuagint
	- Prayer of Manasseh
	1 Esdras (the Greek Ezra)
Ezra	2 Esdras
Nehemiah	
	Tobit
	Judith
Esther	Esther with additional material
	1 Maccabees
	2 Maccabees
	3 Maccabees
Job	Job
Psalms	Psalms
	Psalm 151
Proverbs	Proverbs
Ecclesiastes	Ecclesiastes
Song of Solomon	Song of Solomon or Canticles
	Wisdom, or Wisdom of Solomon
	Sirach or Ecclesiasticus
	Psalms of Solomon[113]
Isaiah	Isaiah
Jeremiah	Jeremiah
	Baruch and the Epistle of Jeremy
Lamentations	Lamentations
Ezekiel	Ezekiel
Daniel	Daniel with additions
	- Susanna
	- Prayer of Azariah
	- Song of the Three Holy Youths
	- Bel and the Dragon

---

[113] The Psalms of Solomon are contained in the Septuagint, but are not generally considered to be Jewish or Christian Scripture. There are some Orthodox clergy who consider them to be Scripture, but the wider Orthodox community does not.

King James Bible	Septuagint
	Minor Prophets (The Twelve)
Hosea	- Hosea
Joel	- Joel
Amos	- Amos
Obadiah	- Obadiah
Jonah	- Jonah
Micah	- Micah
Nahum	- Nahum
Habakkuk	- Habakkuk
Zephaniah	Zephaniah
Haggai	Haggai
Zechariah	Zechariah
Malachi	Malachi

The Septuagint was a boon for the Jewish people, as the Septuagint resulted in large numbers of Gentile adherents known as the God-Fearers. The sociologist Rodney Stark describes the God-Fearers as gentiles who admired "the moral teachings and monotheism of the Jews, but who would not take the final step of fulfilling the law [circumcision, dietary restrictions, and the like]."[114] The Septuagint used by the New Testament authors and the church fathers contained the books Protestants now call the Apocrypha.[115] J.N.D. Kelly writes:

---

[114] (Stark 1996, 58); "The finance minister of the Ethiopian kingdom of Napata-Meroe (Acts 8.27), presumably a godfearer, was one example." (Hengel, The 'Hellenization' of Judea in the First Century after Christ 1989, 13-14) We may also presume Cornelius the Centurian (Acts 10) was a godfearer. Even today, one may be an adherent of Judaism without being a convert. Stories abound of rabbis who attempt to dissuade converts on the grounds that adherents have to keep the 10 commandments, but converts have to keep the entire 613 commandments of the Law.

[115] (Hengel, The Septuagint as Christian Scripture 2002, 22-23)

It should be observed that the Old Testament thus admitted as authoritative in the Church was somewhat bulkier and more comprehensive [than the Protestant Bible]. ...It always included, though with varying degrees of recognition, the so-called apocrypha or deuterocanonical books. The reason for this is that the Old Testament which passed in the first instance into the hands of Christians was not the original Hebrew version, but the Greek translation known as the Septuagint.[116]

Judaism made use of the Septuagint for 250 years before it passed into the hands of Christians, and it only became a problem for Jews after Christians adopted it as scripture.[117]

---

[116] (Kelly 1976, 53) We now know the Septuagint better represents the original text of the Hebrew Scriptures, as demonstrated by the existence of texts in the Dead Sea Scrolls which match the Septuagint version.

[117] There were multiple textual variants (or traditions) circulating in the time of Christ. After the rise of Christianity, and the fall of Jerusalem, everything changed. Dempster writes:

After the fall of Jerusalem in 70 CE changes within Judaism led to the ascendancy of one tradition—what has come to be known as rabbinic Judaism. ...One of the accompanying results was the ascendancy of the form of the Jewish Scriptures used by that group. In the second century CE, revisions of the older [Greek] texts were made by Aquila, Symmachus, Theodotion, and others. Their goal was apparently to bring the translations into line with the authoritative textual stream of their day, the rabbinic text. (Dempster 2008, Kindle Locations 2599-2602; 2628-2633)

5: The Evolutionary History of the Hebrew Text

Robert Alter notes: "It is an old and in some ways unfair cliché to say that translation is always a betrayal."[118] This is because the translator is presented with a text that contains shades of meaning, and has to choose one of those shades to represent in the translated text. In some cases, the translation changes the meaning of the text. Robert Alter notes:

The unacknowledged heresy underlying most modern English versions of the Bible is the use of translation as a vehicle for 'explaining' the Bible instead of representing it in another language, and in the most egregious instances this amounts to explaining away the Bible. This impulse may be attributed not only to a rather reduced sense of the philological enterprise but also to a feeling that the Bible, because of its canonical status, has to be made accessible — indeed, transparent — to all.[119]

The Septuagint is unlike modern English versions of the Bible as the modern concept of canonicity did not exist, nor the modern obsession with understandability. The translation of the Septuagint was not meant for the illiterate masses, but for educated scribes who could read and explain the scriptures. Moreover, as scholars know, today's Hebrew Scriptures are modified versions of the original texts. Even the alphabet has changed from the original Paleo-Hebrew to the so-called Square Script used today. The Jewish Virtual Library notes:

The square script belongs to the Aramaic branch of Semitic writing. ...[By] the second century C.E. it is already possible to speak of the square script proper (figure 7). By the seventh

---

[118] (Alter, The Hebrew Bible 2019, xiii)

[119] (Ibid, xv)

century (figure 8) almost every letter of the alphabet had either a top bar or a head, while many had a base as well.[120]

The Babylonian Talmud mentions there being different scripts: Paleo-Hebrew is called "Ivri," and the script brought back from Babylon by Ezra is called "Ashuri." The Talmud states:

Mar Zutra or, some say, Mar Ukba said: Originally the Torah was given to Israel in Ivri (Paleo-Hebrew) letters and in the sacred Hebrew language. Later, in the times of Ezra, the Torah was given in Ashuri script and Aramaic language. Finally, they selected for Israel the Ashuri script and Hebrew language, leaving the original Hebrew characters and Aramaic language for the ignorant people. Rebbe Yose said: Why is it called Ashuri (Assyrian) script? Because they brought it with them from Assyria.[121]

Robert Alter cites the Israeli linguist Abba ben David (in a text available only in Hebrew) as saying that a "new kind of Hebrew" emerged in the "pre-Christian" (or Second Temple) period.

It is widely recognized that this new Hebrew reflected the influence of the Aramaic vernacular in morphology, in grammar, and in some of its vocabulary, and that, understandably, it also incorporated a vast number of Greek and Latin loanwords. ...Ben David, observing, as have others before him, that there are incipient signs of an emergent rabbinic Hebrew in late biblical books like Jonah and the Song of Songs, makes the bold and, to my mind, convincing proposal that rabbinic Hebrew was built upon an ancient vernacular that for the most part had been excluded from the literary language used for the canonical texts.[122]

---

[120] (The Gale Group 2008)
[121] (Babylonian Talmud: Tractate Sanhedrin n.d.)
[122] (Alter, The Hebrew Bible 2019, xxv)

The alphabet changed, the spelling changed, the language changed, and in some cases, the meaning changed. These language changes are important to understanding both the Septuagint and the importance of the Dead Sea Scrolls. The scholar Martin Hengel notes some Dead Sea Scrolls are manuscripts written in the "paleo-Hebrew script" which dates from the early third century B.C. and seems to be the earliest biblical manuscript in existence. Hengel also notes the Masoretic text is "significantly inferior ...to the LXX exemplar."[123]

The Masoretes wrote using a different script than the one used to write the Old Testament; if Moses were alive today, he would be unable to read the Pentateuch. Not only did the alphabet change, but scribes had altered the texts. First, the spelling changed; second, the manuscripts slowly began using consonants to represent vowels; third, the meaning itself changed.[124]

Of the textual recensions, one of the more noticeable examples is Psalm 14:3. In the King James Version, this verse reads: "They are all gone aside, they are all together become filthy: there is none that doeth good, no, not one." The Septuagint, by contrast, is much longer.

They are all gone out of the way, they are together become good for nothing, there is none that does good, no not one. Their throat is an open sepulchre; with their tongues they have used deceit; the poison of asps is under their lips: whose mouth is full of cursing and bitterness; their feet are swift to shed blood: destruction and misery are in their ways; and the way of peace they have not known: there is no fear of God before their eyes.[125] (Ps 14:3) [English translation by L.C.L. Brenton]

---

[123] (Hengel, The Septuagint as Christian Scripture 2002, 84-85)

[124] (Barrera 1998, 60-64)

[125] (Brenton n.d.)

Deacon Joseph Gleason notes: "In Romans 3:10, St. Paul writes, 'It is written,' a common indicator in the biblical literature that the Scriptures are being referenced. Then, in verses ten through eighteen, he offers an extended quotation from the Psalm."[126] This extended quotation, which the apostle Paul cites as Scripture, is quoting the longer passage from the Septuagint, rather than the shorter passage found in the Masoretic text.

Fundamentalists and Evangelicals may find this problematic. Because they read modern notions of literacy, authorship, and textual authority back into the ancient world, they are unable to comprehend a world in which an author was merely a person whose authority was the basis for which a text was written and maintained. They fail to realize the primacy of oral transmission of knowledge and the inferiority of the written text. They fail to understand a religion where sacred rituals took precedence over sacred text.

People often notice the New Testament quotations usually don't match the Old Testament source texts, as we made clear in the examples cited above. What they don't know is the manuscripts used to create the English translations did not exist; the Masoretic Text was created later. Scholars trace portions of the Masoretic Text back to textual variants within the Dead Sea Scrolls,[127] but the Masoretic Text is an edited version of those texts.

One of the more curious differences between the Septuagint and the Masoretic text is in the ages of the patriarchs. The Oxford scholar James Barr notes the ages of the patriarchs, "at the time when the first son was born ...were different, and in most cases 100 years higher at each birth." Barr goes on to say that the generations of the patriarchs are about 1,000 years longer in the Septuagint than in the Hebrew text.[128]

---

[126] (Gleason, The Apostle Paul's Reading of Psalm 14 2014)

[127] (Barrera 1998, 284)

[128] (Barr 1985, 582)

The version of Ezra in the Masoretic text begins with the last two *verses* of 2 Chronicles. By contrast, the Septuagint version of 1 Esdras begins with the last two *chapters* of 2 Chronicles. 1 Esdras also contains the story of the three youths (1 Esdras 3:4 to 4:4), which turns the core of 1 Esdras into literary chiasmus.[129] Since chiastic structures were a common feature of ancient literature, this suggests the Masoretic text has been artificially truncated.

Table 2 Chiastic Structure of 1 Esdras

EZRA AND I ESDRAS COMPARED		
Masoretic Text	Septuagint	Summary
(II Chr. 35)	(I Esd. 1:1-33)	Continuation of *Paralipomenon* (i.e., "Things Set Off" from Esdras)
(II Chr. 36)	(I Esd. 1:34-58)	
		Begin Ezra
Ezr. 1	I Esd. 2:1-14	Cyrus's edict to rebuild the Temple
Ezr. 4:7-24	I Esd. 2:15-30a	Flash forward to Artaxerxes' reign (prolepsis)
		Core: Chiasm of Celebration
—	I Esd. 2:30b	*Inclusio:* Work hindered until the second year of Darius's reign
—	I Esd. 3	A Feast in the court of Darius with Darius contest
—	I Esd. 4	B Darius vows to repatriate the exiles
—	I Esd. 5:1-6	X The feast of those who returned to Jerusalem
Ezr. 2	I Esd. 5:7-46	B' List of former exiles who returned
Ezr. 3	I Esd. 5:47-65	A' Feast of Tabernacles
Ezr. 4:1-5	I Esd. 5:66-73	*Inclusio:* Work hindered until the second year of Darius's reign
		Conclusion

---

[129] 1 Esdras 3:4 to 4:4. A chiasm (or chiasmus) is a symmetric literary structure whereby a series of ideas are presented (A and B), with variant ideas (A' and B') being presented in reverse order (A, B, B', A'). Sometimes you might have a central idea (X) around which the other ideas are arranged (A, B, X, B', A').

Ezr. 5	I Esd. 6:1-22	In the second year of Darius's reign
Ezr. 6	I Esd. 6:23 — 7	The temple is finished
Ezr. 7	I Esd. 8:1-27	In Artaxerxes' reign
Ezr. 8	I Esd. 8:28-67	List of latter exiles who returned
Ezr. 9	I Esd. 8:68-90	Repentance from miscegenation
Ezr. 10	I Esd. 8:91-9:36	Putting away of foreign wives and children
(Neh. 7:73-8:12)	(I Esd. 9:37-55)	

6: Translation Styles and the Authoritative Text

R. H. Charles states that the Masoretic Text is the result of "conscious recension" and "unconscious change." He writes:

Both before and after the Christian era the Hebrew text did not possess any hard and fast tradition. It will further be obvious that the Massoretic [sic] form of this text, which has so long been generally assumed as conservative of the most ancient tradition and as therefore final, is after all only one of the many phases through which the text passed in the process of over 1,000 years, i.e. 400 B. C. till A. D. 600, or thereabouts.[130]

The Masoretes selected and established a particular strain of Jewish interpretation, and created what Adam Clarke describes as a "gloss" on the text.[131] A curious historical anomaly is that the manuscripts for the Septuagint are older than the manuscripts for the Hebrew Scriptures, and therefore represent the Old Testament text as it existed during the early Second Temple period. By contrast, the Hebrew Scriptures, being the product of the Masoretic tradition, represents the Old Testament as it existed for the Jews during the medieval period. The Septuagint represents the earlier text and is closer to the original text.

The existence of earlier alternate texts presents a problem for those who claim the English language translations are accurate representations of the Scriptures. Bruce Metzger comments:

The importance of the Septuagint as a translation is obvious. Besides being the first translation ever made of the Hebrew Scriptures, it was the medium through which the religious

---

[130] (Charles, The Apocrypha and Pseudepigrapha of the Old Testament in English Vol 2 1913, 5)

[131] (Clarke 1833, iii) A "gloss," in this context, is an interpretation or explanation. We will examine this contention further in Part III of this book.

ideas of the Hebrews were brought to the attention of the world. It was the Bible of the early Christian church, and when the Bible is quoted in the New Testament, it is almost always from the Septuagint version. Furthermore, even when not directly quoted in the New Testament, many of the terms used and partly created by the Septuagint translators became part and parcel of the language of the New Testament.[132]

As Bruce Metzger points out, the Septuagint was the Bible for the earliest Christians. The existence of an earlier and substantially different text pose problems for those who assume their Bible represents the original text and presents a problem for scholars who prefer a literal, word for word English translation. The Septuagint is based on an earlier text and represents a grab bag of translation techniques. Bruce Metzger informs us the translators "avoided literalistic renderings of phrases congenial to another age and another language."[133] Peter J. Gentry describes the translation styles as follows.

Individual books [of the Septuagint] vary in character and quality of translation and exhibit a full spectrum from extreme formal correspondence and literal translation to dynamic and functional translation and even paraphrase.[134]

Bruce Metzger gives us a list of Septuagint books falling into the literal vs. paraphrastic translation styles.

The various books in the Septuagint vary as to literal and free translation. Examples of free (or even sometime paraphrastic) translations are Job, Proverbs, Isaiah, Daniel, and Esther; literal translations are the books of Judges (the B text), Psalms, Ecclesiastes, Lamentations, Ezra-Nehemiah, and Chronicles.[135]

---

[132] (Metzger 2001, Kindle Locations 302-306)
[133] (Ibid, Kindle Locations 266-267)
[134] (Gentry, The Text of the Old Testament 2009, 24)
[135] (Metzger 2001, Kindle Locations 285-287)

Oxford professor Jan Joosten writes concerning the conflicting exegetical tendencies in the Septuagint.

Even within each individual translation unit, a multiplicity of factors comes into play. While most Septuagint translators basically attempt to give a faithful rendering of their Hebrew source text in the target language, several other elements determine the outcome in the translation. To begin with the translators' comprehension of the source text is in many places predetermined by existing interpretative traditions. In many instances, the traditions surfacing in the Septuagint later turn up in Rabbinic sources, which led Zecharia Frankel to speak of the influence of Palestinian exegesis on the hermeneutics of the Septuagint. Another factor influencing the work of the translators is their knowledge of the biblical context in the largest sense of the word. Many renderings reveal the more or less unconscious working of an enormous web of intertextuality, of which the harmonization of parallel passages is only the most prominent symptom. A third factor is the culture, world view and theology of the Diaspora Jews among whom the version came into being. Admittedly, little is known about the culture, world view and theology of Alexandrian Judaism – making it difficult to determine influences with any degree of certainty.

The multiplicity of factors – several others could be thought of – leads to a layering of meanings in the Septuagint as a whole. The plain meaning of a passage may stand in contrast to the vocabulary used; different meanings may emerge according to whether a phrase is read in light of the near or the larger context; a simple and straightforward passage may contain one puzzling expression throwing the meaning of the whole into doubt. [136]

It is not always clear why the translators chose one style over another; within each category of styles, we find historical books and wisdom literature. The translators paraphrased

---

[136] (Joosten 2008)

some of the Major Prophets (Isaiah and Daniel) while translating the Psalms literally. Jesus, the apostles, and the early church used a bible translated using methods that would not pass muster with most scholars today. The New Testament authors referred to the Septuagint as Scripture, and the Septuagint was the Bible of the early church. The style of translation is not as important as we think it is, which suggests problems with the modern idea of verbal, plenary inspiration.[137]

Leaving aside the issue of translation style (or exegetical tendencies), the Septuagint is not a book in the modern sense, but instead a collection of scrolls. Christians began cutting the scrolls into sheets and sewing them together to form what we call a codex. Many examples of codices exist, but they are not books in the modern sense. As Fr. Stephen Freeman notes, these were liturgical items, intended for use in and by the "worshipping Church."

The Orthodox still use the Scriptures in this form - the Gospels as a book (it rests on the altar), and the Epistles as a book (known as the Apostol). They are bound in such a manner for their use in the services of the Church, not as private "Bibles." These are outstanding examples of the Scriptures organized in their liturgical format for their proper use: reading in the Church. They are Churchly items - not "The Book" of later Protestantism. They are the Scriptures of the worshipping Church.[138]

---

[137] Plenary is a term that means unqualified and absolute.

[138] (Freeman, The Church and the Scriptures 2014) The formal name for the Apostol is the *Apostolos*, and it contains the New Testament with markings indicating the lectionary readings — the readings appointed for that day. The Old Testament lectionary readings, which includes what Protestants call the Apocrypha, are contained in a third volume called the *Prophetologion*. The *Psalter* contains the text of the Psalms, along with other texts appropriate to their use both in Church and in prayer.

7: The Septuagint & its Manuscripts

Since the manuscripts of the Septuagint were copied by hand and by people of differing abilities, there were different versions of the Septuagint in existence. The translation of the book of Daniel was so poor that the second-century translation attributed to Theodotion replaced it.[139]

By the 3rd century, the textual problem had become so bad that Origen collected all the existing versions of the Septuagint and created a six-column work called the *Hexapla*.[140] The Hexapla compares different Septuagint texts against the Hebrew texts and other Greek translations. Bruce Metzger (and others) claim the fifth column of the *Hexapla* was Origen's "corrected" text of the Septuagint.[141] Martin Hengel writes:

Origen created the Hexapla to obtain an overview of the confusing chaos. But he too defended the LXX text as approved by the church since it represented the translation that had come into existence by God's providence and was binding in the churches.[142]

In the early 4th century Pamphilus and Eusebius published Origen's corrected text; there were other 4th century recensions of the Septuagint as well.[143] Andrew Louth claims that Origen's purpose was not to determine the correct text

---

[139] (Metzger 2001, Kindle Location 298) For a variety of reasons, scholars now doubt that Theodotion was the actual source of the translation of Daniel we find in the later versions of the Septuagint.

[140] The Hexapla was such a massive work that it seems unlikely the entire work was ever copied. The original was maintained in the library of Pamphilus at Caesarea of Palestine, where it existed until 638 when the city was conquered by the Muslims (Saracens). (Metzger 2001, Kindle Locations 326-330)

[141] (Metzger 2001, Kindle Locations 311-323)

[142] (Hengel, The Septuagint as Christian Scripture 2002, 36)

[143] (Barrera 1998, 330-334)

of the Septuagint. Instead, its purpose was: "to lay bare the richness of meaning contained in the Scriptures of the Old Testament." As evidence, he points to the following:

Passages from the other columns of the Hexapla found their way into Christian copies of the Septuagint — so-called 'Hexaplaric' readings — and it is these readings that we often find in patristic commentaries on Scripture, as well as in the texts included in the services in the Byzantine liturgy.[144]

Our modern Bibles are products of a manuscript tradition.[145] There is no single authoritative text of the Old Testament. Instead, Andrew Louth indicates that part of the manuscript tradition is an exploration of everything contained in the pluriform texts.[146] Constantine Siamakis writes:

The ancient manuscripts of a text, together with quotations from it in other texts of similarly ancient or later date, and any surviving ancient translations of it which are also in ancient manuscript form, constitute the manuscript tradition of that text. Every printed edition of an ancient text derives directly or indirectly from its manuscript tradition.[147]

While we can speak of the manuscript tradition as a whole, there are different ways of interpreting that tradition. The

---

[144] (Louth 2013, 12)

[145] Some, like Martin Hengel, draw different conclusions from the Hexapla, conclusions that are unsupported by the evidence, and are based on a preexisting bias.

Nevertheless, he never mentions the [Septuagint] translation or even the inspiration legend. For him, the Hebrew original gained a certain importance once again. Indeed, the first two columns of his magnum opus were devoted to it. Thereby the church was continually reminded that the LXX is only a translation that can never exceed the Hebrew original in dignity, but must, rather, always succeed it." (Hengel, The Septuagint as Christian Scripture 2002, 34)

[146] (Louth 2013, 12)

[147] (Siamakis 1997, 8)

different methods have different criteria, leading to variant authoritative texts. Today there are three families of texts used to translate the New Testament: the *Textus Receptus*, the Critical Text, and the Majority Text.

The *Textus Receptus* was created by the 16th-century scholar Erasmus using the best texts available at the time and is the basis for most of the vernacular translations produced during the Reformation, including the King James Bible.[148] Later manuscript discoveries and scholarship resulted in the Critical Text, which nearly all modern translations and scholarship uses. The Critical Text is based upon Alexandrian manuscripts which constitute only about 10% of the manuscripts in existence. By contrast, the Majority Text, also known as the Byzantine Majority text, is supported by around 90% of the existing manuscripts.[149] The *Textus Receptus* is based on the Byzantine Majority family of New Testament texts.

There are two basic textual families within the Old Testament manuscript tradition. The Masoretic Text is the text produced by medieval Jewish scholars and is the basis for their Hebrew Scriptures as well as the Protestant Old Testament. The Septuagint, as we have been discussing, was the Greek Translation of earlier editions of the Hebrew Scriptures; this was the text used by most New Testament writers for their quotations from the Old Testament.

There are some Fundamentalists who dismiss the importance of the Septuagint. Samuel C. Gipp, Th. D. calls the Septuagint: "A figment of someone's imagination."[150] Gipp considers the Letter of Aristeas to be: "the **sole** evidence for the existence of this mystical document [emphasis in the original.]"[151] He dismisses the textual evidence for the Septuagint as follows: "There are absolutely **NO** Greek Old

---

[148] (Samworth n.d.)
[149] (Fores 1996)
[150] (Gipp 2016)
[151] Ibid

Testament manuscripts existent with a date of 250 BC or anywhere near it. Neither is there any record in Jewish history of such a work being contemplated or performed [emphasis in the original.]"[152] Gipp's arguments are widespread among the King James Only movement.[153] Beginning with the proposition that the King James Version is the only inspired translation, they must then discredit all others, including the biblical manuscripts used by other translations.

We will not address his issues point by point, as the contents of this chapter have already done that. However, we should note that the test of an ancient document's authenticity is *not* the existence of manuscripts from the time of the document's creation. If that were the case, we would have to dismiss the entire Old Testament.[154] The oldest manuscript evidence for the Masoretic text is from the 9th and 10th century AD, while the manuscript evidence for the Septuagint dates from 150 BC – 70 AD. When Samuel C. Gipp says there are no Greek manuscripts going back to the 3rd

---

[152] Ibid

[153] Our KJV is *not* the original 1611 version. Benjamin Blayney's Oxford edition of 1769 is a reworking of Francis Sawyer Parris' Cambridge edition. The King James Only movement praises the King James Version of 1611 as being inspired, but uses the Oxford edition of 1769. They claim the Oxford edition merely corrected errors, but never address how an inspired text can be edited to correct errors.

[154] If we dismissed the Septuagint because we have no examples dating to the time of their writing, we would also have to dismiss most of the Bible. The Hebrew Scriptures are among the best-attested ancient documents, with more than ten thousand manuscripts. However, because the Jews destroy worn out scrolls, few manuscripts exist earlier than the 13th century, and most of those exist in fragments. By way of contrast, Homer's Iliad is preserved in 647 manuscripts; the history of Rome composed by Velleius Paterculus survived in a single incomplete copy which was lost after being copied; the only manuscript of the *Epistle to Diognetus* was destroyed in a library fire.

century BC, the same is also true of Hebrew manuscripts. Samuel C. Gipp is arguing against the King James Version.

Even Protestants who accept the importance of the Septuagint generally choose not to use it for their bible texts. When I was Lutheran, I raised the question of why we didn't use the Septuagint instead of the Masoretic text as the basis for our new Lutheran Study Bible, to which one pastor replied: "Which Septuagint?" This is a reasonable question for a Protestant to ask, especially given what we now know about the translation and copying of the Septuagint during the first four centuries of the Christian era.[155] But we could just as well ask which Bible, as there are multiple canons in use among the different Christian communities. Moreover, there are differing textual families, each with seemingly valid arguments for their use. When confronted by multiple Old Testament canons, each authoritative for different Christian communities, the standard question is which canon is correct? But instead, what if we asked ourselves why the question of canon is so important? It may help to examine the question of how the canon(s) were formed in the first place.

---

[155] The answer, which no right-thinking Protestant would accept, is to use the version of the Septuagint delivered to us by the Church. This is, however, the basis upon which Protestants accept their canon — it is the canon delivered to them.

8: Flavius Josephus and the Canon

The Jewish historian Josephus is often cited as providing the first written canon of the Hebrew Scriptures. Conservative Bible scholars approvingly cite Josephus as evidence of a settled canon of Scripture among the Jews. However, as we shall see, things are not quite as simple as they appear. In "Flavius Josephus Against Apion" we read:

For we have not an innumerable multitude of books among us, disagreeing from and contradicting one another [as the Greeks have], but only twenty-two books, which contain the records of all the past times; which are justly believed to be divine; and of them five belong to Moses, which contain his laws and the traditions of the origin of mankind until his death. ...The prophets, who were after Moses, wrote down what was done in their thirteen books. The remaining four books contain hymns to God, and precepts for the conduct of human life. It is true, our history hath been written since Artaxerxes very particularly, but hath not been esteemed of like authority with the former by our forefathers, because there hath not been an exact succession of prophets since that time.[156]

Gleason Archer, in his "A Survey of Old Testament Introduction," provides the following points regarding the above quote:

Note three important features of this statement: (1) Josephus includes the same three divisions of the Hebrew Scriptures as does the MT [Masoretic text] (although restricting the third group to 'hymns' and hokhmah), and he limits the number of canonical books in these three divisions to twenty-two. (2) No more canonical writings have been composed since the reign of Artaxerxes, son of Xerxes (464-424 B.C.), that is, since the time of Malachi. (3) No additional material was ever included in the canonical twenty-two books during the centuries

---

[156] (Josephus 1987, Against Apion, 1.8.42)

between (i.e., from 425 B.C. to A.D. 90). Rationalist higher critics emphatically deny the last two points, but they have to do with the witness of such an early author as Josephus and explain how the knowledge of the allegedly post-Malachi date of sizable portions, such as Daniel, Ecclesiastes, Song of Solomon, and many of the psalms, had been kept from this learned Jew in the first century A.D. It is true that Josephus also alludes to apocryphal material (as from 1 Esdras and 1 Maccabees); but in view of the statement quoted above, it is plain that he was using it merely a historical source, not as divinely inspired books.[157]

The conclusions of Archer are incorrect. There were different canons in use among the Jewish people at the time of Christ, from the truncated canon of the Samaritans to the expansive canon represented by the Dead Sea Scrolls. Alfred Edersheim mentions that the Septuagint, including its Messianic implications, was widely accepted as Scripture 250 years before the Christian era, and that it was accepted for use in Jewish worship in Palestine at the time of Christ.[158] Francis Ernest Charles Gigot describes the larger Alexandrian canon as follows:

[B]efore Our Lord's time the Jews of Alexandria—and indeed all the Greek-speaking Jews—numbered among their sacred writings both proto-and deutero-canonical books, can hardly be doubted. For on the one hand, all the extant manuscripts of the Septuagint Version comprise both classes of books without the least trace of difference of authority between them, and on the other hand, as we shall see later, both deutero-and proto-canonical books stood on the same footing at the very beginning of the Church, that is at a time when no deviation from Jewish tradition can seriously be supposed.[159]

---

[157] (Archer 1974, 71)
[158] (Edersheim 1993, 16)
[159] (Gigot 1900, 32)

Historically, it is clear that the Jews did not reject the Septuagint until it was taken up by Christians. In place of the Septuagint, Judaism chose a newer Greek translation of the Hebrew Scriptures by Aquila the Proselyte, a translation which reflected the change in Judaism in response to the destruction of the temple and the challenge of Christianity.[160]

Alfred Edersheim notes that just as the Septuagint was the product of Hellenistic Jews (and could provide the date for the start of the Hellenistic era), so too was the Apocrypha the result of or response to Hellenism.[161] The Apocrypha were either written in Greek or, as we know from certain of the Dead Sea Scrolls, were written in Hebrew or Aramaic and translated into Greek. Alfred Edersheim writes:

[The] general object [of the Apocrypha] was twofold. First, of course, it was apologetic — intended to fill in gaps in Jewish history or thought, but especially to strengthen the Jewish mind against attacks from without, and generally to extol the dignity of Israel. ...But the next object was to show that the deeper and purer thinking of heathenism in its highest philosophy supported — nay, in some respects, was identical with — the fundamental teaching of the Old Testament. This, of course, was apologetic of the Old Testament, but it also prepared the way for a reconciliation with Greek philosophy.[162]

The canon of the LXX was itself quite fluid, being a collection of scrolls including books the Protestants now consider Apocryphal. Whoever deposited the Dead Sea Scrolls (popularly identified as the Essenes, although more likely to have been Jews from Jerusalem), also appears to have used the Septuagint canon (with the possible exception of the book of Esther). Given all this, what are we to make of the following statement from Josephus?

---

[160] (Edersheim 1993, 20-21)
[161] (Ibid, 16-20; 22- 24)
[162] (Ibid, 22)

How firmly we have given credit to those books of our own nation, is evident by what we do; for during so many ages as have already passed, no one has been so bold as either to add anything to them, to take anything from them, or to make any change in them; but it becomes natural to all Jews, immediately and from their very birth, to esteem those books to contain divine doctrines, and to persist in them, and, if occasion be, willingly to die for them.[163]

F. F. Bruce cites the first half of this quote approvingly, and states: "This language can scarcely signify anything other than a closed canon."[164] Unfortunately, F. F. Bruce is writing from within his Evangelical framework and fails to note the importance of the second half of what Josephus said. Josephus is not writing about the text of Scripture, but the "divine doctrines" contained therein. No one can add to the divine doctrine, nor take anything from them, nor change anything in them. Moreover, Josephus is writing after the destruction of Jerusalem and is reading the new importance of the texts back into Jewish history.

It is important to examine the quote from *Against Apion* in context and to compare that context with other of Josephus' writings. First, Josephus was writing to correct Apion, a man who claimed that since the Greek historians didn't mention the events of the Old Testament, the Old Testament was untrustworthy. It was within this context that Josephus defined the proto-canonical books. However, it should be noted that the books Josephus cites include Esdras instead of Ezra and Nehemiah. Also, at the end of *The Antiquities of the Jews*, Josephus writes:

I shall now, therefore, make an end here of my Antiquities; ...I have also carried down the succession of our kings, and related their actions, and political administration, with [considerable]

---

[163] (Josephus 1987, Against Apion, 1.8.42)
[164] (Bruce, The Canon of Scripture 2010)

errors, as also the power of our monarchs; and all according to what is written in our sacred books; for this it was that I promised to do in the beginning of this history.[165]

Francis Gigot notes that *The Antiquities of the Jews* freely uses 1 Maccabees, and quotes from the version of Esther found in the Septuagint instead of the version included by the Masoretes.[166] It seems Josephus used a different and larger canon than that admitted by Protestants.

We know the current Hebrew canon was established in response to the Christian's use of the wider canon of the Jewish diaspora. But if Josephus is speaking about Jewish doctrine, he clearly was arguing against the Christian writings — especially as they introduced new doctrines which diverged from the interpretations of Judaism developed in response to Christianity. Therefore, any argument from Josephus is an argument against Christianity itself. We cannot rely upon Josephus to delimit the Christian catalog of Sacred Scriptures.

---

[165] (Josephus 1987, The Antiquities of the Jews, 20.9.22)
[166] (Gigot 1900, 33)

9: The Christian Old Testament

F. F. Bruce believes the canon of the Old Testament was closed by the time of Christ; he argues that our Lord and His apostles knew what they meant when they used the term scripture.[167] However, we can say with confidence that our Lord and His apostles did not equate Scripture with a list of inspired texts. Nowhere in the New Testament writings do we come across anything resembling a list or catalog of books. And even if — for the sake of argument — even if we assume our Lord and his apostles had anything resembling a list, is there any way to recover that list? To put it another way: when was the canon of the Old Testament closed, and by whom?

Peter J. Gentry, professor of OT Interpretation at The Southern Baptist Theological Seminary, provides the standard argument for the closing of the canon before the time of Christ.

The text of the OT in arrangement, content, and stability was fixed by the time of Ben Sira or more probably, at the end of the fifth century BC by Ezra and Nehemiah. According to 2 Macc 2:13–14, Judas collected the books as a library after the war, following the example of Nehemiah before him.[168]

This sounds convincing until you realize that having a library of religious texts does not imply a standard catalog. Two pastor's libraries may contain many of the same books, but no two pastor's libraries are identical. As we shall discuss later, the culture at the time of Christ was primarily a scribal one. Scribes kept libraries for use in the temple and the government. Scribes wrote material for other scribes and not

---

[167] (Bruce, The Canon of Scripture 2010, 28-29)
[168] (Gentry, The Text of the Old Testament 2009, 19)

for public consumption.[169] The libraries of Nehemiah and Judas Maccabaeus would have been reference libraries containing materials useful for the ministration to and administration of the people. The establishment of a scribal library in no way implies a fixed canon.

The focus of Judaism during Christ's day was temple rather than text; Jews were not yet "people of the book." The idea of being a people of the book would not make sense until after the temple was destroyed.[170] During Jesus' day texts were read in the synagogue and temple worship used portions of the text, but it was the temple liturgy itself that was the center of Judaism. Subdeacon Gabe Martini describes the relationship between text and temple in ancient Judaism in this way.

Despite the advent of synagogues across both the diaspora and Palestine, the primary focus of Judaism—even in the diaspora—was the temple cult. Anyone that lived remotely near Jerusalem would make pilgrimage several times a year for the festal celebrations. The temple was at the heart of the Jewish faith. And as a result, there was not the same level of textual study as seen in both Christianity and Judaism today. Scriptural commentary was just beginning to take shape by the first century, and still only the scribes and priests could actually make sense of the ancient, Hebrew language.[171]

---

[169] The function of a Jewish scribe was the study of "the law, the prophets, and the other books," and the "translation and explication" of same. (Lim 2012, Kindle Locations 2340, 2344)

[170] The Jewish Encyclopedia, in its article on Jesus of Nazareth, makes the following comment: "It is doubtful whether he received any definite intellectual training, the great system of Jewish education not being carried into effect till after the destruction of Jerusalem." (Jewish Encyclopedia 1906) Thus formal education of the scriptures, that which became Talmudic Judaism, did not begin in earnest until after the destruction of the Temple.

[171] (Martini 2014)

The earliest evidence for the current list of Old Testament books comes from the period after the fall of Jerusalem. The Babylonian Talmud contains the first statement of the three divisions of the Hebrew Scriptures: The Law, the Prophets, and the Writings. F. F. Bruce writes:

> *One of the clearest and earliest statements of these three divisions and their respective contents comes in a baraitha (a tradition from the period AD 70—200) quoted in the Babylonian Talmud, in the tractate Baba Bathra. This tradition assigns inspired or authoritative authors to all twenty-four books, and discusses their order.*[172]

One problem with this reference to the Babylonian Talmud is the timing. A tradition dating from between the fall of Jerusalem and the end of the 2nd century can scarcely be used to describe the state of Judaism in Christ's day. This is especially true because Judaism changed in response to the destruction of the temple. After the fall of Jerusalem, the center of Judaism could no longer be the temple but instead focused on the sacred texts. The texts themselves changed in response to the growth of Christianity as a rival sect, a sect that used the Septuagint as its own Sacred Scriptures. This change in the Hebrew Scriptures was well underway in the mid-2nd century, as showed by Justin Martyr in his Dialogue with Trypho the Jew.[173]

Another problem is that the *baraitha* (independent oral tradition) quoted in the Babylonian Talmud was not authoritative. The *baraitha* was one of many voices in an ongoing discussion. This particular *baraitha* was not included in the Mishnah (completed ca. 200 – 220 AD). Also, the Christian community did not adopt the threefold division of the Scriptures and devised their own ordering and division of books.[174] Christians can hardly argue for the canonicity of

---

[172] (Bruce, The Canon of Scripture 2010, 29-30)
[173] (Schaff, ANF01 1884, Chapters LXXI - LXXIII)
[174] (McDonald 2007, 164-165)

The Christian Old Testament

the three-fold division of the Hebrew Scriptures when we reject that division in our Old Testament. We cannot derive the pre-Christian status of the Jewish canon from post-Christian Jewish sources. Post-Christian sources are all arguing a point of view influenced both by Christianity and Jewish hostility to Christianity.

Epiphanius of Salamis (c. 170-235 AD) is another important source of Jewish canonical information. In his *Panarion* (aka *Adversus Haereses*, or Against Heresies), Epiphanius provides a list of the books accepted by the Jews. This list contains all the books now accepted in the Hebrew Scriptures, but also includes Sirach and the Wisdom of Solomon as "books of disputed canonicity."[175] This list represents the works accepted by the Jews in the 3rd century, and should not be used to describe either the Hebrew Scriptures in the time of Christ or to describe the Christian Old Testament. However, it does indicate that even in the 3rd century some of the Apocryphal books were still in use within Judaism.

There was no early Christian consensus on the canon of Old Testament Scriptures. The scholar Martin Hengel notes the canonical limits were fluid at least up to the 3rd century. He writes:

The uncertainty with respect to the delineation of the 'Scriptures of the Old Covenant' ...in this period attempted for the first time to work carefully through the rich Jewish literature which was originally in Greek or had been translated into Greek and to investigate its usefulness for church doctrine and practice and theological speculation.[176]

Henkel also says there was a disagreement between using only those Scriptures written in Hebrew and those supported

---

[175] (Epiphanius of Salamis 2012, Book 1, Part 8, Section 8, 6:1 - 6:4) The reference to "canonicity" can only be a reading of our current usage of the word back into antiquity.

[176] (Hengel, The Septuagint as Christian Scripture 2002, 55)

by the "LXX legend."[177] The Jewish translation legend is first seen in the Letter of Aristeas, likely written sometime between 150-100 B.C.; the purpose of Aristeas, according to Martin Hengel, is to "legitimize a certain version of the LXX as solely valid."[178] According to Aristeas, six men were chosen from each of the twelve tribes of Israel and sent to Egypt to translate the law into Greek. These seventy-two men completed their task in seventy-two days. This legend was spoken of by the Jewish scholar Philo of Alexander (c. 25 B.C. to 50 AD), and also paraphrased by Josephus in his *Antiquities of the Jews*.

It is perhaps interesting to note that a number of early Christian writers used the LXX legend of Aristeas to show the Christian Scriptures of the Old Covenant were at least the equal of their Hebrew counterparts, and potentially superior. The first Christian author to lay this out clearly is Justin Martyr. In his *The First Apology*, Justin Martyr uses the translation legend to suggest the entire Old Testament was translated into Greek.[179] Then, in his *Dialogue*, Justin Martyr uses the Septuagint translation legend to indicate it was as authoritative as the Hebrew originals.[180] Other Christian additions to the LXX legend include the idea that the seventy (the customary way of referring to the seventy-two) translated not only the Law, but also the entire Old Testament. Christians also added a miraculous element to the story, such that the translators were kept in individual seclusion, but at the completion of their work all their translations agreed down to the smallest detail. Epiphanius of Salamis writes:

For while they were seventy-two in number and on the Pharian island, but called Anoge, opposite Alexandria, they were in thirty-six cells, two in each cell. From morning to evening they

---
[177] (Hengel, The Septuagint as Christian Scripture 2002, 56)
[178] (Ibid, 25)
[179] (Schaff, ANF01 1884, 266)
[180] (Ibid, 377)

were shut up, and in the evening they would cross over in thirty-six small boats and go again to the palace of Ptolemy Philadelphus and dine with him. And each pair slept in (one of) thirty-six bedchambers, so that they might not talk with one another, but might produce an unadulterated translation. Thus they conducted themselves. ...And when they were completed, the king sat on a lofty throne; and thirty-six readers also sat below, holding thirty-six duplicates of each book, and one had a copy of the Hebrew Scriptures. Each reader read alone, and the others kept watch. No disagreement was found, but it was such an amazing work of God that it was recognized that these men possessed the gift of the Holy Spirit, because they agreed in translation.[181]

The LXX legend developed from a historical event and combining the historical with elaborate fictions to such an extent that we may never know what actually happened. After the coming of Jesus Christ, the Jews created elaborate fictions of their own, such as the legend that the skies were darkened and the sun failed to shine for three days upon the completion of the translation.[182]

Some ancient scholars, reacting against the LXX legend, decided the Hebrew manuscripts were the most reliable. Protestant scholars such as Martin Hengel approvingly cite how individuals such as Origen and St. Jerome[183] preferred Hebrew manuscripts, and particularly those texts originally written in Hebrew. However, as Protestants, these scholars fail to understand the importance of the bishops in this process. While great scholars in their own right, neither Origen[184] or Jerome were bishops, and therefore their

---

[181] (Epiphanius of Salamis 1935, 18-22)

[182] (Wasserstein and Wasserstein 2006, Kindle Locations 2837ff; 3483ff)

[183] (Hengel, The Septuagint as Christian Scripture 2002, 41)

[184] Origen was under the jurisdiction of the Bishop of Alexandria, but was ordained to the clergy in Caesarea. The Bishop of Alexandria convened a synod which declared his ordination

opinions were subject to the judgment of their respective ruling bishop. St. Jerome believed Hebrew was a sacred language and that only those books whose originals were written in Hebrew were Scripture. However, when Jerome was engaged by the Bishop of Rome to translate the Scriptures into Latin, the Bishop of Rome disagreed, and the Vulgate includes Jerome's Latin translations of books Protestants call the Apocrypha.

---

invalid. However, the Alexandrian synod had no jurisdictional authority in Caesarea, and Origen appears to have performed priestly duties until his martyrdom.

10: People of the Book

The Koran (Quran) defines Jews, Sabians,[185] and Christians as being fellow peoples of the book,[186] which makes sense in an Islamic context. Muslims consider the Koran to be the Word of God made text. When Gabriel revealed the Koran to Mohammed, both Jews and Christians already had collections of inspired literature. Jews and Christians both had a way to preserve the inspired text relatively uncorrupted from additions and errors.

Most modern Christians have no trouble with thinking of themselves as people of the book; modern Christians have the Bible, a book which they refer to as the Word of God. Yet it is unlikely either the ancient Jews or the earliest Christians would have defined themselves as people of the book, for they had no such book.

Judaism was in flux at the time of Christ, with multiple canons and textual traditions. The Jews did not agree upon a single list of Hebrew Scriptures until the 3rd century AD. Moreover, the differing textual traditions were not merged into a single text until the 9th century AD. Apostolic Christianity described the Septuagint as Sacred Scripture, and the various New Testament writings only gradually became thought of as Scripture. Christians did not agree upon the canon of the New Testament until the 9th century.

This seems odd to us now, but in the ancient world, the oral word was primary; the written word was of little importance, useful only to a small class of people in

---

[185] The term Sabians seems to refer to a variety of monotheistic faiths that are neither Jewish nor Christian, although they appear to have more in common with Christianity than with Judaism.

[186] The term 'People of the Book' is used throughout the Koran, but there is no single passage that defines who the People of the Book are. Instead, we have a few passages where these peoples are specifically addressed (as in Quran 5:69), and it is understood that this reference is to the 'People of the Book.'

government, religion, or business. John H. Walton and D. Brent Sandy write:

After the discovery of writing, whether for the Egyptians or Sumerians, the Greeks or Romans, it was often only the priestly or commercial elites that acquired enough literacy to carry out their duties (or they purchased slaves who had been trained to read and write on behalf of their masters). Beyond that, the wealthy may have been educated enough to be literate. For the general populace literacy was rare, for it was almost never a necessity.[187]

We grew up in a literate culture, and we think of the illiterate as uneducated, backward, and unintelligent.[188] And yet our children learn to speak before they learn to write. We spend hours watching television and listening to the radio, both of which are primarily oral means of communication. The government funded the creation of the Internet as a tool to transfer and display text, yet the Internet did not become a phenomenon until it began to display audio and video. Speaking and hearing are fundamental; reading and writing are specialized skills. Walton and Sandy write:

Fundamentally, speaking is primary; writing is derivative. So it is in the Bible: nothing in the biblical creation accounts suggests that God wrote or created writing. Speaking was the focus; writing would come later. So it is for children: learning to speak is essential and comes first; learning to write is helpful and comes second. So it has been in history: a society that does not speak to one another has never existed; a society that does not write to one another has always existed.[189]

This may be hard for us to grasp, but the Bible was primarily oral before it became the written text we know today. In the synagogues, the reader would translate the written text on

---

[187] (Walton and Sandy 2013, 90)

[188] For more on literacy and the ancient world, see chapter 19.

[189] (Walton and Sandy 2013, 89-90)

the fly into ordinary language. In the early church, Christians would gather to hear the Gospels and the epistles read to them. Even today, we gather to hear the Scriptures read to us, after which we hear a sermon or a homily based on the text we just heard. The distinction between an oral and a textual culture revolves around the question of authority. Walton and Sandy write: "For oral communication, authority focuses on the persons who transmit the tradition. In written communication, authority shifts to the words on the page."[190]

In an oral culture, the speaker transfers the tradition; the speaker controls what is said and how it is understood. This is why the apostle Paul reminded the Thessalonians to "stand fast, and hold the traditions which ye have been taught, whether by word, or our epistle." (II Th 2:15) However, in a textual culture, readers approach the text with their own ideas and create their own meaning from the text irrespective of any interpretive tradition.[191] Tertullian, the father of Latin theology, understood this long ago. Karlfried Froehlich explains that for Tertullian, the issue was not that scripture could be interpreted differently, but rather that those outside the apostolic church have no "right to use the Scriptures at all."[192]

According to Tertullian, arguing with Gnostics about scriptural interpretation is useless. Even an agreed canon and common exegetical methods do not guarantee unambiguous results for there is always room for heretical intentions to dictate the agenda. Thus, the true battlefield is not interpretation but the very right to use Scriptures at all. Apostolic Scriptures belong to the apostolic church.[193]

---

[190] (Ibid, 89)

[191] (Ibid, 91-92)

[192] Tertullian's argument is interesting in that he died outside the church, having joined the Montanist heresy. This is why the Orthodox do not count Tertullian as a church father.

[193] (Froehlich 1984, Kindle Locations 210-212)

Protestants developed at the same time as the Gutenberg press. It is no wonder that Protestants are in thrall to the written word, and are compelled to disregard the apostolic tradition. (2Th 3:6) It is no wonder that each reader, having discovered some new interpretation of the text, is compelled to create some new denomination, leading directly to the confusion of the tower of Babel.

If, as the Scriptures state, "God is not the author of confusion," could it be that we are approaching Sacred Scripture incorrectly? (1Co 14:33) Is it possible that the God who spoke the worlds into existence, who commanded the prophets to speak the words of God unto the people, and that the God who gave prophets, evangelists, and teachers to the church, also expects the oral transmission of tradition — including the interpretation of Sacred Scripture?

11: Literacy and the Canon

The economist Michael Hudson describes the problem we have with understanding ancient cultures. In the context of economics, he says we modern people read our 'anachronistic fables' back into these ancient eras. He writes: "The Bronze Age Near East was organized on principles so different from those of today that it seems unconnected to modern civilization."[194] What Michael Hudson says of economics is also true when we try and understand the Old Testament scriptures by reading modernity into them.

What Jews call the Hebrew Scriptures is primarily a set of Bronze Age writings, gathered together and maintained by an early Iron Age people.[195] Bronze Age cultures are responsible for year-round systems of agriculture, for writing systems, for legal codes, for systems of government, for organized religion, and the beginnings of science and mathematics. We can trace much of our world back to its Bronze Age foundations, but we would be wrong to read our circumstances back into their world.

In our modern culture, illiteracy is rare. We tend to read our circumstances into the ancient world. It is hard for us to imagine a society without modern technology, to say nothing of a culture that does not require literacy. Bart Ehrman writes:

Studies have shown that what we might think of as modern literacy is a modern phenomenon, one that appeared only with the advent of the Industrial Revolution. ...This applies even to ancient societies that we might associate with reading and writing — for example, Rome during the early Christian

---

[194] (Hudson 2018, xx)

[195] The Bronze Age in the Near East is dated from 3300 – 1200 B.C.; The Iron Age began in the Near East around 1200 B.C. The end of the Bronze Age and the start of the Iron Age is dated differently in different parts of the world, and depends on the spread of iron smelting technology.

centuries, or even Greece during the classical period. The best and most influential study of literacy in ancient times, by Columbia University professor William Harris, indicates that at the very best of times and places — for example, Athens at the height of the classical period in the fifth century B.C.E., — literacy rates were rarely higher than 10-15 percent of the population.[196]

The ancient world had a remarkably different concept of literacy than we do. While the scribes and others had a remarkably high standard of literacy, the idea of literacy was rather broad, encompassing people who could only sign their name. The most famous example of this is a story from 184 AD and involves two "scribes" named Petaus and Ischyrion.

As often happened, Petaus was assigned to duties in a different village, Ptolemais Hormou, where he was given oversight of financial and agricultural affairs. In the year 184 C.E., Petaus had to respond to some complaints about another village scribe from Ptolemais Hormou, a man named Ischyrion, who had been assigned somewhere else to undertake responsibilities as a scribe. The villagers under Ischyrion's jurisdiction were upset that Ischyrion could not fulfill his obligations, because, they charged, he was "illiterate". In dealing with the dispute Petaus argued that Ischyrion wasn't illiterate at all, because he had actually signed his name to a range of official documents. In other words, for Petaus "literacy" meant simply the ability to sign one's name.[197]

Things were much the same for Jesus' apostles, some of whom were illiterate.[198] In another well-known example, the apostle Paul reminds the Corinthians that most of them are illiterate. He writes: "For ye see your calling, brethren, how that not many wise men after the flesh, not many mighty, not

---

[196] (Ehrman 2005, 37)

[197] (Ibid, 38-39)

[198] The book of Acts describes Peter and John as "unlearned and ignorant," meaning unschooled and illiterate. (Ac 4:13)

many noble, are called." (1Co 1:26) Some of them were educated and literate, but not many.

In the ancient world, reading and writing was the province of the scholar, the scribe, of clerks working in government, and of slaves who managed their master's affairs. When the Old Testaments speaks of reading it envisions a situation in which few were literate, and the act of reading was communal; the Scriptures were read aloud to and within the community. Chris Rollston, writing for the Society of Biblical Literature, notes that reading was not a solitary and individual enterprise.

Sometimes scholars will refer to the number of times "reading" and "writing" is mentioned in the Hebrew Bible and assume that this demonstrates that elites and non-elites could read and write. However, I would contend that the Hebrew Bible was primarily a corpus written by elites to elites. That is, it would be difficult to suggest that statements in the Hebrew Bible could be used as a basis for assuming the literacy of non-elites. Significantly, in this connection, Young wrote two seminal articles on the subject of literacy in ancient Israel. Among the most important of his findings is the fact that those referred to in the Hebrew Bible as writing and reading were primarily scribes, royal officials, kings, priests, and prophets. Some skilled craftsmen may have also been able to write and read (Young 1998a; 1998b). Ultimately, Young's analysis demonstrates in a convincing manner that the Hebrew Bible itself attests to literacy of elites, not the non-elite populace. Young's conclusions about "writing in the Hebrew Bible" dovetail with the Old Hebrew epigraphic record quite nicely: elites wrote and read, non-elites did not.[199]

Because literacy was rare in the ancient world, the concept of reading a book was (apart from the scribal community) necessarily communal, and books were read aloud. Bart Ehrman writes:

---

[199] (Rollston 2010, 133)

[C]ommunities of all kinds throughout antiquity generally used the services of the literate for the sake of the illiterate. For in the ancient world "reading" a book did not mean, usually, reading it to oneself; it meant reading it aloud to others. One could be said to have read a book when in fact one had heard it read by others. There seems to be no way around the conclusion that books—as important as they were to the early Christian movement—were almost always read aloud in social settings, such as in settings of worship.[200]

This situation reflects the Hellenistic world — that is to say, the world as it existed after 300 B.C.; before that time, there were no books as such. Professor Karel van der Toorn, a scholar of ancient religions, says that before the Hellenistic era there existed "documents, literary compilations, myths, collections of prayers, ritual prescriptions, chronicles, and the like, but no books, no trade in books, and no reading public of any substance."[201] If it is true that there were no books as such before the Hellenistic era, then we have a problem with stating Moses was the author of the Pentateuch, at least an author in the modern sense.

Even during the Hellenistic period, reading was still primarily oral and communal. To have read a book was to have heard someone reading a book aloud. Bart Ehrman writes:

We should recall here that Paul instructs his Thessalonian hearers that his "letter is to be read to all of the brothers and sisters" (1 Thess. 5:27). This would have happened out loud, in the church community. Paul also instructed the Colossians: "And when you have read this epistle, be sure that it is read in the church of the Laodiceans, and that you read the letter written to Laodicea" (Col. 4:16). Recall, too, Justin Martyr's report that "On the day called Sunday, all who live in cities or in the country gather together to one place, and the memoirs

---

[200] (Ehrman 2005, 41-42)
[201] (Van der Toorn 2007, 5)

of the apostles or the writings of the prophets are read, as long as time permits" (I Apol. 67) The same point is made in other early Christian writings. For example, in the book of Revelation we are told, "Blessed is the one who reads the words of the prophecy and blessed are those who hear the words" (1:3)—obviously referring to the public reading of the text. In a lesser-known book called 2 Clement, from the mid second century, the author indicates, in reference to his words of exhortation, "I am reading you a request to pay attention to what has been written, so that you may save yourselves and the one who is your reader." (S Clem. 19.1)^{202}

Part of our problem is that books, as we know them today, did not exist. Instead, of a book, think of a scroll — a single, long piece of paper rolled around a pair of spindles. Not only was the paper expensive, but the reproduction of the manuscript was a long, laborious, and all too human process. Bart Ehrman writes:

[Books] could not be produced en mass (no printing presses). And since they had to be copied by hand, one at a time, slowly and painstakingly, most books were not mass produced. Those few that were produced in multiple copies were not all alike, for the scribes who copied texts inevitably made alterations in those texts—changing the words they copied either by accident (via a slip of the pen or other carelessness) or by design (when the scribe intentionally altered the words he copied). Anyone reading a book in antiquity could never be completely sure that he or she was reading what the author had written. The words could have been altered. In fact, they probably had been, if only just a little.^{203}

Because the technology for printing did not exist, the concept of book publishing was unknown. A manuscript was widely copied because people found it to be valuable enough to spend the time, energy, and money to make, preserve, and

---

[202] (Ehrman 2005, 42)

[203] (Ibid, 46)

share their copy. Bart Ehrman notes the difficulties inherent in publishing manuscripts in the ancient world.

In the ancient world, since books were not mass produced and there were no publishing companies or bookstores, things were different. Usually an author would write a book, and possibly have a group of friends read it or listen to it being read aloud. This would provide a chance for editing some of the book's contents. Then when the author was finished with the book, he or she would have copies made for a few friends and acquaintances. This, then, was the act of publication, when the book was no longer solely in the author's control but in the hands of others. If these others wanted extra copies ...they would have to arrange to have copies made, say, by a local scribe who made copies for a living, or by a literate slave who copied texts as part of his household duties.[204]

Because copying manuscripts was a laborious, manual process, errors were inevitable and even expected. The written word was not as trustworthy as the word that came directly from the mouth of a teacher. Papius writes on the relative value of books vs. oral teaching: "For I did not think that what was to be gotten from the books would profit me as much as what came from the living and abiding voice."[205] The spoken word was the preferred method of transmitting information. Fr. Maximos Costas describes the situation like this:

An essential element of this [living] experience was the oral transmission of doctrine from master to disciple, for which written texts were but material supports for the spoken word, comprising intermediary moments between two dialogical events. The written logos as such was neither the focus nor the goal of such a life, but rather the living logos, for which written

---

[204] (Ibid, 46)

[205] (Schaff, NPNF2-01 1890, Eusebius, Church History 3.39.4; pp. 312-333)

texts were but preparations and complements: mnemonic devices ancillary to the concrete and practical experience of dialogue.[206]

Because of the inherently error-prone process of copying scrolls, the written word was not as valued as it is today. Written copies could not be trusted. Bart Ehrman relates some interesting examples of the way the ancients viewed the written word.

In a famous essay on the problem of anger, the Roman philosopher Seneca points out that there is a difference between anger directed as what has caused us harm and anger at what can to nothing to hurt us. To illustrate the latter category he mentions "certain inanimate things, such as the manuscript which we often hurl from us because it is written in too small a script or tear up because it is full of mistakes." ...A humorous example comes to us from the epigrams of the witty Roman poet Martial, who, in one poem, lets his reader know "If any poems in those sheets, reader, seem to you either too obscure or not quite good Latin, not mine is the mistake: the copyist spoiled them in his haste to complete for you his tale of verses. But if you think that not he, but I am at fault, then I will believe that you have no intelligence. "Yet, see, those are bad." As if I denied what is plain! They are bad, but you don't make better."[207]

The all-too-human act of copying scrolls rendered those texts less trustworthy. This problem was compounded by the few people who were literate enough to be able to read, interpret, and teach the scrolls. For the great mass of humanity, reading was a communal and participatory process, one that both entertained and enlightened. In this environment, the idea that the Hebrew Scriptures consisted of a closed catalog of manuscripts is absurd.

---

[206] (Constas 2018, 20)
[207] (Ehrman 2005, 46-47)

12: Scribal Culture

How are we to determine the development of the Old Testament canon, to say nothing of the development and preservation of the Scriptures themselves? The first difficulty is our tendency to view antiquity through the lens of the modern age — to assume that people lived, thought, and acted much as we do. But this is a tremendous error, for the ancients were quite unlike us.

For one thing, the ancients did not have our fascination with the printed word and with individual authorship. The ancients had a much different view of the individual than we do — not individual as a means of distinguishing one person from another, but rather as a person occupying a social role. Professor Karel van der Toorn expounds upon this.

We think of a human person as a unique individual distinct from all other human beings. This view is the outcome of a long historical process. Earlier cultures put much greater emphasis on the social role of the individual. In ancient civilizations, such as Mesopotamia and Israel, the human person is understood as a character (personage) rather than as a personality (personne). The individual is indistinguishable from his or her social role and social status.[208]

Since the ancients didn't have our fascination with the individual, our concept of authorship doesn't fit. The ancient author was unconcerned with issues that concern modern publishing such as "authenticity, originality, and intellectual property."[209] Instead, the name attached to a document had to do with the *authority* of the document rather than authorship in the modern sense. The actual author, in the modern sense, may have been an anonymous scribe.[210]

---

[208] (Van der Toorn 2007, 46)

[209] (Ibid, 47)

[210] (Ibid, 47)

The role of the scribe in antiquity was in part a function of that era's widespread illiteracy. In the last chapter, we mentioned a case where a scribe was considered literate since he knew how to sign his name.[211] With few people knew how to read, there could be no trade in books. Scrolls, therefore, were primarily a matter for governance and religion and were kept in the palace and temple libraries. Scribes used manuscripts as an aid to memory rather than a means of passing on knowledge. The writings themselves were largely incomprehensible without prior knowledge of their contents. Paul J. Achtemeier notes:

The written page consisted entirely of lines each containing a similar number of letters, lines that ended and began irrespective of the words themselves. Documents were written without systematic punctuation, without indications of sentence or paragraph structure, indeed without separation of letters into individual words. As a result, no visible indications presented themselves to the ancient readers that would have rendered them aid in their attempt to discern the structure, and hence the meaning, of the piece of literature they confronted.[212]

Reading ancient manuscripts was difficult, and required a person to be acquainted with its contents, to have heard the manuscript read before, and likely to have been taught its contents. Even for manuscripts, we must presume their orality. Paul J. Achtemeier writes of late antiquity: "The oral environment was so pervasive that *no* writing occurred that was not vocalized." [emphasis in the original][213] This means that people didn't read silently, to themselves; instead, they read out loud. Because of the difficulties in reading the texts without already knowing their contents, the transmission of

---

[211] (Ehrman 2005, 38-39)

[212] (Achtemeier 1990, 10-11)

[213] (Ibid, 15)

knowledge was primarily oral. Professor Karel van der Toorn writes:

Scribes wrote scrolls (rather than books) for the benefit of other scribes (rather than for private readers). A book market did not exist, nor were there public libraries; in fact, there was no reading public of any substance. Texts reached the people by being read out loud by someone from the literate elite. Writing and reciting were complementary facets of the scribal craft, and the Bible came into being through the agency of the scribes. In many respects, then, the Bible is the fruit of scribal culture.[214]

Conditioned as we are by Hellenism, this scribal culture is foreign to us — so much so that we read our Hellenistic understandings into the Scriptures, seeing in them the things that fit our Hellenistic mental model. We are like someone learning a foreign language and whose brain cannot 'hear' the phonemes that don't occur in our native tongue. Paul J. Achtemeier describes the period of early Hellenism, where the trade in books coexisted with scribal culture: "We have in the culture of late Western antiquity a culture of high residual orality which nevertheless communicated significantly by means of literary creations."[215] In other words, while they had written manuscripts, communications were still primarily oral. Scribes were needed to read the texts aloud.

Andrei A. Orlov describes the secular role of the scribe as follows.

Besides writing, this occupation also presupposes the ability to understand various scripts and languages, since scribal duties required proficiency in copying, i.e., duplicating written materials.[216]

---

[214] (Van der Toorn 2007, 51)
[215] (Achtemeier 1990, 3)
[216] (Boccaccini 2007, 116) 116)

While not disregarding the function of the scribe in antiquity, scribes also occupied a special place in post-exilic Judaism. Protestant theologian Emile Schürer writes:

The law which Ezra had introduced was essentially a ceremonial law. The religion of Israel is there reduced to strictly legalized forms, in order that it may be made more secure against the influences of heathenism. In the form of a law given by God Himself, the Jew was told what he had to do as a faithful servant of Jehovah, what festivals he should celebrate, what sacrifices he should offer, what tribute he should pay to the priests who conduct the services, and generally what religious ceremonies he should perform. Precision in the observance of all these prescribed rites was to be made henceforth the gauge and measure of piety. And in order to make this precision as exact as possible, it was necessary that an authentic interpretation be supplied. A special order under the name of "Scribes" devoted themselves to the study of the law as a profession, and engaged upon a subtle and refining exposition of it.[217]

Rabbi Jacob Neusner, one of the great scholars of 1st century Judaism, describes the scribal profession for us.

The scribes practiced a profession and were responsible for teaching the Torah, from preparing the documents that made official actions in conformity with the Torah. For example, a woman was entitled to a marriage contract, which specified the husband's responsibilities to her while she was married and also in the event of a divorce or the death of the husband. The scribes would write such a document. ...The scribe on earth was a partner of heaven both in his teaching of the Torah and also in many of the documents that he prepared.[218]

---

[217] (Schürer, A History of the Jewish People, First Division, Volume 1 1890, 193-194)

[218] (Neusner 1993, 101)

The 2nd century BC scribe Ben Sira (a.k.a. Joshua ben Sira, or Jesus son of Sirach), describes the function of the scribe:

But he that giveth his mind to the law of the most High, and is occupied in the meditation thereof, will seek out the wisdom of all the ancient, and be occupied in prophecies. He will keep the sayings of the renowned men: and where subtil parables are, he will be there also. He will seek out the secrets of grave sentences, and be conversant in dark parables. (Sir 39:1-3)

The Book(s) of Enoch and other Second Temple manuscripts such as Jubilees describes Enoch as performing scribal functions. Andrei A. Orlov notes the scribal functions of Enoch operate at both the celestial and terrestrial levels.

The important aspect of the early portrayals of Enoch as a scribe is that they depict him in the capacity of both celestial and terrestrial scribe, as the one who not only records messages from his heavenly guides, but also composes petitions as the request of the creatures from the lower realms.[219]

The ideal scribe's primary interest is the law of the Lord. The meditation upon the law of it "requires study of other kinds of knowledge and writings."[220] These other writings were likely limited to Jewish scribal writings. Timothy H. Lim writes:

The phrase σοφία πάντων ἀρχαίων should be understood as "the wisdom of all Israelite ancestors" and not the wisdom of the ancient ancestors of other peoples in general. Understood in the context of the grandson's Greek usage, [Sirach] 39: 1– 3 is likely to be a reference to Israelite literature.[221]

---

[219] (Boccaccini 2007, 115)
[220] (Lim 2012, Kindle Locations 2276-2277)
[221] (Ibid, Kindle Locations 2297-2300)

Andrei A. Orlov mentions the task of the legal scribe as "settling disputes and writing petitions."[222] Ben Sira describes the life of the scribe as appearing before great men and princes, of traveling through foreign countries, of spending his life in prayer and meditation, and of glorying in the law of the Lord. From the descriptions of Emil Schürer, Rabbi Jacob Neusner, Andrei A. Orlov, Timothy H. Lim, and Ben Sira, we gather that the scribe spent his life in study, in working amongst ordinary people drawing up legal documents, and also guiding the wealthy and powerful to conduct their affairs according to the Law of Moses.[223] The scribe also appears to have been a revealer and explainer of sacred mysteries, something central to the Enochian traditions as developed in the Second Temple period. Andrei A. Orlov writes:

One must not forget that the great bulk of information about Enoch's scribal roles and honorifics found in Enochic literature may implicitly point to the social profile of the authors of these writings. Collins notes that the description of Enoch as "scribe of righteousness" suggests that the author and his circle may have been scribes too. He observes that although we know little about the authors of the Enochic writings, the books of Enoch "often speak of a class of the 'righteous and chosen' and Enoch, the righteous scribe, must be considered their prototype.[224]

---

[222] (Boccaccini 2007, 116)

[223] There is a curious similarity between the function of the scribe in the ancient world and the professional parliamentarian today. The parliamentarian supposedly applies parliamentarian procedure in an impartial manner. As a practical matter, the parliamentarian is charged with finding a way to allow the leaders to do what they want to do — with enforcing the status quo. Likewise, the position of the scribe was to explain and encourage the rule of Mosaic law, but as a practical matter appears to have enabled and enforced the privileges of the elites.

[224] (Boccaccini 2007, 118)

Epiphanius of Salamis (c. 310 – 403 AD) lists the Scribes as one of twelve Jewish sects. He describes their peculiarities of Jewish belief and practice, which helps us to understand Jesus' condemnation of them. Epiphanius informs us that among their peculiarities was the wearing of borders of purple cloth (phylacteries) on their clothing and fringes on the corners of their garments during their periods of celibacy. These special garments informed others of their sanctity and thereby prevented accidental defilement.[225] Epiphanius of Salamis writes:

Scribes were persons who repeated the Law as though they were teaching it as a sort of grammar. They observed the other Jewish customs but introduced a kind of extra, quibbling teaching, if you please. They did not live just by the Law but in addition observed the 'washing of pots, cups, platters[226]' and the other vessels of table service as though they were bent on the pure and holy, if you please—'washing their hands thoroughly,' and also thoroughly cleansing themselves, in natural water and baths, of certain types of pollution. ...Scribes had four 'repetitions.' One was in circulation in the name of the prophet Moses, a second in that of their teacher called Aqiba or Bar Aqiba, another in the name Addan or Annan, also called Judas, and another in the name of the sons of Hasmonaeus. Whatever customs they derive from these four traditions under the impression that they are wisdom—they are unwisdom mostly—are boasted of and praised, and celebrated and acclaimed as the teaching to be given first place.[227]

The mixture of celestial and terrestrial roles described previously, plus the scribe's self-identification as the

---

[225] But all their works they do for to be seen of men: they make broad their phylacteries, and enlarge the borders of their garments (Mt 23:5).

[226] Woe unto you, scribes and Pharisees, hypocrites! for ye make clean the outside of the cup and of the platter, but within they are full of extortion and excess (Mt 23:25).

[227] (Epiphanius of Salamis 2012, Book 1, Section 1, Part 15)

'righteous and chosen,' is important for an understanding of the scribal hostility towards Jesus Christ in the Gospels. Jesus Christ is not only usurping their societal role as a revealer and explainer of sacred mysteries but is doing so as the lower-class son of a rustic peasant worker.

Scribes could also be priests. Priests performed their priestly duties only when their allotted times came up and served in other capacities during the rest of the year. One of the occupations open to priests was that of the scribe. The book of Enoch not only describes the patriarch as a scribe but also shows him performing the functions of a priest. One passage in particular (1 Enoch 14:9-18) shows Enoch passing "through three celestial constructions: a wall, an outer house, and an inner house,"[228] corresponding to the arrangement of the temple with its vestibule, the Holy Place, and the Holy of Holies. Another passage in Jubilees has Enoch burning incense — as in the incense offered in the Holy Place upon the Altar of Incense. "He [Enoch] burnt the incense of the sanctuary, even sweet spices acceptable before the Lord on the Mount."[229] That many scribes were also priests helps us understand their hostility to our Lord — to one who usurped their role by proclaiming forgiveness of sins.

The scribal response to the Babylonian captivity helps explain why the book of Psalms seems so disorganized. Although there are five books, they are not arranged in a manner befitting the Jewish liturgical cycle, nor do they seem to have any thematic scheme. The arrangement of the Psalms seems almost random. Karlfried Froehlich, the emeritus professor at Princeton Theological Seminary, explains why the current order likely doesn't match the original order of the Psalms.

The psalms suffered much displacement because the book was accidentally lost during the Babylonian captivity. Afterwards,

---

[228] (Boccaccini 2007, 119)

[229] (Lumpkin, The Book of Jubilees 2006, 39)

about the time of Ezra, it was rediscovered, though not the whole book at once but piecemeal-one, two, or perhaps three psalms at a time. These were then reassembled in the order in which they were found, not as they were arranged originally.[230]

Following the return of the exiles from Babylon, the individual psalms were found in various scribal libraries and collections. Rather than attempt to recreate the lost order (if we can presume there was one), the psalms were assembled in the order they were found. Thus, the arrangement of the Psalms is arbitrary. Even so, the book of Psalms is inspired.

Another example of the influence scribal culture had upon the content of Sacred Scripture is the passage in Deuteronomy providing regulations for the behavior of the king once the people enter the land. (De 17:14-20) This passage is peculiar because it suggests that God was not opposed to Israel having a king, yet it was normative during the period of the Judges for Israel not have a king. (Jg 18:1; 19:1; 21:25) The prophet Samuel was serving as the last judge of Israel when the people asked for a king. And God said to Samuel: "Hearken unto the voice of the people in all that they say unto thee: for they have not rejected thee, but they have rejected me, that I should not reign over them." (1Sa 8:7) What follows is a passage that details the behavior of the king — his taxation, and the manner of his rule — and describes this behavior in a negative light and much greater detail than the passage in Deuteronomy. Given this, we may well ask why the passage in Deuteronomy exists if Israel was not meant to have a king. The Mosaic law explicitly permits something that, under Samuel, was considered to be a rejection of God. We could discuss this in light of God's perfect will vs. his permissive will, but wouldn't it be easier to suggest the passage in Deuteronomy is a later scribal addition? That perhaps the regulations for the behavior of the king were a later addition to the text of Deuteronomy? If so, the idea that only the original author was inspired and not

---

[230] (Froehlich 1984, Kindle Locations 1069-1071)

the community of the faithful who received and transmitted the writings is flawed.

A historical understanding of scribal culture shocks our sensibilities. We are wedded to an understanding of authorship as an individualistic, creative act. But in the scribal culture, authors didn't exist as such. An author provided the authority for that which was written; the author was not necessarily the person who actually wrote the text. Scribes collected, copied, edited, and maintained reference libraries for use in the temple and in governmental administration. It is reasonable to assume that once Israel had a king, scribes added rules and regulations for having a king to the law, rules which were consistent with the Mosaic tradition.[231]

We should understand the books of Moses as the books compiled and maintained under Moses' authority, rather than the books Moses personally authored by his own hand. Moses would likely have used an amanuensis to transcribe his thoughts. Given the scribal culture, we should expect the original Mosaic material to have been compiled and edited over the centuries, yet still maintaining the basic structure and authority of the original.

To illustrate just one problem with applying the modern concept of authorship to the Old Testament, let us examine the Deuteronomic account of the death of Moses. As a boy, I was taught that Moses included this account as a prophecy. This idea has no scriptural foundation; there is no suggestion of this anywhere in the Hebrew Scriptures nor in the Christian New Testament. There is no reason to assume Moses wrote this account of his death unless you are wedded to later Hellenic ideas of authorship.

---

[231] We should note that while Saul was king, he functioned more like a tribal leader. Under Saul, there was no government as such. The same can be said for David. It wasn't until Solomon that a government existed, one in which the power of the king was delegated to government functionaries whose exercise of power was in accordance with the law.

13: The Curious Case of Jeremiah

Having examined the idea of authorship in scribal cultures, let us now examine the curious case of Jeremiah. The Septuagint version is 3,097 words shorter than the Masoretic text and is organized differently.[232] The material forming chapters 46-51 of the Masoretic text is placed after Jeremiah 25:13 in the Septuagint. The oracles against the nations are ordered differently in the Septuagint than in the Masoretic text.

Before the discovery of the Dead Sea Scrolls, some scholars believed the translators of the Septuagint had redacted and edited the text during the translation process. However, in the Dead Sea Scrolls, 4QJer^{b,d} is more closely aligned to the Septuagint than the Masoretic text.[233] The Dead Sea Scrolls prove that Jeremiah exists in two basic versions; the Septuagint and the Masoretic text. A shorter, earlier, and closer to the original version was used for the Septuagint. The Masoretic text is a longer and reworked version of the original. Regarding the additional material in the Masoretic text, the scribes added "headings to prophecies, repeated sections, added new verses and sections, new details, new arrangements, and clarification of unclear passages."[234]

---

[232] (de Ward 2003, xviii) Bruce Metzger points out that the Greek version of Job is also shorter than the version contained in the Hebrew Scriptures. (Metzger 2001, Kindle Locations 297-298)

[233] (Anonymous, Old Testament: Dead Sea Scrolls 2014) The Manuscript numbering system for the Dead Sea Scrolls is relatively simple. In this case we are dealing with manuscript number 4QJer^{b,d}. 4Q represents Qumran Cave Four. After that we either have a number representing the manuscript number from that cave, or we have an abbreviation for the book, with the superscript representing the different texts. So here we are dealing with Jeremiah texts "b" & "d" from Qumran cave four, also known as 4Q71 and 4Q72. For more information see the Leon Levy Dead Sea Scrolls digital library at http://www.deadseascrolls.org.il.

[234] (Ibid)

Table 3: Jeremiah in the LXX and MT Versions[235]

LXX	MT
1–25:13a	1–25:13a
25:14–20** Elam	49:34–39 Elam
26:2–25 Egypt	46:1–26 Egypt
26:27–28	46:27–28
27–28** Babylon	50–51 Babylon
29 Philistines	47 Philistines
30:1–16 Edom	49:7–22 Edom
30:17–21/22 Ammon	49:1–6 Ammon
30:23–28 Kedar	49:28–33 Kedar
30:29–33 Damascus	49:23–27 Damascus
31* Moab	48 Moab
32:13b–38*	25:13b–38
33	26
34*	27
35	28
36*	29
37*	30
38	31
39	32
40*	33
41	34
42	35
43	36
44	37
45	38
46*	39
47	40
48	41
49	42
50	43
51:1–30	44
51:31–35	45
52*	52

NOTE: *verses missing | **variation in order

---

[235] (B. Davidson 2012, 2)

Chapter 36 of Jeremiah not only mentions the name of Jeremiah's amanuensis but records the suggestion of the scribes and princes that perhaps Baruch had edited the manuscript. Then, after Jehudi burns the scroll in the presence of the king, it is recorded how Jeremiah once again dictated the book to Baruch, and that additional material was added as well (Jer 36:32). Professor W. H. Bennett suggests Baruch may have had a hand in the composition of the book.

It has often been supposed that our present Book of Jeremiah, in some stage of its formation, was edited or compiled by Baruch, and that this book may be ranked with biographies — like Stanley's Life of Arnold — of great teachers by their old disciples. He was certainly the amanuensis of the roll, which must have been the most valuable authority for any editor of Jeremiah's prophecies. And the amanuensis might very easily become the editor. If an edition of the book was compiled in Jeremiah's lifetime we should naturally expect him to use Baruch's assistance; if it first took shape after the prophet's death, and if Baruch survived, no one would be better able to compile the Life and Works of Jeremiah than his favourite and faithful disciple. The personal prophecy about Baruch [Jer 45:1-5] does not occur in its proper place in connection with the episode of the roll, but is appended at the end of the prophecies, possibly as a kind of subscription on the part of the editor. These data do not constitute absolute proof, but they afford strong probability that Baruch compiled a book, which was substantially our Jeremiah.[236]

To put it another way, Jeremiah may not have been the author in the Hellenic sense, but the person under whose authority Baruch wrote. We now know the Jeremiah of the

---

[236] (Bennett 1895, 57-58). Our likely reaction to the discussion of Baruch as the possible editor and author of Jeremiah is an example of how we read our modern concept of authorship back into a culture where authorship was not a creative act, but an assertion of the authority under which something was written.

Septuagint represents an ancient text, one that underwent several centuries of scribal expansion and revision to become the edited version found in the Masoretic text. Given this, which version of Jeremiah is scripture — the version extant in the time of Christ, or the later Masoretic text? If you asked a Roman Catholic, a Copt, or an Eastern Orthodox Christian that same question, they would likely say both are, because the Church considers them to be inspired scripture, profitable for doctrine, for reproof, and instruction in righteousness.

In its liturgy, the Orthodox Church uses the Scriptures preserved in its lectionary. The four Gospels form the Gospel Book, known as the *Evangélion*. The rest of the New Testament (except Revelation)[237] form the *Apostolos*, and the Old Testament readings form the *Prophetologion*. There is currently no authoritative translation of the *Prophetelogion* into English, and the Old Testament liturgical readings come from a variety of sources, including the very Bibles used within the Protestant Churches. Ideally, the Old Testament lectionary would be read from a translation that matches the Septuagint, but if that is not available other translations will do. When we read from the book of Jeremiah, some may read from bibles translated from the Masoretic text, and others may read from bibles translated from the Septuagint. The two texts are organized differently, but both are inspired.

---

[237] Revelation is not included in the Eastern Orthodox lectionary readings because it was not considered to be inspired when, in the 4th century, the lectionary readings were created.

14: The Development of the NT Canon

The development of the New Testament was substantially different from that of the Old Testament. For one thing, the New Testament was written over a much shorter period. The New Testament was written in a different language and uses literary types not found in the Old Testament. And then we come to the literary influences of the New Testament writers. Joseph Lumpkin notes: "Even more extensively than in the Old Testament, the writers of the New Testament were frequently influenced by other [non-canonical] writings." And of course, the canon (so-called) developed differently than that of the Old Testament.

The modern conception of canon as a list began with the dispute between the Church of Rome and the Protestants, each of whom made the issue of the canon part of their dispute. But as there has never been a Reformation among the Orthodox, the issues of canon and canonicity are of no dogmatic importance. Schisms among the Orthodox were about Christology, including the departure of the non-Chalcedonians and the Great Schism between the Orthodox and the Roman Catholics. Each collection of authoritative writings arose by common consent among the different groups rather than as part of a formal dogmatic stance.

The Ecumenical Councils were uninterested in the issues of canon and canonicity. Dr. Eugenia Constantinou writes:

By that time, certain books were unquestioned, while most apocryphal works were recognized as such and universally rejected. But individual churches and bishops exercised their own discretion among disputed works. Clearly the issue was not resolved at [the first council of] Nicea because no pressing need to create a definitive canon was perceived: the question of the canon was simply not a divisive issue. This lack of concern among the participants of the Nicene council with respect to the canon indicates that opinions about the canon were not essentially dogmatic. Two persons could disagree about the canon and both could be entirely orthodox in doctrine.[238]

How were the limits of our current canon determined? At first, Christian writings were shared between the churches. The title of Scripture was reserved for what we call the Old Testament while the boundaries of the Old Testament were left undefined.[239] Dr. Eugenia Constantinou writes:

Until the end of the second century, the term "Scriptures," referred exclusively to the Jewish Scriptures.[240] *Just as they had been the sole Scriptures for Christ and the apostles they remained the only Holy Scripture of the Church for many decades. Christ himself had quoted them, appealed to them, interpreted them and, most of all, fulfilled them. The Law and the Prophets had been normative for so long that it was difficult to conceive of any other writings achieving such high status. Although it appears that Christian documents were read within the context of Christian worship services by the early second century, another hundred years passed before they were recognized as possessing a level of authority that placed them on par with the Old Testament.*[241]

Consider the writings of Ignatius of Antioch (ca. 50 AD – between 98 and 117 AD). Ignatius was the third Bishop of Antioch when the Romans arrested him and transported him to Rome for execution.[242] During his journey, Ignatius wrote

---

[238] (Constantinou, Andrew of Caesarea and the Apocalypse 2008, 38)

[239] (McDonald 2007, 22)

[240] The "Jewish scriptures" used in the 2nd century refers to the Septuagint, not the collection of "Hebrew scriptures" that were edited and redacted by the Masoretes in the early-to-mid Medieval period. As Christianity spread, Christians used the Septuagint in the increasingly gentile and Greek-speaking Church.

[241] (Constantinou, Andrew of Caesarea and the Apocalypse 2008, 32)

[242] Ignatius of Antioch is said to have been (along with Polycarp) a disciple of the Apostle John. (O'Connor 1910) In his Dialogues,

several letters to various churches to encourage them in the faith. In none of his letters does Ignatius refer to the New Testament writings as Scripture. Ignatius scarcely makes use of them. Fr. John Behr writes:

Rarely, however, does Ignatius intimate the source for his proclamation. He knows the letters of Paul, and refers to them in the plural (Eph 12.2), perhaps even as a collection, and his writings are certainly imbued with the thought and vocabulary of both Paul and John, though this is only to be expected, given that they are dealing with the same proclamation. However, Ignatius never appeals to their writings to substantiate his own theological affirmations.[243]

Over time, various churches considered certain writings from the New Testament period to be Scripture. Bishops created lists of books that were acceptable to read during the liturgy. These lists applied only to the churches they were responsible for.[244] Sometimes that status was granted by one bishop and then taken away by his successor. Some bishops thought the *Didache* (also known as *The Teaching of the Twelve Apostles*) should be appended to the Gospel of Matthew. Some bishops accepted *The Shepherd of Hermas* for liturgical reading; others accepted some of the letters of Clement and Ignatius. Lee McDonald writes:

When a particular writing was acknowledged by a religious community to be divinely inspired and authoritative, it was elevated to the status of Scripture, even if the writing was not

---

Theodoret of Cyrrhus says that Ignatius was ordained as bishop of Antioch by the Apostle Peter (Schaff, NPNF2-03 1892, 308), while The Apostolic Constitutions (3rd and 4th century) say that Ignatius was ordained as bishop of Antioch by the Apostle Paul. (Schaff, ANF07 2004, 714)

[243] (Behr 2001, 84-85)

[244] A preposition at the end of the sentence is perfectly acceptable in English. We don't speak Latin.

yet called *"Scripture" and even if that status was only temporary. For example, the noncanonical writings Eldad and Modad, Barnabas, Shepherd of Hermas, 1 Clement, and the letters of Ignatius were initially given this status in the church, but in time that practice ceased. There was limited discussion or agreement in the early church on such matters, and in the first two centuries only selective agreement on books acknowledged as Scripture took place.*[245]

As the Nicene Creed came into existence to counter the Arian heresy, so too the New Testament canon did not become an issue until Marcion. The heretic Marcion is the first person known to devise a list of (so-called) Christian Scriptures.[246] Marcion's list did not include the Old Testament and included only a truncated Gospel of Luke and the non-pastoral letters of Paul as Scripture.[247] While Marcion spurred the interest of the early church in canonical matters, the early church did not take this opportunity to resolve the issue. Instead, the debate continued.

Even the four Gospels, while important in worship and the transmission of the Gospel, were likely not considered to be Scripture until around the end of the 2nd Century. Let us consider Tatian the Assyrian, whose *Diatesseron* harmonized the four gospels into a single book — a book which replaced the four Gospels in the Syriac churches until the 5th century. Eusebius reports that Tatian also tried to rewrite the gospels.[248]

Had the New Testament been considered Scripture, it is unlikely that Marcion's errors would have drawn so many

---

[245] (McDonald 2007, 23-24)

[246] Some recent scholarship suggests that Marcion's editing of extant texts and the robust opposition this incited suggests the importance of the texts, thereby implying their canonical importance. (Ward n.d.) I find this argument unconvincing, as there is no evidence for any authoritative list of NT scriptures prior to Marcion.

[247] (Kirby 2014)

[248] (Constantinou, Andrew of Caesarea and the Apocalypse 2008, 32-35)

away from the orthodox faith. Had the New Testament been considered Scripture, it is unlikely that Tatian would have would have tried to rewrite them. Had the New Testament been considered Scripture, the Syriac Church would not have accepted the *Diatesseron* for use in the liturgy.

In the following centuries, the canon of Scripture gradually coalesced around a common core of books. A few other books remained in dispute, with different bishops and regional councils weighing in. Eugenia Constantinou writes:

It can only be said that by the end of the fourth century a consensus existed in both the East and West for the core of the canon: our present fourfold gospel corpus, Acts of the Apostles, thirteen Epistles of Paul, 1 John and 1 Peter. However, Hebrews, James, 2 and 3 John, Jude, 2 Peter, and Revelation remained disputed at least to the extent that they were not universally accepted. [249]

The Book of Revelation is unique among the New Testament books. Revelation alone claims divine inspiration, yet has a strange canonical history. In the 2nd century, Revelation was widely accepted as authoritative because of its authorship and apostolicity. However, by the 4th century, Revelation had fallen out of favor because of the influence of the Montanist heresy. Eugenia Constantinou writes:

Montanist prophecy was primarily eschatological in orientation. The message contained chiliastic and apocalyptic expectations which were associated with the Revelation of John, such the promise of a New Jerusalem. The three prophets proclaimed the imminent coming of the end of the world and professed to be the divinely appointed agents sent to warn Christians that the second coming of Christ was at hand.[250]

---

[249] (Ibid, 39)

[250] (Ibid, 65)

The Montanist heresy was so pervasive as to have attracted the founder of Latin Christianity, Tertullian. The response of the Christian Churches to the Montanist heresy was to discredit the Book of Revelation.[251] Revelation also lost its appeal because the symbolism was mysterious and no longer understood. John wrote the Revelation to the seven churches of Asia Minor. Those seven churches were presumably familiar with the Jewish apocalyptic genre and with the author's cryptic imagery. Later generations lacked the intimate connection with the author and, being largely gentile, with the Jewish apocalyptic genre. The author's intent was lost, and the book's meaning was easily misinterpreted.[252]

Around 332 AD, the Roman emperor Constantine the Great commissioned Eusebius to provide fifty copies of the Scriptures for the churches in Constantinople. Unfortunately, none of these copies exist today, and Eusebius does not tell us which books he included in these copies. Some authorities contend they only contained the Gospels; others think they would have contained only the books Eusebius considered canonical. Since Eusebius did not consider Revelation to be Scripture, Revelation likely would not have been included.[253]

F. F. Bruce believes the Bibles provided by Eusebius would have contained our current 27 book canon but provides no convincing evidence.[254] Bruce fails to mention the western Church disputed the canonicity of Hebrews (due to its unknown author) for at least another hundred years.[255] Moreover, Bruce fails to provide convincing evidence for the inclusion of the Revelation, supposing that it would have been included because Emperor Constantine the Great used its imagery as "imperial propaganda."[256] Bruce also fails to

---

[251] (Ibid, 68-71)

[252] (Ibid, 72-73)

[253] (Ibid, 92)

[254] (Bruce, The Canon of Scripture 2010, 204)

[255] (Constantinou, Andrew of Caesarea and the Apocalypse 2008, 92)

[256] (Bruce, The Canon of Scripture 2010, 204)

mention the Byzantine lectionary dating from the 4th century did not include the book of Revelation. A convincing argument can be made for both Hebrews and Revelation not being part of the bibles produced by Eusebius. Wishful thinking is no substitute for scholarship.

Some Protestants point to works such as the Synod of Laodicea (363 A.D)., the festal letter of Athanasius (367 A.D)., or the Third Council of Carthage (397 A.D). to prove the catalog of New Testament was complete. Instead, what this shows is the matter was in some dispute, leading various bishops and regional councils to weigh in on the issue. The Council of Trullo (c. 692 A.D)., also known as the Quinisext Council, approved the conflicting lists of the previous councils and apostolic fathers without clearing up the conflicts between them. Eugenia Constantinou writes:

With regard to the canon of Scripture, rather than creating clarification, the Council of Trullo only compounded the confusion. The question of the New Testament canon of the East remained hopelessly muddled and even contradictory because the Quinisext synod did not compose its own list of canonical Scripture but only ratified earlier decisions, ignoring the fact that the canons of Scripture enumerated by earlier councils and various Fathers were not in agreement, especially with respect to Revelation. For example, Athanasius, Basil the Great and the Synod of Carthage accepted Revelation, while the Council at Laodicea and the 85 Apostolic Canons rejected it. They ratified Aniphilochios' canon, but it is unclear whether he accepted or rejected Revelation or the catholic epistles. On the other hand, the 85 Apostolic Canons accepted 1 and 2 Clement as Scripture, something which earlier synods and the ratified Fathers did not. All of these synodal decisions and patristic canons of Scripture were ratified at Trullo. Metzger concludes, and he may be correct, that the representatives at Trullo had not even read all of the texts they ratified.[257]

---

[257] (Constantinou, Andrew of Caesarea and the Apocalypse 2008, 107)

The Development of the NT Canon

When I was a boy, I remember being taught that the New Testament canon was closed with the death of the apostle John; that before his death, the apostle John supposedly granted his apostolic seal of approval to all the New Testament books. However, the historical evidence does not support this idea. Unlike what seems reasonable to the Protestant understanding of the canon, the development of the list of New Testament books took many centuries. The Church gradually came to a consensus on the limits of the New Testament canon, a process guided by the still, small voice of the Holy Spirit. The early church had the *regula fidei*, the rule of faith, as their guide. This guide led them to accept certain books as Scripture over the centuries. In like manner, they rejected other books as not consistent with the rule of faith and therefore not inspired.

No formal agreement settled the issues of the New Testament canon. In the Western Church, the problem was compounded by the standard medieval commentary on Sacred Scripture, the *Glossa Ordinaria*.[258] The *Glossa Ordinaria* was the Ordinary Glosses, the "normal tongue" of scripture. The primary contributor was Jerome, including his introductions to the various books. These introductions included Jerome's thought that those books the Jews consider apocryphal are not to be considered canonical.

Many people, who do not give much attention to the holy Scriptures, think that all the books contained in the Bible should be honored and adored with equal veneration, not knowing how to distinguish among the canonical and non-canonical books, the latter of which the Jews number among the apocrypha. ...Here, then, we distinguish and number distinctly first the canonical books and then the non-

---

[258] The Glossa Ordinaria originally began as Walafric Strabo's written notes in the margins of the Latin Vulgate. In the 12th century Anselm of Laon published an interlinear version. These were expanded upon through the years.

canonical, among which we further distinguish between the certain and the doubtful.

The canonical books have been brought about through the dictation of the Holy Spirit. It is not known, however, at which time or by which authors the non-canonical or apocryphal books were produced. Since, nevertheless, they are very good and useful, and nothing is found in them which contradicts the canonical books, the church reads them and permits them to be read by the faithful for devotion and edification. Their authority, however, is not considered adequate for proving those things which come into doubt or contention, or for confirming the authority of ecclesiastical dogma, as blessed Jerome states in his prologue to Judith and to the books of Solomon. But the canonical books are of such authority that whatever is contained therein is held to be true firmly and indisputably, and likewise that which is clearly demonstrated from them.[259]

While Jerome's ideas were never formally accepted, his Romish status as a Doctor of the Church lent his ideas a great deal of influence. The Roman Catholics waited until the Council of Florence (1422) before declaring which books were considered Scripture, a statement lacking dogmatic significance. Martin Luther, schooled as he was in the *Glossa Ordinaria*, could thus claim the authority of Jerome in support of these eliminating books from the corpus of the New Testament. In Luther's day, the idea of a formal catalog of books was new and was a product of what Luther considered a corrupt church. When Martin Luther came into conflict with the Roman Catholic Church, he deferred to the authority of Jerome and the medieval traditions contained in

---

[259] Biblia cum glosa ordinaria et expositione Lyre litterali et morali (Basel: Petri & Froben, 1498), British Museum IB.37895, Vol. 1, On the canonical and non-canonical books of the Bible. Translation by Dr. Michael Woodward. (Webster n.d.)

the *Glossa Ordinaria* when deciding which books should be in the canon.[260]

In response to the Reformation, the Roman Catholic Church held the *Concilium Tridentinum* or Council of Trent. In its fourth session (8 April 1546 A.D.)., the council published a catalog of biblical books, essentially ratifying the list produced at the Council of Florence in 1422 AD. Since the Latins convened the Council of Trent in response to the Protestant Reformation, this list had dogmatic significance for Catholic and Protestant alike and hardened the positions of each.

---

[260] (Swan 2011)

Part II: Inspiration and Authentication

15: The Self-Authenticating Scriptures

Modern Protestant scholars are fond of saying the Bible is "credible in itself, having credibility from itself."[261] The Sacred Scriptures are "self-authenticating": they are whole unto themselves, and need nothing outside themselves as proof of inspiration. Protestants teach the Scriptures as being the Word of God; as the Word of God, they have the power to convince us of their truth.

The idea of the self-authenticating Scriptures arose in the context of the reformer's conflict with Rome. Specifically, the reformers objected to the Roman Catholic claim that it alone had the authority to interpret Scripture and determine the canon. However, the reformers fail to deal with the implications of their counter-claim, which are two-fold: first, the concept of the self-authentication of Scripture confuses the ideas of authority and revelation as canonical norms; second, the concept of self-authentication effectively divinizes the Scriptures.

Christians often appeal to the Scriptures as an authority. For most Christians, this appeal to authority stands in for an appeal to a "network of claims about special revelation."[262] The source of the Scripture's authority is traced through the witness of "holy tradition, the Church, councils, prophets, reformers, bishops, and the like." Ultimately the source is traced back to God, with the Scriptures as the revelation of God.[263]

Protestant academic William J. Abraham describes the Protestant view of the self-authenticating Scripture as the confusion or separation of canon and revelation. The idea that Scripture functions "primarily or exclusively as an

---

[261] (Gerhard 2006, 68)
[262] (Abraham 1998, 6)
[263] (Ibid, 8)

epistemic norm of morality and theology"[264] diminishes the value of Scripture as the divine revelation and as a means of Grace. Of the concept of Scripture as a means of grace, William J. Abraham writes:

On this alternative reading, Scripture functions to bring one to faith, to make one wise unto salvation, to force one to wrestle with awkward questions about violence and the poor, to comfort those in sorrow, and to nourish hope for the redemption of the world.[265]

William J. Abraham says there has been a transition from "ecclesial canonicity" to "epistemic normativity." Ecclesial canonicity has to do with the involvement of the apostles and prophets, council and community, bishops and reformers — all summed up as the Church's involvement in declaring writings to be inspired and approved for use in the Church. Protestant scholar John C. Peckham dismisses this as the Community-Canon approach.[266] As described by Abraham, epistemic normativity has to do with Scripture having an autonomous justification.

Simply put, the question is whether the Scriptures alone testify to their inspiration, or whether we know the Scriptures are inspired because of the testimony of Christians throughout the ages. The Routledge Encyclopedia of Philosophy further describes the 'Foundational' view of Epistemic Normativity: "The foundational propositions have autonomous justification that does not depend upon any further justification which could be provided by inferential relations to other propositions."[267] This means the Scriptures are self-authenticating in that they do not require the witness

---

[264] (Abraham 1998, 7) Epistemology has to do with the difference between a justified belief and an opinion. In logic, an epistemic norm is a rule guiding the acquisition of beliefs.

[265] (Ibid, 6-7)

[266] (Peckham 2011, 204-205)

[267] (Klein 2005)

of the apostles and prophets, council and community, or bishops and reformers.[268]

The idea that Scripture witnesses to itself has consequences, and is contrary to Scripture. In the Gospel of John, Jesus says: "If I bear witness of myself, my witness is not true. There is another that beareth witness of me; and I know that the witness which he witnesseth of me is true. Ye sent unto John, and he bare witness unto the truth." (Jn 5:31-33) Jesus Christ did not self-authenticate Himself but instead followed the principle that truth is determined by multiple witnesses. How then can the Scriptures authenticate themselves?

The appeal to the self-authenticating Scriptures has the unfortunate effect of turning the Scriptures into a created god. Not God in essence, not a fourth person of the Trinity, but much more than a created being. The Gnostics (and others) described this lesser god as a demiurge. The idea of the self-authenticating Scriptures is mystical, subjective, irrational, and bad theology.

Descriptions of the self-authenticating Scriptures often include the Holy Spirit, but the idea of Scripture authenticating itself is a denial of the person and work of the Holy Spirit. Why do we need the Holy Spirit if the Scriptures authenticate themselves? The term "self-authenticating" is false if it is accomplished by the Holy Spirit. But if the Holy Spirit authenticates the Scriptures, we need to know whether that happens within the community of faith or in the heart of the individual believer. If in the heart of the individual believer, then what need is there of the church, the community of the faithful?

The author of Hebrews says: "The word of God is quick, and powerful, and sharper than any twoedged sword, piercing even to the dividing asunder of soul and spirit, and of the joints and marrow, and is a discerner of the thoughts and intents of the heart." (He 4:12) Unfortunately for Protestants, the Word of God referenced in this passage is not

---

[268] (Klein 2005)

the Scriptures as text. This passage references the Logos (λογος) of God, a term the apostle John uses as a reference to Jesus Christ. This is affirmed in John's Revelation, where we read of the rider on a white horse, one who is called Faithful and True, one clothed in a vesture dipped in blood, and one whose name is called the Word of God. (Re 19:11-13)

We should understand the earlier passage from Hebrews 4:12 as a description of the work of the Holy Spirit testifying of Christ to the world and within the Church. Our Lord Jesus Christ spoke to His disciples concerning the work of the Holy Spirit. "But the Comforter, which is the Holy Ghost, whom the Father will send in my name, he shall teach you all things, and bring all things to your remembrance, whatsoever I have said unto you." (Jo 14:26) And again: "But when the Comforter is come, whom I will send unto you from the Father, even the Spirit of truth, which proceedeth from the Father, he shall testify of me." (Jo 15:26)

The Scriptures are the Word of God because they tell us about Jesus Christ. When we speak of the Word of God, we are speaking about Jesus Christ. When Protestants connect the idea of the self-authenticating Scripture with a formal concept of the Scriptures as the Word of God, this equates Jesus Christ with Sacred Scripture, making scripture into an entity partaking of the divine nature. In this context, the use of the Word of God as a reference to the Scripture contains a hint of polytheism.

It is one thing to use the Word of God (in its secondary sense) as a shorthand for Sacred Scripture. However, the idea that scripture is self-authenticating is to ascribe to Scripture a characteristic contrary to the humility expressed within the Holy Trinity. The Holy Spirit does not draw attention to Himself. Instead, the Holy Spirit draws our attention to Jesus Christ. Jesus Christ draws attention to God the Father and foretells the coming of the Comforter. Yet somehow we are told that the Sacred Scriptures attest to themselves in a way foreign to the nature of God.

While the Holy Spirit ministers to each person, pointing each person to the Christ, this is done in the context of the

Church. When Jesus promised the Comforter, he was speaking to His disciples. The apostle writes that the apostles and prophets make up the Church's foundation, with Jesus as its cornerstone. (Ep 2:20) Also, the Holy Spirit was given to "All with one accord in one place," meaning the fullness of the Church at Pentecost. (Ac 2:1-4) Vladimir Lossky writes:

The first communication of the Holy Spirit was made to the whole Church, to the Church as a body; or, rather, the Spirit was given to the college of the apostles, on whom, at the same time, Christ bestowed the priestly power of binding and loosening. This is a presence of the Holy Spirit which is not so much personal as functional in relation to Christ, by whom the Spirit is given — the bond of unity in the Church, according to St. Gregory of Nyssa.[269] Here the Spirit is bestowed upon all in common as a bond of unity and as sacerdotal power: He remains unknown to persons and imparts to them no personal holiness.[270]

Lossky is not saying the Holy Spirit does not minister to each Christian; instead, that the personal ministry of the Holy Spirit takes place within the context of the Church — as the Church's bond of unity. Vladimir Lossky writes:

The Holy Spirit communicates Himself to persons, marking each member of the Church with a seal of personal and unique relationship to the Trinity, becoming present in each person. How does this come about? That remains a mystery— the mystery of the self-emptying, of the κένωσις [kenosis] of the Holy Spirit's coming into the world.[271]

The Church is not only the body of Christ, but it is also the temple of the living God. (2Co 6:16) The Church is made up of living stones, stones given life by the Holy Spirit. (2Pe 2:5)

---

[269] Lossky provides the following citation: 'In Cant., Hom. XV', P.G. XLIV, 1116– 7.
[270] (Lossky 1958, 167)
[271] (Ibid, 168)

Thus, the Holy Spirit works within the Church using specific persons. Vladimir Lossky writes:

If Christ is 'Head of the Church which is his body', the Holy Spirit is He 'that filleth all in all' (Eph. i, 23). Thus, the two definitions of the Church which St. Paul gives show two different poles within her which correspond to the two divine persons. The Church is body in so far as Christ is her head; she is fullness in so far as the Holy Spirit quickens her and fills her with divinity, for the Godhead dwells within her bodily as it dwelt in the deified humanity of Christ. We may say with Irenaeus: 'where the Church is, there is the Spirit; where the Spirit is, there is the Church.'[272]

With all that in mind, we say the Holy Spirit inspires the authors of Scripture and authenticates the Scripture within the Church, the body of Christ.

In his book *The Theology of Martin Luther*, Paul Althaus says the idea of the self-authenticating Scriptures involves their main focus, which is Christ. The Law serves as a preparation for Christ, and the Gospel speaks of the person and work of Christ. Althaus notes: "Since Christ is its content, this means that in the Holy Spirit Christ authenticates himself to men as the truth and thereby authenticates the Holy Scripture." [273] Note well the role the Holy Spirit plays in authenticating the Sacred Scriptures, which is a wholly orthodox position. The issue is how the Holy Spirit works to authenticate Sacred Scriptures — whether individually (outside of the Church), or corporately (within the Church, through the communion of saints). As pre-modern people did not think of themselves as individuals, but always as part of a community and the social role they played within that community, the idea that the Holy Spirit spoke to individuals apart from and outside the Church would have been anathema to the ancient church.

---

[272] (Lossky 1958, 156-157)

[273] (Althaus 1966, 74-75) In quoting Althaus on Luther's theology, I am not endorsing his support for Adolf Hitler.

In Luther's view, the Holy Spirit always works through means. Althaus writes:

Both Scripture and the spoken word however are external words; that is, they are not primarily a direct mystical communication from God's spirit to man's spirit but a word which comes to men from the outside and is brought and mediated to them by other men. This is closely connected to the fact that Christ in his humanity, that is, in his historicity, is God present with us. Just as he became man bodily, so he also comes to men through the human and historical means of the "external word."[274]

Althaus explains the connection between the external word and the Holy Spirit for us.

God's word, however, is never merely an external word, spoken by human lips and heard with human ears. On the contrary, at the same time that this word is spoken, God speaks his truth in our hearts so that men receive it not only externally but also internally and believe it. This is the work of the Spirit of God. ...God does not give his Spirit until the external word has preceded. Thus he does not give his Spirit directly, "without means," but rather through means.[275]

Luther directed his argument against the "spiritualists and enthusiasts," those who felt the Holy Spirit spoke to them directly. Althaus writes:

The content of the Spirit's speaking is therefore also completely bound to the word. If God would speak without means, as the spiritualists thought he should, and if the Spirit were free from the word, he could inspire anything that one might think of.[276]

---

[274] (Ibid, 35-36)

[275] (Ibid, 36)

[276] (Ibid, 37)

The later Luther's argument is completely at odds with the early Luther. The Roman Catholic apologist Dave Armstrong writes the following concerning the early Luther:

Luther gives the most varied expression to the principle of the free interpretation of Scripture: He declares that the Bible may be interpreted by everyone, even by the "humble miller's maid, nay, by a child of nine if it has the faith." "The sheep must judge whether the pastors teach in Christ's own tone."[277]

While the idea that the Holy Spirit works through means is entirely reasonable, the problem is Luther's artificial restriction of the Holy Spirit to the preached word of a single pastor as opposed to the proclaimed word of the body of Christ. In Luther's view, the Church is not one of the means the Holy Spirit uses to point us to Christ. Paul Althaus tells us Luther is reacting against a Roman Catholic idea:

That the earthly church be related to, and connected with, both the heavenly church and the church suffering in purgatory. This takes place through the veneration of the saints and the use and application of merits.[278]

Luther reacted against this by dividing the Church into the visible Church on earth, and the invisible Church made up of all the saints in heaven.[279] The visible Church is not the Church in its fullness, a fullness found only in the invisible church. Luther's radical ecclesiology is unsupported by Scripture; search as you will, holy writ expresses no such division of the body of Christ. The Orthodox position is that each local Church (or Eucharistic assembly) is the Church in its fullness. The Orthodox position is connected to the idea

---

[277] (Armstrong 2014, 190-191)

[278] (Althaus 1966, 297)

[279] This division between the visible and the invisible was originally a Marcionite position, as was Luther's division of Scripture into Law and Gospel.

that Christ can be fully present within you, fully present within another, and fully present within the Church.

The Reformed (i.e., the spiritual children of Calvin and Zwingli) promote the idea of the self-authenticating Scripture as the way the canon of Scriptures was created and validated. John Calvin admits the role of the Holy Spirit in this process.

Let it therefore be held as fixed, that those who are inwardly taught by the Holy Spirit acquiesce implicitly in Scripture; that Scripture, carrying its own evidence along with it, deigns not to submit to proofs and arguments, but owes the full conviction with which we ought to receive it to the testimony of the Spirit. Enlightened by him, we no longer believe, either on our own Judgment or that of others, that the Scriptures are from God; but, in a way superior to human Judgment, feel perfectly assured—as much so as if we beheld the divine image visibly impressed on it—that it came to us, by the instrumentality of men, from the very mouth of God. We ask not for proofs or probabilities on which to rest our Judgment, but we subject our intellect and Judgment to it as too transcendent for us to estimate.[280]

What John Calvin describes is the manner in which the Holy Spirit works within the individual to authenticate the Scriptures as divinely inspired. We do not deny the person and work of the Holy Spirit in the life of each person; in fact, we insist on it. We also remember the Holy Spirit reveals himself as a still, small voice. Each person can ignore this voice, just as our passions can quench it. The Holy Spirit does not force himself on us, just as He did not force Himself on the Virgin Mary.[281] The Holy Spirit, working through the communion of saints, cannot be ignored. It is for this reason that the Church — and not the Sacred Scriptures — is called the pillar and ground of the truth. (1Ti 3:15)

---

[280] (Calvin, The Institutes of the Christian Religion 2005, I.7.5, p.78)
[281] See my book *Why Mary Matters* for more information.

The Self-Authenticating Scriptures

Church history shows us the work of the Holy Spirit in forming the canon is not as simple as Calvin makes it appear. Different individuals had widely varying ideas of what formed Sacred Scripture. Calvin's idea requires that anyone who disagreed with Calvin was not enlightened by the Holy Spirit. Another less charitable argument is that Calvin (along with the other reformers) set himself up as the *regula fidei*, the rule of faith, the plumb bob used to determine deviations from the truth.

What John Calvin described is different from how other theologians described the self-authenticating Scriptures. For example, the Lutheran scholar Johann Gerhard writes: "Because it is God-breathed, published, and spread by divine inspiration, therefore it is credible in itself, having credibility from itself."[282] Professor David Scaer simplifies this thought: "Because the biblical writers were recipients of immediate illumination, the Bible possesses a self-authenticating authority."[283] Thus, the Bible is "credible in itself, having credibility from itself"; thus, the Sacred Scriptures are "self-authenticating": they are whole unto themselves, and need nothing external to prove their inspiration. However believable the idea of the self-authenticating Scriptures may sound, this is not a useful principle for settling canonicity. The self-authenticating principle can draw one astray into all manner of enthusiasms, allowing an individual or group to fix their own canon of Scripture. The attempt at creating one's own canon was the error of Marcion — the first person to devise a Christian canon that "self-authenticated" his preexisting heresies.

We must determine the principle (or principles) by which the Church determines the scope of the canon. Regarding this process, Dr. Eugenia Constantinou writes:

On what basis were certain books accepted and others rejected? What criteria were used? Did the authority of the

---

[282] (Gerhard 2006, 68)

[283] (Scaer, Baptism as Church Foundation 2003, 118)

book precede its canonization or was it recognized as authoritative because of its history or a particular quality that ultimately rendered it officially canonical? Which qualities were most important? Apostolicity? Prophecy? Spirituality? Perceived inspiration of the writer? Inspired reaction in the reader? Dogmatic importance? Orthodoxy of doctrine? Use by the community of faith? Didactic usefulness? Resonance with Christian experience?[284]

Protestants do not look at the problem historically; they do not use the principles used by the Early Church. Instead, Protestant scholars define two mutually exclusive alternatives. The scholar John C. Peckham defines these as the Community-Canon approach and the Intrinsic-Canon approach. Peckham describes the Community-Canon as "a collection of books deemed authoritative by a given community," and the Intrinsic-Canon as "a collection of authoritative books that are authoritative because God commissioned them."[285] If we use the Community-Canon alternative, the text is canonical because the community declared it to be so. If we use the Intrinsic-Canon alternative, the text is canonical apart from the community's declaration of the text to be Scripture. In the minds of some, any acceptance of the Community-Canon approach amounts to a denial of the Protestant Reformation. We will discuss these two approaches in the following chapters.

---

[284] (Constantinou, Andrew of Caesarea and the Apocalypse 2008, 31)
[285] (Peckham 2011, 204-205)

16: The Community-Canon Approach

According to John C. Peckham, when using the Community-Canon approach, the community says the Scriptures are Scripture because the community declares them to be so. A more extreme description would be to say a text becomes Scripture only *after* the community defines them as Scripture.

The pure Community-Canon approach is something of a straw man. First, there is no evidence for the Community-Canon approach among the early Christian communities. In particular, the early church was more interested in declaring certain books to be outside the canon than to decide the limits of the canon. When pressed by outside forces, and out of necessity, the bishops as spiritual overseers authorized a collection of writings for use in liturgical services. However, the early church as a whole had no interest in defining the extent of the canon. Second, the rhetoric of the Roman Catholic Church in the time of the Reformers may well have argued for the authority of the church to declare which books made up Sacred Scripture. However, even the Council of Trent claimed to be acting under the authority and influence of the Holy Spirit.

For any Church to determine a set of writings to be Scripture, we must first accept the existence of the community, the writing of said books as a witness to the community, and the use of said books within the community. Jesus Christ said when the Comforter comes, He will guide us into all truth. We must accept the Holy Spirit's work within the Church as the body of Christ. (Jo 14:26, Ac 4:31) We are not lively stones existing individually apart from the Church, but lively stones building up a spiritual house. (1Pe 2:5) If we accept this, then the organizational Church is only approving what the Church as a community has already decided upon.

The Reformer John Calvin denies the work of the Holy Spirit within the Roman Catholic Church, but his rationale denies the Holy Spirit works in any way except through individual members of the elect who are members of the body of Christ.[286] In effect, John Calvin denies that the Holy Spirit works within the body of Christ. Following the Reformers, Protestants generally believe that if the church fixes the canon of Scripture, it is the work of the Church as an institution rather than the Holy Spirit working within and through the Church. In Book One of his *Institutes of Christian Religion*, John Calvin writes as though the institutional Church was different than the Church as the body of Christ.

A most pernicious error has very generally prevailed; viz., that Scripture is of importance only in so far as conceded to it by the suffrage of the Church; as if the eternal and inviolable truth of God could depend on the will of men. With great insult to the Holy Spirit, it is asked, Who can assure us that the Scriptures proceeded from God; who guarantee that they have come down safe and unimpaired to our times; who persuade us that this book is to be received with reverence, and that one expunged from the list, did not the Church regulate all these things with certainty? On the determination of the Church, therefore, it is said, depend both the reverence which is due to Scripture, and the books which are to be admitted into the canon.[287]

Calvin's argument is flawed in that he presumes the Holy Spirit does not work through the Church, the body of Christ. The elimination of the Church as an authority leads us inevitably to the dogma at the heart of the Reformation, which is Sola Scriptura, or Scripture Alone. According to the Reformers, the institutional Church has no say in what books are or are not Scripture. Lewis W. Spitz, Sr. writes of Martin Luther:

His study of church history convinced him that councils and popes had erred. Replying to the Dialogue Concerning the Powers of the Pope, prepared by Silvester Prierias in 1518,

---

[286] (Calvin, The Institutes of the Christian Religion 2005, I.7 passim)
[287] (Ibid, I.7.1)

Luther insisted that only the Holy Scriptures were without error.[288]

When Martin Luther was called before to the Diet of Worms, he defended himself with the most famous statement in Reformation history:[289]

Unless I am convinced by the testimonies of the Holy Scriptures or evident reason... (for I believe neither in the pope nor councils alone, since it has been established that they have often erred and contradicted themselves), I am bound by the Scriptures adduced by me, and my conscience has been taken captive by the Word of God, and I am neither able nor willing to recant, since it is neither safe nor right to act against conscience. God help me. Amen.[290]

This statement replaces the Roman Catholic triad of Scripture, Tradition, and the Teaching Magisterium with the Protestant triad of Scripture, Reason, and Conscience. We should note that while Luther's statement lacks any mention of the Holy Spirit, other of Luther's writings indicate the Holy Spirit's role in guiding the believer's reason and conscience. Luther's view aligns well with John Calvin, suggesting we need to examine the role of the Holy Spirit in the inspiration of Scripture.

The apostle Peter writes: "For the prophecy came not in old time by the will of man: but holy men of God spake as they were moved by the Holy Ghost." (2Pe 1:21) Calvin's argument depends on the writing of the various books before the Church existed, meaning the Church had no role in recognizing their inspiration. However, even Calvin recognizes the Church's existence before the writing of the New Testament. In his Commentary on Acts, Calvin states

---

[288] (Spitz, Sr. 1960, 740)

[289] The Diet of Worms was a council presided over by the Holy Roman Emperor, called to decide the fate of Martin Luther.

[290] (Spitz, Sr. 1960, 740 - 741)

Christ first introduced the Church, but that Luke's description of Pentecost reveals the "best form of the Church."[291]

Now, here is most lively painted out the beginning of Christ's kingdom, and as it were the renewing of the world; for although the Son of God had gathered together, by his preaching, a certain Church, before such time as he departed out of the world, yet, nevertheless, that was the best form of the Church which began then, when as the apostles, having new power given them from above, began to preach that that only Shepherd did both die and also rise again, that through his conduct all those which were dispersed, far and wide, (upon the face of the whole earth,) might be gathered unto one sheepfold. Here is, therefore, set down both the beginning and also the increasing of the Church of Christ after his ascension, whereby he was declared to be King both of heaven and earth.[292]

According to Calvin, Christ revealed the existence of the Church, which then assumed its final form at Pentecost. Thus, the Son of God established the Church, and the Holy Spirit empowered the Church. John Calvin credits the "best form of the Church" to the Holy Spirit, but then denies the continued work of the Holy Spirit within and through that Church. Calvin's hostility to the Roman Catholic Church colors his understanding of Scripture and the Church as the body of Christ. He writes:

These ravings are admirably refuted by a single expression of an apostle. Paul testifies that the Church is "built on the foundation of the apostles and prophets," (Eph. 2:20). If the doctrine of the apostles and prophets is the foundation of the Church, the former must have had its certainty before the

---

[291] Hyperdispensationalists, like E.W. Bullinger, claim the Church did not begin until sometime near the end or after the book of Acts. (Bullinger 1909, Appendix 181, pp. 643-646)

[292] (Calvin, Commentary on Acts Volume 1 1585, 14-15)

latter began to exist. Nor is there any room for the cavil, that though the Church derives her first beginning from thence, it still remains doubtful what writings are to be attributed to the apostles and prophets, until her Judgment is interposed. For if the Christian Church was founded at first on the writings of the prophets, and the preaching of the apostles, that doctrine, wheresoever it may be found, was certainly ascertained and sanctioned antecedently to the Church, since, but for this, the Church herself never could have existed.[293]

Calvin's argument is in error due to his faulty Christology. In his *Institutes of the Christian Religion*, Calvin provides an orthodox understanding of the Incarnation, of the two natures in Christ, and the communication of attributes. When Calvin deals with the *implications* of the Incarnation, however, it is clear Calvin is no orthodox theologian. In the orthodox theology of the Incarnation, God becomes a man by assuming humanity into Himself; thus, orthodox Christology recognizes the human nature of Christ does not diminish His divine nature. The idea that God became a man is certainly true, but it is not the whole truth. When we speak of the sun rising and setting, we know the Earth is spinning on its axis, and that the earth is moving about the sun. Likewise, when we say God became a man it is a shorthand encompassing the way God took humanity into Himself while remaining fully God and fully man, yet without diminishing either nature or confusing their attributes.

Because neither nature is diminished by the other, Christ can be locally present and yet everywhere present and filling all things. According to Calvin, Christ is forever limited by His humanity. Our Lord is bodily present "at the right hand of the Father" while His kingdom "is not limited by any intervals of space, nor circumscribed by any dimensions." In this manner, Calvin distinguishes the presence of Christ and the Kingdom of God. Calvin distinguishes between God's economy and God's actual presence in this fashion:

---

[293] (Calvin, The Institutes of the Christian Religion 2005, I.7.2)

Hidden in Plain Sight

Christ can exert his energy wherever he pleases, in earth and heaven, can manifest his presence by the exercise of his power, can always be present with his people, breathing into them his own life, can live in them, sustain, confirm, and invigorate them, and preserve them safe, just as if he were with them in the body.[294]

The Christ of Calvin is not everywhere present and filling all things, meaning His human flesh diminishes his essence; His humanity is a diminution of the Son of God. As the Christ, the Son of God is no longer everywhere present, meaning He is no longer co-equal with the Father and the Holy Spirit. The grace of Christ, being separate from His physical person, must, therefore, be created. (Created grace is a Roman Catholic position, by the way). Calvin indicates this is "only for a time"; that ultimately, we will "enjoy the immediate presence of his Godhead."[295]

Let us examine how Calvin's rationalism affects his understanding of the Church. Calvin admits that Christ set up a "certain Church." This "certain Church" assumed its intended form when the Holy Spirit descended with power on the apostles at Pentecost. Here is the problem with Calvin's argument. Christ's calling of the apostles and His proclamation of the Kingdom of God did not merely occur at the same time but were the same thing. Jesus made many statements about His kingdom: "the kingdom of God is come unto you" (Mt 12:28); "The time is fulfilled, and the kingdom of God is at hand" (Mr 1:15); "The kingdom of God cometh not with observation: Neither shall they say, Lo here! or, lo there! for, behold, the kingdom of God is within you" (Lu 17:20-21). The followers of Jesus made up a community of faith; for them, Jesus was "God with us" (Mt 1:23). During His ministry on earth, our Lord restrained the exercise of His power; He voluntarily hid his power and His glory within His human flesh. However, Jesus also spoke of a time when some would

---

[294] (Ibid, IV.17.18)

[295] (Ibid, II.14.3)

The Community-Canon Approach

see "the kingdom of God come with power" (Mr 9:1). Peter, James, and John witnessed this power on the mount of Transfiguration (Mt 17:2); the entire community witnessed this power when the Holy Spirit descended on the Church at Pentecost (Acts 2:1-4). Jesus' calling of His disciples and the beginning of the Church is the same event. When Paul says, the Church is "built on the foundation of the apostles and the prophets," he is not saying the apostles and prophets came before the Church. Instead, the apostles and prophets are consanguineous with the Church, meaning they share the same blood, the same kinship, the same origin.

The apostle Peter writes: "For the prophecy came not in old time by the will of man: but holy men of God spake as they were moved by the Holy Ghost." (1Pe 1:21) These "holy men of God" were part of a community. The community of faith was the source from which the prophets and apostles came and the community to which they witnessed. The Church existed before the writing of Scripture, and the Scriptures existed before their recognition by the Church as Scripture. Nonetheless, the Scriptures were created by, within, and for the Church.

Decades passed between Pentecost and the writing of the first New Testament Scripture. More decades passed before all the books of our New Testament were written. Centuries passed before the list of New Testament Scriptures was accepted. The process of canonization in the modern sense of the term is the result of a long historical process culminating in a religious authority of some sort formally settling the content of the canon, a decision ratified by the common consent of the Church.

The idea of a canon of Scriptures assumes a community to whom those Scriptures bear witness, a community bearing witness to those Scriptures, and an authoritative body which formalizes the witness on behalf of the community. Julio Trebolle Barrera writes:

The final validation of a canon of sacred books is always the province of a religious authority which, by means of a «conciliar definition» or another form of authoritative decision, fixes the list of canonical books and at the same time excludes books not accepted into the canon. This is an historical event of a social nature, always determined and conditioned by circumstances of a very different kind.[296]

Despite this, there are those who chose to deny the historical and social nature of canonical development and in particular the idea of a religious authority deciding on such matters. In arguing for Sola Scriptura, the Reformers also chose to limit the canon of Scripture, a decision that cannot be justified by Scripture Alone. Nowhere in Scripture is the canon defined. Nor are there any canonical precepts in Scripture that would guide us in determining which books are and are not Scripture. Ultimately, Protestants rely upon their traditions in determining their 66-book canon. To put it another way, Protestants use their Community-Canon approach to justify their 66-book canon of Scripture.

---

[296] (Barrera 1998, 151)

17: Objections to the Community-Canon Approach

Arguments against the Community-Canon approach include the hostile reaction of the community of faith to the prophets and the failure of the community to recognize and declare a text to be Scripture. Did not the Holy Spirit inspire the author to write it? Was the text Scripture before the community declared it to be so? In chapter 10 we discussed how the community did not immediately recognize Jeremiah's writings as Scripture. Instead, the King burned Jeremiah's first manuscript (Jer 36:21-25). If an inspired text can be destroyed, how then can that text be Scripture? The answer to all these questions is that inspiration is about the message, not the text. The prophet is God's herald (the κηρύσσω, kerusso) while the message is the herald's proclamation (the κήρυγμα, kerugma, or kerygma). The prophet is the herald who proclaims God's message. The proclamation is made by a member of a community, to that community. This proclamation is later written down; the record of the prophetic proclamation is recognized by that community (perhaps at a later date) as Scripture.

John C. Peckham argues differently:

The biblical concept of a true prophet refers to one divinely authorized to speak for God (Jer 15:19; Acts 3:18, 21). There is then, by definition, a divinely appointed authority belonging to true prophets that is thereby inconsistent with the epistemological primacy of the community. Yet if the community is considered to be authoritative to determine the validity of prophets, such prophetic authority is logically (if not actually) compromised.[297]

In layman's terms, John C. Peckham claims the prophet's authorization to speak for God exists independently and

---

[297] (Peckham 2011, 209) Epistemology concerns the foundation, scope, and validity of knowledge.

apart from any criteria the community might use to determine the prophetic authority of the prophetic writing. The individual is an authority by being a prophet; the prophetic authority, according to Peckham, is an essential part of the text. In this view, the text is authoritative because God authorized it, and its authority exists apart from the textual witness to and within the community. Peckham refuses to notice the prophet exists within a community, is a product of that community, and is inspired by the Holy Spirit as a witness to that community, and that the text is a record of the prior proclamation.

Protestants in general (and John C. Peckham in particular) lack an understanding of the communion of saints and instead approaches inspiration as applying to individuals. Protestants read the modern, western concept of individualism back into the ancient era, failing to notice that the ancients had no such concept. Reading individualism into the ancient era has profound implications for the Protestant understanding of the Church, whom they view as a collection of individuals. The Scriptures, by contrast, describe each person as a member of the body of Christ (with Christ as its head). The individual member of the body of Christ has no life independent of the body. To use another biblical metaphor, Christians are but one of the living stones. It takes a community of living stones to build a spiritual house, and apart from the house, the stone is not alive. The prophets were but one member of the body of Christ and but one of the lively stones. Just as a flame cannot exist apart from the fire, the prophets (and the textual account of their message) cannot exist apart from the household of faith. The individual Christian is an oxymoron.

John C. Peckham assumes the Holy Spirit either works with the prophet, or works with the community, but not both. By presenting us with only these two options, Peckham is forgetting the Holy Spirit is unbound by time and space, and that He blows where He pleases (Jo 3:8). The Holy Spirit can be simultaneously present with the prophet who speaks, the amanuensis who writes down the prophet's words, and the

Objections to the Community-Canon Approach

community who receives the writing. When the prophet Habakkuk calls down God's judgment on the nation of Judah, he is calling down judgment on himself as a member of that community. The prophet's use of the phrase "Thus saith the Lord" forms part of the witness of that community. Therefore, the question of the epistemological primacy of the community is a lot like asking which came first — the chicken or the egg.

Perhaps the greatest problem with the Intrinsic-Canon approach (as defined by Peckham) is that it uses an epistemic criterion (one determined by propositional knowledge) to decide whether a book is suitable for the Canon.[298] If the Biblical Canon is a list of authoritative and inspired books compiled by the Church through the Holy Spirit, then only the Church can recognize and define that list. If, however, canonicity is an epistemic criterion, then individuals and groups can each use different propositions and reason their way towards different lists. (This is exactly what the Reformers did, by the way). Protestant scholar William J. Abraham describes the key difference between these two views.

The older way was prepared to leave scripture as both a gift of the Holy Spirit and as subject to the ongoing activity of the Spirit without worrying overmuch about epistemology. In my terms, the older way was content to leave scripture as a means of grace. The new fashion was to give primacy to ideas of revelation and inspiration as applying in some unique fashion to the Bible, and to limit scripture to the Bible. However, it is only someone already smitten by epistemology, and more

---

[298] Epistemic criterion are the standards and rules used to determine the accuracy and validity of propositions claiming to be true, and are used to separate justified knowledge from belief. Propositional Knowledge may be described as knowledge-that. It is a proposition or declarative statement that need not be true.

precisely by the kind of epistemology furnished by Aquinas, who can accept the shift identified here so gladly and readily.[299]

For us to understand this argument, we must discuss the development of an epistemological role in theology — the foundation, source, and validity of revelatory truth. Richard Foley comments: "For the medievals, religious authority and tradition were seen as repositories of wisdom"; it was the Enlightenment views of men like Descartes and Locke who "regarded tradition and authority as potential sources of error and took reason to be the corrective."[300] This view did not originate with Locke and Descartes but has its roots in the writings of Aquinas. William Abraham develops this thesis following this quote from the French theologian Yves Marie Joseph Cardinal Congar, who claims Thomas Aquinas inherited the following crucial assumptions from the Middle Ages:

First, the attributing of all true (and holy determinations of the life of the Church, to a «revelation, inspiration, suggestion,» [revelation, inspiration, suggestion] of the Holy Spirit.

Second, the practice of including the Fathers, the conciliar canons and even the pontifical decrees and (more rarely) the more outstanding treatises of the theologians, in the «Scriptura Sacra» [Sacred Scripture], or again, without distinguishing, in the «divina pagina» [interpretation of scripture].[301] *This is a practice of long standing; there seems no doubt but that it arises from the «Decretum Gelasianum»*

---

[299] (Abraham 1998, x-xi)

[300] (Foley 2001, 13)

[301] *Divina pagina* refers to the interpretation of Scripture, (McGinn 1998, 127) and is one of the three early medieval terms used for theology, the other two being *sacra doctrina* and *sacra scriptura* (Fiorenza 1991)

Objections to the Community-Canon Approach

[Gelasian Decree][302], which ...had passed into canonical collections, and into those chapters which dealt with sources and rules.[303]

For William J. Abraham, and likely with Protestants in general, the implications are quite startling.

'Scripture' was not originally confined to the Bible; it had a much wider frame of reference. ...What we see emerging in what follows is a quite different range of sense and reference. Over time, Scripture was cut back to apply materially to the Bible; and its primary function lay in that of operating as an authority.[304]

According to William Abraham, Thomas Aquinas developed that "special kind of rigour in theology," and was, therefore, the first to distinguish the authority of the Bible from that of the Fathers and Doctors of the Church.[305] As a natural

---

[302] Tradition attributes the *Decretum Gelasianum* [Gelasian Decree] to Pope Gelasius I, who was Pope from 492-496. The second part of the *Decretum Gelasianum* is a list of canonical scriptures. The list includes the Old Testament Scriptures which the Protestants consider to be Apocryphal, and the entire New Testament with the exception of 2 Corinthians. The third part discusses the authority of the Bishop of Rome. The fourth part makes the ecumenical councils authoritative and receives the works of a number of the church fathers. Finally, the fifth part contains a list of books compiled or recognized by heretics and schismatics, works which are not received by the church. It is possible that the list of Apocryphal books represents a tradition that can be traced back to Pope Gelasius, but was not actually written by him.

[303] (Abraham 1998, ix)

[304] (Ibid, ix)

[305] (Ibid, x) Thomas Aquinas was merely one practitioner of the style of critical theology developed in the west. Andrew Louth writes in the Forward to John Behr's *The Way to Nicea*: "The science of theology developed in the medieval universities, and then passed through the waves of cultural history that swept through the West."

consequence, the Roman Catholic Church distinguishes between the *ecclesia docens* and *ecclesia discerns*, between the teaching church and the learning church.[306] Everyone is a member of the learning church, but to some are given the special charism as the teaching church — in particular, the Pope of Rome and his "infallible magisterium."[307] According to Aleksei Khomyakov, this "bifurcation of the Church ...has passed into the Reform and is preserved in it as a result of the abrogation of legitimate tradition or the encroachment of knowledge on faith."[308] The rationalism of Thomas Aquinas laid the foundation for the Reformation's outright rejection of the Father's and the Councils and their replacement by Reason and Conscience. The Roman Catholic's division between the teaching church and the learning church has become the division between the educated pastor passing on the Protestant tradition, and the less educated faithful who receive the Protestant tradition. To put it another way, Protestants are following in the footsteps of Aquinas and therefore are unwitting Thomists.

John C. Peckham then raises another interesting question: "What Constitutes a Legitimate and/or Adequate Community?" This question is not as easy to answer as you might think. Multiple canons circulated in the early church; each Bishop seemingly had his own opinion. There were different communities of faith which considered themselves Christian. Many of these we consider heretical, and yet these heretical groups thought they had the authority to decide canonical issues. Prominent among these was the early heretic Marcion whose canon did not include the Old Testament and included only portions of the New Testament. The Gnostics also had their canon containing texts rejected by the Orthodox Christian community. Peckham writes:

This science of theology "had developed as an academic discipline, remote from the life of prayer." (Behr 2001, ix)

[306] (Örsy, Foundations and Context of the Magisterium 1987)

[307] (Pope Paul VI 1964)

[308] (Khomyakov 1977, 55)

Perhaps one might posit that a later community, whether a community of a particular time and place or the collective early Christian community over a period of time, is authoritative to determine canonicity. Yet the same problems apply to later communities. On what grounds should one accept that a later community is more legitimate and/or adequate to determine canonicity? As was the case for the earliest Christian community, the "community" is not monolithic decades or even centuries later. There are now and have been in ages past numerous communities that differ regarding the scope of sacred writings as canon. Examples include the times of the early church (the so-called canon of Marcion and Irenaeus' view of the Scriptures vs. his Gnostic opponents), over one thousand years later (the canon posited by the Council of Trent vs. the Thirty-Nine Articles), and more recent times (the Gospel revisions of the Jesus Seminar). Hence, asserting that a later community might be authoritative to determine the canon likewise raises the question, "which community?"[309]

If the community decides on the canon, the question of which community has that authority is valid. We must then ask on what basis the Protestant community assumes that authority. The most important Protestant objection to the Community-Canon approach is the authority of the Church. Their rationale is the Great Apostasy and the Protestant recovery of the true church.[310] Therefore, we must address

---

[309] (Peckham 2011, 210)

[310] The Great Apostasy: the idea that the church apostatized either immediately upon the death of the apostles or sometime within its first few hundred years. This idea posits a righteous remnant of the true Church hidden within and alongside the apostate Church throughout the centuries leading up to the Reformation. This idea depends upon the Protestant notion of the visible and invisible church, the invisible (spiritual) church having primacy over the visible (material) church. There is no historical evidence for the Great Apostasy. The Great Apostasy is a myth, a rationale created to

the issue of the Great Apostasy and its relationship to the canon of scripture.

---

justify differences between Protestants and the post-Apostolic Church.

18: Canonicity and the Great Apostasy

A great many Protestants think the Church apostatized shortly following the apostolic era, an apostasy the Protestant Reformation resolved. If this is the case, the question of the Community-Canon is moot. And yet history tells us the New Testament canon was not determined during the apostolic era, nor during the period before Emperor Constantine, nor the period of the Ecumenical Councils. The catalog of New Testament books was flexible well into the ninth century, and the book of Revelation's canonical status was in flux between the 4th and the 15th century AD. If we accept the idea of the Great Apostasy, then the New Testament is a creation of that apostasy. The same apostates that determined the contents of the New Testament also determined the Apocrypha was inspired. If Protestants accept the apostate's New Testament, they should logically accept both Testaments. If they reject the one, they should logically reject the other.

The right of a community to authoritatively settle issues of inspiration and canonicity is as important an issue for Protestants as it is for all other Christians. Protestants who presume their Scriptures to be self-authenticating also presume their community to be both legitimate and adequate to the task of receiving those writings. The Protestant's self-identification as the true and legitimate Church provides their authority to settle the canon of Sacred Scripture. Other Church bodies presume the same authority as well. How do we decide which Church is the true Church? The question of canon closely related to the question of which Church is the legitimate successor to the Church of the Apostles. As it turns out, the criteria for deciding the boundaries of the scriptural canon are nearly the same as the criteria for deciding which Church is the true, legitimate Church of God on earth.

The most important criterion for discovering the one, true Church is the witness of the Holy Spirit. Unfortunately, our pride, arrogance, and self-satisfaction often drown out the still, small voice of the Holy Spirit. All Christian bodies are guilty of this whether they be Protestant, Roman Catholic,

Coptic, Eastern Orthodox, etc. We allow our pride to get between ourselves and the Holy Spirit; we confuse our internal monologue for the witness of the Holy Spirit.

The witness of the Holy Spirit is a still, small voice, to be sure, but rarely speaks to us directly, but rather speaks through means. In other words, the Holy Spirit brings the evidence before us and guides others to us, just as He guides our hearts and minds. We can use the tools that God created as a way of uncovering the truth. We can look at the witness of history, for example. We can test our assumptions and presuppositions against the historical record, just as we test everything against the record of God's revelation of Himself to humanity. We can use the canonical standards as a proxy for testing the claims if different Christian bodies to be the legitimate successors to the apostolic Church.

19: Canonical Standards and the New Testament

The assertion that only the community of faith can determine the authoritative collection of inspired Scripture creates another problem: which criteria does the community use? John C. Peckham writes:

If each community is authoritative to determine their own canon, then since mutually exclusive canons of sacred writings are posited by various communities, the "Christian canon" is not authoritative over and against the canon of any other community but is authoritative only within the community or communities that determine and/or recognize it. This amounts to a canonical relativism that is mutually exclusive to a universally authoritative biblical canon (cf. Mt 24:14; 28:19–20; Acts 17:30; 1 Thes 2:13; 2 Tm 3:16).[311]

Modern Christians are unaware that the New Testament has a history. The Christian understanding of New Testament writings as Scripture developed gradually, with some books accepted in one place while rejected in others. Rarely did these lists agree with each other, let alone with our current list of the New Testament books. For several centuries, there were multiple canons in use. Various bishops published canonical lists for the churches under their authority, and canonical lists were published by various church fathers. While some argue the New Testament canon was finalized in the fourth century, there continued to be different lists published into the eighth century, as shown by the following list.

---

[311] (Peckham 2011, 210)

Canonical Lists[312]

1. *The Muratorian Fragment (c. 170)*
2. *Melito (c. 170)*
3. *Origen (c. 240)*
4. *Eusebius of Caesarea (c. 324)*
5. *The Damasine List (c. 328)*
6. *Cyril of Jerusalem (c. 350)*
7. *Hilary of Poitiers (c. 360)*
8. *The Cheltenham List (c. 360)*
9. *Council of Laodicea (c. 363)*
10. *Letter of Athanasius (367)*
11. *Gregory of Nazianzus (c. 380)*
12. *Amphilocius of Iconium (c. 380)*
13. *The "Apostolic Canons" (c. 380)*
14. *Epiphanius (c. 385)*
15. *Jerome (c. 390)*
16. *Augustine (c. 397)*
17. *Third Council of Carthage (397)*
18. *Rufinus of Aquileia (c. 400)*
19. *Codex Claromontanus (c. 400)*
20. *Letter of Innocent I (405)*
21. *Decree of Gelasius (c. 550)*
22. *Synopsis Scripturae Sacrae (c. 550)*
23. *John of Damascus (c. 730)*

These lists differ regarding the makeup of the canon. As late as 730 AD, St. John of Damascus included the Canons of the Holy Apostles in his list of New Testament Scripture. The first complete list of our New Testament canon as we know it today was in the 367 AD Easter Letter of St. Athanasius, Bishop of Alexandria.[313] Unlike what many say, the list was authoritative only for the Alexandrian see. Moreover, the fact that Athanasius felt compelled to create a list is evidence

---

[312] (Marlowe, Ancient Canon Lists n.d.) I added the Damasine List, a.k.a. the *Decretum Gelasianum*, or Decree of Pope Damascus.

[313] (Schaff, NPNF2-04 1892, 1126)

Canonical Standards and the New Testament

of the unsettled nature of the canon. In the West, some scholars cite the Third Council of Carthage (397 AD) as fixing the complete canon of the New Testament. However, this council was only authoritative for the regional Church in Northern Africa. Also, the council's canon of Sacred Scripture begins with the Old Testament and includes what Protestants now refer to as the Apocrypha. It should be impossible to accept the New Testament list without accepting the Old Testament list created at the same council.

Michael D. Marlowe provides us with a list of Canonical Scriptures from the Third Council of Carthage that includes much of what Protestants call the Apocrypha.

It was also determined that besides the Canonical Scriptures nothing be read in the Church under the title of divine Scriptures. The Canonical Scriptures are these: Genesis, Exodus, Leviticus, Numbers, Deuteronomy, Joshua the son of Nun, Judges, Ruth, four books of Kings [I & II Samuel; I & II Kings], two books of Paraleipomena (Chronicles], Job, the Psalter, five books of Solomon [Proverbs, Ecclesiastes, Song of Songs, Wisdom of Solomon, and Sirach, also known as Ecclesiasticus], the books of the twelve prophets, Isaiah, Jeremiah, Ezechiel, Daniel, Tobit, Judith, Esther, two books of Esdras [1 Esdras and 2 Esdras being the longer Greek versions of Ezra and Nehemiah], two books of the Maccabees. Of the New Testament: four books of the Gospels, one book of the Acts of the Apostles, thirteen Epistles of the Apostle Paul, one epistle of the same [writer] to the Hebrews, two Epistles of the Apostle Peter, three of John, one of James, one of Jude, one book of the Apocalypse of John. Let this be made known also to our brother and fellow-priest Boniface, or to other bishops of those parts, for the purpose of confirming that Canon, because we have received from our fathers that those books must be read in the Church. Let it also be allowed that the Passions of Martyrs be read when their festivals are kept.[314]

---

[314] (Marlowe, Third Council of Carthage (A.D. 397) n.d.)

Between the apostolic era and the establishment of the New Testament canon, there were controversies over which books were inspired and which were not. The Eastern Church rejected Revelation because of the propensity of heretics to weave apocalyptic fantasies from its strange imagery. The Western Church rejected Hebrews because no one knew who wrote it. Many rejected Jude because it quotes from the apocryphal book of Enoch.[315] Some thought II Peter was spurious, along with II and III John, and rejected them on that basis. The canon of Alexandria always included James, but few knew of the book elsewhere. The late fourth-century *Codex Sinaiticus* includes the Shepherd of Hermas and the Epistle of Barnabas.[316] The early fifth-century *Codex Alexandrinus* contains I and II Clement.[317]

The idea of the self-authenticating Scriptures doesn't square with the history of the New Testament canon. Far from being self-authenticating, it turns out the process of determining an authoritative list of inspired scriptures was a long, arduous, and all-too-human process. Given that the Holy Spirit works through human beings, why would we expect this to happen any other way?

---

[315] S. Jerome, in his account of Jude in «De Viris Illustribus», says that inasmuch as in the Epistle a testimony is quoted from "Enoch," an apocryphal Book, it is rejected by most. ...Part of the reason that led some distinguished scholars to put the Epistle of Jude in the 2nd century A.D., and to question the right of its author to call himself the brother of James, was derived from the approval with which it seemed to stamp an 'apocryphal' writing. (Burkitt 1914, 17)

[316] In his account of the discovery in 1844 of the Codex Siniaticus, Lobegott Friedrich Constantin (von) Tischendorf (c. 1815 – 1874) notes that the Epistle of Barnabas and the Shepherd (Pastor) of Hermas had "an extensive authority" in the 2nd through the 4th centuries, and were placed "side by side" with the inspired writings. What Tischendorf does not say, but should have said, is that many Christians of the 2nd through the 4th centuries considered both to be scripture. (Vincent 1899, 16-17)

[317] (Lieuwen 1995)

20: The NT use of the OT Scriptures

Jesus Christ rarely uses the term "scripture." Matthew's Gospel does not use the term. In Mark's Gospel, Jesus uses the term once when he says: "And have ye not read this scripture; The stone which the builders rejected is become the head of the corner" (Mk 12:10; Psa 118:22). In Luke's Gospel, Jesus reads from the prophet Isaiah and then states: "This day is this scripture fulfilled in your ears" (Luk 4:21). Mark's Gospel contains an editorial comment on Jesus' crucifixion between two thieves: "And the scripture was fulfilled, which saith, And he was numbered with the transgressors" (Mk 15:28; cf Isa 52:9, 12). The Gospel of John, which contains eleven references to "scripture," only contains four places where Jesus references the Scriptures. The rest are editorial comments by the apostle John or comments by the crowd.

Jesus Christ treats the Old Testament as Scripture in some places, but never represents Scripture as a list of books. What we have instead are a few places where Jesus cites or alludes to this book or that text as Scripture — what we would today call the Old Testament. But which Old Testament is Christ using? As we shall see, often he quotes or alludes to the Apocrypha in the same manner as he quotes or alludes to the books contained in the Protestant Old Testament. F. F. Bruce writes: "Jesus, according to all the strata of the gospel tradition, regularly appealed to the Hebrew Scriptures to validate his mission, his words and his actions."[318] We have already established that Jesus rarely used the term Scripture. In what way, then, did Jesus appeal to the Jewish writings and assumed their authority for Himself?

Consider how Jesus Christ announced the beginning of his ministry: "The time is fulfilled, and the kingdom of God is at hand: repent ye, and believe the gospel" (Mk 1:15). According to F. F. Bruce, the Jews would have understood this as a reference to the book of Daniel; specifically, to its

---

[318] (Bruce, The Canon of Scripture 2010, 27) We should note that Jesus primarily quoted from the Septuagint.

apocalyptic reference to Nebuchadnezzar's vision of the kingdom of God. The vision of Nebuchadnezzar ends as follows:

And in the days of these kings shall the God of heaven set up a kingdom, which shall never be destroyed: and the kingdom shall not be left to other people, but it shall break in pieces and consume all these kingdoms, and it shall stand for ever (Dan 2:44).

While Jesus Christ is alluding to the Kingdom mentioned by Daniel, He does not use any introductory formulae indicating the scriptural nature of the passage. Jesus does not use the phrase "It is written," although the phrase is used 26 times in the gospels alone. Nor does he use the related terms "it was written" (3 times), "it was said" (3 times), "it is said" (1 time), and "it hath been said" (4 times). And finally, Jesus does not quote the book of Daniel. Instead, Jesus makes use of its themes and phrases.

In the Gospel of Luke, Jesus Christ says to His disciples: "It is your Father's good pleasure to give you the kingdom" (Lk 12:32). Jesus uses no introductory formulae, nor is He directly quoting any specific passage. Jesus expects His disciples to make the connection between His words and the thematic material provided by the prophet Daniel, as follows:

And there was given him dominion, and glory, and a kingdom, that all people, nations, and languages, should serve him: his dominion is an everlasting dominion, which shall not pass away, and his kingdom that which shall not be destroyed. ...But the saints of the most High shall take the kingdom, and possess the kingdom for ever, even for ever and ever. ...Until the Ancient of days came, and judgment was given to the saints of the most High; and the time came that the saints possessed the kingdom. ...And the kingdom and dominion, and the greatness of the kingdom under the whole heaven, shall be given to the people of the saints of the most High, whose kingdom is an everlasting kingdom, and all dominions shall serve and obey him. (Dan 7:14, 18, 22, 27)

The NT Use of the OT Scriptures

Jesus alludes to Daniel, indicating the Father's kingdom is an everlasting kingdom. This everlasting kingdom, dominion, and judgment will be given to the saints of the most High. If Jesus alludes to the book of Daniel in this manner, how do we to differentiate this from His allusions to the books Protestants call the Apocrypha? Although exegetes claim Jesus is alluding to Daniel, he could very well be alluding to prophetic material in the Apocrypha.[319] We will discuss this subject more in Part IV; however, now would be a good place for a preview.

- Mt 16:18 - Jesus' reference to the "power of death" and "gates of Hades" references Wisdom 16:13 – "For thou hast power of life and death: thou leadest to the gates of hell, and bringest up again."
- Mt 24:15 - the "desolating sacrilege" Jesus refers to is taken from 1 Macc. 1:54 – "Now the fifteenth day of the month Casleu, in the hundred forty and fifth year, they set up the abomination of desolation upon the altar, and builded idol altars throughout the cities of Juda on every side"; see also 2 Macc. 8:17.
- Mt 24:16 – Jesus warning to let those "flee to the mountains" is taken from 1 Macc. 2:27-28 – "And Mattathias cried throughout the city with a loud voice, saying, Whosoever is zealous of the law, and maintaineth the covenant, let him follow me. So he and his sons fled into the mountains, and left all that ever they had in the city."
- Mk 4:5, 16-17 - Jesus' description of seeds falling on rocky ground and having no root follows Sirach 40:15 – "The children of the ungodly shall not bring forth many branches: but are as unclean roots upon a hard rock."
- Lk 13:29 - Jesus' description of men "come from the east, and from the west, and from the north, and from the

---

[319] Jesus could also have been alluding to the general understanding of the kingdom that was expressed in the wealth of Second Temple literature. See Appendix A for more information.

south, and shall sit down in the kingdom of God" follows Baruch 4:37 – "Lo, thy sons come, whom thou sentest away, they come gathered together from the east to the west by the word of the Holy One, rejoicing in the glory of God."

- Lk 21:24 - Jesus' usage of the phrase "fall by the edge of the sword" follows Sirach 28:18 – "Many have fallen by the edge of the sword: but not so many as have fallen by the tongue."
- Jn 3:13 – Jesus' usage of the phrase "who has ascended into heaven but He who descended from heaven" references Baruch 3:29 – "Who hath gone up into heaven, and taken her, and brought her down from the clouds?" (This is a reference to the personification of Wisdom, which is commonly an adumbration or foreshadowing of Christ, which belies the contention that the Apocrypha contain no prophecies about Christ).
- Jn 4:48; Acts 5:12; 15:12; 2 Cor. 12:12 - Jesus', Luke's and Paul's usage of the phrase "signs and wonders" follows Wisdom 8:8 – "If a man desire much experience, she knoweth things of old, and conjectureth aright what is to come: she knoweth the subtilties of speeches, and can expound dark sentences: she foreseeth signs and wonders, and the events of seasons and times."
- Jn 5:18 - Jesus claiming that God is His Father follows Wisdom 2:16 – "We are esteemed of him as counterfeits: he abstaineth from our ways as from filthiness: he pronounceth the end of the just to be blessed, and maketh his boast that God is his father."

None of the preceding matters if scholars can prove the canon of the Hebrew Scriptures was closed at the time of Christ and that the canon did not contain the books considered as apocryphal. As we have previously demonstrated, this is not the case, which presents a problem for the Protestant understanding of Scripture.

21: The Intrinsic-Canon Approach

The Intrinsic-Canon approach is the accepted method in Protestant churches. John C. Peckham provides the following definition.

God determines the scope of the canon, and the community recognizes it. The canon is a collection of authoritative books that are authoritative because God commissioned them. Recognizing the canon does not bear on its canonicity but determines only whether that given community will allow the canon to function as authority.[320]

A difference exists between what Peckham is describing here and the pure Intrinsic-Canon approach. The pure Intrinsic-Canon approach says the God inspired the texts, the texts are self-authenticating, and the texts need no recognition by the community to certify their inspiration. The pure approach has radical implications: it is a denial of the Church as a community, as the body of Christ, as the building fitly framed together on the foundations of the apostles and the prophets. The pure Intrinsic-Canon approach is a denial of the person and work of the Holy Spirit within the Church and a denial of the Church as the pillar and ground of the truth. Peckham describes a hybrid approach when he gives the community the role of recognizing the canon.

Peckham defines the Intrinsic-Canon approach as "a collection of authoritative books that are authoritative because God commissioned [inspired] them." Peckham fails to explore the practical implications of his approach. Conservative scholars believe the Old Testament came together over 1,000 years. It is difficult to speak of a canonical collection of authoritative books when the canon itself was incomplete and (seemingly) open-ended. Practically speaking, the inspiration of a book is meaningless apart from its witness to and within a community. There can be no

---

[320] (Peckham 2011, 205)

collection of canonical books apart from the community who accepted the authority of the books and who preserved them, copied them, and used them in worship.[321] Likewise, there can be no inspired writings without a community to receive them. God does not reveal Himself for His own sake, but ours.

We should also note that John C. Peckham's arguments against the Community-Approach apply to the Intrinsic-Canon approach as well. Peckham's explanation of his hybrid Intrinsic-Canon approach argues for the community's recognition of certain texts as authoritative. Inspiration of the text is pointless until the text is recognized and used. The Holy Spirit inspires the author and bears witness to the inspired text; the this witness takes place within and to the community of believers — the Church. The Holy Spirit works both within persons and within the Church.[322]

If we independently deal with the two views, they seem like alternate and opposing approaches. However, we have already noted that hybrid Intrinsic-Canon approach does not preclude the community's involvement in recognizing that a particular book is authoritative and inspired. In practical terms, the two approaches are related, and any attempt to separate them is shortsighted at best.

---

[321] Regardless of a book's inspiration, it wouldn't exist for long unless the community thought enough of it to go to the expense of copying it so that it could be shared within the community and across the centuries.

[322] The Church is an entity, not an organization or assembly of individuals. The metaphors used of the Church speak of its organic unity. The Church is made up of persons distinguished by their particularity, but united in their essence. This is a true hypostatic union. If your conception of the Church is different, you will likely not agree with the idea that the Holy Spirit works within persons and within the Church; you will likely say that the Holy Spirit's working within the Church is merely an amalgam of the Holy Spirit's work within individuals.

22: Objections to the Intrinsic-Canon Approach

Some say the scriptural text is inspired apart from and before the community's recognition of said inspiration. This pure Intrinsic-Canon approach is conceptually flawed. An inspired text has never existed apart from the community for whom it serves as a witness. Historically a prophet from a community would speak to that community. Afterward, either the prophet, his amanuensis, or his followers would write down he had said. From that point, the continued existence of the text depended on the community copying it by hand; the community undertook this expensive and laborious process when the manuscript's worth was recognized. Therefore, a text's continued existence is dependent upon its recognition by and usefulness within the community.[323]

The history of the book of Jeremiah is important in this regard. As previously discussed, Jehoiakim, king of Judah destroyed the original text of Jeremiah; Jeremiah then dictated another scroll to his scribe, Baruch (Jeremiah 36). If we accept the intrinsic-canon approach, we now have a problem. Which manuscript was inspired: the first scroll or the second? There is a reason to think both of them were inspired, but only one is canonical. The proclamation (the κήρυγμα, kerugma, or kerygma) convicted Jehoiakim who destroyed the original manuscript. The destruction of the first edition of Jeremiah does not invalidate Jeremiah as the

---

[323] The idea that the preservation of a text is related to the community's acceptance of the text leads to the idea that the number of preserved or extant manuscripts reflects the importance of that manuscript to the community. Michael J. Kruger describes this as "Extant Manuscript" evidence, which concept us used to demonstrate the canonicity of the New Testament books over against the New Testament apocryphal writings — in particular, the gnostic texts recently discovered in the Nag Hammadi library. (Kruger 2013)

Herald (the κηρύσσω, *kerusso*), and suggests the first text of Jeremiah was inspired. Therefore, a pure Intrinsic-Canon approach will not do, as it does not account for the problem of the two Jeremiahs — in particular, the destruction of an inspired revelatory text.

The pure Intrinsic-Canon approach has other problems, the most important of which is that the community uses certain guidelines or standards to judge whether a book is canonical or not. According to F.F. Bruce, the community decided that "the teaching of the apostles in the Acts and Epistles was regarded as vested with His [Christ's] authority."[324] The realization that a book was vested with Christ's authority became the standard used to judge against the disputed books of Hebrews, II Peter, and II & III John. Eventually, the community recognized the disputed books as authoritative and inspired despite their not meeting the community's initial guidelines.

The idea of an inspired text existing apart from the community's recognition of its inspiration presents a serious textual problem. The same standards which argue for and against certain books being part of the canon can be used to argue that other books should also be part of the canon. Take, for example, the idea that if a book of Scripture references another book, that book may be assumed to be Scripture as well. However logical this may appear, it nonetheless false. The Old Testament names several authoritative books, yet these books are not part of the canon. Despite being mentioned and used as reference material, none of these books are part of the Old Testament. It is clear that most of them are government records and were authoritative on that basis without requiring inspiration. Others of these are records that were likely useful to the priestly class but did not rise to the level of Scripture, much like the books that fill a pastor's library.

---

[324] (Bruce, The Canon of Scripture 2008)

Objections to the Intrinsic-Canon Approach

Table 4: Books Referenced in the Old Testament[325]

Book	Citation
The Book of Records (Book of the Chronicles of Ahasuerus)	Est 2:23; 6:1
Samuel's Book	1 Sm 10:25
The Book of Jasher	2 Sm 1:18
The Acts of Solomon	1 Kgs 11:41
The Chronicles of King David	1 Chr 27:24
The Chronicles of Samuel, Nathan, Gad	1 Chr 29:29
The Records of Nathan the Prophet	2 Chr 9:29
The Prophecy of Ahijah the Shilonite	2 Chr 9:29
The Treatise of the Prophet Iddo	2 Chr 13:22
The Annals of Jehu	2 Chr 20:34
The Book of the Kings	2 Chr 24:27
The Sayings of Hozai	2 Chr 33:19

We also know of epistles referenced in the New Testament but not accepted as Scripture. One such is Paul's epistle to the Laodiceans,[326] referenced in his epistle to the Colossians:

And when this epistle is read among you, cause that it be read also in the church of the Laodiceans; and that ye likewise read the epistle from Laodicea. (Col 4:16)

While the primitive church did not have a fixed canon of New Testament writings, the post-apostolic church quickly divided books into those that were read in church and those that were not. For Paul to tell the Colossians to read his letter to the Laodiceans in church suggests the idea of canonicity. And yet the letter to the Laodiceans was lost.

---

[325] (Lumpkin, The Books of Enoch 2011, 7-8)

[326] There are various spurious versions of this Epistle to the Laodiceans, one of which became part of Wycliffe's translation of the New Testament.

Paul may have written four letters to the Corinthians, of which only two remain. In 1 Corinthians, Paul references an earlier letter (1 Cor 5:9). Then in 2 Corinthians, we have a reference to another letter, the details of which are not clear (2 Cor 2:3-4). This letter, coming between 1 and 2 Corinthians, is different from the pseudepigraphical 3rd Epistle to the Corinthians, which was composed sometime in the mid-to-late 2nd century.

We also have the Book of Enoch, a Jewish text that is quoted in the book of Revelation and which the book of Jude cites. Thus, four extra-biblical texts are either cited, quoted, or mentioned in five different New Testament Scriptures. At least two of those books have a troubled canonical history, which suggests the difficulty with using a rules-based approach to determining canonicity.

A related canonical standard is that if a suspect book references a book that is acknowledged not to be scripture, the suspect book is therefore assumed not to be scripture. While not a hard and fast rule, the latter idea kept the book of Jude from being widely acknowledged as part of the canon, as it cites the Book of Enoch.

Another example of a canonical standard is the argument of some that the canon of the Old Testament was closed around 400 B.C. — after the reign of Artaxerxes, according to Flavius Josephus, and after the book of Malachi was written, according to any number of Protestant authors. Unfortunately, this canonical standard is wholly arbitrary. The argument seems to be that no canonical books were written after 400 B.C., so any book written after 400 B.C. is not canonical. This is kind of like saying all swans are white, so any swan that isn't white isn't a swan.

Another way of stating the previous argument is that Malachi was the last prophet and ushered in the intertestamental period. Even people who argue for this position recognize its weaknesses. Rabbi Hayyim Angel writes:

Even if Malachi were the last of the biblical prophets, there is no statement at the end of his book or anywhere else in the Bible stating categorically that prophecy had ceased. For example, Nehemiah battled false prophets (Neh. 6:5–7, 11–13) but did not negate the existence of prophecy in principle.[327]

Nevertheless, Rabbi Angel assumes a definite end to the prophetic era. Protestants tend to borrow this Jewish line of thinking, saying the prophetic witness ended with Malachi and did not begin again until to the coming of John the Baptist. We will return to this argument further in chapters 20 & 40. For now, it is enough to mention the argument I heard as a youth — that the intertestamental period was typologically connected to the Old Testament period when prophecy had ceased, the period before the coming of Samuel the Prophet. This is a rather weak argument as analogies do not constitute proof.

---

[327] (Angel 2011)

23: The Verbal Icon and the Holy Spirit

Karl Barth, the most important Protestant theologian of the twentieth century, states: "the Bible is the witness of divine revelation." Barth thus draws a distinction between the revelation of God and the Bible as the witness to that revelation, a distinction that should apply to the Intrinsic-Canon approach. Barth goes on to state: "there is a Word of God for the Church: in that it receives in the Bible, the witness of divine revelation."[328] Thus, the Bible is the Word of God *for the Church* precisely because of its witness to divine revelation. Regarding this proposition, Barth writes:

A witness is not absolutely identical with that to which it witnesses. This corresponds with the facts upon which the truth of the whole proposition is based. In the Bible we meet with human words written in human speech, and in these words, and therefore by means of them, we hear of the lordship of the triune God. Therefore when we have to do with the Bible, we have to do primarily with this means, with these words, with the witness which as such is not itself a revelation, but only — and this is the limitation — the witness to it.[329]

Barth is careful to say that the Bible mediates the original revelation; that it is the means by which the revelation comes to us, the means by which the revelation accommodates itself to us, and the means by which the revelation of God becomes "an actual presence and event."[330] In other words, the revelation of God is primary; the text of the Bible is absolutely dependent upon the initial revelation. The text is a faithful witness to that revelation, but must be distinguished from it.

Georges Florovsky, Emeritus Professor of Eastern Church History at Harvard University, (c. 1972) has a related but

---

[328] (Barth, Church Dogmatics I.2 2004, 462)

[329] (Ibid, 463)

[330] (Ibid, 463)

different take on this subject. In reaction to liberalism, and to some extent neo-orthodoxy, Florovsky notes that we cannot separate the message from the manuscript.

It has recently been suggested that we should radically "demythologize" Scripture, meaning to replace the more antiquated categories of the Holy Writ by something more modern. Yet the question cannot be evaded: Is the language of Scripture really nothing else than an accidental and external wrapping out of which some "eternal idea" is to be extricated and disentangled, or is it rather a perennial vehicle for the divine message, which was once delivered for all time?[331]

In another passage, Florovsky says:

The message is divine; it comes from God; it is the Word of God. But it is the faithful community that acknowledges the Word spoken and testifies to its truth. The sacred character of the Bible is ascertained by faith. The Bible, as a book, has been composed in the community and was meant primarily for its edification. The book and the Church cannot be separated.[332]

There is a connection between the message and the text. The text is inspired because of the message, yet the message cannot be removed from the text. The two are separate, yet the two are bound together in such a way that even though the text is translated or transmuted into other forms, the reader finds the revelation of God within the text. The revelation of God is found in its purest form in the original language and explained most clearly using the original idiom. Georges Florovsky writes: "How can we interpret at all if we have forgotten the original language? Would it not be safer to bend our thought to the mental habits of the biblical language and to relearn the idiom of the Bible?"[333]

---

[331] (Florovsky 1972, 10)

[332] (Ibid, 18)

[333] (Ibid, 10)

In the same way, there is a connection between the message and the Church. The message was written for the Church and is properly understood by and within the Church. The revelation is not subject to private interpretation (2Pe 1:20). Both the holy men of God and the false prophets spoke: "among the people" (2Pe 2:1). The false prophets beguile "unstable souls" (2Pe 2:14) away from the community of faith while the community remains "mindful of the words which were spoken before by the holy prophets and of the commandment of us the apostles of the Lord and Saviour (2Pe 3:2).

The message, text, and Church: the three are inextricably interwoven, such that neither can be properly understood without the other two. St. Irenaeus (c. 130-202 AD], in Book I of *Against Heresies*, demonstrates this using his famous metaphor of Scripture as a mosaic. He writes:

By transferring passages, and dressing them up anew, and making one thing out of another, they succeed in deluding many through their wicked art in adapting the oracles of the Lord to their opinions. Their manner of acting is just as if one, when a beautiful image of a king has been constructed by some skilful artist out of precious jewels, should then take this likeness of the man all to pieces, should rearrange the gems, and so fit them together as to make them into the form of a dog or of a fox, and even that but poorly executed; and should then maintain and declare that this was the beautiful image of the king which the skilful artist constructed, pointing to the jewels which had been admirably fitted together by the first artist to form the image of the king, but have been with bad effect transferred by the latter one to the shape of a dog, and by thus exhibiting the jewels, should deceive the ignorant who had no conception what a king's form was like, and persuade them that that miserable likeness of the fox was, in fact, the beautiful image of the king. In like manner do these persons patch together old wives' fables, and then endeavour, by violently drawing away from their proper connection, words, expressions, and parables whenever found, to adapt the oracles of God to their baseless fictions.[334]

Irenaeus is arguing against the near-universal tendency towards proof-texting. Our natural tendency is to search for ways to validate our own opinions or to interpret things according to our pre-existing mental framework. Many of the things we think we know are influenced by tacit knowledge, which is knowledge absorbed without conscious knowledge, and without our ability to verbalize how we know what we know. According to the philosopher Michael Polanyi, many of the propositions we assume to be true are the product of tacit knowledge. We attend from our tacit knowledge to something else; from the *proximal* to the *distal*.[335] In this way, we use our mental framework to incorporate new facts. Suppose someone uses a set of Scrabble® tiles to create a quote from Shakespeare, while someone else mixes up those tiles and uses them to create a quote from Bruce Springsteen. The individual tiles are the same, but it would be wrong to assume that the second quote is equivalent to the first.

Here would be a good place to develop the idea of the "Verbal Icon." William Wimsatt and Monroe Beardsley write:

The term icon is used today by semeiotic writers to refer to a verbal sign which somehow shares the properties of, or resembles, the objects which it denotes. The same term in its more usual meaning refers to a visual image and especially to one which is a religious symbol. The verbal image which most fully realizes its verbal capacities is that which is not merely a bright picture (in the usual modern meaning of the term image) but also an interpretation of reality in its metaphoric and symbolic dimensions. Thus: The Verbal Icon.[336]

The icon is an image of a thing and not the thing itself. Thus, the icon is symbolic of the object to which it refers; the icon

---

[334] (Schaff, ANF01 1884, Against Heresies, I.8.1, pp. 534-535)

[335] (Polanyi 1966, 10)

[336] (Wimsatt and Beardsley 1953, Kindle Locations 35-38)

interprets and illumines reality. The icon is not less than real; its reality is reinforced by its referent. When God says "Let us make man in our image" (Gen 1:26), the Hebrew word used is צלם (tselem, pronounced tseh'- lem). The Greek translation of that term is εικων (eikon, pronounced i-kone'), which is the source for our English word icon. Thus, an icon is not, as is often thought, merely a visual symbolic representation. Humans are the created icon of God; paintings may be icons of Jesus, of saints, and angels; and the Bible may be a "verbal icon" of God.[337] Georges Florovsky writes of the Evangelists and Apostles as not writing histories, but creators of verbal icons.

The Evangelists and Apostles were no chroniclers. It was not their mission to keep the full record of all that Jesus had done, day by day, years by year.[338] They describe his life and relate his works, so as to give us his image: an historic, and yet a divine image. It is no portrait, but rather an ikon — but surely an historic ikon, an image of the Incarnate Lord.[339]

The Scriptures are written in human language. Words are not the thing itself; words are symbols of the thing itself. The word "running" represents the act of running; the word "love" represents an abstract concept but is not the essence or experience of love; the word "God" represents many things, none of which capture the essence of divinity. The writer Frank Schaeffer says, "The problem with theology is its words to describe stuff, and the words are never as valuable as the thing they are trying to describe."[340] Because of the consideration and condescension of God, we have this

---

[337] (Constantinou, Introduction to the Bible Lesson 2 2008)

[338] This is why the Evangelists present the events of Christ's life in different ways and in different orders. The Gospels are arranged theologically, not chronologically. The Gospels are teaching tools rather than biographies.

[339] (Florovsky 1972, 25)

[340] (Schaeffer 2014)

verbal icon called Sacred Scripture. As St. John Chrysostom says in his Homily 17 on Genesis:

Let us follow the direction of Sacred Scripture in the interpretation it gives of itself, provided we don't get completely absorbed in the concreteness of the words, but realize that our limitations are the reason for the concreteness of the language. Human senses, you see, would never be able to grasp what is said if they had not the benefit of such great considerateness.

Robert C. Hill, the translator of Chrysostom's *Homilies on Genesis 1-17*, writes of Chrysostom's theology of the Word as displaying: "the delicate balance of the two correlatives[:] ...divine transcendence and considerateness for human limitations."[341] Sacred Scripture represents both the immanence and transcendence of God through the limitations of human language. Using an idea from C.S. Lewis (or Dr. Who), the inside is larger than the outside.[342] St. John of Damascus writes of the "womb in which the Uncontained dwelt."[343] Germanos of Constantinople describes infant Jesus as being "wider than the heavens."[344] Our Lord Jesus Christ was both locally present according to his humanity, and at the same time everywhere present and filling all things according to his divinity. We should therefore not be astonished at the idea that God, who is ineffable, inconceivable, invisible, incomprehensible, ever existing and eternally the same, nevertheless shows consideration of human weakness by allowing His divinity to be circumscribed in human language, just as He allowed his divinity to be contained in human flesh. The Bible is the verbal icon of Christ, just as Christ is the icon of God the Father.

---

[341] (St John Chrysostom 1999, 228)
[342] (Lewis 1970, 180)
[343] (Cunningham 2011, Kindle Location 1458)
[344] (Ibid, Kindle Location 3328)

If we accept the idea that the initial revelation of God is separate and distinct from the capture of that witness in the pages of Sacred Scripture, then we have a problem, for the Bible is witness to that revelation, and therefore not that revelation itself. Thus, the Intrinsic-Canon approach to canonicity will not work. But the Community-Canon approach will not work either, for the revelation of God predates the community's recognition of its witness in the text.

Professor John Behr, writing in *The Way to Nicaea*, describes the problem with both the Community-Canon and the Intrinsic-Canon approach.

If we are to understand the particular contours of this debate and its resolution, we must avoid reading its terms in the manner set by the polemics of the Reformation and Counter-Reformation, in which Scriptures is opposed to tradition, as two distinct sources of authority. Separating Scripture and tradition in this way introduces an inevitable quandary: if the locus of authority is fixed solely in Scripture, and "canon" is understood exclusively in the sense of a "list" of authoritative books, then accounting for that list becomes problematic; if, on the other hand, Scripture is subsumed under tradition, on the grounds that the Church predates the writings of the New Testament (Conveniently forgetting, in a Marcionite fashion, the existence of Scripture — the Law, the Psalms and the Prophets), then again a problem arises from the lack of a criterion or canon, this time for differentiating, as is often done, between "Tradition" and "traditions"—all traditions are venerable, though some more so than others, yet the basis for this distinctions is never clarified.[345]

The two descriptions of canonicity have similar difficulties. The Intrinsic-Canon approach does not provide a means for differentiating between different canonical lists, nor evaluating the truth claims of each. Likewise, the Community-Canon approach provides no basis for

---

[345] (Behr 2001, 12-13)

differentiating between different traditions, nor evaluating the veracity and value of differing traditions. Both approaches to canonicity give lip service to the person and work of the Holy Spirit.

If we accept the Holy Spirit's role as working with "holy men of God" (2 Pet 1:21) apart from their witness to the community as a whole, then we must accept the possibility of an inspired text existing apart from its recognition as Scripture by the community. We know that it took time after a book was written and in use by the community before the community began to refer to it as Scripture. In nearly every case (with the possible exception of 2 Pet 3:15-16 and Revelation), what the New Testament authors speak of as Scripture is the Old Testament, even while using the books that would become the New Testament in their services. And, as we have mentioned previously, Paul referred to his writings as "traditions" and "epistles" (meaning letters), rather than as Scripture (2 Th 2:15).[346]

The account of the Holy Spirit working with "holy men of God" might indicate that the primary work of the Holy Spirit is with individuals. However, the thesis that the Holy Spirit's ministry is primarily individual is a problem. The very concept of the individual is a recent western phenomenon. The ancients considered themselves to be persons, but persons who were part of a larger whole. Their identity as persons, their self-worth and reason for living, was tied to the community they were part of and their position within that community. Thus, the prophet was moved by the Holy Spirit (2 Pt 1:21) to be a witness to the community. Eventually, the prophet's witness was accepted as such by that same community, as influenced by that same Holy Spirit. The Protestant conception of the Holy Spirit's working primarily through individuals was unknown to the biblical authors, for

---

[346] The recognition that Paul did not refer to his own writings as Scripture is significant. Paul was forced to defend his apostleship as he was not one of the original twelve. We might expect Paul to defend his epistles as scripture, but he does not.

whom inspiration developed within a community, and functioned as a witness to that community. Thus, the inspiration of Sacred Scripture was the Holy Spirit's witness to the community using the prophets and the inspired record of the original revelation of God. The Holy Spirit doesn't work solely at the one level, through the individual, but within and through the community as well.

The prophet writes

The prophet speaks

The community accepts

The community fails

Figure 1 The Prophetic Cycle

If we accept the idea that the Holy Spirit works within the community, and in a special way to persons as a witness to that community, then a text can be inspired apart from the community's initial recognition of such. However, the Holy Spirit works within the community towards its recognition of the Scriptures. While the western idea of time is linear, the people who wrote the bible had a more cyclical view of time. The prophet's writing and the community's acceptance are one half of the cycle, the other half being the community's failure to live up to the prophecy, and God's raising of another prophet. Moreover, although we are limited by time, the Holy Spirit is not. From God's perspective, it is unlikely there is any difference between the Scripture's recording of

The Verbal Icon and the Holy Spirit

revelation and the community's recognition of that record as inspired.[347]

In his argument against the Community-Canon approach, John C. Peckham fails to notice his point also applies to the Reformation. The idea that the Reformers could determine for themselves the canon of Scripture raises the question of their authority to do so. Did the Holy Spirit reveal Himself to the Reformers in a way that He had not revealed Himself to the previous 1,500 years of the body of Christ? By what authority were the Reformers able to make that decision on behalf of themselves and their followers, over against the authority of the witness of the Holy Spirit to the Church of the first millennium? What were the criteria the Reformers used to determine which books the Holy Spirit inspired? It is hard to see how the Reformation's recognition and reception of books as inspired is any different from that of the historical Church. The terms are different, but the process is the same — making it an act of sophistry to assert such a difference.

The Confession of Patriarch Dositheos (c. 1672) references this issue. He writes:

We believe the Divine and Sacred Scriptures to be God-taught; and, therefore, we ought to believe the same without doubting; yet not otherwise than as the Catholic Church[348] hath interpreted and delivered the same. For every foul heresy receiveth, indeed, the Divine Scriptures, but perversely interpreteth the same, using metaphors, and homonymies, and sophistries of man's wisdom, confounding what ought to be distinguished, and trifling with what ought not to be trifled with. For if otherwise, each man holding every day a different sense concerning the same, the Catholic Church would not by the grace of Christ continue to be the Church until this day,

---

[347] Although God created time and is aware of its effect upon us, God is apart from time, seeing the particular moment and the sweep of history all at once.

[348] When Patriarch Dositheos mentions the Catholic Church, he is referring to the Orthodox Catholic Church (or church catholic), not the Roman Catholic Church (which left Orthodoxy in 1054 A.D).

holding the same doctrine of faith, and always identically and steadfastly believing, but would be rent into innumerable parties, and subject to heresies; neither would the Church be holy, the pillar and ground of the truth, without spot or wrinkle; but would be the Church of the malignant as it is manifest that of the heretics undoubtedly is, and especially that of Calvin, who are not ashamed to learn from the Church, and then to wickedly repudiate her. Wherefore, the witness also of the Catholic Church is, we believe, not of inferior authority to that of the Divine Scriptures. For one and the same Holy Spirit being the author of both, it is quite the same to be taught by the Scriptures and by the Catholic Church.[349]

The question of which community has the authority to decide can be difficult for some.[350] The question of which community determine the canon was answered in different ways by different communities in the early church. Some churches used books that were later dropped from the canon by the larger community. Other books that were later included in the canon which had been rejected at some point by large parts of the Christian world. Different bishops produced different canonical lists, lists which in some cases were changed by their successors using different criteria. What criteria were used? Georges Florovsky writes:

Whatever the origin of particular documents included in the book may have been, it is obvious that the book, as a whole,

---

[349] (Trenham 2015, 318-319)

[350] There are a variety of ways to approach the issue. For myself, the question was answered when I became convinced through the pages of Scripture, the witness of the church fathers, and the evidence of Church history that the fullness of the Church was to be found only in Eastern Orthodoxy. Your response is between you and the Holy Spirit. Once you prayerfully examine the evidence, it may well be that the Holy Spirit wants you to stay where you are. I do not believe that to be the case, but I dare not presume to tell the Holy Spirit what to do.

was a creation of the community, both in the old dispensation and in the Christian Church. The Bible is by no means a complete collection of all historical, legislative and devotional writings available, but a selection of some, authorized and authenticated by the use (first of all liturgical) in the community, and finally by the formal authority of the church. And there was some very definite purpose by which this "selection" was guided and checked.[351]

How then was this canonical process guided and checked? What were the criteria used? The primary criterion was apostolicity. Not every New Testament book was written by an apostle, but every New Testament book was consistent with the witness of the apostles. While this may seem a highly subjective assessment, it was considerably more objective in the primitive church, as it contained people who had been taught by the apostles themselves. As the earliest canonical testimonies contained the core of the New Testament as we know it today, we can safely say these books were confirmed by those who were taught by the apostles.

Part of apostolicity has to do with orthodoxy, with the *regula fidei* — the rule (or deposit) of faith. When the apostle Paul reminded the Thessalonians of all that he had taught them concerning the Gospel, he used the term "traditions," which is a way of referring to the apostolic deposit, the rule of faith.

But we are bound to give thanks alway to God for you, brethren beloved of the Lord, because God hath from the beginning chosen you to salvation through sanctification of the Spirit and belief of the truth: Whereunto he called you by our gospel, to the obtaining of the glory of our Lord Jesus Christ. Therefore, brethren, stand fast, and hold the traditions which ye have been taught, whether by word, or our epistle. (2 Th 2:13-15)

---

[351] (Florovsky 1972, 17-18)

Paul uses a similar line of thought when he addresses the Corinthians, telling them he is sending Timothy to remind them of "his ways" which he teaches everywhere, and to every church.[352] In this extended passage he tells them not to follow the teachings of men, but to follow the rule of faith which is held in common among the churches — the faith which we call orthodox doctrine.

I beseech you, be ye followers of me. For this cause have I sent unto you Timotheus, who is my beloved son, and faithful in the Lord, who shall bring you into remembrance of my ways which be in Christ, as I teach every where in every church. (1 Cor 4:16-17)

Related to the criterion of the rule of faith is the criterion that the text must be consistent and free of contradiction. We are speaking of more than mere internal consistency; more important was that the writing did not contradict other writings considered to be Scripture. In this vein, Justin Martyr argues that Scripture does not contradict itself.

If a Scripture which appears to be of such a kind be brought forward, and if there be a pretext [for saying] that it is contrary [to some other], since I am entirely convinced that no Scripture contradicts another, I shall admit rather that I do not understand what is recorded, and shall strive to persuade

---

[352] A brief discussion of the church is necessary. The church is not a voluntary community of like-minded individuals who adhere to the church out of custom, family ties, or common doctrinal understandings. Scripture tells us the Church is the body of Christ. Scripture does not distinguish between the visible and the invisible church, as some Protestants define it. The Church is an entity, a "corporate reality", a community. No one is a Christian by themselves, but only as part of the community. Christianity is a life shared with the community. Christ Himself is a member of this community; He is the head, we are the members of the body, all knit together through the abiding and dwelling of the Holy Spirit. (Florovsky 1972, 59-60)

those who imagine that the Scriptures are contradictory, to be rather of the same opinion as myself.[353]

Another element of apostolicity is its antiquity. One of Tertullian's arguments against the truncated canon of Marcion is that it doesn't pass the test of antiquity. Tertullian argues the Church had accepted the unedited version of Luke from the time Luke wrote it, while Marcion's edited version was unknown to the Church. In his writing, he links apostolicity with antiquity.

That Gospel of Luke which we are defending with all our might has stood its ground from its very first publication; whereas Marcion's Gospel is not known to most people, and to none whatever is it known without being at the same time condemned. It too, of course, has its churches, but specially its own—as late as they are spurious; and should you want to know their original, you will more easily discover apostasy in it than apostolicity, with Marcion forsooth as their founder, or some one of Marcion's swarm. Even wasps make combs; so also these Marcionites make churches. The same authority of the apostolic churches will afford evidence to the other Gospels also, which we possess equally through their means, and according to their usage — I mean the Gospels of John and Matthew — whilst that which Mark published may be affirmed to be Peter's whose interpreter Mark was. For even Luke's form of the Gospel men usually ascribe to Paul.[354]

Another important criterion was authorship. Was the author of a particular book known and accepted as an authority? The book of Hebrews was troubling because the book does not state who wrote it; moreover, the book's authorship has been lost. Some, such as Eusebius, attribute the book of Hebrews to the apostle Paul. The Pauline authorship is doubtful, and the Western Church did not include the book in its list of approved texts because of its disputed authorship.

---

[353] (Schaff, ANF01 1884, 370)
[354] (Schaff and Menzies, ANF03 2006, 581-582)

Eventually, Hebrews was accepted as Sacred Scripture. The important thing to note is that authorship is a criterion while the status of a book is in doubt. Once the general consensus of the Church declares this or that book to be Scripture, the issue of authorship is no longer relevant.

Today various books of the Old and New Testament are disputed. Many scholars believe that II Peter was not written by Peter, but instead by Peter's disciples after his death. Some scholars believe the Revelation and the Gospel of John were written by different people. The authorship (in the modern sense) of the five books of Moses is in dispute. All this is troubling to the Protestant mind, and some have even lost their faith over issues such as these. These issues are unimportant to the Orthodox, and indeed to other non-Protestant Christians. For them, the Church settled these issues. The books of Hebrews, II Peter, Revelation, and the Pentateuch are Scripture no matter the author.

Another important canonical criterion is that the writings churches read these books during worship. Texts read in Church needed to be authoritative. For example, Paul's letters were written to be read aloud in the church; they were then copied and passed on to other churches, who found them to be valuable and worthy of being read in church. The material regularly used in Church became our New Testament. Steve Rudd writes:

The regular use of writings in the ancient churches was also an important factor in their selection for the New Testament canon. This is what Eusebius had in mind when he mentioned that certain writings were "recognized" (homolegoumena) among the churches and became "encovenanted" (endiathekoi = "testamented" or "canonical").[355]

One criterion applied to the book of Jude was that inspired writings should not cite books that were not part of the canon. Since Jude quotes the Book of Enoch, some argued that the book of Jude should not be read in church.

---

[355] (Rudd n.d.) (Schaff, NPNF2-01 1890, III, XXV, 3)

Eventually, this argument was deemed unpersuasive; Jude became part of the New Testament canon.

These different criteria were not applied one at a time as part of some algorithmic process. There are books that seemingly meet these criterions yet did not make it into the canon. *The Didache* was written before 70 AD and the destruction of the temple.[356] Some wanted to attach it to the end of the Gospel of Matthew where it seems a natural fit.[357] As it describes the regular functioning of the church, its use was normative in the early church. It certainly does not contradict any other Scripture text, and yet it did not make it into the canon. Some books like *Clement 1*, the epistles of Ignatius, and the *Shepherd of Hermas* were fully orthodox in doctrine, were often read in church, and yet were left out of the canon.

---

[356] For a number of reasons, some date the Didache as early as 50 AD. First, its discussion of the two ways is Jewish in origin, suggesting a composition date before gentiles were a majority (see Deut 30:19; Jer 21:8; and Mt 7:13-15). Paul and Barnabas were not sent to the Gentiles until 47 AD, and reported to the council in Jerusalem in 49 AD, after which Christianity slowly began to be a Gentile phenomenon. The thesis proposed by Aaron Milavec (and others) is that the Didache is a program of catechesis for gentile converts. (Milavec, The Didache 2003, passim) Second, Christianity was first called "The Way", and only later called Christianity (Acts 9:2; 11:26). Third, the Didache mentions the "Gospel of our Lord", but fails to mention or quote the Gospels, indicating it was written before the Gospels themselves. (The supposed citations of Matthew are contextually different). (Milavec, The Didache 2003, Kindle Edition Kindle Location 2053 ff) Fourth, there is no indication the writer knows anything about Paul's epistles or any of the rest of the New Testament. Fifth, the baptismal and Eucharistic rites are quite primitive. And sixth, there is no hint of the fall of Jerusalem.

[357] Matthew appears to have functioned as an early catechesis, organized as it is around the five discourses. (Scaer, Discourse in Matthew: Jesus Teaches the Church 2004) Aaron Milavec makes a persuasive argument that the Didache was a Gentile catechesis. (Milavec, The Didache: Faith, Hope, & Life 2003, 53) The two catechetical writings may have seemed a natural fit.

The process of canonical formation is not a smooth, logical process. The rules were applied loosely and sometimes were bent or ignored. The only rules applied across the board were that a document had to be consistent with other Scripture and be fully orthodox in doctrine. The rest of the rules were applied in a seemingly haphazard fashion, a process that suggests a supra-rational approach, following the leading of the Holy Spirit working within the community of faith.

John C. Peckham asserts the difficulty in determining which community has the authority to determine the bounds of Sacred Scripture, particularly as different communities decide upon very different things. He also asserts, with the apostle Peter, that inspiration of the holy men of God is the work of the Holy Spirit. Thus, we have two positions, seemingly opposed to one another. Peckham writes of the "division between those who believe that the canon is a community-determined construction and those who believe that the canon is divinely appointed and thus merely recognized, but not determined, by any given community."[358]

While the terms Peckham uses may be his own, the distinction between these two positions is at the heart of the Protestant argument. I submit that we have here an example of the logical fallacy known as the "false dilemma," where an issue is described as having only two possible solutions when in fact there may be others. I also submit that the description of the position Peckham disagrees with — the Community-Canon — is wholly artificial, and an example of the logical fallacy known as the "straw man." As mentioned before, the issue of canon and canonicity is peculiar to Protestants.

The solution to Peckham's dilemma is found in the person and work of the Holy Spirit. The Holy Spirit is not limited to working linearly; first this, then that. God is everywhere present and filling all things; this includes time as well as space. The Holy Spirit inspires the prophet to write and inspires the community of faith to respond. The witness

---

[358] (Peckham 2011, 203)

of the Holy Spirit comes as a still, small voice, working within the heart of the community, just as He is at work in the heart of the prophet. As dripping water bores a hole through rock, so also the voice of the Holy Spirit bears witness to the Scriptures, leading the community of faith to their recognition.

The question of Community-Canon vs. Intrinsic-Canon is an example of Systematic Theology (or Dogmatics) run amuck. The Church has a long history of organizing its dogma around various themes, but the Western Church has taken this to extremes. The Western way of doing theology, going back further than Aquinas, has promoted the use of one's reasoning faculties as the way to the truth. This tendency has increased with the Protestant Reformation and its insistence on the primacy of reason and the individual conscience as a means of interpreting Scripture. What began as a way to organize dogma around simple themes has developed into uncountable definitions of terms and increasingly complex theological taxonomies. The question of canonicity is part of that pattern.

The question of canonicity is not interesting for the Eastern Orthodox. In the second volume of his book, *Orthodox Christianity*, Metropolitan Hilarion Alfeyev discusses the differences between the Protestant, Catholic, and Orthodox canons. He describes the differences between the canons and the reasons why they might be different. But the issue of canonicity itself, being primarily a Protestant issue, is mentioned not at all.[359] The church settled these issues long ago, and there is no need to justify the Orthodox canon.

---

[359] (Alfeyev, Orthodox Christianity Vol. II 2012, 33-41)

24: The New Testament Witness

Peter writes approvingly of Paul's epistles:

And account that the longsuffering of our Lord is salvation; even as our beloved brother Paul also according to the wisdom given unto him hath written unto you; As also in all his epistles, speaking in them of these things; in which are some things hard to be understood, which they that are unlearned and unstable wrest, as they do also the other Scriptures, unto their own destruction" (2 Pet 3:15-16).

What Peter refers to as "other Scriptures" clearly refers to the Old Testament. Dr. Benjamin B. Warfield, the late professor of theology at Princeton Seminary, makes an argument that Peter was indeed declaring Paul's epistles to be Scripture.[360] Although this may be inferred from the link between the "other Scriptures" and Paul's writings, it is not certain that Peter intends to place Paul's writings into that category. Peter does not say which of Paul's many epistles were Scripture; we know that Paul wrote more letters than just the ones preserved in the New Testament. Indeed, we can say that Peter refers to Paul's epistles, but does not directly call them Scripture. Even if we were to suppose that Peter meant to lump Paul's epistles in with the "other Scriptures, that does not mean they were part of the Church's "collection of authoritative books." He may have been first among the apostles, but that does not equate to primacy — first among equals is more like it. (Roman Catholics would beg to differ, of course). We note from both Acts and Galatians that Peter was led astray and was rebuked for his error by the apostle Paul. Given that, we need not assume any pronouncement of Peter was, on that basis alone, accepted by the Church at large.

Dr. Benjamin B. Warfield claims the apostle Paul as a witness to Luke's gospel when he writes: "Beyond what witness one apostolic book was to bear to another — as Paul

---

[360] (B. B. Warfield 1882, passim)

in 1 Tim. v. 18 authenticates Luke — and what witness an apostolic book may bear to itself, we cannot appeal at this day to immediate apostolic authorisation."[361] Even if we accept that the apostles Peter and Paul are bearing witness to the inspiration of some of the New Testament books, what does that say about the self-authenticating Scriptures? We note that neither Peter nor Paul is authenticating their work, but rather the work of another. Neither is Peter or Paul authenticating the entire corpus of the New Testament, but at best only a limited and uncertain portion.

What are we to make of the many references of the New Testament to the Scriptures? Clearly, when Jesus and others speak of the Scriptures, they are referring to the Old Testament. While the Canon as a *regula fidei* [rule of faith] existed, the Canon as a catalog of books did not. Therefore, although the reference is clearly to the Old Testament, it does not help us define the contents of the catalog. Ultimately, if the self-authentication of the Sacred Scriptures is based on epistemological criteria, initial assumptions, and subjective reasonings, then the idea of self-authentication falls apart.

---

[361] (Ibid, 45) Warfield's citation is in error; the cited passage has nothing to do with Luke's writings: "For the scripture saith, Thou shalt not muzzle the ox that treadeth out the corn. And, The labourer is worthy of his reward" (1 Tim 5:18). Warfield likely meant 2 Tim 2:8: "Remember that Jesus Christ of the seed of David was raised from the dead according to my gospel." Paul's reference to "my gospel" could be an endorsement of the *Gospel According to Luke*. The Church Fathers sometimes refer to Luke as "Paul's gospel" because Luke was Paul's disciple.

25: John Calvin, the Church, and the Canon

John Calvin, in his argument against the role of the Church in the canonical process, does discuss the role of the Holy Spirit. However, he indicates that the Holy Spirit works in the individual rather than in and through the Church. Calvin writes: "A most pernicious error has very generally prevailed—viz. that Scripture is of importance only in so far as conceded to it by the suffrage of the Church."[362] Calvin then argues that since the apostles and prophets existed before the Church, that the inspiration of the Scriptures is intrinsic apart from the Church.

These ravings are admirably refuted by a single expression of an apostle. Paul testifies that the Church is "built on the foundation of the apostles and prophets," (Eph. 2:20). If the doctrine of the apostles and prophets is the foundation of the Church, the former must have had its certainty before the latter began to exist. Nor is there any room for the cavil, that though the Church derives her first beginning from thence, it still remains doubtful what writings are to be attributed to the apostles and prophets, until her Judgment is interposed. For if the Christian Church was founded at first on the writings of the prophets, and the preaching of the apostles, that doctrine, wheresoever it may be found, was certainly ascertained and sanctioned antecedently to the Church, since, but for this, the Church herself never could have existed. Nothing therefore can be more absurd than the fiction, that the power of judging Scripture is in the Church, and that on her nod its certainty depends.[363]

---

[362] (Calvin, The Institutes of the Christian Religion 2005, I.7.1) Please note that while Paul references the "foundation of the apostles and prophets", it is Calvin who assumes this references "the writings of the prophets", as though the preaching of the prophets was not inspired until it was written down.

[363] (Ibid, I.7.2)

John Calvin, the Church, and the Canon

John Calvin notes that the inspiration of the Scriptures precedes its recognition by the Church. Since the Church's determination of the canon is invalid, John Calvin replaces the Church with the Holy Spirit who enlightens the individual believer's heart.

Let it therefore be held as fixed, that those who are inwardly taught by the Holy Spirit acquiesce implicitly in Scripture; that Scripture, carrying its own evidence along with it, deigns not to submit to proofs and arguments, but owes the full conviction with which we ought to receive it to the testimony of the Spirit. Enlightened by him, we no longer believe, either on our own Judgment or that of others, that the Scriptures are from God; but, in a way superior to human Judgment, feel perfectly assured—as much so as if we beheld the divine image visibly impressed on it—that it came to us, by the instrumentality of men, from the very mouth of God. We ask not for proofs or probabilities on which to rest our Judgment, but we subject our intellect and Judgment to it as too transcendent for us to estimate.

Such, then, is a conviction which asks not for reasons; such, a knowledge which accords with the highest reason, namely knowledge in which the mind rests more firmly and securely than in any reasons; such in fine, the conviction which revelation from heaven alone can produce. I say nothing more than every believer experiences in himself, though my words fall far short of the reality. I do not dwell on this subject at present, because we will return to it again: only let us now understand that the only true faith is that which the Spirit of God seals on our hearts.[364]

It is curious that John Calvin reason's his way to a dismissal of human reason and posits some ephemeral, mystical revelation of inspiration to the individual believer. Of course, John Calvin then modifies this by reference to the "children of the renovated Church" made up of the "elect

---

[364] (Ibid, I.7.5)

only," who "shall be taught of the Lord" (Isaiah 54:13). Calvin's argument isn't so much against the Church bearing witness to the canon of Scripture, but against the Roman Catholic Church doing so.

In essence, John Calvin's predisposition against the Roman Catholic Church colors his view of canonicity. We can break down his argument like this: 1) The Holy Spirit works within His true church. 2) The Roman Catholics do not constitute a true Church. 3) Therefore, the Holy Spirit does not work within the Roman Catholic Church. Calvin makes another argument: 1) The Holy Spirit works upon the hearts of the elect. 2) The Roman Catholic Church contains none of the elect. 3) Therefore, the Holy Spirit does not work within the Roman Catholic Church. Regarding the canon of Scripture, Calvin's argument goes: 1) The Holy Spirit works to reveal the canon of Scripture to the elect. 2) The Church is the assembly of the elect and not an entity. 3) Therefore, the Holy Spirit works through an assemblage of individuals rather than through the Church as an entity.

Of course, a syllogism can be logically true and yet be false. In these syllogisms, the middle statement, known as the minor premise, must be true for the conclusion to be true. But these minor premises are not themselves evidence, nor are they self-evidentially true. An Anti-Catholic bias has no evidentiary standing.[365] More importantly, Calvin fails to reckon that the prophets and apostles were members of the Church, the mystical body of Christ and that the Church was a continuation of the covenant people.[366] As such, it is difficult to separate the inspiration of scripture from its ministry to and within the church. Indeed, the inspired

---

[365] The Eastern Orthodox do not consider Roman Catholicism to be the true Church either, but for different reasons than the Protestants.

[366] In the 1970s and 80s, Protestant theologians developed a concept called Supercessionism to describe the historic position that the Church supercedes, replaces, and/or is the fulfillment of Judaism.

Scriptures bore witness to divine revelation before that witness was formally recognized.

The same Holy Spirit who inspired the prophets and apostles to write also inspired the bride of Christ to recognize what John Calvin calls "the testimony of the Spirit" when examining the Sacred Scriptures. When discussing issues of inspiration and canonicity, John Calvin denies the existence of the Church as an entity, or at least as an entity that supersedes the individual. Regarding theological anthropology and ecclesiology, John Calvin is arguing for the primacy of the individual over against the institutions to which the individual may belong. John Calvin is known to have declared those who disagreed with him to be heretics, making himself the infallible Pope of his Church. The ascendancy of the individual over against the Church is the spirit of the Protestant Reformation.

26: Canonicity and the Holy Spirit

Protestant discussions of canonicity largely ignore the role of the Holy Spirit in creating and maintaining the canon of Scripture. The concept of the self-authenticating Scripture provides little room for God to act. John C. Peckham's description of the Intrinsic-Canon approach, when carried to its logical conclusion, would seem to deify the Scriptures themselves. John Calvin makes a different claim when he argues the Holy Spirit works in the hearts of the elect, allowing them to mystically and individually recognize the Scriptures. Both claims are problematic. The first claim leads to the *de facto* divinization of Scripture; the second claim is a prescription for a highly individualistic religion, one which marginalizes the idea of the Church as the body of Christ.

How might we begin to properly describe the role of the Holy Spirit in the canonical process? With the idea of Inspiration, as described in the Bible. The apostle Peter writes: "Prophecy came not in old time by the will of man: but holy men of God spake as they were moved by the Holy Ghost" (2 Pet 1:21). The Holy Ghost is described in the Old Testament as the breath of God, giving us the idea of inspiration, or "God-breathed."[367] Of the inspiration of Scripture, the apostle Paul writes:

But continue thou in the things which thou hast learned and hast been assured of, knowing of whom thou hast learned them; And that from a child thou hast known the holy Scriptures, which are able to make thee wise unto salvation through faith which is in Christ Jesus. All scripture is given by inspiration of God, and is profitable for doctrine, for reproof, for correction, for instruction in righteousness: That the man of God may be perfect, thoroughly furnished unto all good works. (2 Pet 3:14-17)

All Scripture is "given by inspiration of God." It is the aspiration or breath of God, the manifestation of the Holy

---

[367] Ruach Elohim (Spirit or Breath of God)

Spirit. The function of scripture is to "make us wise unto salvation," which salvation comes "through faith which is in Christ Jesus." Peter's description of role of scripture aligns well with Christ's description of the Holy Spirit's role: "When the Comforter is come, whom I will send unto you from the Father, even the Spirit of truth, which proceedeth from the Father, he shall testify of me" (Jn 15:26). Just as Jesus reveals the Father to us, the Holy Spirit reveals to us the person and work of Christ Jesus.

Jesus calls the Comforter "the Spirit of Truth" (Jn 14:17). To the Father, Jesus prays: "Thy word is truth" (Jn 17:17). Of the Holy Spirit, Jesus says: "He shall teach you all things, and bring all things to your remembrance, whatsoever I have said unto you" (Jn 14:26). The Holy Spirit both inspires the Hebrew Scriptures and teaches us all things *within the Church*. Jude writes:

These be they who separate themselves, sensual, having not the Spirit. But ye, beloved, building up yourselves on your most holy faith, praying in the Holy Ghost, Keep yourselves in the love of God, looking for the mercy of our Lord Jesus Christ unto eternal life" (Jude 19-21).

From this, we understand that those who separate themselves from the Church separate themselves from the Holy Spirit. As they have not the Spirit, they are unable to pray in the Holy Spirit. The Holy Spirit, the Spirit of Truth, works in and through the Church, which is Christ's body, just as He works in and through the Scriptures to minister to the people of God. Christianity is not a matter of the individual's relationship with God apart from the Church; no, Christianity makes the individual part of the Church.

The apostle Paul writes to Timothy of the Church: "These things write I unto thee, ...that thou mayest know how thou oughtest to behave thyself in the house of God, which is the church of the living God, the pillar and ground of the truth" (1 Tim 14-15). The "church of the living God" is "the pillar and ground of the truth." We need to unpack this a bit. The pillar and ground both refer to the metaphor of the church as a building made up of living stones, with Christ as the cornerstone and the apostles as the foundation (1 Pet 2:5-7; Eph 2:20). We should understand the ground as providing stability; it does not shift, which would cause the edifice to collapse (Mt 7:24-27). The ground also refers to the "good ground" that brings forth much fruit (Mt 13:23). The role of a pillar is to hold up and support the roof and refers to God's "upholding all things by the word of his power" (Heb 1:3). Thus, the idea of the pillar and the ground refers to the role of the Church in providing stability, support, and a structure within which persons may bring forth much fruit. We cannot ignore or otherwise diminish the existence of the Church in our discussions of the formation of the canon.

Returning to the subject of canonicity, we see the Holy Spirit working in and through the Scripture (the Intrinsic-Canon), just as we see the Holy Spirit working in and through the Church (the Community-Canon). These two explanations of canonicity are not mutually exclusive; neither makes any sense apart from the person and work of the Holy Spirit. So how does the Holy Spirit work through Scripture and the Church to produce and maintain the canon?

The work of the Holy Spirit is a mystery. We can't define it, we can't categorize it, and we can't explain it. As Jesus said to Nicodemus: "The wind bloweth where it listeth, and thou hearest the sound thereof, but canst not tell whence it cometh, and whither it goeth: so is every one that is born of the Spirit" (Jn 3:8). When we try to define, categorize, and explain canonicity apart from the person and work of the Holy Spirit, we are raising human reason to a place of primacy. We are telling God how to do His job. As the Church is the pillar and ground of the Truth, it is certain that the Holy Spirit works in and through the Church to preserve the Truth, such that "the gates of hell shall not prevail against it" (Mt 16:18). More than that we ought not to say.

Part III: Inspiration and Inerrancy

27: The Recent Invention of Verbal Inerrancy

The current enthusiasm for the idea of verbal inerrancy — as indeed the word itself—is relatively recent. Lutheran professor Arthur Carl Piepkorn points out that while the word bears a superficial resemblance to the ancient Latin word *inerrantia*, it is in fact "a kind of do-it-yourself [or manufactured] term, ...with *in-* meaning 'not' and *errantia* meaning 'the act of wandering about." Piepkorn cites the Oxford English Dictionary as pointing out that the first use of the English word inerrant was in 1834, and its first use in a religious context was in 1865 when describing the manner in which the Pope was preserved from error.[368]

Michael Horton, professor of apologetics and systematic theology at Westminster Seminary California, describes the "Princeton Formulation of Inerrancy" as the "best formulation of inerrancy" because "it anticipates and challenges caricatures."[369] While Michael Horton is fond of reading modern formulations of inerrancy back into the early church fathers; he is as wrong about the church fathers as he is about the "Princeton Formulation of Inerrancy." For one thing, the word "inerrancy" never occurs in Warfield and Hodge's book, *Inspiration*. This should not be surprising, given that the word "inerrancy' was newly minted when Warfield and Hodge wrote in 1881. For another, the supposed "inerrancy" described by Warfield and Hodge is nothing like that of the modern Fundamentalist and Evangelical.[370]

Warfield and Hodge write: "[I]n all the affirmations of Scripture of every kind, there is no more error in the words

---

[368] (Piepkorn, What Does "Innerancy" Mean? 2007, 29)

[369] (Horton 2010)

[370] In his introduction to the 2007 edition, the Swiss theologian Roger R. Nicole reads his own views on inerrancy back into Hodge and Warfield's book. (Hodge and Warfield 2007, xiv)

of the original autographs than in the thoughts they were chosen to express."[371] If they stopped there, the modern evangelical would be happy. But then they gradually expose a more nuanced position. Instead of speaking of "all the affirmations of Scripture of every kind," they later refer to "all their real affirmations."

In view of all the facts known to us, we affirm that a candid inspection of all the ascertained phenomena of the original text of Scripture will leave unmodified the ancient faith of the Church. In all their real affirmations these books are without error.[372]

What is the content of these "real affirmations" anyway? Do they in any way conform to the modern understanding of inerrancy? Warfield and Hodge tell us these "real affirmations" concern the "ancient faith of the Church." In other words, they are revelatory affirmations. Warfield and Hodge write:

It must be remembered that it is not claimed that the Scriptures any more than their authors are omniscient. The information they convey is in the forms of human thought, and limited on all sides. **They were not designed to teach philosophy, science, or human history as such.** *They were not designed to furnish an infallible system of speculative theology. They are written in human languages, whose words, inflections, constructions, and idioms bear everywhere indelible traces of human error. The record itself furnishes evidence that the writers were in large measure dependent for their knowledge upon sources and methods in themselves fallible; and that their personal knowledge and judgments were in many matters hesitating and defective, or even wrong. [emphasis added]*[373]

---

[371] (Ibid, 19)
[372] (Ibid, 27)
[373] (Ibid, 78)

In making this statement, Warfield and Hodge have made a rather dramatic shift from the "Scottish realism" of Princeton's founders, theologians for whom the Bible was "a sourcebook on every area of knowledge including science and history."[374]

While Warfield and Hodge state the scriptural affirmations are without error in matters of historical fact, they have already mentioned this is not a reference to human history. Thus, what is in view is the history of the relationship between God and man, and in particular the gospel of Jesus Christ. The Princeton Formulation is a long way from the modern concept of inerrancy. Warfield and Hodge summarize their position as follows:

There is a vast difference between exactness of statement, which includes an exhaustive rendering of details, an absolute literalness, which the Scriptures never profess, and accuracy, on the other hand, which secures a correct statement of facts or principles intended to be affirmed. It is this accuracy and this alone, as distinct from exactness, which the Church doctrine maintains of every affirmation in the original text of Scripture without exception. Every statement accurately corresponds to truth just as far forth as affirmed.[375]

There is a vast gulf fixed between the accuracy of the Scriptures as affirmed by Warfield and Hodge and the "absolute literalness" approach of modern Fundamentalists and large numbers of Evangelicals. But the absolutely literal approach is the approach of modernity. As David Bentley Hart writes, the ancients used a different approach to texts in general, including but not limited to spiritual texts.

For ancient and medieval exegetes, however, the very question of whether the events recounted in the text had ever actually happened was largely a matter of indifference for how to go about reading the text literally—or, more precisely, reading it

---

[374] (Rogers and McKim 1979, 309)

[375] (Hodge and Warfield 2007, 27)

ad litteram: that is, with an exactingly scrupulous attention to what was written on the page, in every detail, and with every discernible shade of significance. For them the difference between the literal and the allegorical was simply the difference between what was there to be seen and what was given to be discovered. And their somewhat insouciant attitude to the question of "fact" can prove terribly confusing to modern readers who do not share their presuppositions.[376]

It may well be that the works entitled *The Fundamentals: A Testimony to the Truth* (1910-15) is the first major work to formally equate inspiration with verbal inerrancy, although this assertion is made in only two of the seven essays on the Sacred Scriptures.[377] If so, the idea of verbal inerrancy is an American invention, made by those who came to be known as Fundamentalists.[378] Despite the feeble attempt by L. W. Munhall to find support for this position from the writings of Justin Martyr, Irenaeus, Clement of Alexandria, Origen, and Augustine, it is clear that their understanding of inerrancy concerned the *forma* (doctrine), and not the *materia* (text).[379]

Lutheran theologians of the twentieth century quickly adopted the Fundamentalist definition of inerrancy. In his book, *Luther and the Scriptures*, J. Michael Reu developed his thesis that Martin Luther provides support for the recently developed Fundamentalist definitions of inerrancy. Despite his valiant effort, he is unable to provide a single instance of Luther's use of the word inerrant (or its Latin or German equivalent) in the manner with which Fundamentalists use the word. Despite this failure, the lawyer, professor, Lutheran theologian, and author John Warwick Montgomery

---

[376] (Hart 2015)

[377] See "The Inspiration of the Bible — Definition, Extent and Proof" by Rev. James M. Gray (Gray 2005), and "Inspiration" by Evangelist L. W. Munhall. (Munhall 2005)

[378] (Portier 1994, 130)

[379] (Munhall 2005)

approvingly cites Reu as concluding that Luther "did indeed hold to the inerrancy of the Bible."[380] Reu and Montgomery's arguments are cast in 20th-century terms, not in terms used by Martin Luther and the Lutheran Confessors. The claim that Luther supports a dogma that was developed over 400 years after his death is at best an appeal to authority. At worst, it puts words in his mouth and besmirches his reputation.

John Calvin himself would have affirmed the accuracy of Sacred Scripture while rejecting the modern formulations of "verbal inspiration" as well as inerrancy. Take, for example, the following passage of Scripture:

Then was fulfilled that which was spoken by Jeremy the prophet, saying, And they took the thirty pieces of silver, the price of him that was valued, whom they of the children of Israel did value. (Matt 27:9)

In his commentary on this passage, John Calvin notes that the attribution of the quoted passage is in error.

How the name of Jeremiah crept in, I confess that I do not know nor do I give myself much trouble to inquire. The passage itself plainly shows that the name of Jeremiah has been put down by mistake, instead of Zechariah, (11:13;) for in Jeremiah we find nothing of this sort, nor any thing that even approaches to it.[381]

Having announced the attribution to Jeremiah instead of Zechariah[382] as a mistake, Calvin rightly ignores it. The error is immaterial, irrelevant, and the inspiration of the text suffers not one whit.

---

[380] (Montgomery n.d.)

[381] (Calvin, Commentary on Matthew, Mark, Luke - Volume 3 1999, 188)

[382] And I said unto them, If ye think good, give me my price; and if not, forbear. So they weighed for my price thirty pieces of silver. And the LORD said unto me, Cast it unto the potter: a goodly price that I was prised at of them. And I took the thirty pieces of silver, and cast them to the potter in the house of the LORD. (Zec 11:12-13)

28: Inerrancy: A Protestant Shibboleth

"I can't imagine a more rationalistic account of the Christian faith than some forms of how scriptural inspiration is understood." Dr. Stanley Hauerwas[383]

When we discuss the concept of the canon of Scripture, we must deal with both the concept of Inspiration and the Evangelical Protestant shibboleth of Inerrancy. As we already mentioned, the concept of verbal inerrancy is a modern invention — as is the word inerrancy itself. Conservative Christians created the concept of verbal inerrancy of the Scriptures in the early 1900s in reaction to the perceived threat of Higher Criticism. The concept of inerrancy and its connection to inspiration is barely one hundred years old. We need to understand what was meant by the inspiration of Sacred Scripture before the Fundamentalists redefined of the term.

The New Testament attests to the inspiration of scripture and quotes the apostle Paul's words to Timothy that "All scripture is given by inspiration of God" (2 Tim 3:16). Diodore of Tarsus (died c. 390), in the Prologue to his *Commentary on the Psalms*, writes:

According to the blessed Paul, "all Scripture is inspired by God and profitable for teaching, for reproof, for correction, for training in righteousness" [2 Tim. 3:16]. Indeed, Scripture teaches what is useful, exposes what is sinful, corrects what is deficient, and thus it completes the perfect human being; for Paul adds: "that the man of God may be complete, equipped for every good work" [v. 17].[384]

The Apostle Paul's statement on the inspiration of Scripture is full of difficulties for Protestants. At the time of Paul's letter to Timothy, little of the New Testament had been written.

---

[383] (Mohler 2012)
[384] (Froehlich 1984, Kindle Locations 1029-1031)

Moreover, Paul never claims his own writings to be scripture. The apostle was clearly referring to the Scriptures used by both Jews and Christians, the Scriptures to which Paul appealed when proclaiming Christ as the Messiah, the Scriptures which today we would call the Old Testament. While we use Paul's words as though they apply to both the Old and New Testament, the plain, literal meaning applies only to the Old Testament. In other words, our understanding of Paul is a church tradition that has been passed down to us — a tradition allowing us to recognize the New Testament texts as inspired by God.

The statement of the Assemblies of God on *The Inerrancy of Scripture* cites various church fathers as supporting the idea that this passage is speaking of the inerrancy of scripture.

During the Patristic Period, the Scriptures were considered to be the unique work of the Holy Spirit carrying forth a divine message. To the church fathers, inspiration extended even to the phraseology of the Bible. Thus, Clement of Alexandria underscores Christ's words in Matthew 5:18 by saying that not a jot or tittle shall pass away because the Lord had spoken it (Proteptics, IX, 82, 1). Gregory Nazianzus suggests that the smallest lines in the Scriptures are due to the care of the Holy Spirit, and that we must be careful to consider every slightest shade of meaning (Orat., 2, 105). Justin Martyr distinguished between human and divine inspiration and spoke of the divine word that moved the writers of Scripture (Apology I, Ch. 36). Irenaeus thought of the Scriptures as "beyond all falsehood" (Apology, Ch. 18). There can be little doubt that the early fathers had a very high view of inspiration, and that this view extended to the minutia of Scripture.[385]

The Position Paper of the Assemblies of God equates inspiration and inerrancy and appeals to church history and the church fathers: "The church generally has held to a high

---

[385] (General Council of the Assemblies of God. 1976, 2)

view of inspiration, holding to the inseparability of inspiration and inerrancy."[386] This statement assumes facts not in evidence. The citation from Gregory of Nazianzus states that the "jot and tittle" refers to the "slightest shade of meaning." This is equivalent to the *forma* (the meaning found within the text) rather than the *materia* (the text, being the *ipsissima verba*, the very words themselves). The authors of this Position Paper are reading the modern conception of inerrancy back into the church fathers.

It is clear from the Gospel of Matthew that Jesus Christ is not referring to the inerrancy of Sacred Scripture.

Think not that I am come to destroy the law, or the prophets: I am not come to destroy, but to fulfil. For verily I say unto you, Till heaven and earth pass, one jot or one tittle shall in no wise pass from the law, till all be fulfilled. Whosoever therefore shall break one of these least commandments, and shall teach men so, he shall be called the least in the kingdom of heaven: but whosoever shall do and teach them, the same shall be called great in the kingdom of heaven. For I say unto you, That except your righteousness shall exceed the righteousness of the scribes and Pharisees, ye shall in no case enter into the kingdom of heaven. (Mt 5:17-20)

First, Jesus is not speaking of the Scriptures in their entirety but is referring to the Torah, the five books of Moses. Rabbi Jacob Neusner, in his book, *A Rabbi Talks with Jesus*, replaces the Matthean term *law* with the rabbinic term *Torah*.[387] Jesus states that he has come to fulfill the *Torah*, and is referring to the immutability of the *Torah*, being the words spoken by Moses from Mt. Sinai. The term *torah* with a lower-case "t" has reference to "the instruction of a master — in the context of the teaching of the Torah."[388] When Jesus says "Heaven and earth shall pass away, but my words shall not pass away"

---

[386] (Ibid, 5)

[387] (Neusner 1993, 21)

[388] (Ibid, 4)

(Mt 24:35), He is referring to his teaching (*torah*) as being Torah; He is claiming to be the Torah in person — which equates to the Johannine use of the term *Logos*. Thus, the reference to the law and the prophets in Matthew 5 has to do with the revelation of God incarnate in the text — being the meaning and content of the Torah — rather than the actual text.

The idea that inspiration requires some assertion of inerrancy is not found in Sacred Scripture, and its derivation from Sacred Scripture is suspect at best. This modern conceit was unknown to the early church — and indeed, to the Reformers themselves. As an example of the modern point of view, Lutheran scholar Dr. Robert Preus claims the passages used to support inspiration are also used to support inerrancy.[389] Inspiration and inerrancy are at least referential (if not synonymous) when in fact the two terms mean substantially different things. Even less well supported are the formulae by which Protestants attempt to expound, expand, and enhance a dogmatic assertion of the inerrancy of Sacred Scripture.

Introducing inerrancy into the topic of the inspiration of Sacred Scriptures detracts from our understanding of Sacred Scripture, introduces all manner of problems for scriptural interpretation, and creates serious problems for the doctrine of inspiration. Adding *verbal* inerrancy into our understanding of inspiration tends to change our understanding of canonicity from that of the Word contained within the text (the *forma*) to the actual text (or *materia*) written by a particular author. When canonicity is a matter of the actual written text, we think of Jeremiah (the author) as inspired to produce a text (the *materia*), instead of thinking of the extant text of Jeremiah as the inspired Word of God.[390]

Once we have focused our attention on the actual words on the page, we have to address the fact that we do not

---

[389] (Piepkorn, What Does "Innerancy" Mean? 2007)

[390] (Sanders, English Translation of the Psalms Scroll (Tehillim) 11QPs n.d., xvi-xvii)

possess the original inspired text. Our lack of the originals raises issues as to the inspiration and authority of our imperfectly preserved and translated text. How can the extant text be inspired when it does not contain the exact words written by the holy men of God under the inspiration of the Holy Spirit? If we have variant textual readings, how then can the text be inerrant?

The modern concept of verbal inerrancy could not have arisen before the advent of the printing press because every hand-written copy contained errors.[391] Lee McDonald, retired president of Acadia Divinity College in Nova Scotia, writes:

Until the invention of the printing press, the church employed scribes to make individual copies of their Sacred Scriptures. Until the invention of the printing press no two biblical manuscripts were exactly alike, and yet each manuscript that the scribes produced functioned as Scripture for the communities for which they were copied and preserved. The copiers had differing abilities, and some copies were better than others and some were worse, but each copy functioned as Scripture in the community that authorized or was responsible for their production.[392]

The idea of inerrancy necessitates certain approaches to scripture. The first of these is a literalistic approach; the second is the approach of lower criticism — particularly, the attempt to recover the original, unaltered text. These two approaches are difficult to reconcile, even applying the supposedly scientific rules used in literary criticism. Emanuel Tov writes:

---

[391] Even with careful copyediting, errors are sometimes found in printed scriptures. *The Wicked Bible*, sometimes called *The Sinner's Bible* or *The Adulterous Bible*, contained printer's errors in the seventh commandment where the word "not" was omitted. Thus *The Wicked Bible* commanded: "Thou shalt commit adultery."

[392] (McDonald 2007, 45)

What appears to one scholar to be a safely reconstructed Hebrew variant text is for another a translator's tendentious rendering. Literary analysis of the Hebrew Bible is only interested in evidence of the first type, since it sheds light on the background of the different Hebrew texts that were once circulating. The translator's tendentious changes are also interesting, but at a different level, that of scriptural exegesis. Since a specific rendering either represents a greatly deviating Hebrew text or displays the translator's exegesis, one wonders how to differentiate between the two.[393]

In other words, two scholars can apply the rules of lower criticism and come up with variant readings, each of which can be supported by appealing to different rules. The rules of textual criticism are subject to interpretation and manipulation, intentional or otherwise. The problem is that the textual critic focuses on the wrong thing. The problems with textual criticism are often the same as scriptural exegesis, being the critical interpretation of the text. Fr. John Behr says the Evangelical preoccupation with exegesis is its involvement with the Scriptural text instead of Christ.

It is important to note that it is Christ who is being explained through the medium of Scripture, not Scripture itself that is being exegeted; the object is not to understand the "original meaning" of an ancient test, as in modern historical-critical scholarship, but to understand Christ, who, by being explained "according to the Scriptures," becomes the sole subject of Scripture throughout.[394]

The difficulty in applying the rules of literary criticism, and of reconciling the different applications of the rules of scriptural exegesis, result in all manner of problems. The inspiration of a specific author rather than subject matter has important implications for the canon of Sacred Scripture, leading scholars to excise (or at least discount) passages they

---

[393] (Tov 2008, Kindle Locations 460-464)

[394] (Behr 2001, 27-28)

believe are corruptions of the earliest, best-attested texts. However, if we are using a corrupted text, then in what way is Sacred Scripture the inspired, inerrant, and infallible Word of God? Protestants lack a doctrine of inspiration that that preserves the mystery and the power of inspiration without diminution by scholasticism and sophistry; a doctrine that allows us to understand the extant text as the inspired and authoritative Word of God; an approach that explains Christ "according to the Scriptures" rather than simply dealing with the text as text.

The most troubling problem with the concept of inerrancy is that modern atheists adopt the same concept of inspiration to support their rejection of the Scriptures. If you assume God's revelation of Himself to be without error, then any supposed error is evidence that the Scriptures are entirely a human enterprise. H. L. Mencken writes:

The simple fact is that the New Testament, as we know it, is a helter-skelter accumulation of more or less discordant documents, some of them probably of respectable origin but others palpably apocryphal, and that most of them, the good along with the bad, show unmistakable signs of having been tampered with.[395]

If I held to the fundamentalist view of inspiration, I would be forced to agree with Mencken. However, since the idea the Bible is completely without error — whether of words or the subjects it addresses — is a modern conceit, I must conclude that either the New Atheists such as Richard Dawkins, Sam Harris, and Christopher Hitchens are correct, or that perhaps the idea of inspiration has been misunderstood. For example, Christopher Hitchens, in his book, *God is not Great*, argues that the gospel writers: "cannot agree on anything of importance." He cites the differences in the genealogies, differences concerning the flight to Egypt, and the historical

---

[395] (Mencken 1946, 176)

problems with the supposed world-wide census ordered by Caesar Augustus.[396]

The gospels are not histories, although they cover historical events. The gospels are not biographies, although they cover events in the life of a historical person. What Mencken, Hitchens, and the rest fail to understand is that the Gospels are organized theologically. Moreover, bible critics assume the gospels should agree in all details, but if they did, there would be no need for the four different accounts — each coming from a different theological perspective. Moreover, bible critics assume the modern concept of authorship, rather than viewing the manuscripts as the ancients would have. And finally, Mencken and the rest assume verbal, plenary inerrancy as a requirement for inspiration, which is the same view as most Protestants.

---

[396] (Hitchens 2007, 190)

29: On the Seeming Errancy of Sacred Scripture

As the Sacred Scriptures are full of apparent inconsistencies, seeming contradictions, pre-scientific descriptions, anthropomorphisms, and even what may be called (by some) errors, the issue of inerrancy introduces all manner of problems—of which Biblical scholars are well aware. Lutheran academic Arthur Carl Piepkorn provides us with a long (and nevertheless partial) list of these issues.[397] Moreover, atheists and agnostics delight in producing long lists of inconsistencies and contradictions contained in Sacred Scripture; some of these are silly while others are substantive and deserving of serious consideration.[398]

It is possible to explain away the individual issues within Sacred Scripture, but the accumulated weight of these apparent inconsistencies, seeming contradictions, and other problems present great difficulty for the evangelical and fundamentalist formulae regarding verbal, plenary inspiration.[399] Different manuscripts contain textual

---

[397] (Piepkorn, What Does "Innerancy" Mean? 2007, 34-39) I use Arthur Karl Piepkorn as a source for the following list of pre-scientific descriptions:

The Bible speaks of the sun's rising and setting. Is this metaphorical, or is this evidence of a pre-Copernican understanding of science? (Mal 1:11, Jos 10:13; Ps 19:4-6; Matt 5:45)

The Bible speaks of the four corners of the earth. Is this metaphorical, or evidence of a belief in a flat earth? (Isa 11:12; Rv 7:1)

The Bible describes the constellations of the zodiac. Is this a tacit acceptance of astrology, or is astrology a corruption of God's original plan of redemption written in the stars for all men to see? (Job 38:31-33)

[398] (Morgan n.d.)

[399] Multnomah University uses the following statement: "We believe in the verbal, plenary inspiration of Scripture. This means the Holy

variations, the existence of which presents problems for the concept of verbal inerrancy. It is not enough to appeal to the autographs, as we shall discover in the next chapter.

The term inerrancy not only means something less than inspiration but diminishes the concept of inspiration. A statement that I am an overweight Caucasian with brown hair and blue eyes is inerrant. The same statement—although inerrant—is not inspired. Inerrancy, therefore, means something other than inspiration, but proponents of the verbal inerrancy of Sacred Scripture seem to treat the two statements as though they are synonymous, or at least statements of equivalent importance.

The doctrine of inerrancy forces Protestants to reject the existence of errors in the text. Since there are obvious errors, Protestant scholars develop tortured logic to explain them away. While each explanation by itself seems reasonable, when taken as a whole they are nothing more than a desperate attempt at maintaining an untenable ideology. An appeal to the autographs is a ridiculous argument, an argument we will take up in the next chapter.

Spirit dynamically superintended the verbal expressions of the human authors of Scripture so that the very thoughts God intended were accurately penned in the wording of the original manuscripts. (2 Tim. 3:16-17; 2 Pet. 1:20-21; 1 Cor. 2:13)" (Multnomah University n.d.) Wheaton College uses a similar statement: "WE BELIEVE that God has revealed Himself and His truth in the created order, in the Scriptures, and supremely in Jesus Christ; and that the Scriptures of the Old and New Testaments are verbally inspired by God and inerrant in the original writing, so that they are fully trustworthy and of supreme and final authority in all they say." (Wheaton College n.d.) A directory of similar statements may be found at: http://www.wholesomewords.org/direc.html.

Some of these statements imply the inspiration and therefore the inerrancy of the Masoretic Hebrew text and the Textus Receptus Greek text; some go so far as to imply inspiration and inerrancy apply to the translation of these texts known as the King James Version; others state these texts come closest to the inspired autographs.

30: Inerrancy and the Autographs

Our surviving (or extant) biblical texts have problems. The ancient manuscripts differ from one another, usually in trivial ways, but sometimes in ways with some theological significance. For example, the ending to the Gospel of Mark (Mark 16:9-20) does not appear in the most ancient manuscripts (the Codex Sinaiticus and Codex Vaticanus). In other ancient manuscripts, the ending to the Gospel of Mark occurs with variations and omissions. Without the problematic ending, the book ends rather abruptly with only the myrrh-bearing women being witnesses to the resurrection. What are we to make of this? Do we leave it in, acknowledging the problems in a footnote as is done in the Scofield Reference Bible? Do we add a subheading saying "Endings Added Later" or "One Old Ending to Mark's Gospel" as is done in the Common English Bible and the Contemporary English Version? Should we leave the passage out entirely? What do we do with this problematic passage?

Today, a literary work can be produced and reproduced seemingly without error. This historically recent innovation colors our understanding of the ancient world. Part of our problem is that books, as we know them today, did not exist. Instead, of a book, think of a scroll — a single, long piece of paper rolled around a pair of spindles. Not only was the paper expensive, but the reproduction of the book was a long, laborious process.

Moreover, in the scribal culture that existed before the Hellenistic era, literary texts did not exist as we know them today. Let us focus on the production of scrolls in the Hellenistic era, primarily using the arguments of Bart Ehrman, the popular author and James A. Gray Distinguished Professor of Religious Studies at the University of North Carolina.

[Books] could not be produced en mass (no printing presses). And since they had to be copied by hand, one at a time, slowly and painstakingly, most books were not mass produced. Those

few that were produced in multiple copies were not all alike, for the scribes who copied texts inevitably made alterations in those texts—changing the words they copied either by accident (via a slip of the pen or other carelessness) or by design (when the scribe intentionally altered the words he copied). Anyone reading a book in antiquity could never be completely sure that he or she was reading what the author had written. The words could have been altered. In fact, they probably had been, if only just a little.[400]

The production of books in the ancient world was much different. Today, most authors write books on a computer. The book goes through an editorial process, whereby third parties go over the book to find flaws in its spelling, grammar, content, and presentation. Eventually, the book is electronically typeset, printed, and the galley's edited by the author to ensure the book is what the author intended. Finally, the book is mass-produced and made available for sale, with each copy identical to the others.

Authorship in the ancient world was much different. As we have mentioned before, there often was no author in the modern sense. But in the ancient world, even if there were an author, once a manuscript was passed on to others it was outside the author's control. Anything could happen to the text, and anything often did. Bart Ehrman writes: "Copying texts allowed for the possibilities of manual error; and the problem was widely recognized throughout antiquity."[401] The reproduction of the biblical texts was fraught with problems, leading to different families of texts containing different readings.[402] The typical Protestant answer to this

---

[400] (Ehrman 2005, 46)

[401] (Ibid, 47)

[402] It wasn't until the development of the scriptorium by the Masoretes that manuscript production became more professional. The scriptorium used professional copyists, using a process that counted each letter to prevent additions and omissions. This system, while not perfect, nonetheless cut down on the number of copyist errors.

problem is that inerrancy applies only to the autographs — to the original texts created by the original authors. Presbyterian professor Dr. Marvin R. Vincent provides an introduction to the problems inherent in this idea.

Nothing can be more puerile or more desperate than the effort to vindicate the divine inspiration of Scripture by the assertion of the verbal inerrancy of the autographs, and to erect that assertion into a test of orthodoxy. For:

1. There is no possible means of verifying the assertion, since the autographs have utterly disappeared.

2. It assumes a mechanical dictation of the «ipsissima verba» [the very words] to the writers, which is contradicted by the whole character and structure of the Bible.

3. It is of no practical value, since it furnishes no means of deciding between various readings or discrepant statements.

4. It is founded upon a pure assumption as to the character of inspiration - namely, that inspiration involves verbal inerrancy, which is the very thing to be proved, and which could only be proved only by producing inerrant autographs. [In other words, the definition is a tautology.]

5. If a written, inspired revelation is necessary for mankind, and if such a revelation, in order to be inspired, must be verbally inerrant, the necessity has not been met. There is no verbally inerrant, and therefore no inspired, revelation in writing. The autographs have vanished, and no divine guidance or interposition has prevented mistakes in transcription or in printing. The text of Scripture, in the best form in which critical scholarship can exhibit it, presents numerous errors and discrepancies.[403]

Suppose inspiration required the production and supernatural maintenance of the text without error. Our

---

[403] (Vincent 1899, 3)

current text contains all manner of contradictions, errors, and mistakes. Since the extant text has *not* been preserved without error, either verbal inspiration cannot require the supernatural maintenance of the text without error or the extant text is not inspired (given our presupposition). Moreover, even if we had the autographs, we would have no way of knowing it, or of verifying their authenticity. Dr. Constantine Siamakis writes:

Only autographs dating from the 12th century A.D. onwards exist, and these are only of Greek and Latin authors. ...The texts of the most ancient authors survive only in copies. Yet even if a very ancient autograph were unexpectedly found today, such as the letter to the Galatians in St. Paul's own hand, nobody could know or prove that is was the apostle's autograph.[404]

Modern formulations of verbal inerrancy are based on the idea that the original manuscripts (or autographs) were without error. Since no autographs exist, we cannot know if they were without error. Because the evangelical and fundamentalist insist the autographs were without error, and because the same formulae claim an equivalence between inspiration and inerrancy, the proposition cannot be proven. Therefore, given the formulae, we cannot know if the extant text is inspired.[405]

- Suppose an inspired and verbally inerrant revelatory text is necessary to the validity of the Christian faith. As we have no inspired and verbally inerrant revelatory text, this presupposition can result in questioning the validity of the Christian faith.
- If verbal inerrancy and infallibility are necessary components of inspiration, and the extant text contains errors (even if they are merely copyist errors), then the extant text (as opposed to the revelation contained within

---

[404] (Siamakis 1997, 10)

[405] Absence of evidence is not evidence of absence. On the other hand, the burden of proof is on the person making the proposition.

it) cannot be inspired. The extant text, therefore, cannot be said to be profitable for doctrine, for reproof, for correction, and for instruction in righteousness (2 Tim 3:16).

- If inspiration and infallibility require verbal inerrancy, the requirement has not been met, and we cannot demonstrate the inspiration of Scriptures.

The modern Protestant doctrine of verbal inerrancy is much the same as the position taken by the Muslim faith, a faith which claims the verbal inerrancy of the Quran. Islamic dogma insists the Quran has been supernaturally maintained in its purity (unlike the Bible), by which the Muslims are assured they have the revelation of Allah. But note the middle term depends on upon there being no variant readings of the Quran. While textual criticism of the Quran is in its infancy, it is well known even among Muslim scholars that variant readings exist. Therefore, by their standard of inspiration, the Quran is not inspired and is not a true and faithful revelation of Allah.[406] In this way, the arguments of the Muslim scholars against the Christian Scriptures is turned against themselves.

But let us suppose the proposition of the Muslim faith is true, that the Quran is verbally inerrant and has been preserved free from error. Would this then serve as proof of its inspiration? Of course not, for as we have demonstrated, inerrancy is not the same thing as inspiration; the two are not synonymous, nor is one the proof of the other. Moreover, modern printing technology has the capability of producing multiple copies of a document without error and of preserving a document free from corruption. Does this mean that said documents are therefore inspired? Again, of course not; inspiration is a matter of content, and it is the content that is inspired. The method by which the content is reproduced and transmitted may change; the text may be more or less accurate without affecting the content in any formal way.

---

[406] (Reformed Internet Ministries n.d.)

The same people who proclaim the verbal inerrancy of Scripture are fond of pointing to the preservation of the text, noting the textual differences between different manuscripts are minor and never affect the meaning of the text. This argument is exactly that of those who argue against verbal, plenary inerrancy, who claim that inspiration is about the meaning of the text (the *forma*) rather than the text itself (the *materia*). Which is it? Is inspiration about the revelation of God contained within the text, or about the text itself?

God did not see fit to protect His revelation from corruption by human error, which means that if inspiration requires inerrancy, we have no inspired revelation of the Word of God.[407]

---

[407] (Vincent 1899, 3)

31: Inerrancy and the Nature of God

Victor Kuligin claims the evangelical insistence upon the inerrancy of Sacred Scripture is rooted in the very nature of God. He writes: "Because evangelicals believe God to be without error, they believe that his Word is also without error."[408] The argument goes something like this:
- God is without error;
- The Word is God;
- Therefore, the Word is without error.

We could all agree that Kuligin's argument is true if the Word refers to Jesus Christ, for John's Gospel claims the Logos of God to be God (Jn 1:1). However, Kuligin's argument is based not upon the unity of essence within the Trinity, but an equivalence between the Word of God and the text of Sacred Scripture. But as we have mentioned earlier, these two are hardly the same thing; and if they were, we would have either a fourth person of the Godhead or some created deity — a 'god' if you will.

When speaking of the Sacred Scriptures as the Word of God, Arthur Carl Piepkorn notes this is a maximal statement.[409] Adding adjectives, clarifications, and modifying clauses serve to limit a maximal statement, to make it something less than maximal.[410] Calling the Scriptures the "inerrant, infallible Word of God" adds nothing to the maximal statement, but instead qualifies it and reduces it to meaninglessness. Failing to deal properly with maximal statements is a sign of faulty thinking.

Moreover, we must be careful when we call the Bible the Word of God, for what is the Word of God, and to what does the Word of God refer — to the text of Sacred Scripture, or

---

[408] (Kuligin 2008, 96)

[409] (Piepkorn, What Does "Innerancy" Mean? 2007, 41)

[410] For example, the word "unique" is a maximum statement, such that modifying it detracts from its power. Nothing can be *more* than unique, and if something is *less* than unique it ceases to *be* unique.

something else? Jesus appears to equate scripture and the Word when he accuses the Pharisees of "making the word of God of none effect through your tradition" (Mk 7:13). But then in Luke, it is said that the Word of God came to John the Baptist in the wilderness (Lu 3:2). Since John the Baptist wrote no sacred text, in what sense can we say the Word of God came to him?[411]

Jesus said that man cannot live by "bread alone, but by every word of God" (Lu 4:4); in a different place, Jesus states: "I am the bread of life" (Jn 6:35). The bread that gives life is Christ, and Christ is the Word of God. The most interesting passage is in the Gospel of John: "Jesus answered them, Is it not written in your law, I said, Ye are gods? If he called them gods, unto whom the word of God came, and the scripture cannot be broken..." (Jn 10:34-35). Jesus is quoting Psalms 82:6, which He refers to as both the law and the Word of God. This word of God came unto the "holy men of God" (2Pe 1:21), who then wrote the text of scripture. There is a connection between the Word of God and scripture, but the two are neither identical nor equivalent.

The Word of God is the incarnate Son of God — the Logos, the Son of God made Flesh. The phrase "Word of God" is a reference to the Incarnation, because Jesus Christ is the revelation of God the Father. Thus, the "Word of God" refers specifically to Jesus Christ, but generally refers to the revelation of God. The revelation of God came to John the Baptist as he was in the wilderness; the revelation of God came to the prophets; the revelation of God came to the authors of Sacred Scripture. Properly speaking, the "Word of God" refers not to the text, the *materia*, the actual marks on the paper, but to the *forma*, the revelation of Christ as the Lamb of God who takes away the sin of the world (Jn 1:29). In general, we may say this revelation is contained in the Sacred Scriptures, but we cannot separate the general understanding of the term from the person of the Word made

---

[411] There are some who think Jesus was at one time a disciple of John the Baptist.

flesh. It is incorrect to add anything to the maximal statement — the Word of God — for defining the Incarnate Word using human language is to limit God, to bring God down to our level.[412]

With this in mind, there is a world of difference between saying the Bible is the Word of God, and saying the Bible is the "verbally inspired and infallible, authoritative Word of God,"[413] or the "inerrant Word of God."[414] The modifiers are not only superfluous but diminish the status of the Sacred Scriptures. Moreover, since equating the Scriptures with the Logos of God lends itself to the divinization of Sacred Scripture, the use of these modifiers serves either to diminish the concept of divinity or to elevate the scripture to the level of a deity.

To return to Victor Kuligin's argument for scriptural inerrancy from the nature of God, it is clear that claiming equivalence or correspondence between the Sacred Scriptures and the essence of God ends up equating Scripture with God. Equating scripture with God makes a God of scripture, adding a fourth element to the Trinity of Father, Son, and Holy Spirit. Equating scripture with God is equivalent to the Muslim claim that the Quran existed from eternity with Allah. As such, it cannot stand.

As we previously mentioned, the term "Word of God" has to do with the revelation of God, whether in the person of Jesus Christ as the incarnate Word, in the proclamations of the prophets, or the writings of the authors of Sacred

---

[412] The Bible and the Church fathers speak of God's humility in the Incarnation of the Son, and in the crucifixion (Phil 2:5-11). This humility is also expressed through God's condescension in the expressing of Himself using the limitations of human language. This is why the ancient church fathers speak of God apophatically — by saying what God is not, rather than what God is. By doing so they are refusing to anthropomorphize God.

[413] (Pensicola Christian College n.d.)

[414] (LCMS n.d.)

Scripture. Karl Barth provides a nice summary of this position: "The Bible is God's Word to the extent that God causes it to be His Word, to the extent that He speaks through it."[415] The Word of God, then, is not the *material* [text] of scripture, but the *forma* [content], the God, who is revealed in the text.

---

[415] (Barth, Church Dogmatics I.1 2009, 109)

32: Inerrancy and the Hebrew Autograph of Matthew

A statement that the Sacred Scriptures are inspired and verbally inerrant in the autographs is a problem for the reasons previously stated. But it should also be noted that at least one of the New Testament Greek texts we have today may not be the language in which the books were originally conceived, let alone written. For example, history tells us Matthew wrote his gospel in Hebrew.

The earliest church fathers are generally known as the Ante-Nicene Fathers, who form a continuous chain from the Apostles to the First Ecumenical Council (325 AD), also known as the Council of Nicaea. They provide a consistent testimony to the Hebraic origins of Matthew's Gospel.

The earliest witness to the Hebraic origin of Matthew is Papias, Bishop of Hierapolis, in Asia Minor. The church historian Eusebius references Papias' (now lost) *Exposition of the Sayings of the Lord* (c. 100) of Papias, where he speaks concerning the Hebrew origin of the Gospels. Eusebius quotes Papias:

Matthew put down the words of the Lord in the Hebrew language, and others have translated them, each as best he could.[416]

The church historian Eusebius also writes of Saint Pantaenus the Philosopher, a 2nd-century convert from the Stoics who for a time was a missionary to India.[417] The apostle Bartholomew had preached to the Indian Christians and left with them the writing of Matthew in the Hebrew language, which they had preserved till that time.[418]

---

[416] (Schaff, NPNF2-01 1890, 317)

[417] (Ibid, 445-446)

[418] (Schaff, ANF05 2004, 462). The Romans maintained a trade route to India. A sizeable Jewish population existed there, and remnants exist today.

Hidden in Plain Sight

St. Irenaeus (120-202 AD) was Bishop of Lyons in France. Most of his writings are from the last quarter of the 2nd century. Irenaeus states:

Matthew also issued a written Gospel among the Hebrews in their own dialect, while Peter and Paul were preaching at Rome, and laying the foundations of the Church.[419]

Origen (first quarter of the third century), in his commentary on Matthew, states:

"Among the four Gospels, which are the only indisputable ones in the Church of God under heaven, I have learned by tradition that the first was written by Matthew, who was once a publican, but afterwards an apostle of Jesus Christ, and it was prepared for the converts from Judaism, and published in the Hebrew language.[420]

Eusebius, Bishop of Caesarea (c. 325 AD), writes:

For Matthew, who had at first preached to the Hebrews, when he was about to go to other peoples, committed his Gospel to writing in his native tongue, and thus compensated those whom he was obliged to leave for the loss of his presence.[421]

There are additional references in the later church fathers (generally known as the Post-Nicene Fathers, dating from approximately 325 A.D). St. Epiphanius, for instance, writes at length about the Jewish-Christian sect of the Nazarenes: *"They have the entire Gospel of Matthew in Hebrew. It is*

---

[419] (Schaff, ANF01 1884, 685)
[420] (Schaff, NPNF2-01 1890, 571)
[421] (Ibid, 265)

Inerrancy and the Hebrew Autograph of Matthew

carefully preserved by them as it was originally written, in Hebrew script."[422]

St. Epiphanius also writes about the Ebionites, another Messianic sect:

And they too accept the Gospel of Matthew. ...They call it "according to the Hebrews," and that is the correct way of speaking since Matthew alone of the New Testament writers presents the gospel in Hebrew and in the Hebrew script.[423]

St. Cyril of Jerusalem, in his Catechetical Lectures, makes the following statement: "Matthew who wrote the Gospel wrote it in the Hebrew tongue."[424]

The great Bible scholar St. Jerome provides some of the most compelling testimony to the Hebraic origin of Matthew's Gospel. In his *De Viris Illustribus*, or *On Illustrious Men* (492 AD) Jerome writes of extant copies of the Gospel of Matthew that still existed in the library at Caesarea and among the Nazarenes.

Matthew, also called Levi, apostle and aforetimes publican, composed a gospel of Christ at first published in Judea in Hebrew for the sake of those of the circumcision who believed, but this was afterwards translated into Greek though by what author is uncertain. The Hebrew itself has been preserved until the present day in the library at Cæsarea which Pamphilus so diligently gathered. I have also had the opportunity of having the volume described to me by the Nazarenes of Berœa, a city of Syria, who use it. In this it is to be noted that wherever the Evangelist, whether on his own account or in the person of our Lord the Saviour quotes the testimony of the Old Testament he does not follow the authority of the translators of the

---

[422] (Bivin and Blizzard Jr. 1994, Kindle Locations 214-215) I apologize for not using primary sources, but the primary source material is quite expensive and not readily available.

[423] (Ibid, Kindle Locations 215-217)

[424] (St Cyril of Jerusalem 2013, Kindle Locations 4317-4318)

Septuagint but the Hebrew. Wherefore these two forms exist "Out of Egypt have I called my son," and "for he shall be called a Nazarene.[425]

David Blivin and Roy Blizzard Jr., in their book, *Understanding the Difficult Words of Jesus*, write of the Hebraic background of the New Testament. They point out that although the New Testament documents are written in Greek, they are thoroughly Hebrew in their grammatical construction. In other words, Hebrew was their first language; when they wrote in Greek, they used Hebrew idioms and grammar.[426] This likely accounts for what many scholars call the "poor Greek" of the New Testament

It should be emphasized that the Bible (both Old and New Testaments) is, in its entirety, highly Hebraic. In spite of the fact that portions of the New Testament were communicated in Greek, the background is thoroughly Hebrew. The writers are Hebrew, the culture is Hebrew, the religion is Hebrew, the traditions are Hebrew, and the concepts are Hebrew.[427]

What does this matter, you may ask? It matters very little if you have a theologically orthodox understanding of inspiration. But if you hold to the innovative concept of the

---

[425] (Schaff, NPNF2-03 1892, 626)

[426] The argument that the language of Palestine in the time of Christ was Aramaic is outdated. During the Hasmonean dynasty (140 BC to 37 BC), Hebrew became the official language, as is demonstrated by the Hebrew coinage and inscriptions of that period, as well as the predominance of Hebrew manuscripts contained in the Dead Sea Scrolls — which outnumber the Aramaic manuscripts by 10 to 1. In addition, the Hebrew manuscripts have fewer transcription errors, indicating the scribes were more familiar with Hebrew than Aramaic. On the other hand, the great scholar Martin Hengel suggests Aramaic was spoken by the common people, Hebrew was the "sacred language" used in the temple and by the scribes, and Greek was the "linguistic medium" used by all. (Hengel, The 'Hellenization' of Judea in the First Century after Christ 1989, 7-8)

[427] (Bivin and Blizzard Jr. 1994, Kindle Locations 82-84)

verbal inspiration of Scripture, inerrant in the original autographs, it matters a great deal. If Scripture is inerrant in the autograph, and the autograph was written in Hebrew, then you need to recover the original Hebrew rather than the original Greek. But if you have a different understanding of inspiration, the fact that certain books of the New Testament may have been originally conceived and potentially written in Hebrew rather than Greek is not germane to the faith once delivered to the saints — for the inspiration of the Sacred Scriptures neither implies nor demands an inerrant text. Moreover, if we accept Matthew as Scripture even though it is a Greek translation of a Hebrew original, then what is the problem with accepting the Apocrypha because some of them were written in Greek instead of Hebrew?

33: Inerrancy and the Loss of Faith

If you believe inspiration requires inerrancy, then any suspicion that the Scriptures might not be inerrant has grave consequences, such that a person may begin to doubt the authenticity and reliability of the Scriptures. If you read atheist's arguments against the Bible, you should quickly realize they have the same view of inspiration as Protestant fundamentalists, and indeed of most evangelicals. Atheists argue that for Scripture to be trustworthy, it must be inerrant. They then produce copious lists of errors, thereby proving to themselves that the Bible is not inspired. In essence, atheists and conservative Protestants both approach the Bible with the same presuppositions; they simply draw different conclusions.

Biblical scholar Dr. Bart Ehrman is one such person. In his teen years, Ehrman became a "born again" Christian through Campus Life Youth for Christ, an evangelical parachurch ministry. Ehrman majored in Bible Theology while attending Moody Bible Institute was taught the strict fundamentalist understanding of inspiration. He completed his bachelor's degree at Wheaton College, where he began to have doubts about verbal inerrancy. What good did it do to speak of the inspiration and verbal inerrancy of the autographs when Christians relied upon different versions and translations into different languages? Gradually he became aware of the issues raised by textual criticism and began to question how a document that is inspired and verbally inerrant only in the autographs could be relevant after two millennia of scribal corruption. His search ultimately drove him to accept the position that the Sacred Scriptures contained errors.[428] Since his fundamentalist view

---

[428] Some of the explanations of various problems become quite convoluted, and it is simpler to say that the author erred. Occam's razor suggests that the simplest solution to the problem is more likely to be right. Yet saying the author erred raises a whole host of

of inspiration precluded the possibility of errors in the text, this led to his loss of faith and his belief that what we call Sacred Scriptures are flawed products of human authorship.[429]

There is plenty of evidence that the Protestant insistence upon scriptural inerrancy fuels atheism. A simple Internet search for the phrase "why I am an atheist" will bring up site after site of people whose primary reason is their difficulty with the errors in the Bible. However, getting rid of the concept of inerrancy does nothing to the biblical doctrine of inspiration. Elder Sophrony notes:

It is possible in the Orthodox Church for there to be translations of the New Testament with mistakes, but they do not cause problems, because there is life, the Divine Eucharist. Among the Protestants, on the contrary, who regard Holy Scripture as the source of faith, one translation error alters their whole mentality.[430]

A text containing minor errors may still be profitable for doctrine, for reproof, for instructions in righteousness. If we can adopt a doctrine of inspiration that does not include the concept of inerrancy we get rid of some of the fuel that fires modern atheist thought.

---

other issues, and suggests our understanding may be lacking in some fundamental way. The answer that the author erred is not as simple as it might appear; "The author erred" is often a hypothesis rather than a conclusion.

[429] (Ehrman 2005, 1-14)

[430] (Metropolitan Hiertheos of Nafpaktos 2015, 337)

34: Inerrancy vs. Infallibility

The Committee on Theology and Church Relations of the Lutheran Church-Missouri Synod, writes: "Faith confesses the Bible to be the inerrant Word of God."[431] This statement is in error because inerrancy has to do with the *materia* (text). It is the inspiration of the *forma* (doctrine) that makes the text into Sacred Scripture. Inerrancy of the text is not a necessary component of inspiration, nor is it what the Sacred Scriptures declare to be the nature of inspiration. Peter tells us that prophecy, which is an inspired discourse declaring the purposes of God, comes when holy men of God speak as they were moved by the Holy Ghost. (2 Pet 1:20-21). And all prophecy, which in the context of our current discussion means the Sacred Scriptures, speaks of Christ (Luke 24:27).

Just as Christ is slain from the foundation of the world (Re 13:8), the Sacred Scriptures are inspired because they declare unto us the things concerning the Christ, and are thus the salvific Word of God. The Christian faith does not confess the Sacred Scriptures to be inerrant; no, faith confesses the revelation concerning our Lord and Savior Jesus Christ through whom we are saved, and whose divine expression makes us wise unto salvation. The Sacred Scriptures are the record of the divine expression contained within the limitations of human language; it is the divine expression that is inerrant, not the tools by which the expression was preserved.

"God cannot lie" (Heb 6:18). Thus, the Sacred Scriptures make us wise unto salvation and are profitable for doctrine, for reproof, for correction, and instruction in righteousness (2Pe 1:21). This is most certainly true, but this does not mean the Sacred Scriptures must be inerrant in every detail. When the authors of Sacred Scriptures speak of the four corners of the earth (Isa 11:12, Re 7:1), or the pillars of the earth (1 Sam 2:8), they were not using what they understood to be

---

[431] (Committee on Theology and Church Relations (LCMS) 1995, 8)

metaphors, but what they understood to be scientific fact. When we try to reconcile these statements with today's scientific understanding, we declare them to be metaphors, which is certainly not the understanding of the author. We are trapped: If the Sacred Scripture is inspired by the Holy Spirit and inerrant in every detail, and if the author included information he believed to be true but was actually false, did the Holy Spirit inspire a falsehood? Or did the Holy Spirit allow the author to make the occasional erroneous scientific statement and still use that statement to make us wise unto salvation? Or perhaps the author intended one thing and the Holy Spirit another, which itself suggests problems with the literal interpretation of scripture.

God works through and in spite of human weakness. We accept this principle in our lives but reject its implications in the text of scripture. Isaiah was wrong about the earth resting on pillars. He was not speaking metaphorically; he was proclaiming that which he believed to be true. That Sacred Scripture contains problems of this type does not affect its status as the inspired Word of God. We can even speak of inerrancy and infallibility regarding the purpose for which scripture was written. We are wrong to define inspiration (a maximal statement) using terms that delimit inspiration and mean something other than what Scripture says of itself.

35: Inspiration, Doctrine, Text

It is possible to describe Sacred Scripture as inspired and infallible and not include any reference to verbal inerrancy. Inspiration and Infallibility have to do with doctrine, with the intrinsic *forma* of Scripture. Inerrancy has to do with the text itself, with the *materia*, with the letters, syllables, words, sentences, paragraphs, and the entire grammatical structure, and is, therefore, extrinsic to (or outside of) the doctrinal content of Scripture. Inspiration concerns the intrinsic *forma* of Scripture, the revelation of God contained and expressed in feeble human language.[432] The text serves to signify and reveal the doctrine, but does not constitute the doctrine; in fact, the doctrine of God is indescribably greater than the tongue can express. A 2000-year-old text containing corruptions and possibly errors is still inspired, and we can discern the doctrine of scripture from a corrupted text. Hannu Lehtonen writes:

Regarding the doctrine of Scripture as taught by the Lutheran orthodoxy it is important to pay attention to the distinction they made between the materia and the forma of Scripture. By the materia of Scripture they mean the letters, syllables, words, phrases etc. in Scripture. In this sense Scripture doesn't differ from any other book. By the intrinsic forma of Scripture they mean the inspiration of Scripture or the inspired meaning of Scripture. This forma makes Scripture to be what it is, Scripture, and it also distinguishes it from all other books in the world. When the dogmaticians speak about Scripture as the Word of God they speak about the inspired content of Scripture when they speak exactly. On the other hand the

---

[432] Francis Pieper writes: "God has deigned, as Luther again and again reminds us, to 'become incarnate' in Scripture (*Scriptura Sacra est Deus incarnates*)". (Pieper 1950, 198) The divinization of the text is a theological error. God did not become incarnate in scripture, but in the flesh. (Jn 1:14)

letters and words in Scripture don't only signify the inspired content of Scripture but they actually reveal this divine meaning and therefore it is impossible to separate them from it.[433]

Modern evangelical statements of faith insist upon the connection between inspiration and inerrancy. Evangelical Christianity believes the concept of inspiration includes inerrancy, and that inerrancy is necessary to the definition of inspiration. But this is an ahistorical position and a sign of faulty thinking. The idea that the Scriptures are trustworthy and infallible is an *ancient* Christian teaching, whereas the idea that the Scriptures are inerrant is a *modern* conceit.

First, it depends on what exactly is meant by the term inerrant. Are the Sacred Scriptures that make us wise unto salvation inerrant (the *forma*), or is it the text—the particular combination of marks on a page (the *materia*), which change from language to language and from translation to translation? These textual differences can be significant. A particular word may have a range of meanings in Hebrew, but when that word is translated into Greek, the translator picks one word to represent what the translator considers the primary meaning. The act of translation is, therefore, an act of textual interpretation. When that Greek text is then translated into English, more shades of meaning are lost, while others appear.

Second, if one postulates the verbal (and plenary) inerrancy of the autographs (being the original peculiar combination of marks on a page), this postulate then drives the task of textual criticism. No longer do textual critics seek to determine the *authoritative* text (a theological enterprise), but instead seek the recovery of the *original* text (a critical enterprise), which they deem authoritative because of its

---

[433] (Lehtonen 1999)

being original.[434] When the critical enterprise trumps the theological, we are treading on dangerous ground. The search for the original text is itself an act of textual interpretation. Although textual criticism has rules and therefore presents the appearance of being scientific, the rules are arbitrary and based on assumptions made before one approaches the text. For example, if you favor the Masoretic text of the Old Testament, you will choose rules giving primacy to that text and giving short shrift to alternate texts and textual histories.[435]

The doctrine of *the verbal, plenary inspiration of the Scriptures, inerrant in the autographs*, necessarily requires only the original author to have been inspired by the Holy Spirit and requires that subsequent corrections, additions, and deletions by later copyists and churchmen are corruptions.[436] The clear implication is that the words

---

[434] The search for the original text ignores the fact that the bible has a history, and that the collection of texts into the canon existing today was curated by the Church. The search for the original text must yield to the search for the authoritative text. In turn, this means that we can only understand the bible within the community that curated it, within the "matrix that includes the thoughts and writings of the early church: its bishops, priests, poets, monks, theologians, and artists." (Miller 2012)

[435] Favoring the Masoretic text may seem reasonable, as (apart from the Dead Sea Scrolls) it is the most ancient complete Hebrew text. There is a marked preference for translating the Old Testament from the Hebrew text, a preference that goes back to the Renaissance Humanists who argued for a return to the sources. The rallying cry of this movement was the Latin phrase "*ad fontes*," meaning "to the sources." The reformers, being products of their time, thought that using Hebrew sources rather than the Greek translation was right and proper.

[436] Interesting examples include the following: 1) The epilogue of John 21 may have been added later. The original Gospel appears to end at Jn 20:31; 2) The pericope on the woman taken in adultery (Jn 7:53 – 8:11) is not in the oldest and best-attested manuscripts; and 3) The oldest manuscripts for the Gospel of Mark do not include Mk

Inspiration, Doctrine, Text

written by a particular man (the author) are inspired; indeed, that the author was himself inspired to write them. The Apostle Peter writes of the "holy men of God who spake as they were moved by the Holy Ghost" (2Pe 1:21). The teaching of the inerrancy of the autographs assumes this applies to the particular man or prophet who initially produced the writing, as opposed to the later copyists and churchmen who modified the text in one way or another. The passages deemed by both conservative and liberal scholars to not be part of the original text are suspect, even though they form the extant text which then forms the canon of Sacred Scripture. This approach is similar to that of the Jesus Seminar[437] where scholars voted as to whether this or that text was authentic. The natural result is the re-opening of the canon of scripture and the excision of suspect texts from Sacred Scripture. The obsession with verbal inerrancy logically leads to the error of Marcion.

There is another way of thinking about all this. What if we ignore the minor errors of scripture? As a practical matter, we do that already. Do we care that 1 Kings 4:26 says that Solomon had forty thousand stalls of horses, whereas 2 Chron 9:25 says Solomon had four thousand? No, of course not. We recognize that a copyist made an error. It is not germane to the subject at hand and represents no threat to the inspiration and trustworthiness of Scripture. The only way this becomes a problem is if we begin to incorporate modern understandings of inspiration into our thinking.

16:9-20; instead, it ends rather abruptly with the resurrection appearance to Mary Magdalene.

This all results in the following question: if the Sacred Scriptures were inerrant in the original manuscripts, and these texts were not part of the original text, are they then Scripture? Do we excise them from our bibles? And if so, in what way is this different from what the heretic Marcion tried to do?

[437] (Westar Institute n.d.)

Requiring an inerrant text requires a series of rationales and tendentious arguments for every difficult passage.

How do we deal with the historical anachronisms of the Bible? In Genesis 11:28 & 31, Abram (later renames Abraham) is said to have lived in Ur of the Chaldees. While Abram was born as early as 2000 BC or as late as 1800 BC, the Chaldeans as a tribe did not exist until the late 10th or early 9th century BC. Moreover, the Chaldeans were originally from the Tigris and Euphrates delta at the head of the Persian Gulf and did not occupy Mesopotamia (the region or the city of Ur) until the 8th century BC.[438] What are we to make of this, since we cannot square the biblical text with the actual events of history?[439]

A literalistic understanding of Sacred Scripture can lead to all sorts of problems with the text. For example, the United Methodist Minister Richard Hagenston writes of the contradiction found in the final verses of Psalm 51. In his analysis of this passage, verses 16-17 indicate that God does not want sacrifice while verses 18-19 say that God will be pleased with sacrifices. So, which is it?[440]

For thou desirest not sacrifice; else would I give it: thou delightest not in burnt offering.

The sacrifices of God are a broken spirit: a broken and a contrite heart, O God, thou wilt not despise.

Do good in thy good pleasure unto Zion: build thou the walls of Jerusalem.

---

[438] While there are innumerable sources for these dates, Vladika Lazar Puhalo put it all together nicely. (Puhalo 2014)

[439] I recognize that a similar argument was once made regarding the biblical references to the Hittites; it wasn't until archeological discoveries in the latter half of the 19th century that the biblical record was validated. It is unlikely that anything similar to that will be found to radically change the history of the Chaldean people.

[440] (Hagenston 2014)

Then shalt thou be pleased with the sacrifices of righteousness, with burnt offering and whole burnt offering: then shall they offer bullocks upon thine altar. (Ps 51:16-19)

Let us compare different approaches to this passage. Richard Hagenston's approach is a simplistic attempt to take the text at face value. The text means exactly what it says, and has no deeper meaning attached to it. The literal interpretation is the only interpretation, you might say. If that is the case, we have a contradiction: God does not desire sacrifice. and God is pleased with sacrifice.

Most other Bible scholars would look at this passage in the context of the Psalm as a whole. Since the overall theme is of repentance, verses 16-17 would indicate that God prefers repentance to sacrifice; verses 18–19 says that God is pleased with sacrifices when they are offered with a repentant heart. But note that this interpretation goes beyond the literal meaning of the text, and depends on the idea that the text contains deeper meanings than the mere literal reading will provide. To a strict literalist such as Richard Hagenston, the passage in Psalm 51 represents a contradiction and is an error, with the latter two verses added later.

The accumulated weight of the typographical errors, anachronisms, and seeming contradictions drives some, like Bart Ehrman, to a loss of faith in God; for others, like Richard Hagenston, these errors drive them to a loss of faith in the Bible and questioning of doctrinal orthodoxy. All because we conflate inspiration and inerrancy. God help us.

36: Inerrancy and Lutheran Orthodoxy

The Reformation is generally dated from 1517 when an Augustinian monk and Theology Professor fastened his 95 theses to the church door in Wittenberg, Germany. Since it was Martin Luther and his followers who confronted the Roman Catholic establishment and asserted their claims based on Sacred Scripture, it would be wise for us to consider what Lutheran Orthodoxy has to say about inspiration and inerrancy.

Lutheran Orthodoxy does not include the Fundamentalist concept of verbal inerrancy in their understandings of inspiration. In this, they stand with orthodox Christianity against those who assert verbal inerrancy. Simply because Lutheran Orthodoxy does not assert verbal inerrancy does not mean they promote the opposite argument — that the Scriptures are errant. Lutherans have until recently not participated in the entire errant/inerrant argument. The Lutheran Confessions, their argument against the Roman Catholics, never asserts verbal inerrancy — nor is verbal inerrancy asserted by the Lutheran Scholastics.[441] (Remember, inerrancy is a modern term). Instead, the confessors state that Sacred Scriptures are the sole "rule and norm" by which all teachers and teachings are alike judged.[442]

Jacob Andreae (et al.) wrote the following in the first theological exchange between the Lutherans and the Eastern Orthodox:

There is, indeed, no more sure, nor truer, nor better standard rule for judging all dogmas, all institutes, and usages of faith and human traditions and works, than the Word of the

---

[441] Lutheran Scholasticism began in the 17th century, and came about due to conflicts with the Jesuits. (Preus 1957, Kindle Locations 180-182)

[442] (The Book of Concord: The Confessions of the Evangelical Lutheran Church, Ep 1; SD Rule and Norm, Summary, 1)

Almighty God of all; the Word, which has been revealed to the human race by the Prophets and Christ and the Apostles and written in the Old and New Testaments for the benefit and the salvation of the entire Church. ...When in matters of religion a controversy arises, it is to be answered by both the Old and the New Testaments, as heavenly documents and schools, both of which have been guaranteed and made sure by admirable signs and wonders—with seals, as it were.

...It is altogether evident, that none of the prophetic and apostolic Scriptures have been intermixed with error; no deceit has come out of them for anyone. Since they have been written under the inspiration of and brought to mind by the Holy Spirit (who is the Spirit of Truth) [cf. Jn 15:26], as the same Apostle Peter bears witness. He says: "no prophecy of the scripture ever came by the impulse of man, but men moved by the Holy Spirit spoke from God" [2 Pet 1:20-21].[443]

According to Jacob Andreae, the Sacred Scriptures have not been intermixed with error; from the context, it is clear Andreae is referring to the Scripture's ability to stand as a rule of dogma, of institutes, and usages of faith, human traditions, and good works. This is not an assertion of verbal inerrancy, but rather an assertion regarding the nature of divine revelation. Andreae says the Sacred Scriptures are the Word of God and therefore without error in matters with which the divine revelation concerns itself: doctrine, reproof, correction, instruction in righteousness and salvation by faith in Christ Jesus. (2 Tim 3:15-16).[444]

Johann Gerhard (c. 1582-1637) greatly expanded upon this idea:

From the efficient cause and goal of Holy Scripture results its perfection and clarity. Because God, the Creator of mind and language, wanted to inform people in and through Scripture

---

[443] (Mastrantonis 1982, 110-111)

[444] (Ibid, 111)

about his essence and will and in its instruction about faith and mores to make them wise to eternal salvation, therefore he also wanted Scripture to be perfect and clear. Were it not perfect and clear, it could not have instructed us fully about the essence and will of God nor could it have made us wise to eternal life. **Our churches affirm that Scripture is perfect;** *and with that word perfect, they mean the fact that* **Scripture instructs us fully and perfectly about all things necessary for attaining salvation.***[emphasis added]*[445]

David Hollaz (c. 1646-1713) writes:

In the definition of the Holy Scriptures, The Word of God signifies formally the purpose of God, or the conception of the divine mind, revealed for the salvation of men immediately to the prophets and apostles, and mediately, through their ministrations, to the whole race of man.[446]

Johann Gerhard again says:

The absolutely wise and perfect God ...wanted the Scriptures to appear and exist for this purpose: that they might instruct us fully about his essence and will for our salvation. ...Scripture, then, as the effect of a perfect cause of this sort, is perfect.[447]

The careful reader will note that in ascribing perfection to the Sacred Scriptures, Gerhard is not asserting verbal inerrancy. Instead, he is saying that "the absolutely wise and perfect God" is the "perfect cause" of Sacred Scripture, and that the Word of God informs us regarding God's essence and will, containing such instructions about faith and mores as will make us wise unto salvation.

Gerhard points out that the text itself is only the external form of the divine revelation, and the divine revelation is the most important thing.

---

[445] (Gerhard 2006, 333)
[446] (Schmid 1875, 40)
[447] (Gerhard 2006, 335-336)

By the term Scripture, we are not to understand so much the external form, or sign, i.e., the particular letters employed, the art of writing and the expressions by which the divine revelation is described, as the matter itself or the thing signified, just that which is marked and represented by the writing, viz., the Word of God itself, which instructs us concerning the nature and will of God. For, as in all writing, performed by an intelligent agent, so also in these prophetic and apostolic writings, two things are to be considered, viz., in the first place, the letters, syllables, and sentences which are written, and which are external symbols signifying and expressing conceptions of the mind; and, secondly, those conceptions themselves, which are the thing signified, expressed by these external symbols of letters, syllables, and sentences; wherefore in the term Scriptures we embrace both of these, and the latter especially.[448]

Franz August Otto Pieper (c. 1852-1931), in his *Christian Dogmatics*, writes not of inerrancy, but of the "perfection, or sufficiency, of Holy Scripture" over and against those who deny their "normative or judicial authority." Scripture does not tell us everything we can know about "earthly or civil life," nor does Scripture "reveal all divine matters." The Scriptures do teach us "perfectly whatever we need to know to obtain eternal life." This is the normative function of Holy Scripture.[449]

---

[448] (Schmid 1875, 41)

[449] Pieper does seem to provide some slight support for inerrancy: "But remember: When Scripture incidentally treats a scientific subject, it is always right, let "science" say what it pleases." (Pieper 1950) We should not argue for science or history over and against the Bible. "In the beginning" means the universe is not eternal, but time, space, energy, and matter had a beginning. "God created the heavens and the earth" means exactly what it says. But we must not base our Christian apologetics on the Biblical account of creation, as do the Fundamentalists, but on Christ.

And so, having determined what inspiration is not, we must finally describe the content and the meaning of inspiration. Sacred Scripture is inspired because it makes us wise unto salvation (2 Tim 3:15).

Johann Gerhard remarks:

Scripture is nothing other than the divine revelation reduced to sacred writing, for the revealed Word of God and Holy Scripture really are not different because holy men of God reduced into the Scriptures those actual divine revelations.[450]

Franz August Otto Pieper writes:

The Scriptures not only tell us that they are the Word of God, but they also teach very clearly why they are the Word of God, namely, because they were inspired, or breathed into the writers, by God. ...This divine act of inspiration establishes the fact that the Holy Scriptures, though written by men, are the Word of God.[451]

Because the Sacred Scriptures are the inspired revelation, the very Word of God, they make us wise unto salvation and are profitable for doctrine, for reproof, for correction, and instruction in righteousness (2 Tim 3:15-16). The plain words of Scripture regarding the nature and content of inspiration constitutes that which Aiden Nichols calls the formal perspective of inerrancy, "that of relevance to human salvation."[452]

The "relevance to human salvation" is not Gospel-Reductionism — the reduction of Biblical authority to matters that are either part of the Gospel or derived from it.[453] We know this cannot be the case; the resurrected Christ,

---

[450] (Gerhard 2006, 49)

[451] (Pieper 1950, 217)

[452] (Nichols 1991, 137)

[453] Edmund Schlink writes regarding the treatment of Scripture in the Lutheran Confessions: "This intense concern with the Gospel

on the road to Emmaus, began with Moses and the prophets and showed how the entire Scriptures were about Him (Luke 24:27). From this, we know that the entirety of Sacred Scripture is a testimony to the Christ, "who is our life" (Col 3:4). Christ (and Christology) is the center of Sacred Scripture. Christ is the *Logos*, the Word made flesh, and the *Logos* is the essence of the Gospel message. Therefore, Christ is the Gospel (in the broadest sense), the formal element of Sacred Scripture, for all Scripture testifies of Christ and is, therefore, profitable for salvation. How then may we say that this or that portion of Sacred Scripture is not Gospel, and therefore not authoritative? And by what authority could we say it? Down that path lies the diminution of the most perfect and holy Word of God, and the destruction of "the faith which was once delivered unto the saints" (Jude 1:3).

---

suggests that the Gospel is the norm in Scripture and Scripture is the norm for the sake of the Gospel." (Schlink 1961, 6) The statement is made within a Law/Gospel context, and suggests support for the use of Law/Gospel Reductionism as the ruling hermeneutical principle; however, Schlink seems to be using "norm" in its philosophical sense, as described by Piepkorn: "The norm is in a sense the form which the tangible, palpable matter seeks to express, by which the matter is informed, and to which it is conformed. Thus in the Sacred Scriptures, in the Symbols, and in the concrete expressions of the Church's continuing ministry, we have a material element which changes from language to language, from situation to situation and from generation to generation, and we have a formal element[,] the unalterable Word of God". (Piepkorn, The Significance of the Lutheran Symbols for Today 2007, 86) Holsten Fagerberg notes the Confessions speak of the "Holy Scriptures" as "God's Word," which is sometimes used as a synonym for the Gospel. (Fagerberg 1972, 16-17) Thus Schlink's statement is true because he appears to use the term Gospel in its broad sense: as being the Logos which is the formal element of Sacred Scripture. By contrast, Law/Gospel Reductionism (normally referred to as Gospel Reductionism) expresses the Law/Gospel as the "ruling or only hermeneutical presupposition in Lutheran theology". (Murray 2001, 128) Gospel Reductionism replaces Christology with the Law-Gospel principle as the ruling hermeneutical principle.

The inspiration of Sacred Scriptures, which are the Word of God, requires that word to speak with consistency and unanimity regarding the divine revelation. Writing on the subject of inspiration, the Commission on Theology and Church Relations of the Lutheran Church-Missouri Synod makes the point that the unity of Sacred Scripture is both Christological and doctrinal. The unity of Sacred Scripture is the content, the subject matter, and the purpose of inspiration:

The unity of the Scriptures is Christological. Jesus said that the Old Testament testifies of Him (John 5:39) and that Moses wrote of Him (John 5:46). In the parable of the householder (Matt. 21:33-46) He cited Ps. 118:22-23 as applying to Himself. In Mark 14:27 He refers to Himself as the subject of Zech. 13:7. He went up to Jerusalem that everything written of the Son of Man in the prophets might be fulfilled in Him (Luke 18:31-33). Beginning at Moses and all the prophets He expounded to the disciples on the Emmaus road the things concerning Himself in all the Scriptures (Luke 24:27).[454]

The unity of the Scriptures is doctrinal. Throughout the Scriptures, wherever such topics are treated whether as the specific subject of discussion or only incidentally mentioned, the same doctrine is taught concerning creation, anthropology, justification, sacraments, church, the end of the world, resurrection of the dead, judgment, eternal life, eternal death, or any other article of the Christian faith.[455]

Because the Sacred Scriptures are the inspired Word of God, and because the many authors all testified concerning Christ and are unified in doctrine, the *forma* (doctrinal matters) of the Sacred Scriptures is reliable. However, the reliability of the Sacred Scriptures is not demonstrated by the inerrancy of the *materia* (text), nor would an inerrant text be

---

[454] (Committee on Theology and Church Relations (LCMS) 1995, 12)
[455] (Ibid, 13)

evidence of inspiration. It is not the Sacred Scriptures that are inerrant; rather, the divine revelation is inerrant. The Sacred Scriptures are a reliable, authoritative, and trustworthy source of knowledge concerning the divine revelation, which is understood by faith in Christ. Lutheran theologian Samuel Nafziger writes:

[We] believe that confidence in the reliability of the Bible is not possible apart from faith in Jesus Christ. Christians believe what the Scriptures teach because they first believe in Jesus Christ. Christ is the object of faith, not the Bible. We believe that the inversion of this order compromises "scripture alone" and results in rationalistic fundamentalism, as if an accepted demonstration of the Bible's truthfulness and reliability -- perhaps a piece of Noah's ark, for example -- could provide a foundation for faith in the Gospel. The Bible remains a dark book apart from faith in Christ, for He is its true content. But when sinners are brought to faith in Him, Christ points them back to the writings of the prophets and apostles as the sole authoritative source for all the church believes, teaches and confesses.[456]

---

[456] (Nafziger 1994, 6)

37: On the Doctrine of Inspiration

We err when we assume inspiration requires inerrancy, as though the doctrine of Sacred Scriptures would be unreliable if the Scriptures contained errors. When Protestants ascribe inerrancy (in its modern theological formulation and understanding) to Sacred Scripture, they are subscribing to a view of inspiration that goes beyond what Sacred Scripture says about itself. Moreover, the concept of inerrancy is not derived from Sacred Scripture but is a theological proposition imposed upon the Word of God. As such, it is a divinization of the text and a desacralization of the divine revelation. Practically speaking, the divinization of the text forces us to spend time and energy focusing on side issues (like proving that the Bible is scientifically accurate) instead of focusing on Jesus Christ. And what did Jesus say about himself? "I am the way, the truth, and the life: no man cometh unto the Father, but by me" (John 14:6). The Sacred Scriptures are not the way, but rather the means through which the way is revealed. Christ alone is the divine self-expression of the Father; the text is the guidepost pointing us to Christ; the text is the medium through which the Holy Spirit works to bring us to faith in Christ. For this purpose, the Sacred Scriptures were given to us as the inspired revelation of God the Word — to make us wise unto salvation.

The Bible is unique because it is God's revelation recorded in human language. According to II Timothy 3:16–17 the words of Scripture are "God-breathed" or inspired. God is the source or origin of what is recorded in Scripture. God, through the Holy Spirit, used human authors and human language to make himself known to men. Unfortunately, many Fundamentalists and Evangelicals assume inspiration requires inerrancy. If you extract the material regarding inerrancy from their statements, what is left is an entirely inadequate description of inspiration. As an example, the following is the statement of Moody Bible

Institute, modified to remove the references to (and consequences of) inerrancy.

The Bible, including both the Old and New Testaments, is a divine revelation. Revelation is God's making Himself known to men. God has revealed himself in a limited way in creation. But the Bible is a form of special revelation. The Bible is "special" revelation in the sense that it goes beyond what may be known about God through nature. It is divine in origin, since in the Bible God makes known things which otherwise could never be known.

There is nothing in this altered statement about the Scriptures making us wise unto salvation. The statement fails to unpack the statement that Scripture is profitable for doctrine, for reproof, for instruction in righteousness. The statement says nothing about the manner in which Scripture brings us to perfection, or how using the Scripture, we are thoroughly furnished unto good works (2 Tim 3:15-16). There is no mention of how the special revelation of the ineffable, inconceivable, invisible, and incomprehensible God can be contained within the limits of human language, and no discussion of how the infinite God can be circumscribed by the finite mind. In other words, the doctrinal statement of Moody Bible Institute asserts inerrancy rather than inspiration.

I have tried this experiment with a variety of doctrinal statements and have come up short every time. The 20th century Evangelical Protestant Church has replaced inspiration with inerrancy (and its corollary, infallibility). In doing so, they began to argue over trivial issues (like science vs. religion) that have nothing to do with the Christ revealed in the Scriptures. It is past time to remove the false idol of inerrancy from the temple of our hearts.

Part IV: Inerrancy, Canonicity, and the Dead Sea Scrolls

38: The Need for the Dead Sea Scrolls

Between 1946 and 1952, what became known as the Dead Sea Scrolls were discovered in caves near the ancient settlement of Qumran. Since then scholars have differed as to their importance. Many years ago, I asked a bible scholar what we had learned from the Dead Sea Scrolls. His answer: "We learned that we didn't need them," meaning the Dead Sea Scrolls had confirmed everything conservative Bible scholars had been saying about the reliability, inerrancy, and canonicity of the Protestant Scriptures. When I began to study these issues for myself, I discovered this was a faulty assessment of the Dead Sea Scrolls.

Beginning with the first Dead Sea Scrolls discovered by a Bedouin shepherd, scholars found themselves with a group of texts that were around one thousand years older than the existing Masoretic texts — texts which date from the 9th and 10th centuries. The importance of this finding would be difficult to overstate. Julio Trebolle Barrera writes:

Analysis of the biblical Dead Sea scrolls has «important repercussions in a wide range of fields:» the history of the Hebrew language, the history of the transmission of the biblical text, the historical process of the translation of the Bible into other languages, the development of biblical and Jewish interpretation of the biblical text, textual criticism which aims to trace «original» variants and lastly, literary criticism which has the aim of reconstructing the history of the formation of the biblical books.[457]

Conservative Protestant scholars often claim the Masoretic texts were passed on relatively unchanged around since the time of Christ. From this faulty claim some theological conservatives — such as Dr. Will Varner, writing for BiblicalArcheology.org — draw faulty conclusions. Varner writes:

---

[457] (Barrera 1998, 285)

Now we have manuscripts around a thousand years older than those. The amazing truth is that these manuscripts are almost identical! Here is a strong example of the tender care which the Jewish scribes down through the centuries took in an effort to accurately copy the Sacred Scriptures. We can have confidence that our Old Testament Scriptures faithfully represent the words given to Moses, David and the prophets.[458]

Gleason L. Archer Jr., writing in 1974 (and quoted approvingly by many since then), indicates the Dead Sea Scrolls reinforce the reliability of the Masoretic Text.

It should be understood that the existence of these non-Masoretic manuscript families does not necessarily mean that the proto-Masoretic does not represent the purest textual tradition of all. Nothing in the new discoveries from the Qumran caves endangers the essential reliability and authority of our standard Hebrew Bible text.[459]

The claim that the Scriptures changed little between the Dead Sea Scrolls and the Masoretic texts provides us no insight into the potential for the development or alteration of the texts in the centuries before Christ. Moses lived around 1300 years before Christ, and 1100 years before the earliest of the Dead Sea Scrolls were written, yet Will Varner & Gleason Archer ignore this entire period (the implication being that the Masoretic text, being the same as the Dead Sea Scrolls, is also the same as the text produced by Moses). The concept of the scriptorium, designed by the Masoretes to preserve (as much as possible) the text of the Hebrew Scriptures, had not yet come into existence. During the Hellenistic era, the reproduction of manuscripts was error prone. As Alfred Edersheim notes, the reproduction of Greek manuscripts (as in the Septuagint) was accomplished with one hundred

---

[458] (Varner, What is the importance of the Dead Sea Scrolls? 2008)

[459] (Archer 1974, 41)

slaves copying what one person read.[460] There is no evidence for careful error-checking until the Masoretic scriptorium. In the scribal culture of the pre-Hellenic era, scrolls were rare, and scribes wrote for other scribes, rather than for the greater (and mostly illiterate) populace.[461] The scribes were already familiar with the content of the texts and used them as memory aids more than anything else.

Despite the overwhelming evidence of the Dead Sea Scrolls, scholars like Varner and Archer falsely claim that nothing has changed, when in fact our entire understanding of Second Temple Judaism has been altered.[462] Professor Norman Golb writes:

These scrolls, along with the many other biblical texts and text fragments discovered in the caves, show that at the time the scrolls were hidden, there was not yet a single authoritative text of scriptural writings but rather different versions of the same texts that circulated widely among the Palestinian Jews.

---

[460] (Edersheim 1993, 16)

[461] (Van der Toorn 2007, 51)

[462] Margaret Barker describes a number of alternative Jewish movements, many of which were hostile to the form of Judaism imposed by Ezra. First among these are the Rechabites, first mentioned in Jeremiah 35. (Barker, The Mother of the Lord, Volume 1 2012, Kindle Locations 328-343) In the Church History of Eusebius, a group of Rechabites objected to the stoning of James the Just, the brother (kinsman) of Jesus. (Schaff, NPNF2-01 1890, 199) The Jewish Encyclopedia says their descendants were found in Arabia in the 12th and 19th century. (Board, et al. 1906) Next we have a group of Jews, either refugees from Josiah's reforms or from the Babylonian invasion, who by 525 BC had their own temple in Egypt. (Barker, The Mother of the Lord, Volume 1 2012, Kindle Locations 486-495) There are still more groups of people whose culture has Hebraic elements, and whose communities may have split from official Judaism in reaction to second temple Judaism. Among these are the Qemant people of Ethiopia and the Chiang Min people of the Szechuan province of China. (Barker, The Mother of the Lord, Volume 1 2012, Kindle Locations 524-594)

Some of these versions were closer to that of the (Greek) Septuagint version of the Bible, others to the Samaritan tradition, and still others to the traditional Massoretic text of the Hebrew scriptures.[463]

Professor Karel van der Toorn writes that our understanding of the scribal culture and their ecclesiastical libraries has expanded enormously.

The most important archaeological event for biblical scholarship in the twentieth century was the discovery of the Dead Sea Scrolls at Qumran. This extraordinary collection of texts gives us an idea of what a major Jewish library of the Hellenistic era may have looked like. The Qumran library was, broadly speaking, comprehensive; it contained copies of works with opposite views, such as the Aramaic Levi document, Jubilees, and I Enoch, on the one hand, and Ben Sira, on the other. Except for the Scroll of Esther, we know of no other Jewish literary text clearly dating from before 150 B.C.E. that was not represented. In fact, Qumran has yielded many Hebrew texts that never made it into the Bible.[464]

The number of Hebrew texts found among the Dead Sea Scrolls suggests that the language of Judea in the time of Christ was not Aramaic, as is commonly taught, but Hebrew (we began this discussion in chapters 4 and 29.) The Scriptures themselves tell us that the language was Hebrew: for example, the book of Acts says Jesus spoke in Hebrew (Acts 26:14), and that Paul spoke in Hebrew (Acts 21:40). Pilate's inscription above Jesus' cross was written in Greek, Latin, and Hebrew (Lk 23:38). Julio Trebolle Barrera writes:

The linguistic map of Palestine around the turn of the era and at the moment when Christianity was born is marked by great differences in language. In Jerusalem and Judaea, Hebrew was spoken for preference, with Aramaic as a second language.

---

[463] (Golb 2012, Kindle Locations 7937-7941)
[464] (Van der Toorn 2007, 241-242)

Hebrew underwent a period of renaissance starting [from] the nationalistic revolt by the Maccabees (mid-2nd cent. BCE). At the same time there was a true renaissance of Hebrew Literature (Ben Sira, Tobit, «Jubilees, Testament of Naphtali,» writing of the Qumran [community], etc.). The coining of money with Hebrew inscriptions is further proof of the revival of Hebrew and of its official importance.[465]

Professor Norman Golb agrees. He writes:

From it [the «Paean to Alexander Jannaeus»], as from the others, we may note the lyrical richness of ancient Hebrew up to the very destruction of the Second Temple in A.D. 70; and we observe that virtually all of this poetry, as well as over three quarters of the prose texts, was composed in Hebrew, disproving the view that Aramaic had overtaken Hebrew as the main language of the Jews of Palestine in the first century A.D.[466]

There are numerous Aramaic loan words used in the New Testament, such as the word *Abba*, meaning father. The word Abba is used today in modern Israel, but no one claims the Israelis speak Aramaic today.[467] The existence of Aramaic loan words cannot account for the historical evidence for Hebrew as the Jewish language at the time of Christ, which includes the number of Hebrew manuscripts hidden away as part of the Dead Sea Scrolls, the Hebrew inscriptions found throughout Jerusalem, and the Hebrew script found on the coinage. Bivin and Blizzard provide an account of when and how the switch from Aramaic to Hebrew took place.

In 167 B.C., the Temple was desecrated by Antiochus IV Epiphanes, the Syrian Selucid ruler over Palestine. Shortly thereafter, the Jews, led by Judas Maccabaeus, revolted against the tyranny and harsh policies of Antiochus. There seems little

---

[465] (Barrera 1998, 74)
[466] (Golb 2012, Kindle Locations 7909-7913)
[467] (Bivin and Blizzard Jr. 1994, Kindle Locations 115-117)

doubt that this revolt, which culminated in the cleansing of the Temple in December of 164 B.C., spurred a religious revival among the Jews. It was the Maccabean victory which gradually led to a reinstatement of the ancestral language, Hebrew, as the dominant language in the whole of Palestine. Similarly, in recent times, it was Hebrew that won the struggle over which language would be the national language of the Jews living once again in their homeland, later to become the modern-day State of Israel.[468]

The Dead Sea Scrolls have thoroughly transformed our idea of what Judaism was like in the time of Christ. They have revealed not only were there many different forms of Judaism in existence at that time but many different textual traditions. They have provided additional evidence that the language used by Jesus Christ and the Apostles was indeed Hebrew, as described in the New Testament. They reveal that multiple families of texts were in use at the time of Christ, which tells us that the canon of the Old Testament had not been closed. The evidence of the Dead Sea Scrolls makes it clear that the notion of a fixed, three-part canon of the Hebrew Scriptures in the time of Christ is demonstrably faulty, as is the idea that the scribal libraries were the progenitor of the Masoretic text of the Hebrew Scriptures as we know them today.

---

[468] (Ibid, Kindle Locations 271-276)

39: Vowel Points and Textual Interpretation

The earliest writing systems (such as the Sumerian cuneiform script) used logographs (pictures or symbols) to represent words or phrases. Egyptian Hieroglyphics used a variety of logographs, syllabic, and alphabetic elements. The Semitic family of languages is based on the Proto-Canaanite alphabet, which is a consonantal alphabet. Consonantal alphabets get their name because they have characters for all the consonants, but no vowel characters. Professor Julio Trebolle Barrera notes that around 900 BC the Aramaeans began experimenting with using consonants to represent the vowels. This system is called *matres lectionis*, or mothers of reading. Barrera writes: "This system was also used by the Israelites from the beginning of the 9th cent BCE."[469]

The Dead Sea Scrolls use the *matres lectionis*, and the manuscripts have a different spelling than that found in the Masoretic text. Masoretic texts use points over the consonants to represent the vowels, while the most ancient Hebrew texts did not contain the vowel points and used no spacing between the letters. Even with the use of consonants to represent vowels, it was still difficult to read an unfamiliar text. It was necessary for an oral tradition to be transmitted side-by-side with the written text. The oral tradition consisted of the actual division of the text into words and their pronunciation. Jaroslav Pelikan writes:

It would be ridiculous to suppose that because it was only the consonants that had been written down in the received text of the Tanakh, only they were transmitted. The Hebrew words did have to be pronounced, and for that they needed vowels. And so there has existed from the very beginning an oral tradition, handed down from teacher to pupil through countless generations, of precisely which vowels went with the

---

[469] (Barrera 1998, 60)

consonants that appeared on the page. The only difference was that these vowels had to be committed to memory instead of being part of the transmitted written text.[470]

Since the Hebrew Scriptures had neither vowel points, punctuation, nor spaces between words, an oral tradition had to have existed side-by-side with the text.[471] The existence of an oral interpretive tradition presents a problem for Protestants; their acceptance of the Masoretic vowel pointing should require them to accept the existence of an oral tradition in Judaism. If the Masoretic vowel pointing is accepted, then Protestants have no reason to reject both Judaic and Christian oral tradition, but if oral tradition is rejected, the Masoretic text is called into question. Deacon Joseph Gleason writes:

The vowel points of the Masoretic Text put Protestants in a precarious position. If they believe that the Masoretic vowels are not trustworthy, then they call the Masoretic Text itself into question. But if they believe that the Masoretic vowels are trustworthy, then they are forced to believe that the Jews successfully preserved the vowels of Scripture for thousands of years, through oral tradition alone, until the Masoretes finally invented the vowel points hundreds of years after Christ. Either conclusion is at odds with mainstream Protestant thought.[472]

The French Protestant scholar Louis Cappel (c. 1584 – 1658 AD) made a study of the Hebrew Language. In his book *Hoc Est Arcanum Punctationis Revelatum* (a.k.a. *Arcanum Punctationis Revelatum*, or 'The Secret is Revealed

---

[470] (Pelikan 2005, 68)

[471] The *matres lectionis*, or mothers of reading, represents an early attempt at capturing this oral tradition in written form. As we shall see in later chapters, the Dead Sea Scrolls represent an early manuscript tradition, and thus an interpretive tradition much older than that represented by the Masoretic text.

[472] (Gleason, Masoretic Text vs. Original Hebrew 2012)

Punctuation'), Louis Cappel holds that the Masoretes inserted the vowel points and accents no earlier than the 5th century. This posed a problem for the Reformed scholars, as this compromised their idea of Scripture as the sole authority.[473]

While Louis Cappel argues the Masoretes were active in the 5th century, others argue they worked between the 6th and 10th century to "preserve and transmit" the Hebrew Scriptures.[474] This process involved editing together various textual families (The Babylonian, the Palestinian, and the Egyptian) and adding vowel pointing and word spacing. As is clear from the Dead Sea Scrolls, there were different textual families and different oral traditions, each of which was considered to be scripture. What the Masoretes did is to eliminate and replace the extant textual variations, thus fixing a particular interpretation of the text.[475] The 18th Century Anglican Scholar Adam Clarke, in the Preface to Volume 1 of his *Commentary on the Whole Bible*, writes the following:

The Mazoretes were the most extensive Jewish Commentators which that nation could ever boast. The system of punctuation, probably invented by them, is a continual gloss on the Law and the Prophets; their vowel points, and prosaic and metrical accents, give every word to which they are affixed a peculiar kind of meaning, which in their simple state, multitudes of them can by no means bear. The vowel points alone, add whole conjugations to the language. This system is one of the most artificial, particular, and extensive comments ever written on the Word of God; for there is not one word in the Bible that is not the subject of a particular gloss, through its influence.[476]

It should be noted that the Hebrew word from which the term Masoretes is derived, *mesorah* (מסורה, alt. מסורת), is a

---

[473] (Ibid)
[474] (Bromiley 1988, 799)
[475] (Boadt 1984, 73)
[476] (Clarke 1833, iii)

reference to the transmission of a tradition. Therefore, we should understand the Masoretic text as fixing a particular strain of Jewish thought. When the Masoretes required the destruction of all other versions of the text, they ensured that their interpretation would become the only version of the Hebrew Scriptures.[477] The Masoretic text, used as the basis for the King James Bible, is at a minimum an edited text. Protestants should question the use of the Masoretic text as the basis for the critical task of recovering the original text, as well as the theological task of determining the authoritative text.

There are those who argue that the ancient Hebrew text contained vowel pointing. This argument is easily countered. First, the Dead Sea Scrolls are unpointed texts. Second, the Scriptures themselves contain evidence that vowel pointing did not exist. John Calvin points to one such place where the Masoretic text is incorrectly pointed.

By faith Jacob, when he was a dying, blessed both the sons of Joseph; and worshipped, leaning upon the top of his staff. (Heb 11:27)

Of this, Calvin writes:

And worshipped on the top, etc. This is one of those places from which we may conclude that the points were not formerly used by the Hebrews; for the Greek translators could not have made such a mistake as to put staff here for a bed, if the mode of writing was then the same as now. No doubt Moses spoke of the head of his couch, when he said על ראש המטה *but the Greek*

---

[477] The Masoretic text used by the scholars of the Renaissance and the Reformation was not the same as the Hebrew texts used by Jerome when he translated the Scriptures to create the Vulgate in the late 4th century. Justin Martyr noted in the 2nd century that the Jewish textual revision was already under way. See chapter 5 for details.

translators rendered the words, "On the top of his staff" as though the last word was written, *mathaeh*.[478]

John Calvin points out that the Masoretes pointed the word incorrectly, causing the dying Jacob to bless the sons of Joseph while leaning on his staff, rather than leaning on the head of his couch (or leaning up in bed.) The Masoretic text contains an error of transmission, not an error in the original text.

The Masoretic text is not the same as the original text, and the vowel points were added later — just like the spaces between words, the punctuation, the verse and chapter divisions, and the chapter headings in our English Bibles. All such constitute a gloss on the text, a means of fixing a particular strain of interpretation. In the words of Pavel Florensky: "The Apostle Paul did not write in organized sections. To organize by heading is to distort the essence of Holy Scripture."[479]

As previously stated, manuscripts from the time of Christ were written without divisions between the words. More text was able to be written on any particular scroll, but the text was unintelligible without an interpretive guide. We fine evidence in the first book of *The Shepherd of Hermas*, a Christian text from the 2nd century AD. The first book consists of a series of visions; in one of the visions, Hermas is given a text to copy.

On rising from prayer, I see opposite me that old woman, whom I had seen the year before, walking and reading some book. And she says to me, "Can you carry a report of these things to the elect of God?" I say to her, "Lady, so much I cannot retain in my memory, but give me the book and I shall transcribe it." "Take it," says she, "and you will give it back to

---

[478] (Calvin, Commentary on Matthew, Mark, Luke - Volume 3 1999, 254)

[479] (Florensky 2014, 10)

me." Thereupon I took it, and going away into a certain part of the country, I transcribed the whole of it letter by letter; but the syllables of it I did not catch.[480]

Being unfamiliar with the text, Hermas was unable to read it. He was able to copy it letter-by-letter but was unable to understand it, as he couldn't make out the individual syllables.

There are other ways of subtly modifying text to support a preferred interpretation. Punctuation, for example, can change the entire meaning of a text. We tend to think of the punctuation of our English translations of the Bible as part of the text, rather than a commentary or gloss on the text. However, the original texts had no punctuation, no separation between words, and in the case of the Hebrew Scriptures, no vowels.

The difficulty with punctuating an unpunctuated text, like the Bible, is well known, as illustrated by Lynn Truss in her book, *Eats, Shoots & Leaves*.

Consider the following:

"Verily, I say unto thee, This day Thou shalt be with me in Paradise."

and:

"Verily I say unto thee this day, Thou shalt be with me in Paradise."

Now, huge doctrinal differences hang on the placing of this comma. The first version, which is how Protestants interpret this passage, (Luke xxiii, 43), lightly skips over the whole unpleasant business of Purgatory and takes the crucified thief straight to heaven with Our Lord. The second promises Paradise at some later date (to be confirmed, as it were), and

---

[480] The meaning of the text was later miraculously revealed to him. (Schaff, ANF02 2004, 13-14)

leaves Purgatory nicely in the picture for the Catholics, who believe in it.[481]

None of the Catholic bibles I've checked punctuate the Luke 23:43 passage the way Lynne Truss suggests. Nevertheless, the point is valid; the punctuation is not in the original. Our English punctuation may be based on the best approximation of the mood or case of the original language. The meaning can also be determined from the context, which would then suggest ways of punctuating the text. But, as illustrated by Lynn Truss, there are alternative ways of punctuating a text. Without an interpretive standard, we rewrite the text to suit ourselves.

As with punctuation, the chapter and verse divisions are also not in the original text. They are artificial devices, serving in some manner as a gloss or commentary on the text.[482] The artificiality of the chapter divisions can be seen using modern bibles with subheadings, where the subject matter extends into the first few verses of the following chapter. You won't typically see this using older bibles, such as the Scofield Reference Bible, which tend to organize their subheadings by chapter number.[483] However, there is one example that exists in every Protestant Bible: the division of Psalm 9 in the Septuagint into Psalm 9 & 10 in the Masoretic text. In his translation of the Psalms, the American professor of Hebrew Robert Alter points out that Psalm 9 and 10 form a single Hebraic acrostic poem.[484] Fr. Joseph Gleason notes a similar issue with Psalm 145:

---

[481] (Truss 2006, 74-75)

[482] (Edgecomb 1880)

[483] The subheadings are their own gloss upon scripture, an attempt to guide the reader into a preferred interpretation of the text.

[484] Alter also notes that some verses no longer fit the acrostic, indicating our current text is not the original text. (Alter 2007, 25)

Psalm 145 is also an acrostic poem. Each verse beginning with the successive letter of the alphabet, except that in the Masoretic text, the verse beginning with the Hebrew letter nun (נ) is missing. The missing verse, found in both the Septuagint and the Dead Sea Scrolls, reads as follows: "The Lord is faithful in His words and holy in all His works."[485]

Another modern gloss on the text is the use of red lettering to represent the words of Christ, presenting certain theological problems. The red lettering fixes a certain interpretation of which words Christ said and which words are the author's commentary. It is unclear whether John 3:16 and following are spoken by Jesus, or are a commentary by the apostle John; the red lettering fixes the first interpretation. The red lettering also highlights the words of Christ over against the words of the Father. In the account of John's baptism of Jesus, the words of Jesus are in red, but the words of the Father ("This is my beloved Son, in whom I am well pleased") are not. Fr. Ephrem Lash calls this a "wholly unorthodox inverted Arianism."[486]

The Masoretic text presents a problem for Protestants. Either they have to argue the vowel points, accents, and word divisions have always existed and are divinely inspired, or they have to argue the vowels, accents, and word divisions were preserved unchanged through oral tradition. If such a tradition preserved the Masoretic text, this brings into question the Protestant dismissal of Holy Tradition. Philip Schaff notes the work of Louis Cappel in dispelling the Reformation dogma of the "literal integrity and sacredness of the Masoretic text" by proving the Masoretic vowels were added sometime after the completion of the Babylonian Talmud. Since the Masoretic vowels were added rather late in the text's development, the Reformer's concept of

---

[485] (Gleason, Masoretic Text vs. Original Hebrew 2012)
[486] (Archimandrite Ephrem Lash 2008)

Scripture Alone is questionable; the lack of an infallible text left little room for verbal inspiration.[487]

---

[487] (Schaff, Creeds of Christendom, Volume 1 1876, 487 - 488)

40: Textual Alterations

The Masoretic text differs from the Dead Sea Scrolls not simply in the area of vowel points and word spacing, but because entire texts have undergone extensive editorial changes. These changes are of such magnitude that they cannot be simple copyist mistakes. The Book of Psalms as found in the Dead Sea Scrolls is different, including psalms missing from both the Masoretic text and the LXX.[488] The book of Jeremiah is consistent with the version preserved in the Septuagint rather than the one found in the Masoretic text. (We have already discussed *The Curious Case of Jeremiah* in Chapter 10).

Lawrence Boadt, in his book, *Reading the Old Testament*, writes:

There were quite a variety of copies of the Hebrew Old Testament available by the time of Jesus. Since copying had gone on for a long time already, many different editions circulated, some longer with sections added in, some shorter with sections omitted. All had some change or error in them. Since a scribe in one area often copied from a local text, the same error or change often appeared regularly in one place, say, Babylon, but not in text copied in Egypt. Thus, at the time of Christ, three major "families" or groupings of text types could be found: The Babylonian, the Palestinian, and the Egyptian. ...Only at the end of the first century A.D. did the rabbis decide to end the confusion and select one text, the best they could find, for each part of the Bible. In the Pentateuch they chose the Babylonian tradition, but in other books, such as the prophets Jeremiah and Isaiah, they followed the Palestinian-type text.[489]

---

[488] (Sanders, English Translation of the Psalms Scroll (Tehillim) 11QPs n.d.)

[489] (Boadt 1984, 73)

In the time of Christ not only was the canon not fixed but the form of each book could differ based on location. For those who insist upon the modern concept of verbal, plenary inspiration this is quite troubling; it suggests the revelation of God is not contained within or constrained by any particular text, just as God Himself cannot be circumscribed by human language. This understanding does not prevent us from the theological task of discovering the authoritative text, nor does it prevent us from preserving the extant text. We have already described Origen's *Hexapla*, his six-column work which attempted to collect and compare all the textual variants of the Septuagint.[490] Similarly, once the temple had been destroyed the rabbis began *their* work of consolidating and preserving their sacred writings. Lawrence Boadt writes:

These first century rabbis also inaugurated a method of guaranteeing the text from any more glosses and additions, though not completely from copying errors. They counted words, syllables, and sections, and wrote the totals at the end of each book of the Old Testament. ...The standard Hebrew text that resulted from the decisions of these early rabbis has become known as the "Masoretic text," named after a later group of Jewish scholars of the eighth to eleventh centuries A.D., the masoretes, or "interpreters," who put vowels into the text, and thus "fixed" the words in a definitive form. No longer could a reader be confused by whether the word qtl in the text meant qotel, "the killer," or qatal, "he killed."[491]

Before the discovery of the Dead Sea Scrolls, the earliest known manuscripts of the Hebrew Bible were from the 10th or 11th century. The fact that these manuscripts exist at all is something of a miracle; Jews have a tradition of destroying old, worn manuscripts.

During the Renaissance, humanist scholars were guided by their cry: "*ad fontes*" — to the sources. Because the only

---

[490] (Metzger 2001, Kindle Locations 326-330)
[491] (Boadt 1984, 73-74)

extant manuscripts they had were in Hebrew, and because the humanists influenced the Reformers, the Reformers chose the Hebrew texts over the Septuagint. However, the Dead Sea Scrolls are far older than the Masoretic text and support Justin Martyr's charge that the Jewish rabbis were engaged not only in the preservation of their sacred writings but in altering their content in response to the challenge of Christianity.[492] The Reformers were wrong. Hershel Shanks writes:

Before the discovery of the Dead Sea Scrolls, the oldest texts of the Hebrew Bible were in two manuscripts from the 10th or possibly the early 11th century known as the Aleppo Codex and the Leningrad Codex. These manuscripts—the Aleppo Codex, which was recovered partially after a fire and somehow brought to Jerusalem, and the Leningrad Codex, which is now in St. Petersburg—both of these nearly identical texts are what scholars call the rabbinic recension.[493]

The problem is this. The Masoretes fixed the text in a form significantly different than that used by the Jewish people in the time of Christ. The radical emendation of the text, when coupled with the Masoretic vowel pointing, fixed the wording and interpretation of the text. As Judaism underwent substantial changes after the destruction of the temple, so too did the text used as the basis for their faith. The question we should ask ourselves is whether we are using a corrupted text and whether we would be better off using a text that is closer to that used by the apostles, prophets, and our Lord Jesus Christ.

---

[492] (Schaff, ANF01 1884, Dialogue with Trypho, Chapters LXXI and LXXII)

[493] (Shanks 2007, 19) The rabbinic recension is the revised text of the Hebrew scriptures promoted by Hillel and others. This revised text is assumed to have been completed by 70 CE., and does not match the texts contained in the Dead Sea Scrolls. (Cross 1998, 216-217)

41: Canonical Differences

We have learned from the Dead Sea Scrolls that the canon of the Hebrew Scriptures was quite fluid in the years leading up to the fall of Jerusalem.[494] Judaism is now understood to have been more accepting of a diverse canon in the time of Christ than it was to become after the Masoretes completed their work. In part, this was because Judaism was itself a rather fluid concept. Hegesippus, the 2nd century Church historian, mentions seven different Jewish sects that existed at the time of Christ: "Essenes, Galileans, Hemerobaptists, Masbothæans, Samaritans, Sadducees, Pharisees."[495] In chapter 2, we quoted Epiphanius of Salamis list of twelve different Jewish sects existing at the time of Christ; we also quoted the Jerusalem Talmud as saying there were 24 heretical Jewish sects in the time of Ezekiel. What we see in the books of Ezra and Nehemiah is the suppression of alternate forms of Judaism.

The Anglican Bishop Joseph Barclay, writing in his book *The Talmud*, notes that there were two schools of the

---

[494] (Tigchelaar 2009)

[495] (Schaff, NPNF2-01 1890, 381) The Essenes were a Jewish sect opposed to the Hasmonean dynasty, which had supplanted the hereditary Aaronic priesthood. The Galileans are the Zealots, a group of Jews who opposed Roman rule by force of arms. The Hemerobaptists were a sect of the Essenes who bathed every morning so they could pronounce the name of God in their prayers with a clean body. Little is known about the Masbothæans. The Samaritans were (are) the remnants of the Northern Kingdom of Israel. The Sadducees were originally the descendants of the high priest in the time of David and Solomon, but by the time of Christ were not only the party of the law and the temple, but in a broader sense comprised the Hellenistic Jewish aristocracy. The Pharisees opposed the Sadducees, and were known for their scrupulous adherence to the law, and for a more democratic understanding of the people of God; the synagogue is (in part) one of the Pharisaic contributions to modern Judaism.

Pharisees: that of Shammai and that of Hillel. These two schools are often contradictory, yet of equal authority. Opposed to the Pharisees, on the one hand, were the Sadducees; opposed on the other hand were the Mehestanites whose Judaism was combined with the doctrines of Zoroaster. Barclay also adds the Misraimites who studied the Kabbala; the Essenes who allegorized the law; the Hellenists who combined the law with Greek philosophy; the Therapeutists for whom meditation was the 'supreme happiness;' the 'political Herodians;' the Zealots; and other 'petty sects' that either supported or opposed the two main schools of Judaism.[496]

While the Samaritans are generally not considered to be part of Judaism, the fact remains that they considered themselves to be the true followers of the law. The Samaritans held that only the five books of Moses were scripture. The Samaritan Pentateuch is a more ancient form of the Torah than the Masoretic text but also agrees more closely with the Dead Sea Scrolls.[497]

It has been widely (although not universally) understood that the Sadducees considered only the first five books of Moses to be scripture.[498] This view was prevalent among some of the church fathers, but modern scholars think the fathers were conflating the Samaritans and the Sadducees. If the latest scholarship is correct, the canon for both the Sadducees and Pharisees covered what we know today as the Hebrew Scriptures, or what Christians call the Old Testament. By contrast, the Jewish Diaspora, sometimes called the Hellenists, used the Septuagint (LXX) in their synagogues. The canon of the LXX was itself quite fluid, containing numerous books written after the time of Ezra.

The Essenes are thought to have a very wide canon, including books that were of importance only to their sect. the attribution of a large canon to the Essenes is because they

---

[496] (Barclay 1878, 15-17)

[497] (Lieber 2013)

[498] (Ross 2006)

are popularly thought to have deposited the Dead Sea Scrolls in the caves near one of their outposts at Qumran. However, Israeli archeologist Yuval Peleg and others cast doubt upon the supposed connection between Qumran and the Essenes.

After digging at the site for ten years, he [Yuvan Peleg] also believes that Qumran was originally a fort designed to protect a growing Jewish population from threats to the east. Later, it was converted into a pottery factory to serve nearby towns like Jericho, he says. Other scholars describe Qumran variously as a manor house, a perfume manufacturing center and even a tannery. Despite decades of excavations and careful analysis, there is no consensus about who lived there—and, consequently, no consensus about who actually wrote the Dead Sea Scrolls.[499]

What is clear, according to Yuvan Peleg, is that Qumran is not an Essene outpost. "There is no connection to the Essenes at this site." Instead, Peleg believes that Jews escaping from the Roman invasion of 70 AD stored their scrolls in the caves outside Qumran for safekeeping.[500] For scholars, this is an increasingly popular view.

Norman Golb, a University of Chicago professor of Jewish history, provides evidence that Qumran was a military outpost, and Roman forces took the outpost by force sometime around the fall of Jerusalem. Graveyards were found containing men, women, and children, indicating the celibate Essenes did not occupy the site.[501] There are geographical problems with the description of the Essenes given by Pliny the Elder, in that their location north of Engedi could not have been Qumran, because by the time Pliny the Elder wrote the Romans occupied Qumran. In other words, the connection between Qumran and the Essenes makes no sense.

---

[499] (Lawler 2010)

[500] (Ibid)

[501] (Golb 2012, Kindle Locations 230-368; 416-424; 461-482)

Jodi Magness notes there is no textual evidence to suggest a connection between the Qumran community and the Dead Sea Scrolls: "If the inhabitants of Qumran were Essenes, why does this term not appear in the Dead Sea Scrolls?" She suggests the possibility they used nicknames such as "Sons of Light," or perhaps did not refer to themselves at all.[502] Another problem she mentions is the lack of texts at the Qumran site: "No scrolls were discovered in the settlement at Qumran. Instead, all of the scrolls come from the caves surrounding the site." She notes, however, that the pottery at Qumran matches the pottery in which the Dead Sea Scrolls were deposited. (If Qumran were a pottery factory, as Yuval Peleg suggests, this would account for the similarity in pottery between Qumran and the Dead Sea Scrolls). Jodie Magness suggests that the pottery, plus the physical proximity of some of the caves to Qumran, suggests a connection to the Qumran community. She suggests the lack of texts at Qumran can be accounted for by two conflagrations: the first on 9/8 BCE, and the second destruction by the Romans in 68 CE[503]

Despite the similarities between the pottery between Qumran and the containers in which the Dead Sea Scrolls were stored, more and more evidence suggests the source of the scrolls was Jerusalem rather than the Essene community. First, Yizhar Hirschfeld says the over 500 scrolls found were too many to have been used by a sect as small as the Essenes. Qumran itself only supported 200 people, and both Pliny the Elder and Josephus say the total number of Essenes was around 4,000.[504] Second, Hirschfeld notes two previous historical discoveries of scrolls hidden in the Judean desert. Origen reports the 4th-century finding of scrolls hidden away in Judean caves, and Timothy I, Patriarch of Seleucia (northern Syria, 779 AD – 823 AD) reports additional scrolls

---

[502] (Magness 2002, 41-42)

[503] (Ibid, 43-44)

[504] (Grabbe 2010, Kindle Location 776)

were recovered from caves near Jericho. All this suggests a large-scale effort to hide scribal libraries before the destruction of Jerusalem in 70 AD.[505]

The historical evidence suggests that although the Jewish leaders in Jerusalem *may* have been conservative as regards the canon, Judaism as a whole was not. This runs counter to the position of earlier scholars like F. F. Bruce, who claims the early Christians used a different and larger canon than did the Jews.[506] The Jews of Jerusalem and its environs now appear to have used the larger and more inclusive canon of the Septuagint, which F. F. Bruce calls "Septuagint plus" (with the possible exception of the book of Esther, which does not appear in the Dead Sea Scrolls).[507]

The Essenes and the Sadducees disappeared following the destruction of Israel in 70 AD. The only Jewish sects to survive? The Pharisees, the Samaritans, and the Christians, of which only the Pharisees and Christians were active among the Jewish Diaspora.[508] However, as John Bowker notes, the relationship between the Pharisees and later Rabbinic Judaism is complicated.

Nothing could be more misleading than to refer to the Pharisees without further qualification as the predecessors of the rabbis, for the fact remains that 'Pharisees' are attacked in rabbinic sources as vigorously as 'Pharisees' are attacked in the Gospels, and often for similar reasons.[509]

---

[505] (Hirschfeld 2004, 45-48)

[506] (Bruce, The Canon of Scripture 2010, 44-46)

[507] (Ibid, 47)

[508] Although the Jews and the Samaritans were bitter enemies, in a sense this was more of an internal squabble within Judaism. It is increasingly clear that the Samaritan Pentateuch is based on a more ancient manuscript tradition than the Masoretic text, and many problematic Masoretic texts are clarified in the Samaritan text.

[509] (Bowker 1973, 1)

John Bowker (and others) suggest the Hebrew word commonly translated as 'Pharisee' may refer to a different group, and that the rabbinic sources refer to their predecessors as "Hakamim (the Wise, or the Sages)" instead of as 'perushim,' the Semitic word commonly translated as Pharisee.[510] Thus the Hakamim and the Pharisees may be roughly similar.

Professor Norman Golb describes the radical shift in thinking that took place following the destruction of the temple, a shift that saw the downfall of the priests and the rise of the heirs of the Pharisees.

There can be no doubt that a radical shift in both Jewish hegemony and religion and social thinking occurred during the decades following the destruction of the Second Temple. The message of the priests had been that the Jews could count on the Lord to save them if only, in accordance with the biblical precepts, the animal sacrifices were faithfully performed; and when this failed to happen in A.D. 70, the priests suffered a disastrous loss of credibility. ...In an agreement apparently worked out with the Roman government several decades after the fall of Jerusalem, the Jewish leadership was, instead, vested in a new governing figure, the Palestinian Patriarch, who granted not only religious but also both legislative and judicial authority to the heirs of the Pharisees — i.e., the rabbis or, more specifically, the Tannaim.[511]

Historical evidence suggests the Jews were actively hostile to the Christians, as described in the book of Acts (Acts 13:43-50; 14:1-5,19; 19:33). Some have suggested the Hebrew canon was restricted in an attempt to remove support for the Messiahship of Jesus.[512] This process was once thought to have begun with the school of Jewish law founded by Rabbi

---

[510] (Ibid, 2-42)

[511] (Golb 2012, Kindle Locations 8096-8100; 8104-8107)

[512] For example, Baruch 3 can be interpreted as supporting the identification of Wisdom with Christ, especially as regards the Incarnation.

Yohanan ben Zakkai in the city of Jamnia. Late 19th to mid-20th biblical scholarship suggested the existence of a Council of Jamnia which decided on a definitive Jewish canon. F.F. Bruce describes their work as follows:

After the fall of Jerusalem in A.D. 70, a new Sanhedrin or council of elders, consisting of Jewish scholars, was constituted at Jamnia in Western Palestine. They reviewed the whole field of Jewish religion and law, and held long discussions on the scope of the Canon of Hebrew Scripture. They debated whether certain books should not be excluded, and whether certain others should not he admitted: but in the end they did not exclude any book which already enjoyed canonical recognition, nor did they admit any book which had not previously received such recognition.[513]

Although F.F. Bruce describes the makeup and work of the Council of Jamnia, it is no longer certain that such a council took place; in fact, the myth of Jamnia appears to have been created by the Jewish Historian Heinrich Graetz in 1871; he put forth his "novel thesis," yet provided no evidence whatsoever.[514] Protestant appeals to the discredited Council of Jamnia substitutes wishful thinking for evidence.

We do not know exactly when the editorial process began, nor do we know if there was anyone to authorize such a thing.[515] We do know that alterations of the text of the Hebrew Scriptures were underway after the fall of Jerusalem,[516] and these changes were significant enough to have been mentioned by Justin Martyr (c. 100 – 165 AD). Justin Martyr argues forcefully that the Jews artificially

---

[513] (Bruce, The Canon of Scripture 2008, 20)

[514] (Aune 1991)

[515] While the Christians had an ecclesial hierarchy, and even in the book of Acts settled doctrinal disputes in councils, such a framework was unknown to Judaism.

[516] (Boadt 1984, 73-74)

truncated their canon of Scripture to eliminate passages that demonstrate that Jesus was the promised Messiah.[517] It is clear that the Christians used the Septuagint as their scripture while the Jews gradually settled on their more restricted catalog, one intentionally created out of hostility to the claims of Christ. This is one reason why the Bible for early Christians was the Septuagint: it better supported the claim that Jesus Christ was the long-promised Messiah.

---

[517] (Schaff, ANF01 1884, Dialogue with Trypho, Chapters LXXI and LXXII)

42: Theology and the Apocrypha

If God is all-powerful, ever-present and filling all things, why does evil exist? This is a question that is never directly addressed in the Protestant Scriptures. Closely related to the problem of evil is the existence of suffering. On this lesser question, the Protestant Scriptures do have something to say, although the answer must be teased out. On the larger and more important question, the Protestant Scriptures are silent.

So why do the righteous suffer? The entire book of Job has this as its theme but does not provide a satisfactory answer (from our perspective, of course). Ultimately the answer of God to Job comes down to this:

Then the LORD *answered Job ...Who is this...? Where wast thou...? Hast thou commanded the morning since thy days...? Have the gates of death been opened unto thee? ...Hast thou perceived the breadth of the earth? declare if thou knowest it all (Job 38 2-3, 12, 17-18).*

God is saying through Job: *Who do you think you are to even ask that question?* After which Job abhors himself and repents (Job 42:6). But God does not leave the question there, as we shall see.

The story of Joseph is instructive on this question. Joseph was the then youngest and most beloved son of his father, who his brothers sold into slavery in Egypt. There he suffered greatly before rising to a position of great power and authority. Many years later, during a famine where his brothers came to Egypt to buy grain, Joseph revealed himself to them. He said: "But as for you, ye thought evil against me; but God meant it unto good, to bring to pass, as it is this day, to save much people alive" (Gen 50:20). And so we see that God allowed Joseph to suffer evil and brought good from it. This is not a situation of God using evil to do good, or even requiring the existence of evil to do good, but rather that although evil exists, God works in the midst of it. Ultimately, however, this does not resolve the main question of why evil exists in the first place.

The corollary to the question of why the righteous suffer is this: Why do the wicked prosper? (Jer 12:1). This question finds a partial answer when God pronounces judgment upon those who "touch the inheritance which I have caused my people Israel to inherit. Behold, I will pluck them out of their land..." (Jer 12:14). The issue for Jeremiah is the prosperity of wicked Judah and the prosperity of those who would soon take them into captivity for their many sins.

Because of their sins, the prophet Habakkuk cries out to God to judge His people (Hab 1:2-4). When the impending captivity by the Babylonians is revealed to the prophet, he is distraught, because the Chaldeans are even worse. How can a holy God use an evil nation to punish His chosen people? (Hab 1:13). Interestingly, God does not answer Habakkuk's question at all. Instead, God pronounces five woes, not only upon the Babylonians, and not only upon Judah, but upon all sinners. These woes are for usury & greed (Hab 2:6); coveteousness & pride (Hab 2:9); wrath & murder (Hab 2:12); drunkenness and lust (Hab 2:15); and idolatry (Hab 2:19).

Connected to these woes are three pronouncements about God and His people. The first pronouncement is that the just shall live by his faith (Hab 2:4). That this comes first, even before any of the woes, is significant. It suggests the just live by faith even when evil men prosper, and the righteous suffer. When God pronounces the second woe upon those who build a town by blood and iniquity, He then suggests that the people weary themselves in vain, "For the earth shall be filled with the knowledge of the glory of the Lord" (Hab 2:14). This brings us out of the consideration of our troubles, suggesting the apocalyptic end of all evil and the eschatological hope. But God does not suggest all judgment is reserved until the end of time; no, for we finally come to the third woe: "the cup of the LORD's right hand shall be turned unto thee, and shameful spewing shall be on thy glory" (Hab 2:16). But finally, the answer to Habakkuk is the same as that given to Job: "[T]he Lord is in his holy temple: let all the earth keep silence before him" (Hab 2:20).

Asaph too asked this question. In Psalm 73 he says he "was envious at the foolish when he saw the prosperity of the wicked" (Psa 73:3). He describes their strength, their prosperity, their pride and violence, their corruption and oppression, and the way they speak out against God and abuse His people. He is so cast down that he begins to think he has "cleansed his heart in vain, and washed my hands in innocency. For all the day long have I been plagued, and chastened every morning" (Psa 73:13-14). In great pain and turmoil of soul, he comes into the sanctuary, where he finally understands. In light of eternity, the wicked have been set "in slippery places." The wicked are about to slip; but then Asaph notes that God has already cast them down into destruction (Psa 73:18). In temporal terms, they are about to slip; but in light of eternity, they have already been condemned, and "brought into desolation, as in a moment! They are utterly consumed with terrors" (Psa 73:19). In light of eternity, Asaph sees he has been ignorant, and his doubts have been foolish. "I am continually with thee: thou has holden me by my right hand. Thou shalt guide me with thy counsel, and afterward receive me to glory" (Psa 73:23-24). The more difficult question of why evil exists is left unanswered.

Regarding the existence of evil, what in the Protestant Scriptures must be painstakingly drawn out is more clear in the Apocryphal books. "For God formed man to be imperishable; the image of his own nature he made him. But by the envy of the devil, death entered the world, and they who are in his possession experience it" (Wis 2:23-24). And again: "It was the wicked who with hands and words invited death, considered it a friend, and pined for it, and made a covenant with it, because they deserve to be in its possession" (Wis 1:16). The problem of evil is explained: sin entered into the world, and death by sin, through the influence of the devil. Moreover, those who are in the grips of the devil are subject to death, deserve death, choose death, pined for death, and make a covenant with death. Although the devil introduced sin, death, evil, and suffering, mankind chose and continues to choose death and suffering over life and righteousness.

Now regarding the suffering of the righteous, once again the Apocrypha have an answer. The same answer can be teased out of the Protestant Scriptures but made clear and plain in the Apocrypha, as seen in this excerpt from a much longer dissertation on the hidden counsels of God, regarding suffering, childlessness, and early death.

But the souls of the just are in the hand of God, and no torment shall touch them. They seemed, in the view of the foolish, to be dead; and their passing away was thought an affliction and their going forth from us, utter destruction. But they are in peace. For if before men, indeed, they be punished, yet is their hope full of immortality; Chastised a little, they shall be greatly blessed, because God tried them and found them worthy of himself. (Wis 3:1-5)

Wisdom equates suffering with peace, hope, blessing, and immortality. The peace that God gives is found in trials and chastisement and is full of hope. There is hope for this life, and hope for the life to come, both of which come through suffering. Indeed, the blessings of God do not result in an easy life but introduce us to the life to come. There is more that can be said here, but explaining the problem of evil is outside the scope of this book.

Suffice it to say that without what the Protestants call the Apocrypha and Catholics call the Deuterocanonical books, the Scriptures are veiled on a variety of the most important and troubling issues.

Part V: References to the Apocrypha in the Scriptures

43: The New Testament Witness

Among the Protestant arguments against the Apocrypha are that the New Testament never quoted from them and never used them as scripture. The Reformed teacher Michael Marlow categorically states: "The apostles never quote from these writings."[518] This canonical argument seemed so obvious and unquestioned as to be axiomatic. F.F. Bruce writes:

Our Lord and the apostles certainly did not regard the apocryphal books as part of Holy Scripture; the evidence is that they acknowledged as canonical only the books of the Hebrew Bible, and that is the justification for the Protestant Evangelical attitude. Our supreme reason for acknowledging the divine authority of the thirty-nine books of the Old Testament is the fact that Christ and (following Him) His apostles acknowledged it.[519]

As with many things in life, the unexamined truth turns out to be false. The evidence that our Lord and the Apostles regarded the Apocrypha as Scripture is quite extensive. There are numbers of direct references to the Apocryphal books in the New Testament. Moreover, the themes found in the Apocrypha inform the content of the New.

Merrill C. Tenney, writing in *Bibliotheca Sacra* (a publication of Dallas Theological Seminary), provides us with a way to categorize these different references.

Scriptural references can be generally classified under three heads: citations, which are almost exact verbally and which are definitely referred to a given author; quotations, which are sufficiently close to the original to leave no doubt concerning

---

[518] (Marlowe, A Brief Introduction to the Canon and Ancient Versions of Scripture 2012)

[519] (Bruce, The Canon of Scripture 2008, 20-21)

their derivation, but which are not attributed explicitly to a definite source; and allusions, which are often so loosely constructed that only one or two words out of a sentence parallel the Biblical text.[520]

These direct and indirect references can be prophetic, as in the case of the allusion to the slaying of the holy innocents in the Wisdom of Solomon, or provide sources for various New Testament doctrines such as the resurrection of the dead. The Doctrinal Sources are treated separately for clarity's sake.

The Bible contains numerous references to books that are not part of Sacred Scripture.[521] The Apostle quotes two pagan philosophers in his Areopagus speech (Acts 17:28).[522] In 1st Corinthians, he quotes Menander when he writes: "Evil communications corrupt good manners" (1Co 15:33). In his letter to Titus Paul quotes Epimenides when he writes: "The Cretians are always liars, evil beasts, slow bellies" (Ti 1:12).[523] A reference in Sacred Scripture to another writing does not automatically add that work to the catalog of Sacred Scriptures. We must examine these references carefully and prayerfully; we must consider how the references were made and used. We must also consider the number of times a work was referenced: whether it was an isolated passage, or whether there were numerous passages referenced. And we must consider the witness of the Church; or if you like, the historical witness of Christians living closest to the time of Christ. Ultimately, we must always remember: "This is the Lord's doing; it is marvellous in our eyes" (Ps 118:23).

---

[520] (Tenney 1963, 301)

[521] Wikipedia has a partial list in their article entitled "Non-canonical books referenced in the Bible":

https://en.wikipedia.org/wiki/Non-canonical_books_referenced_in_the_Bible

[522] Dr. Riemer Faber has an interesting discussion of these citations in his article, *The Apostle and the Poet: Paul and Aratus* (Faber 1993)

[523] (Jamieson, Fausset and Brown 1871, 3578;4010)

44: Citations

Using Merrill C. Tenney's definition of a citation as being "almost exact verbally and which are definitely referred to a given author," there are virtually no direct citations of the Old Testament Apocrypha in the New Testament.[524] Many quotations, but few citations. The lack of citations is not a problem; the New Testament quotes and alludes to the Old Testament often, but rarely cites its sources. The writers of the New Testament were not preparing academic papers, and the Chicago Manual of Style did not exist. They used quotations and allusions freely, assuming a degree of scriptural familiarity on the part of their readers.

Another issue with citations is that Jude cites a source outside the canon.

It was also about these men that Enoch, in the seventh generation from Adam, prophesied, saying, "Behold, the Lord came with many thousands of His holy ones, to execute judgment upon all, and to convict all the ungodly of all their ungodly deeds which they have done in an ungodly way, and of all the harsh things which ungodly sinners have spoken against Him." (Jude 1:14-15)

This citation of the book of Enoch was one reason why the canonicity of Jude was a matter of dispute among the early church. Henry Chadwick writes:

More problematic was the presence of a quotation [citation] from the book of Enoch in the epistle of Jude, some thinking that this guaranteed Enoch's place in the Christian canon, while others disagreed because the book was not included in the Septuagint.[525]

---

[524] (Tenney 1963, 301)

[525] (Chadwick 2001, 28)

In the fifth century, the Syriac Church settled on a 22 book canon that does not contain the book of Jude, nor other disputed books (II Peter, II & III John, and Revelation).[526] This canon is still in use today among the Nestorians. Only the Ethiopian Orthodox Tewahedo Church and the Eritrean Orthodox Tewahedo Church accept the Book of Enoch as being part of the canon. Michael Marlow states the apostles never quoted from the Apocrypha;[527] this is only true if Marlow is using "quotation" as a replacement for Merrill C. Tenney's use of the term "citation." It is true the apostles never cited from the Apocrypha, but they rarely cited from the books of the Protestant Old Testament. If a direct citation is an essential part of canonicity, why is the Book of Enoch not in the canon?

---

[526] (Lieuwen 1995)

[527] (Marlowe, A Brief Introduction to the Canon and Ancient Versions of Scripture 2012)

45: Quotations

In this chapter, we will first read a portion from the Apocrypha and the corresponding passage from the New Testament. In many cases, the relevant passages will be in bold text. Any such emphasis is not in the original text. Following these texts will be a commentary on the text, and why it is important. Some of these quotations are more important than others, either because of the subject matter, the context, or who is speaking. Let the reader understand.

The Lord's Prayer

Forgive thy neighbour the hurt that he hath done unto thee, so shall thy sins also be forgiven when thou prayest (Sirach 28:2).

And forgive us our debts, as we forgive our debtors (Matt 6:12).

The citation from Sirach is the most intriguing of the quotations from the Apocrypha, as it forms part of what has come down to us as either The Lord's Prayer or the Our Father. The Lord's Prayer is not a pure quotation from Sirach, but neither is it simply an allusion. Instead, Jesus is inverting the two clauses from Sirach, creating the parallel statements characteristic of Hebrew poetry.

Dr. David Scaer's book, *The Sermon on the Mount* contains a typical Protestant understanding of The Lord's Prayer. Scaer writes:

The Matthean version of the Prayer does not suggest that God's forgiving us is caused by our forgiving others; the word "as" is used, not "because." "As" means "like" or "similar." We ask that God would forgive us as, not because we forgive others. Some hold the view that our forgiving precedes God's, but this is done more from a theological and not a grammatical consideration.[528]

---

[528] (Scaer, The Sermon on the Mount 2000, 184)

Scaer is correct if we do not consider the source for this passage. In Sirach's version, forgiveness of the neighbor is necessary for God to hear our prayers of forgiveness. Sirach's interpretation is demonstrated in Matthew's gospel by the Parable of the Unforgiving Debtor (Matt 18:23-34). A servant owed his master a great debt and asked to be forgiven. When the servant refused to forgive a minor debt owed to him, the master refused to forgive the servant. Jesus sums up the parable by saying: "So likewise shall my heavenly Father do also unto you if ye from your hearts forgive not every one his brother their trespasses" (Matt 18:35). Jesus is indicating that the passage from Sirach represents the proper interpretation — God forgives us to the extent we forgive others. The apostle writes: "For if, when we were enemies, we were reconciled to God by the death of his Son, much more, being reconciled, we shall be saved by his life" (Ro 5:10). Forgiving our enemies is the essence of a Christ-like life.

Blessed Theophylact, in his commentary *The Gospel According to St. Matthew*, writes:

Because we sin even after our baptism, we beseech Him to forgive us. But forgive us as we forgive others: if we remember wrongs, God will not forgive us. God takes me as the pattern He will follow: what I do to another, He does to me.[529]

God, therefore, respects our free will. He does not respond in kind, but responds overabundantly. When we truly repent — when we truly change our mind, rejecting the evil and seeking the good — the angels rejoice and the Holy Spirit fills us, empowering us for service. When we seek God half-heartedly, we quench the Holy Spirit and God seems far from us. It is all God's work and none of ours. Nothing we do is meritorious in and of itself. But God is merciful, bestowing great mercy upon us at the least sign that we are responsive to Him, and that we desire communion with Him. This, then, is the meaning of the forgiveness clause in The Lord's Prayer.

---

[529] (Blessed Theophylact 1992, 58)

Sheep Without a Shepherd

And I will lead thee through the midst of Judea, until thou come before Jerusalem; and I will set thy throne in the midst thereof; and thou shalt drive them **as sheep that have no shepherd**, *and a dog shall not so much as open his mouth at thee: for these things were told me according to my foreknowledge, and they were declared unto me, and I am sent to tell thee (Jdt 11:19).*

But when he saw the multitudes, he was moved with compassion on them, because they fainted, and were scattered abroad, **as sheep having no shepherd** *(Mt 9:36).*

When Jesus describes the multitudes as "like sheep without a shepherd," he is quoting Judith 11:19. The context seems very different, but the metaphor from Judith provides depths of meaning to Jesus' words. In the passage from Judith, she is setting up Holofernes, the general of the armies threatening Israel. She tells him that with her help, he will "drive them as sheep that have no shepherd." When Jesus uses the same phrase, the image is not simply of sheep without a leader to guide them, but of sheep with no protector, with no one to take care of them.

The military metaphor from Judith has a twofold meaning. On the one hand, it could be a sign of Jesus' concern over the Roman military occupation. But since Judith functions more as a myth than as history, it is clear that Jesus is alluding to spiritual warfare. Jesus reserves his harshest words for the spiritual leadership of the Jewish people, those who lay heavy burdens upon their people but are unwilling to carry those burdens themselves. The oppressed the people instead of protecting them, leaving them open to the predations of the devil. The multitudes were fainting under their spiritual onslaught and were scattered because they had no one who cared for their souls.

Lord of Heaven and Earth

Be of good comfort, my daughter; the **Lord of heaven and earth** *give thee joy for this thy sorrow: be of good comfort, my daughter [emphasis added] (Tobit 7:18).*

At that time Jesus answered and said, I thank thee, O Father, **Lord of heaven and earth**, *because thou hast hid these things from the wise and prudent, and hast revealed them unto babes [emphasis added] (Mt 11:25).*

The imprisoned John the Baptist sent his disciples to Jesus, asking: "Art thou he that should come, or do we look for another" (Matt 11:3)? Jesus reply was to look at what they can see and hear: "The blind receive their sight, and the lame walk, the lepers are cleansed, and the deaf hear, the dead are raised up, and the poor have the gospel preached to them" (Matt 11:5).

Following this, Jesus begins a lengthy discourse beginning with an apologetic for John the Baptist. He then pronounces woes upon the cities in which He performed these great works and to whom He had preached the gospel, and yet the people had not repented. Finally, Jesus lifted his eyes to heaven and praised the "Lord of heaven and earth," a phrase borrowed from the book of Tobit.

John the Baptist was in great sorrow, as were the Jewish people themselves. Jesus' prayer is both an expression of praise to God and a means of comfort to those around him. The comfort comes from the central story in the book of Tobit. The man Tobit is about to marry Sara, a woman tormented by a demon who has threatened to kill any man she marries. Tobit is visited by the archangel Raphael who tells Tobit how to defeat the demon. On the evening of her wedding day, Sara is sorrowful; she is sure she will be a widow in the morning. However, her father blesses her by reminding her that God is the Lord of heaven and earth, and can turn her weeping into joy. Those listening to Jesus' prayer would Jesus' words and their context.

The demon was defeated with the help of God. Tobit gained not only a wife but great wealth. Sara's sorrow was turned into joy, a reminder that would have been a comfort to the imprisoned John the Baptist, to Jesus' disciples, and to the multitudes of Roman subjects who followed Jesus.

Take My Yoke Upon You

Draw near unto me, ye unlearned, and dwell in the house of learning. Wherefore are ye slow, and what say ye to these things, seeing your souls are very thirsty? I opened my mouth, and said, Buy her for yourselves without money. **Put your neck under the yoke**, and let your soul receive instruction: she is hard at hand to find. ...Behold with your eyes, how that **I have but little labour, and have gotten unto me much rest.** [emphasis added] (Sirach 51:23-27).

Come unto me, all ye that labour and are heavy laden, and I will give you rest. Take my yoke upon you, and learn of me; for I am meek and lowly in heart: and ye shall find rest unto your souls. **For my yoke is easy, and my burden is light** [emphasis added] (Mt 11:28-30).

The scholar Henry Chadwick states:

Among Greek-speaking Christians ...The wisdom of Ben Sira became so popular that in the west it acquired the title 'Ecclesiasticus,' and a famous saying of Jesus in Matt 11:28 directly quotes from Sirach 51:27.[530]

In our day, we speak of blue collar and white collar workers, meaning those who work with their hands and those who work at their desks. In general, white collar work requires a greater degree of education than does blue collar work. This distinction was even more pronounced in Jesus' day when literacy was rare — when most people were unlearned, and therefore laborers. Jesus is speaking directly to those of low estate, not those of high degree (Ja 1:9).

The two passages are not direct quotations; Jesus is restating the verse from Sirach. The two passage form a

---

[530] (Chadwick 2001, 28) While Chadwick refers only to Sirach 51:27, it is reasonable to include the entire passage beginning at verse 23.

parallelism, a literary technique used in Hebrew poetry. The call to the unlearned to dwell in the house of learning is a call for them to rest from their labors. But the context of Sirach is even more interesting. Chapter 51 is a prayer, and beginning at verse 13, Jesus ben Sirach begins to describe his search for wisdom. Thus, when Jesus is quoting from Sirach, He is identifying Himself as Wisdom incarnate.

This connection between Jesus Christ and Wisdom becomes even clearer when we discover Jesus' reference to the yoke comes from Sirach injunction to "Put your neck under the yoke." In Sirach, this is the yoke of Wisdom; in Matthew, the yoke of Wisdom belongs to Jesus. He, Jesus, is Wisdom personified, and only in Him do we find rest for our souls.

Power of Death

*For thou hast power of life and death: thou leadest to the **gates of hell**, and bringest up again [emphasis added] (Wisdom 16:13).*

*And I say also unto thee, That thou art Peter, and upon this rock I will build my church; and the **gates of hell** shall not prevail against it [emphasis added] (Matt 16:18).*

Jesus' reference to the 'gates of hell' quotes from Wisdom. The idea of God leading to the gates of hell and bringing up again refers both to the resurrection of the dead and to the Harrowing of Hell. The Harrowing of Hell is the theological term for Christ's descent into Hades (Eph 4:9-10; 1 Peter 3:19-20), from which He led captivity captive (Eph 4:8).

Flee to the Mountains

*So he and his sons **fled into the mountains**, and left all that ever they had in the city [emphasis added] (1 Macc 2:28).*

When ye therefore shall see the abomination of desolation, spoken of by Daniel the prophet, stand in the holy place, (whoso readeth, let him understand:) Then let them which be in Judaea **flee into the mountains** *[emphasis added] (Mt 24:15-16).*

The events described in 1 Maccabees occurred after the temple had been desecrated by Antiochus IV Epiphanes, who set up an altar to Zeus and had pigs sacrificed upon the altar. As if that was not enough, one of the Jews came and sacrificed on the altar, an action that infuriated the priest Mattathias. Mattathias and his sons killed both the Jewish man and the King's commissioner, after which they tore down the altar and "fled into the mountains."

Jesus alludes to this in his use of the term "abomination of desolation" (described in the chapter on "Allusions") and follows this up with a direct quote from 1 Maccabees. Thus, Jesus made it clear to his disciples that when they saw a similar desolation of the temple, they were to flee to the mountains. The disciples would have understood the reference as coming from the 1st book of Maccabees. Historically, the Romans fulfilled this prophecy when they leveled Jerusalem in 70 AD.

Signs and Wonders

If a man desire much experience, she [wisdom] knoweth things of old, and conjectureth aright what is to come: she knoweth the subtilties of speeches, and can expound dark sentences: she foreseeth **signs and wonders**, *and the events of seasons and times [emphasis added] (Wisdom 8:8).*

For there shall arise false Christs, and false prophets, and shall shew great **signs and wonders**; *insomuch that, if it were possible, they shall deceive the very elect [emphasis added] (Mt 24:24).*

For false Christs and false prophets shall rise, and shall shew **signs and wonders**, *to seduce, if it were possible, even the elect [emphasis added] (Mr 13:22).*

Then said Jesus unto him, Except ye see **signs and wonders**, *ye will not believe [emphasis added] (Jn 4:48).*

*By stretching forth thine hand to heal; and that **signs and wonders** may be done by the name of thy holy child Jesus [emphasis added] (Acts 4:30).*

*And by the hands of the apostles were many **signs and wonders** wrought among the people; (and they were all with one accord in Solomon's porch [emphasis added] (Acts 5:12).*

*Long time therefore abode they speaking boldly in the Lord, which gave testimony unto the word of his grace, and granted **signs and wonders** to be done by their hands [emphasis added] (Acts 14:3).*

*Through mighty **signs and wonders**, by the power of the Spirit of God; so that from Jerusalem, and round about unto Illyricum, I have fully preached the gospel of Christ [emphasis added] (Ro 15:19).*

*Truly the signs of an apostle were wrought among you in all patience, in **signs, and wonders**, and mighty deeds [emphasis added] (2Co 12:12).*

*God also bearing them witness, both with **signs and wonders**, and with divers miracles, and gifts of the Holy Ghost, according to his own will [emphasis added] (Heb 2:4)?*

The phrase "signs and wonders" is used nine times in the New Testament, but never used in the Hebrew Scriptures. The phrase comes from the Wisdom of Solomon as part of an extended monologue on wisdom. Wisdom is allegorically associated with Jesus Christ; therefore, it is clear that Jesus Christ is the one who both foresees signs and wonders. Without the quotation from the Wisdom of Solomon, it is not clear what the difference is between the signs and wonders performed by Christ and His disciples and the signs and wonders performed by the false prophets.

In Wisdom chapter 8, we see the growth of an individual who desires wisdom, which gives us a way of discerning between false prophets and true disciples.

- The true disciple loves wisdom and seeks her out (v. 2)

- The true disciple seeks wisdom rather than riches (v. 5)[531]
- The true disciple is prudent (v. 6)
- The true disciple loves righteousness (v. 7)
- The true disciple practices the virtues (temperance, prudence, justice, and fortitude) (v. 7)[532]
- The true disciple lives with wisdom, is counseled by wisdom, and is comforted by wisdom (v. 9)

The false prophet is no lover of wisdom, is no true disciple, and will seek to profit from the gospel. The false prophet will be extravagant rather than prudent and will surround himself (or herself) with the things of this world. The false prophet will be self-indulgent and reckless, will show partiality, and will lack courage and strength.

Notice that Jesus warns against those who seek to persuade the faithful through signs and wonders, and those who seek after signs and wonders instead of Christ. Those whose preaching is focused on signs and wonders, and those whose desire is for signs and wonders instead of Christ, are equally in error. Signs and wonders are not salvific, nor do signs and wonders validate the teaching of a prophet. When the nobleman approached Jesus and besought him to heal his son, Jesus stated: "Except ye see signs and wonders, ye will not believe." The nobleman's reply demonstrated his belief: "Sir, come down ere [before] my child die." Instead of asking for a sign, the father was now expressing his faith. In seeking after healing, he received neither healing nor the presence of

---

[531] Note the implicit rebuke of the prosperity gospel.

[532] The Greek word translated here as fortitude (ἀνδρείαν, *andreian*) can be translated in a variety of ways. The short definitions are *manliness, manhood, manly spirit*. Please note that these are to be interpreted in the fashion of the ancient world, in which certain characteristics were thought to be "manly virtues". In fact, the Latin translation for ἀνδρείαν is *virtus*, from the root word *vir*, meaning man. Thus the opposite of the manly virtues would be the feminine weaknesses (according to the ancient accounting, not the modern approach to gender distinctions).

Christ; in seeking after Christ, the nobleman received both Christ and the healing of his son.

Your House is Left to you Desolate

Thus saith the Almighty Lord, Your house is desolate, I will cast you out as the wind doth stubble (2 Esd 1:33).

Behold, your house is left unto you desolate (Mt 23:38).

The first two chapters of 2 Esdras are known to scholars as 5 Ezra. These chapters are a Christian interpolation written sometime in the 2nd century.[533] Thus, this section was written after the time of Christ, such that 2 Esdras is quoting Christ, rather than Christ quoting 2 Esdras. The interesting thing is that Christ is using an unusual turn of phrase. In the Old Testament, we read many times of the land being made desolate as a punishment for sin, but never of the house of Israel being left desolate. This suggests there may be something to the concept of Supersessionism.[534]

He Trusted in God to Deliver Him

Let us see if his words be true: and let us prove what shall happen in the end of him. **For if the just man be the son of God, he will help him, and deliver him from the hand of his enemies** *[emphasis added] (Wisdom 2:17-18).*

Likewise also the chief priests mocking him, with the scribes and elders, said, He saved others; himself he cannot save. If he be the King of Israel, let him now come down from the cross, and we will believe him. **He trusted in God; let him deliver him now, if he will have him: for he said, I am the Son of God** *[emphasis added] (Mt 27:41-43).*

---

[533] (Davila 2007)

[534] Supersessionism is the teaching that the Church fulfills, replaces, or supersedes the nation of Israel. Some Protestants reject Supersessionism, believing God has one plan for the Jews, another for the Christians. See chapter 46 for more information.

This is a telling passage from the Gospel of Matthew, for the chief priests are using a passage from the Wisdom of Solomon against Jesus, saying that if he is the Son of God, God will deliver Him. There are three things to note here. First, the passage from Wisdom defines its subject as a just man, something the chief priests don't acknowledge. Second, the chief priests are defining themselves as the just man's enemies; this is most certainly inadvertent. Third, the passage containing the phrase used by the chief priests is a lengthy monologue by the ungodly against the just man; this is a clear attempt by Matthew to declare the chief priests to be not only the enemies of Jesus but explicitly aligns the priestly class with the ungodly men described by Ben Sira. (We will discuss the extended passage from Wisdom in greater detail in the next chapter). And finally, like ungodly men always do, the chief priests are not accounting for the resurrection from the dead. They could kill the humanity of the Theanthropos, the God-man Jesus Christ, but the divinity of Jesus Christ could not allow His humanity to stay in the grave. Thus, God did indeed save the just man, just not in the manner the ungodly expected.

Blessed Among Women

Then said Ozias unto her, O daughter, **blessed art thou of the most high God above all the women upon the earth***; and blessed be the Lord God, which hath created the heavens and the earth, which hath directed thee to the cutting off of the head of the chief of our enemies [emphasis added] (Jdt 13:18).*

And she [Elizabeth] spake out with a loud voice, and said, **Blessed art thou among women***, and blessed is the fruit of thy womb [emphasis added] (Lk 1:42).*

After saving her city by beheading Holofernes, the commanding general of the Assyrian army, Judith brings the head to Ozias, one of the governors of Bethulia. This happens in much the same way as the story of the death of Sisera at the hand of Jael, the wife of Heber the Kenite (Jud 5:24). A great deal of similarity exists between the praise heaped upon Jael by Deborah and Barak, and the praise heaped upon Judith by Ozias.

In her greeting of the Virgin Mary, Elizabeth is quoting from Judith, whereas Ozias — in his praise of Judith — is alluding to the praise of Jael. By including this detail, Luke is making the greatness of Mary clear. Whereas both Jael and Judith saved their nation by killing the leader of the nation's enemies, Mary bruised Satan's head by giving birth to the Christ (Ge 3:15).

The Magnificat

The Lord hath cast down the thrones of proud princes, and set up the meek in their stead (Sirach 10:14).

He hath put down the mighty from their seats, and exalted them of low degree (Lk 1:52).

Mary's Magnificat is one of the most well-known prayers in all of the Scriptures. What is less well known is that it is one scripture quotation or citation after another. Given that context, it would be hard to say that citations from Judith and Sirach are not scripture when everything else is. Here is the text of the Magnificat, verse by verse, with all its scriptural quotations and allusions.[535]

46 And Mary said, My soul doth magnify the Lord,
- 1 Sa 2:1 My heart rejoices in the LORD; in the LORD my horn is lifted high.
- Ps 34:2,3 My soul will boast in the LORD; let the afflicted hear and rejoice. Glorify the LORD with me; let us exalt his name together.
- Ps 103:1 Praise the LORD, O my soul; all my inmost being, praise his holy name.

47 *And my spirit hath rejoiced in God my Saviour.*

---

[535] (Jahn 1997, 14-15) The cross-references for the Magnificat come from a number of sources. The versification is from an essay by Curtis A. Jahn.

- Ps 18:46b Exalted be God my Savior!
- Isa 61:10 I delight greatly in the LORD; my soul rejoices in my God. For he has clothed me with garments of salvation and arrayed me in a robe of righteousness.

48a For he hath regarded the low estate of his handmaiden:
- 1 Sam 1:11 And she vowed a vow, and said, O LORD of hosts, if thou wilt indeed look on the affliction of thine handmaid, and remember me, and not forget thine handmaid, but wilt give unto thine handmaid a man child, then I will give him unto the LORD all the days of his life, and there shall no razor come upon his head.
- Ps 138:6 Though the LORD is on high, he looks upon the lowly, but the proud he knows from afar.

48b For, behold, from henceforth all generations shall call me blessed.
- Gen 30:13 And Leah said, Happy am I, for the daughters will call me blessed: and she called his name Asher.
- Lk 1:28 And the angel came in unto her, and said, Hail, thou that art highly favoured, the Lord is with thee: blessed art thou among women.
- Lk 1:42 And she spake out with a loud voice, and said, Blessed art thou among women, and blessed is the fruit of thy womb.

49a For he that is mighty hath done to me great things;
- 1 Sam 2:1 And Hannah prayed, and said, My heart rejoiceth in the LORD, mine horn is exalted in the LORD: my mouth is enlarged over mine enemies; because I rejoice in thy salvation.
- Ps 71:19 Your righteousness reaches to the skies, O God, you who have done great things. Who, O God, is like you?
- Isa 61:10 I will greatly rejoice in the LORD, my soul shall be joyful in my God; for he hath clothed me with the garments of salvation, he hath covered me with the robe of righteousness, as a bridegroom decketh himself with ornaments, and as a bride adorneth herself with her jewels.

- Hab 3:18 Yet I will rejoice in the LORD, I will joy in the God of my salvation.

49b And holy is his name.
- 1 Sa 2:2 There is no one holy like the LORD; there is no one besides you.
- Ps 22:3 You are enthroned as the Holy One; you are the praise of Israel.
- Ps 71:22b I will sing praise to you with the lyre, O Holy One of Israel.
- Ps 89:18 Indeed, our shield belongs to the LORD, our king to the Holy One of Israel.
- Ps 99:3 Let them praise your great and awesome name – he is holy.
- Ps 103:1b Praise his holy name.

50 And his mercy is on them that fear him from generation to generation.
- Ps 103:17 From everlasting to everlasting the LORD's love is with those who fear him, and his righteousness with their children's children.

51a He hath shewed strength with his arm;
- Ps 89:10 Thou hast broken Rahab in pieces, as one that is slain; thou hast scattered thine enemies with thy strong arm.

51b He hath scattered the proud in the imagination of their hearts.
- 1 Sa 2:3 Do not keep talking so proudly or let your mouth speak such arrogance, for the LORD is a God who knows, and by him deeds are weighed.
- 2 Sa 22:28 You save the humble, but your eyes are on the haughty to bring them low.
- Ps 89:10 You crushed Rahab like one of the slain; with your strong arm you scattered your enemies.

52 He hath put down the mighty from their seats, and exalted them of low degree.
- Sirach 10:14 The Lord hath cast down the thrones of proud princes, and set up the meek in their stead.

53a He hath filled the hungry with good things;
- 1 Sa 2:5b but those who were hungry hunger no more.

- Ps 103:5 who satisfies your desires with good things.
- Ps 107:8,9 Let them give thanks to the LORD for his unfailing love and his wonderful deeds for men, for he satisfies the thirsty and fills the hungry with good things.

53b And the rich he hath sent empty away.
- 1 Sam 2:5 Those who were full hire themselves out for food. (Note: This was the prayer of the barren Hannah when she was blessed with a child).

54 He hath holpen his servant Israel, in remembrance of his mercy;
- Ps 98:3 He hath remembered his mercy and his truth toward the house of Israel: all the ends of the earth have seen the salvation of our God.

55a As he spake to our fathers,
- Ps 25:6 Remember, O LORD, your great mercy and love, for they are from of old.
- Ps 98:3 He has remembered his love and his faithfulness to the house of Israel.
- Ps 105:8-11 He remembers his covenant forever, the word he commanded, for a thousand generations, the covenant he made with Abraham, the oath he swore to Isaac. He confirmed it to Jacob as a decree, to Israel as an everlasting covenant: "To you I will give the land of Canaan as the portion you will inherit."
- Ps 136Aff. His love [mercy] endures forever.

55b To Abraham, and to his seed for ever.
- Gen 12:2-3 And I will make of thee a great nation, and I will bless thee, and make thy name great; and thou shalt be a blessing: And I will bless them that bless thee, and curse him that curseth thee: and in thee shall all families of the earth be blessed.
- Ps 147:19 He has revealed his word to Jacob, his laws and decrees to Israel.
- Mic 7:20 You will be true to Jacob, and show mercy to Abraham, as you pledged on oath to our fathers in days long ago.

- Sirach 44:19-22 Abraham was a great father of many people: in glory was there none like unto him; Who kept the law of the most High, and was in covenant with him: he established the covenant in his flesh; and when he was proved, he was found faithful. Therefore he assured him by an oath, that he would bless the nations in his seed, and that he would multiply him as the dust of the earth, and exalt his seed as the stars, and cause them to inherit from sea to sea, and from the river unto the utmost part of the land. With Isaac did he establish likewise for Abraham his father's sake the blessing of all men, and the covenant, And made it rest upon the head of Jacob. He acknowledged him in his blessing, and gave him an heritage, and divided his portions; among the twelve tribes did he part them.

From the East and West

O Jerusalem, look about thee toward the east, and behold the joy that cometh unto thee from God. Lo, thy sons come, whom thou sentest away, **they come gathered together from the east to the west by the word of the Holy One, rejoicing in the glory of God** *[emphasis added] (Baruch 4:36-37).*

There shall be weeping and gnashing of teeth, when ye shall see Abraham, and Isaac, and Jacob, and all the prophets, in the kingdom of God, and you yourselves thrust out. **And they shall come from the east, and from the west, and from the north, and from the south, and shall sit down in the kingdom of God** *[emphasis added] (Luke 13:28-29).*

Our Lord's description of men coming from east and west to rejoice in God quotes Baruch 4:37. Baruch states that those who despoiled Jerusalem will be miserable while Jerusalem will be regathered from the east to the west. However, Jesus turns this around, indicating that the Jewish people will be left out of the Kingdom of God while those who "come gathered together from the east to the west" will be the Gentiles; it is the Gentile nations who will enter into the

Kingdom of God. Baruch spoke of the drawing of the sons of Jerusalem from the east to the west — the return of all the Jewish people to Jerusalem, including those who stayed behind in Babylon and those who had escaped the captivity by hiding in Egypt. Jesus cries out to the Jerusalem that killed the prophets, announcing his constant desire to gather them together (from the east to the west) but they would not.

Jesus does not apply this passage from Baruch literally, but allegorically. For Jesus, this was not the literal Jerusalem, nor were the sons who returned the sons of Abraham after the flesh. Those who insist "the literal interpretation is the only interpretation" are misguided at best. Despite what the dispensationalists will say, the Church has indeed superseded the Jewish people, just as the "natural branches" were broken off and the "wild olive tree" was grafted in (Rom 11:16-24). Our Lord sought to gather the people of Israel together, to invite them to His wedding feast, but they would not come (Lk 14:16-25). Instead, he gathered in the Gentiles "from the east, and from the west, and from the north, and from the south," into his wedding feast, into the Kingdom of God, into the spiritual Jerusalem.

Fall by the Edge of the Sword

The stroke of the whip maketh marks in the flesh: but the stroke of the tongue breaketh the bones. Many have **fallen by the edge of the sword***: but not so many as have fallen by the tongue [emphasis added] (Sirach 28:17-18).*

And they shall **fall by the edge of the sword***, and shall be led away captive into all nations: and Jerusalem shall be trodden down of the Gentiles, until the times of the Gentiles be fulfilled [emphasis added] (Lk 21:24).*

There are 27 verses in the Hebrew Scriptures having to do with being killed by the sword, slain by the sword, or dying by the sword.[536] The specific idea of the "edge of the sword" is not found in the Hebrew Scriptures, but in the book of Sirach. It is interesting to me that Jesus removes this phrase from its context and repurposes it. In its original context, Sirach is talking about the power of the tongue to harm, saying the tongue destroys more people than the sword ever could.[537] Jesus is not speaking morally but is instead prophesying about the coming destruction of Jerusalem. The words of the chief priests and the people — "Crucify Him" — would lead to the destruction of Jerusalem and the end of the Hebrew people as a nation.

Who has Ascended into Heaven

Who hath gone up into heaven, and taken her, and brought her down from the clouds? (Baruch 3:29)

And no man hath ascended up to heaven, but he that came down from heaven, even the Son of man which is in heaven (Jn 3:13).[538]

Baruch is speaking here of Wisdom dwelling in the heavens and which is, therefore, unobtainable to humanity (in an ultimate sense, of course). Christians understand Wisdom to be an adumbration of Christ — that is to say, Wisdom is a faint representation in human terms of the glory that is the

---

[536] (Anonymous, 28 Bible verses about Killed With The Sword n.d.) Numbers 14:43; Jeremiah 42:16; 44:12,13,27; Job 15:22; Ezekiel 17:21; 21:12; 23:25; 24:21; 26:6,8, 11; 28:23; 29:8; 30:4,6; 32:12,20; 33:27; 35:8; Daniel 11:33; Hosea 7:16; 13:16; Amos 7:17; 9:10.

[537] James expresses a similar notion about the tongue in James 3:1-13.

[538] Scholars disagree as to whether Jesus answer to Nicodemus, which begins at verse ten, continues through to verse 21. Some hold that it does, while others believe that the majority of this passage is John's commentary on Jesus' words. The use of the conjunction "and" to begin sentences is consistent with the way Hebrew uses "and" to connect clauses, suggesting verse 10-21 may well be a single unbroken speech.

Son of God. John is drawing our attention to the connection between the passage in Baruch, which then makes the allegorical connection between Wisdom and Christ plain. Thus, while no one could ascend into heaven and bring Wisdom down to earth, Wisdom personified could come to us, become one with us, and ascend to heaven, thereby opening the pathway for us to attain Wisdom — which is Christ Himself.

God Shows No Partiality

Give unto the most High according as he hath enriched thee; and as thou hast gotten, give with a cheerful eye. For the Lord recompenseth, and will give thee seven times as much. Do not think to corrupt with gifts; for such he will not receive: and trust not to unrighteous sacrifices; for **the Lord is judge, and with him is no respect of persons** *[emphasis added] (Sirach 35:10-12).*

Then Peter opened his mouth, and said, Of a truth I perceive that **God is no respecter of persons** *[emphasis added] (Act 10:34).*

Glory, honour, and peace, to every man that worketh good, to the Jew first, and also to the Gentile: For **there is no respect of persons with God** *[emphasis added] (Rom 2:10-11).*

But of these who seemed to be somewhat, (whatsoever they were [Judaizers], it maketh no matter to me: **God accepteth no man's person**:) *for they who seemed to be somewhat in conference added nothing to me [emphasis added] (Gal 2:6).*

The statement by Peter that God is no respecter of persons is a direct quote from Sirach 35:12. The statement by Paul alludes to it. The idea in Sirach has to do with true vs. false righteousness. Jesus expresses this using the example of the widow's mite. The widow's gift was greater by far than those of the rich men who gave from their disposable income, whereas the widow gave that which might well have gone for food, shelter, and clothing (Lu 21:1-4). The idea that God does not prefer the wealthy over the poor was just as radical in Jesus day as it is today. The disciples were astonished at Jesus' teaching that the rich have a harder time getting into heaven than the poor; they assumed wealth was a sign of God's blessing (Mt 20:24-26).

The idea contained in Sirach was enlarged in Acts to include not just the difference between the righteous and the unrighteous, or between the rich and the poor. We see Peter and Paul talking about the Jew and the Gentile, and how God does not prefer one over the other. The concept the Jews had of themselves was that they were God's chosen people and therefore superior to the Gentiles; when Peter quoted from Sirach and applied this to the Gentiles, it represented a fundamental shift and was something many Jewish Christians had difficulty accepting. Paul also combated the Judaizers throughout much of his ministry and alluded to Sirach as part of his argument against them.

False Gods of God and Silver

But miserable are they, and in dead things is their hope, **who call them gods, which are the works of men's hands, gold and silver***, to shew art in, and resemblances of beasts, or a stone good for nothing, the work of an ancient hand [emphasis added] (Wisdom 13:10).*

Forasmuch then as we are the offspring of God, we ought not to think that the Godhead is like unto **gold, or silver, or stone, graven by art and man's device** *[emphasis added] (Acts 17:29).*

In Paul's speech on Mars Hill, the phrase "gold and silver" comes directly from Wisdom 13:10. The phrase "gold and silver" is used elsewhere in the New Testament, but only Paul uses the phrase in connection with the argument from Wisdom. Paul's use of this argument is interesting. Despite its being available in the Greek language, the Greek philosophers would not be expected to have intimate knowledge of Jewish wisdom literature and would likely not have caught the reference. Paul is not using this quotation purely as a rhetorical device, but rather because the text had so permeated his thinking that its words became his words.

A similar thing happens in the opening of the epistle to the Romans, where Paul writes: "[the ungodly] changed the glory of the uncorruptible God into an image made like to corruptible man, and to birds, and fourfooted beasts, and creeping things" (Rom 1:23). This verse sums up the entire passage in Wisdom 13:1-19, which describes a man who takes some wood and uses it to make serving dishes and uses the leftover wood to make an idol unto which he prays. Of the same tree, he makes for himself something praiseworthy and something useless.

Besides the passage in Wisdom 13, the same thought is repeated elsewhere in Wisdom, and the allusion would have been clear to Paul's readers.

But for the foolish devices of their wickedness, wherewith being deceived they worshipped serpents void of reason, and vile beasts, thou didst send a multitude of unreasonable beasts upon them for vengeance (Wisdom 11:15).

For they went astray very far in the ways of error, and held them for gods, which even among the beasts of their enemies were despised, being deceived, as children of no understanding (Wisdom 12:24).

The Mind of the Lord

For what man is he that can know **the counsel of God***? or who can think what the will of the Lord is [emphasis added] (Wisdom 9:13)?*

For who hath known the **mind of the Lord***? or who hath been his counsellor [emphasis added] (Rom 11:34)?*

For who hath known the **mind of the Lord***, that he may instruct him? But we have the mind of Christ [emphasis added] (1 Cor 2:16).*

Paul is paraphrasing this passage — but it is such a close paraphrase that it must of necessity be counted among the quotations rather than the allusions. The phrase "mind of the Lord" is used in the book of Leviticus (Lev 24:12) but in the context of judging a man who had used the Lord's name in vain. Paul's use of the phrase comes from Wisdom, where the idea is an indication of the distance between God and us. If God is greater than us, is truly the creator of all, and transcends this plane of existence, then by what right do we judge God, or instruct Him in the outworking of His plans? On the other hand, we have the mind of Christ in the Scriptures as preserved by the Church.

All Things are not Expedient

The belly devoureth all meats, yet is one meat better than another. ...My son, prove thy soul in thy life, and see what is evil for it, and give not that unto it. **For all things are not profitable** *for all men, neither hath every soul pleasure in every thing. Be not unsatiable in any dainty thing, nor too greedy upon meats: For excess of meats bringeth sickness, and surfeiting will turn into choler. By surfeiting have many perished; but he that taketh heed prolongeth his life [emphasis added] (Sirach 36:18; 37:27-31).*

All things are lawful unto me, but **all things are not expedient***: all things are lawful for me, but I will not be brought under the power of any. Meats for the belly, and the belly for meats: but God shall destroy both it and them [emphasis added] (1 Cor 6:12-13).*

While we find warnings against gluttony in the Old Testament (as in Proverbs 23), Paul appears to be using Sirach as his source material. There is a close correlation between "all things are not profitable" and "all things are not expedient," so much so that they approach unto balanced parallelism. Paul repeats himself by yet again copying Sirach when he says: "All things are lawful for me, but all things are not expedient: all things are lawful for me, but all things edify not" (1 Cor 10:23). Moreover, in Sirach we have the idea that excess brings sickness, choler, and death; in 1 Corinthians we have the idea that to be a glutton is to fall under their power; to fall under the power of temporal things is to fall under the power of death.

Fathers Under the Cloud

For the whole creature in his proper kind was fashioned again anew, serving the peculiar commandments that were given unto them, that thy children might be kept without hurt: As namely, **a cloud shadowing the camp***; and where water stood before, dry land appeared; and out of the Red sea a way without impediment; and out of the violent stream a green field: Wherethrough all the people went that were defended with thy hand, seeing thy marvellous strange wonders. For they went at large like horses, and leaped like lambs, praising thee, O Lord, who hadst delivered them. For they were yet mindful of the things that were done while they sojourned in the strange land, how the ground brought forth flies instead of cattle, and how the river cast up a multitude of frogs instead of fishes.* **But afterwards they saw a new generation of fowls, when, being led with their appetite, they asked delicate meats. For quails came up unto them from the sea for their contentment.** *And punishments came upon the sinners not without former signs by the force of thunders: for they suffered justly according to their own wickedness, insomuch as they used a more hard and hateful behaviour toward strangers [emphasis added] (Wisdom 19:6-13).*

Moreover, brethren, I would not that ye should be ignorant, how that **all our fathers were under the cloud**,[539] *and all passed through the sea; And were all baptized unto Moses in the cloud and in the sea; And did all eat the same spiritual*

---

[539] (Spence-Jones and Exell, Pulpit Commentary 1897) One of the few Protestant commentaries to reference the Wisdom of Solomon in their explanation of 1 Corinthians is Spence-Jones and Exell's Pulpit Commentary.

meat; And did all drink the same spiritual drink: for they drank of that spiritual Rock that followed them: and that Rock was Christ. **But with many of them God was not well pleased: for they were overthrown in the wilderness. Now these things were our examples, to the intent we should not lust after evil things, as they also lusted.** *Neither be ye idolaters, as were some of them; as it is written, The people sat down to eat and drink, and rose up to play. Neither let us commit fornication, as some of them committed, and fell in one day three and twenty thousand. Neither let us tempt Christ, as some of them also tempted, and were destroyed of serpents [emphasis added] (1 Cor 10:1-9).*

While there are references to the glory cloud and the pillar of cloud in the Torah and the Psalms, these are not used by Paul as his source material. Paul is drawing from the Wisdom of Solomon and prividing a Christological focus. Paul is more descriptive of the sins the people committed and their punishments, and he is using them as examples to keep in mind during this life as an encouragement to holy living.

Sacrifices to Devils

For ye provoked him that made you by sacrificing unto devils, and not to God (Baruch 4:7).

But I say, that the things which the Gentiles sacrifice, they sacrifice to devils, and not to God: and I would not that ye should have fellowship with devils (1 Cor 10:20).

In the early part of 1 Corinthians chapter 10, Paul reminds the Corinthians of the exodus of the Hebrews from the land of Egypt, using Wisdom as his source material. Paul is continuing with that theme here by reminding us that while Moses was on Mt. Sinai receiving the Ten Commandments, the children of Israel had made for themselves an idol and were worshipping it. Paul expands upon the passage from Baruch by stating that all the Gentile gods were demons; that the meat purchased from the pagan temples had been offered to demons.

Prayer for a Spirit of Wisdom

Wherefore I prayed, and understanding was given me: I called upon God, and the **spirit of wisdom** *came to me [emphasis added] (Wisdom 7:7).*

That the God of our Lord Jesus Christ, the Father of glory, may give unto you the **spirit of wisdom** *and revelation in the knowledge of him [emphasis added] (Eph 1:17).*

Paul uses the Old Testament example from Wisdom when writing to the Ephesians. However, unlike the Old Testament exemplar, Paul does not pray for himself. Instead prays for the Ephesians, that *they* would receive the "spirit of wisdom and revelation." This is a wonderful example of intercessory prayer, the type of prayer that is to be normative for Christians. The goal is not to pray for ourselves; instead, we pray for others.

Breastplate of Righteousness

He shall put on **righteousness as a breastplate**, *and true judgment instead of an helmet [emphasis added] (Wis. 5:18).*

Stand therefore, having your loins girt about with truth, and having on the **breastplate of righteousness** *[emphasis added] (Eph 6:14).*

Paul's exhortation to "Put on the whole armour of God" uses a metaphor that comes from the Wisdom of Solomon. We will discuss this in greater detail later, but for now, it is enough to point out that Paul's use of the phrase "breastplate of righteousness" quotes the Wisdom of Solomon.

King of Kings

But the **King of kings** *moved Antiochus' mind against this wicked wretch, and Lysias informed the king that this man was the cause of all mischief, so that the king commanded to bring him unto Berea, and to put him to death, as the manner is in that place [emphasis added] (2 Macc. 13:4).*

*Which in his times he shall shew, who is the blessed and only Potentate, the **King of kings**, and Lord of lords [emphasis added] (1 Tim 6:15).*

*These shall make war with the Lamb, and the Lamb shall overcome them: for he is Lord of lords, and **King of kings**: and they that are with him are called, and chosen, and faithful [emphasis added] (Re 17:14).*

*And he hath on his vesture and on his thigh a name written, **KING OF KINGS**, AND LORD OF LORDS [emphasis added] (Re 19:16).*

The Protestant Old Testament contains three uses of the phrase "King of Kings": Ezra 7:12; Eze 26:7; and Da 2:37. In each case, the reference is to the pagan kings Nebuchadnezzar and Artaxerxes. The only time "King of Kings" is used of God is in 2 Maccabees 13:14. The New Testament use of this phrase comes from 2 Maccabees, not from the Hebrew Scriptures.

Enoch

He pleased God, and was beloved of him: so that living among sinners he was translated (Wis 4:10).

Enoch pleased the Lord, and was translated, being an example of repentance to all generations (Sir 44:16).

By faith Enoch was translated that he should not see death; and was not found, because God had translated him: for before his translation he had this testimony, that he pleased God (Heb 11:5).

In Genesis, we read of Enoch: "And Enoch walked with God: and he was not; for God took him" (Ge 5:24). The description of Enoch in the book of Hebrews as one who "pleased God" and of his being "translated" comes from the Apocrypha. For additional information on Enoch and the New Testament, see the Appendix: Second Temple Writings and the Bible.

Drooping Hands and Weak Knees

*A wicked woman abateth the courage, maketh an heavy countenance and a wounded heart: a woman that will not comfort her husband in distress maketh **weak hands and feeble knees** [emphasis added] (Sirach 25:23).*

*Wherefore lift up the **hands which hang down, and the feeble knees** [emphasis added] (Heb 12:12).*

The description of "drooping hands" and "weak knees" comes from Sirach 25:23. In this passage Sirach is referencing the "wicked woman," and his description is similar to that used when the prophets referred to the Hebrew nation as an adulterous wife. The writer of Hebrews intends to bring to mind the passage from Sirach, which serves as a warning against being dragged down by the Hebrews, who are the adulterous wife.

Quick to Hear, Slow to Respond

*Be **swift to hear**; and let thy life be sincere; and **with patience give answer** [emphasis added] (Sirach 5:11).*

*Wherefore, my beloved brethren, let every man be **swift to hear, slow to speak**, slow to wrath: For the wrath of man worketh not the righteousness of God [emphasis added] (Jas 1:19-20).*

When James quotes Sirach, he expands upon the specific quote when to the phrase "slow to speak," he adds "slow to wrath." James seems to be saying that our wrath makes us quick to speak; and likewise, being quick to speak makes us wrathful. It is a vicious cycle. However, there is more to this passage than meets the eye. The larger context of Sirach has to do with not inviting the wrath of God. Therefore, being slow to speak serves to avoid adding sin unto sin, thereby falling under the wrath of God. Both mercy and wrath come from the Lord, as it says in Sirach. Therefore, let us not presume upon the mercy and forbearance of God; let us not take God for granted.

Faith Reckoned as Righteousness

Was not Abraham found faithful in temptation, and **it was imputed unto him for righteousness** [emphasis added] (1 Macc 2:52)?

Was not Abraham our father justified by works, when he had offered Isaac his son upon the altar? Seest thou how faith wrought with his works, and by works was faith made perfect? **And the scripture was fulfilled which saith,** Abraham believed God, and **it was imputed unto him for righteousness**: and he was called the Friend of God [emphasis added] (James 2:21-23).

James cites as scripture a passage found in the first book of Maccabees. The apostle Paul also uses the same passage from 1 Maccabees in his extended argument regarding Abraham's faith (Rom 4:13-22). You well might argue that James is quoting from Genesis 15:6: "And he believed in the LORD; and he counted it to him for righteousness." The Genesis passage is a close approximation to the one James quotes, but the exact quotation is from 1 Maccabees.

Judgment According to Works

As his mercy is great, so is his correction also: **he judgeth a man according to his works**. The sinner shall not escape with his spoils: and the patience of the godly shall not be frustrate [emphasis added] (Sirach 16:12-13).

And if ye call on the Father, **who without respect of persons judgeth according to every man's work**, pass the time of your sojourning here in fear [emphasis added] (1 Pet 1:17).

The passage from 1 Peter is a difficult one for many Protestants because Peter seems to be arguing for works righteousness, the idea that we can work our way to heaven.

A satisfactory exploration of the matter is outside the scope of this book.[540] Peter is quoting from Sirach, a method which was used to bring to mind the extended meditation from Sirach on the mercy and judgment of God. We find the key to 1 Peter in Sirach 16:13, which states the sinner shall not escape, nor shall the righteous be frustrated. The apostle Paul speaks of those who with "patient continuance in well doing seek for glory and honour and immortality, eternal life" (Rom 2:7). Paul exhorts the Galatians to "not be weary in well doing: for in due season we shall reap, if we faint not" (Gal 6:9). Peter himself reminds those who suffer to "commit the keeping of their souls to him in well doing, as unto a faithful Creator" (1 Pet 4:19).

---

[540] It is worth noting that none of those accused of teaching "works righteousness" are doing any such thing. Roman Catholics may come the closest, but this is due to a selective reading of Roman Catholic doctrine, cherry-picking texts that appear to reinforce existing prejudices and ignoring the more nuanced passages. James says, "faith without works is dead" (Jas 2:20, 26), but James never says those same works are righteous or salvific.

46: Allusions

Often in the New Testament we allusions to an Old Testament passage. We understand the New Testament passage in connection with a related passage from the Old Testament. The allusion is not formally stated, but is implicit in the text; the hearer was expected to be familiar with the Old Testament and to understand the context.

In addition, there are more allusions to the Apocrypha in the book of Revelation than in any other New Testament book. It gives one pause when considering the importance of the book of Revelation in the Protestant mind.

Prophetic Passages

Some of the passages from the Apocrypha speak prophetically of Christ and are comparable in importance to those in the book of Isaiah — in particular when the godly or the righteous man is compared against the ungodly or unrighteous. Additional Christological source material comes from the various personifications of Wisdom; just as in the Hebrew Scriptures, these passages are an adumbration of Christ.

The Gospels and the Wisdom of Solomon

Regarding the allusions to the Apocrypha in the New Testament, let us begin our discussion with an examination of an extended passage from the Wisdom of Solomon. In Wisdom chapter 2, we have a description of the ungodly man and his reaction to and oppression of the righteous. This passage is generally applicable to the relationship between the ungodly and the righteous person, whoever he (or she) may be; however, this passage is specifically applicable to the relationship between Jesus (the ultimate Righteous Man), and the religious and political leaders of His day. I would argue that the gospels are the fulfillment of this passage from the Wisdom of Solomon. With that in mind, let us examine this passage.

Let us oppress the poor righteous man, let us not spare the widow, nor reverence the ancient gray hairs of the aged. (Wisdom 2:10)

This passage begins with the oppression of the poor, which is a recurring theme of the Old and New Testaments. The book of Proverbs goes so far as to say: "A righteous man regardeth the life of his beast: but the tender mercies of the wicked are cruel" (Pr 12:10). Not only does a righteous man care for the poor man and the aged, but also the creatures entrusted to his care (Gen 1:26).

Let our strength be the law of justice: for that which is feeble is found to be nothing worth (Wisdom 2:11).

The ungodly use the law as a weapon against the poor, the aged, and all creation. To the ungodly, obedience to the letter of the law excuses a lack of mercy. Against this argument, the prophet Hosea argues that God desires mercy rather than sacrifice (Hos 6:6). To those who pride themselves on their adherence to the law, Jesus argues that judgment, mercy, and faith are the "weightier matters of the law," which must be done without neglecting the law itself (Matt 23:23).

Therefore let us lie in wait for the righteous; because he is not for our turn, and he is clean contrary to our doings: he upbraideth us with our offending the law, and objecteth to our infamy the transgressings of our education (Wisdom 2:12).

Here is where this passage takes a turn; while generally applicable to the relationship between the ungodly and the righteous, from this point onward this passage applies to the relationship between the ungodly and The Righteous One, who is Jesus Christ. In the Gospels, we read how Jesus upbraided the religious leaders, and how they, in turn, plotted against him. We read how they tried to trap Jesus with questions designed to elicit answers which would have been unsatisfactory to the people or would have put Him at odds with the Roman authorities.[541]

He professeth to have the knowledge of God: and he calleth himself the child of the Lord (Wisdom 2:13).

This is most certainly true of Our Lord. We find the first example in the story of the boy Jesus in the temple. Not only were the teachers astonished at His understanding, but when His parents upbraided Him Jesus asked them why they didn't know He must be about His Father's business (Lk 2:41-50).

He was made to reprove our thoughts (Wisdom 2:14).

Jesus fulfills this passage in the healing of the man with palsy (Matt 9:1-8). Jesus first announces to the man the forgiveness of sins; the scribes thought was blasphemous because only God can forgive sins. Jesus reproved them for their thoughts, after which he demonstrated His power to forgive sins by healing the palsied man.

He is grievous unto us even to behold: for his life is not like other men's, his ways are of another fashion (Wisdom 2:15).

In the Gospel of Luke, we read how Jesus called Levi the tax collector. Levi then gave a great feast at his house with other tax collectors present. Seeing this, the scribes and Pharisees complained: "Why do You eat and drink with tax collectors and sinners?" Jesus response was that just as a doctor takes care of those who are sick; so too He ministers to those who know themselves to be sinners (Lk 5:30-31). While dining with Simon the Pharisee, a sinful women "began to wash His feet with her tears, and wiped them with the hair of her head: and she kissed His feet and anointed them with the fragrant oil." At this, the Pharisee murmured in his heart against Jesus for allowing Himself to be touched by a sinful woman. Jesus then rebuked the Pharisee for

---

[541] The question regarding whether it was lawful to pay taxes to the Roman authorities comes to mind; see Matt 22:17ff

failing to follow the standards of hospitality by having Jesus' feet washed before dinner, whereas the sinful woman had done this and more. To the woman, he said her sins were forgiven and that her faith had saved her (Lk 7:36-50). To the Lawyer who sought to justify himself in his own eyes, Jesus gave the Parable of the Good Samaritan, a parable in which the Priest and Levite are the villains, while the hated Samaritan was the hero for showing mercy to someone to whom he had no relationship, no kinship, and no expectation of reward (Lk 10:25-37).

We are esteemed of him as counterfeits: he abstaineth from our ways as from filthiness: he pronounceth the end of the just to be blessed, and maketh his boast that God is his father (Wisdom 2:16).

In the Gospel of Matthew, Jesus denounces the counterfeit religiosity of the Pharisees, those who clean the outside of the cup and platter, while inside they are full of extortion and excess. (Matt 23:25) In the Beatitudes, Jesus pronounces the blessedness of the righteous (Matt 5:3-12). The gospels use the life of Christ as an illustration of this passage from Wisdom; the good works that Jesus does enrage the ungodly, as does his description of God as His Father (Luke 10:22; John 5:28; 10:30). Thus, the three clauses from this verse apply to the life of Christ.

Let us see if his words be true: and let us prove what shall happen in the end of him. For if the just man be the son of God, he will help him, and deliver him from the hand of his enemies. Let us examine him with despitefulness and torture, that we may know his meekness, and prove his patience. Let us condemn him with a shameful death: for by his own saying he shall be respected. (Wisdom 2:17-20)

These final verses describe the state of mind and the actions of the Chief Priests and Pharisees regarding the death of Christ, and specifically foretell the words of the rulers of the Jews at the foot of the cross.

The Jewish trial was done contrary to the law, using false witnesses (Matt 26:59). After accusing Jesus of blasphemy, the scribes and elders spit in Jesus' face and beat him with their hands, mocking him by saying: "Prophesy unto us, thou Christ, Who is he that smote thee? (Matt 26:67-68). After delivering Jesus to the Pontius Pilate, the Romans stripped him, whipped him, put a crown of thorns on His head, mocked Him, and crucified Him (Mt 27:27-31; Jn 19:1-18).

During Jesus' examination before the Sanhedrin, Jesus said nothing until he was asked whether he was "the Christ, the Son of God" (Mk 14:53-62). During Jesus' examination before Herod, Jesus said nothing (Lk 23:6-9). Jesus did not try to justify Himself, nor did he beg for mercy, but "as a sheep before her shearers is dumb, so he openeth not his mouth" (Isa 53:7).

There was nothing more shameful than to be stripped naked and die a criminal's death on the cross. The gospels state not only that the Jewish leaders desired the death of Jesus, but they specifically wanted the Romans to crucify Him (Jn 19:6). The author of Hebrews states that Jesus "endured the cross, despising the shame," and is now seated at the right hand of God. (Heb 12:2).

Finally, at the foot of the cross, the rulers of the Jews use the words from Wisdom to mock Christ. They sneer: "He saved others; let him save himself, if he be Christ, the chosen of God" (Lk 23:35). The soldiers mock Christ, saying: "If thou be the king of the Jews, save thyself" (Lk 23:37). Finally, one of the thieves crucified with Christ blasphemes: "If thou be Christ, save thyself and us" (Lk 23:39).

It is quite clear that this passage from Wisdom is prophetic, in that it is broadly descriptive of the life and death of Christ. Therefore, the arguments of some that the Apocrypha are not prophetic and therefore are not scripture fall to the ground.[542]

---

[542] (Geisler and MacKenzie 1995, 196-197) Normal Geisler and Ralph MacKenzie write: "Contrary to the Roman Catholic argument from

The Slaughter of the Holy Innocents

For a manifest reproof of that commandment, whereby the infants were slain, thou gavest unto them abundance of water by a means which they hoped not for (Wis 11:7).

Then Herod, when he saw that he was mocked of the wise men, was exceeding wroth, and sent forth, and slew all the children that were in Bethlehem, and in all the coasts thereof, from two years old and under, according to the time which he had diligently enquired of the wise men (Matt 2:16).

Jesus answered and said unto her, If thou knewest the gift of God, and who it is that saith to thee, Give me to drink; thou wouldest have asked of him, and he would have given thee living water. The woman saith unto him, Sir, thou hast nothing to draw with, and the well is deep: from whence then hast thou that living water? Art thou greater than our father Jacob, which gave us the well, and drank thereof himself, and his children, and his cattle? Jesus answered and said unto her, Whosoever drinketh of this water shall thirst again: But whosoever drinketh of the water that I shall give him shall never thirst; but the water that I shall give him shall be in him a well of water springing up into everlasting life (Jn 4:11-14).

This passage from the Wisdom of Solomon is part of a paean to Wisdom. The specific passage in Wisdom references the tenth plague upon Egypt, the death of the firstborn, as well as the many ways in which God provided water in the desert to the Israelites fleeing the land of Egypt. Typologically speaking, the slain infants foreshadow the death of the Holy Innocents at the hands of Herod the Great. We should note

---

Christian usage, the true test of canonicity is propheticity. ... There is strong evidence that the apocryphal books are not prophetic. But since propheticity is the test for canonicity, this would eliminate the Apocrypha from the canon." But Geisler and MacKenzie are wrong, for not only are there prophetic passages in the Apocrypha, but there are books in the Protestant Old Testament, like Esther, which contain no prophetic elements.

that Matthew specifically references the prophecy of Jeremiah. This does not, however, prevent us from noting the typological connection between Wisdom and the Gospel of Matthew.

But this does not exhaust the riches of this passage from the Wisdom of Solomon. Besides the reference to the tenth plague upon Egypt, Wisdom also mentions the abundance of water given God's people in the desert. The abundance of water prefigures the rivers of living water Jesus spoke of to the Samaritan woman.

Source Material

The New Testament often uses phrases or ideas from the Apocrypha as source material. Our Lord uses phrases or concepts which come directly from the Apocrypha (such as the Golden Rule). In other cases, the Jewish leaders raise questions derived from the Apocrypha (such as the women with seven husbands). None of these cases, taken individually, constitute proof that the Apocrypha are part of Sacred Scripture. When taken collectively, these passages are more difficult to dismiss.

Treasures in Heaven

Many therefore have refused to lend for other men's ill dealing, fearing to be defrauded. Yet have thou patience with a man in poor estate, and delay not to shew him mercy. Help the poor for the commandment's sake, and turn him not away because of his poverty. Lose thy money for thy brother and thy friend, and let it not rust under a stone to be lost. **Lay up thy treasure according to the commandments of the most High***, and it shall bring thee more profit than gold. Shut up alms in thy storehouses: and it shall deliver thee from all affliction. It shall fight for thee against thine enemies better than a mighty shield and strong spear [emphasis added] (Sir 29:7-13).*

Lay not up for yourselves treasures upon earth, where moth and rust doth corrupt, and where thieves break through and *steal: But **lay up for yourselves treasures in heaven**, where neither moth nor rust doth corrupt, and where thieves do not break through nor steal: For where your treasure is, there will your heart be also [emphasis added] (Matt 6:19-21).*

This passage from Sirach (a.k.a. Ecclesiasticus) is alluded to by Jesus in the Gospel of Matthew when he tells his followers to "lay up for yourselves treasures in heaven." As is common in Jesus' teachings, he expects his hearers to understand that he is alluding to a larger teaching and interpreting it for them. Thus, Jesus words in this passage from the Sermon on the Mount refer to the context of the statement in Sirach, expounding and expanding upon it.

Interestingly, the passage in Sirach is part of a larger passage regarding not hoarding wealth but instead helping the poor. Sirach tells us to "Lay up thy treasure according to the commandments of the most High," and to "Shut up alms in thy storehouses." To lay up treasure according to God's commandments is to lay up treasures in heaven, and to build a storehouse of alms.

The storehouse of alms is not a storehouse of merits. These are the good works spoken of in the book of James, where he writes: "Faith without works is dead" (Jas 2:20). The man of faith will lay up for himself treasures in heaven by helping the poor and needy, in the same manner in which God helped us by sending us his Only Begotten Son.

The Woman with Seven Husbands

*It came to pass the same day, that in Ecbatana a city of Média Sara the daughter of Ragúel was also reproached by her father's maids; because that she had been married to seven husbands, whom Asmodéus the evil spirit had killed, before they had lain with her. Dost thou not know, said they, that thou hast strangled thine husbands? **thou hast had already seven husbands**, neither wast thou named after any of them [emphasis added] (Tobit 3:7-8).*

The same day came to him the Sadducees, which say that there is no resurrection, and asked him, Saying, Master, Moses said, If a man die, having no children, his brother shall marry his wife, and raise up seed unto his brother. **Now there were with us seven brethren:** *and the first, when he had married a wife, deceased, and, having no issue, left his wife unto his brother: Likewise the second also, and the third, unto the seventh. And last of all the woman died also.* **Therefore in the resurrection whose wife shall she be of the seven?** *for they all had her [emphasis added] (Mt 22:23-28; cf Mk 12:18-23; Lk 20:27-33).*

The Pharisees, Sadducees, lawyers, and scribes would often ask Jesus difficult and tricky questions in an attempt to force Jesus into saying something that would alienate Him from one or the other factions of Judaism. In this particular case, the Sadducees question Jesus about the validity of the resurrection. The question they ask references the story of Sara around which the book of Tobit revolves. This particular reference is found in the three synoptic gospels, indicating its importance. The Sadducees' story uses the framework of the story of Sara, along with the Mosaic law that a brother is to raise a son to his brother's widow (Deu 25:5-6).

The Desolating Sacrilege

Now the fifteenth day of the month Casleu, in the hundred forty and fifth year, they set up **the abomination of desolation** *upon the altar, and builded idol altars throughout the cities of Juda on every side [emphasis added] (1 Macc 1:54).*

So Maccabeus called his men together unto the number of six thousand, and exhorted them not to be stricken with terror of the enemy, nor to fear the great multitude of the heathen, who came wrongly against them; but to fight manfully, And to set before their eyes the injury that they had unjustly done to the holy place, and the cruel handling of the city, whereof they made a mockery, and also the taking away of the government of their forefathers (2 Macc. 8:16-17).

*When ye therefore shall see **the abomination of desolation**, spoken of by Daniel the prophet, stand in the holy place, (whoso readeth, let him understand). **Then let them which be in Judaea flee into the mountains** [emphasis added] (Mt 24:15-16).*

Jesus specifically refers to the "abomination of desolation" as coming from the book of Daniel. Indeed, this abomination is described in three passages: Dan 9:27; 11:31; and 12:11. In the book of Daniel, it is not clear exactly what this is referring to. The reference would have been clear to the Jews of Jesus' day, as the events described in the books of the Maccabees were well known. Jesus is tying the prophecy of Daniel with its fulfillment during the reign of Antiochus IV Epiphanies. Antiochus set up an altar to Zeus in the Second Temple and sacrificed pigs on the altar. Jesus is prophesying a second abomination of desolation, which occurred when the Romans destroyed Jerusalem, torn down the temple, and the Christians fled into the wilderness.

The Parable of the Sower

The children of the ungodly shall not bring forth many branches: but are as unclean roots upon a hard rock. The weed growing upon every water and bank of a river shall be pulled up before all grass. Bountifulness is as a most fruitful garden, and mercifulness endureth for ever (Sirach 40:15-17).

Hearken; Behold, there went out a sower to sow: And it came to pass, as he sowed, some fell by the way side, and the fowls of the air came and devoured it up. And some fell on stony ground, where it had not much earth; and immediately it sprang up, because it had no depth of earth: But when the sun was up, it was scorched; and because it had no root, it withered away. And some fell among thorns, and the thorns grew up, and choked it, and it yielded no fruit. And other fell on good ground, and did yield fruit that sprang up and increased; and brought forth, some thirty, and some sixty, and some an hundred. And he said unto them, He that hath ears to hear, let him hear (Mk 4:5-9).

In the Parable of the Sower, Jesus is alluding to the passage from Sirach, which has some of the same thematic material, as well as some of the same metaphors (in particular, the seed that fell upon the rock. Jesus uses this same imagery in the Parable of the Tares: at the time of harvest, the tares are separated from the wheat; in like fashion, Sirach mentions the weeds growing on the bank of the river being pulled up before the grass.

Jesus does not stop at using the existing imagery, but expands upon it, providing more detail and advancing the thematic content, thereby connecting it with the spreading of the Gospel.

Where Their Worm Does Not Die

Woe to the nations that rise up against my kindred! the Lord Almighty will take vengeance of them in the day of judgment, in **putting fire and worms in their flesh; and they shall feel them, and weep for ever** *[emphasis added] (Jdt 16:17).*

And if thy hand offend thee, cut it off: it is better for thee to enter into life maimed, than having two hands to go into hell, into the fire that never shall be quenched: **Where their worm dieth not, and the fire is not quenched.**

And if thy foot offend thee, cut it off: it is better for thee to enter halt into life, than having two feet to be cast into hell, into the fire that never shall be quenched: **Where their worm dieth not, and the fire is not quenched.**

And if thine eye offend thee, pluck it out: it is better for thee to enter into the kingdom of God with one eye, than having two eyes to be cast into hell fire: **Where their worm dieth not, and the fire is not quenched** *[emphasis added] (Mk 9:43-48).*

Jesus uses a Semitic metaphor when He states that it if your hand causes you to sin, it would be better to lose your hand than be cast into Hell: "Where their worm dieth not, and the fire is not quenched."[543] Some have taken this metaphor literally and have mutilated themselves, not understanding the underlying meaning.[544] J. Vernon McGee once said the best way for a child to avoid stealing cookies is not to stand near the cookie jar. In other words, cut yourself off from whatever is tempting you to sin. The interesting thing here is that Jesus borrows His imagery of Hell directly from Judith's song of thanksgiving. The imagery of hellfire used by Christ does not appear in the Hebrew Scriptures, but appears in Judith. This does not require Judith to be scripture but certainly brings the issue into question.

The Declaration of Simon

Then Anna ran forth, and fell upon the neck of her son, and said unto him, **Seeing I have seen thee, my son, from henceforth I am content to die.** *And they wept both [emphasis added] (Tobit 11:1,9).*

Lord, now lettest thou thy servant depart in peace, *according to thy word. For mine eyes have seen thy salvation, Which thou hast prepared before the face of all people; A light to lighten the Gentiles, and the glory of thy people Israel [emphasis added] (Luke 2:29-32).*

Upon seeing the Christ child, Simeon responds with a canticle that plays an important part in Christian liturgies. In western

---

[543] The description appears to be that of the Guinae worm (Dracunculus medinensis,) a parasitic larvae found in drinking water. The larvae grows into a long worm that emerges through an ulcer and causes an intense burning sensation. The intense burning causes people to seek relief by dipping the infected area in water; the worm then releases its eggs, continuing its life cycle. https://www.who.int/dracunculiasis/disease/en/

[544] (Schaff, NPNF2-01 1890, 518-520) The church historian Eusebius tells us that Origen, out of immaturity and youth, castrated himself so as to make himself a eunuch "for the kingdom of heaven's sake."

Christianity, this is known as the *Nunc dimittis*; in Eastern Christianity, this is known as the Song of Simeon. While this is not a direct quotation from Tobit, it is close enough that we may assume Simeon is paraphrasing Tobit and expands upon the thought. Having seen God's son, he is content to die.

Two Men in Bright Array

Nevertheless Heliodorus executed that which was decreed. Now as he was there present himself with his guard about the treasury, the Lord of spirits, and the Prince of all power, caused a great apparition, so that all that presumed to come in with him were astonished at the power of God, and fainted, and were sore afraid. For there appeared unto them an horse with a terrible rider upon him, and adorned with a very fair covering, and he ran fiercely, and smote at Heliodorus with his forefeet, and it seemed that he that sat upon the horse had complete harness of gold. **Moreover two other young men appeared before him, notable in strength, excellent in beauty, and comely in apparel,** *who stood by him on either side; and scourged him continually, and gave him many sore stripes. And Heliodorus fell suddenly unto the ground, and was compassed with great darkness: but they that were with him took him up, and put him into a litter. Thus him, that lately came with a great train and with all his guard into the said treasury, they carried out, being unable to help himself with his weapons: and manifestly they acknowledged the power of God. For he by the hand of God was cast down, and lay speechless without all hope of life [emphasis added] (2 Macc 3:23-29).*

And it came to pass, as they were much perplexed thereabout, **behold, two men stood by them in shining garments:** *And as they were afraid, and bowed down their faces to the earth, they said unto them, Why seek ye the living among the dead [emphasis added] (Lk 24:4-5)?*

And while they looked stedfastly toward heaven as he went up, **behold, two men stood by them in white apparel;** *Which also said, Ye men of Galilee, why stand ye gazing up into* heaven? this same Jesus, which is taken up from you into heaven, shall so come in like manner as ye have seen him go into heaven [emphasis added] (Acts 1:10-11).

And I saw heaven opened, and **behold a white horse; and he that sat upon him was called Faithful and True**, and in righteousness he doth judge and make war. His eyes were as a flame of fire, and on his head were many crowns; and he had a name written, that no man knew, but he himself. And he was clothed with a vesture dipped in blood: and his name is called The Word of God [emphasis added] (Re 19:11-13).

In 2 Maccabees is a story of Heliodorus, a man charged to take the money given to the temple for charitable purposes and place the funds into the King's treasury. As Heliodorus presented himself with the guard before the Treasury, a horse and rider appeared before him, and Heliodorus was smitten with the horse's forefeet. Accompanying the horse and rider were by two men described as "notable in strength, and excellent in beauty"; these two men proceeded to scourge Heliodorus in the presence of his guard and all the people. These same two men appear at Jesus' resurrection and His ascension. It is clear that the "horse with a terrible rider" is none other than Jesus Christ, and that the two men in the resurrection accounts are the same two young men seen in 2 Maccabees.

All Things Were Made by Him

O God of my fathers, and Lord of mercy, **who hast made all things with thy word** [emphasis added] (Wis 9:1).

In the beginning was the Word, and the Word was with God, and the Word was God. The same was in the beginning with God. **All things were made by him**; and without him was not any thing made that was made [emphasis added] (Jn 1:1-3).

The apostle John is clearly alluding to the Wisdom of Solomon when he speaks of Jesus Christ as the Word through whom all things were made. This allusion is so close as to be a near quotation in English. In Greek, the word choice and sentence structure are somewhat different, but the idea is the same. St. John the Theologian expands upon the source material, revealing Christ to be the Word through whom all things were made.

The Bread of Life

They that eat me shall yet be hungry, and they that drink me shall yet be thirsty (Sir 24:21).

And Jesus said unto them, **I am the bread of life: he that cometh to me shall never hunger; and he that believeth on me shall never thirst.** ...*I am that bread of life. Your fathers did eat manna in the wilderness, and are dead. This is the bread which cometh down from heaven, that a man may eat thereof, and not die. I am the living bread which came down from heaven: if any man eat of this bread, he shall live for ever: and the bread that I will give is my flesh, which I will give for the life of the world. ... Verily, verily, I say unto you, Except ye eat the flesh of the Son of man, and drink his blood, ye have no life in you.* **Whoso eateth my flesh, and drinketh my blood, hath eternal life; and I will raise him up at the last day. For my flesh is meat indeed, and my blood is drink indeed. He that eateth my flesh, and drinketh my blood, dwelleth in me, and I in him.** *As the living Father hath sent me, and I live by the Father: so he that eateth me, even he shall live by me. This is that bread which came down from heaven: not as your fathers did eat manna, and are dead: he that eateth of this bread shall live for ever [emphasis added] (Jn 6:35: 48-51; 53-58).*

In Jesus' Eucharistic Discourse from John's Gospel, Jesus plays off of the passage in Sirach. The idea in Sirach is that those who desire Wisdom will never be satiated, but will always want more. In John's Gospel, Jesus is claiming to be the only one who can fill that desire; that those who eat his flesh and drink his blood will live forever.

The Feast of Hanukkah

Moreover, Judas and his brethren with the whole congregation of Israel ordained, that the days of the dedication of the altar should be kept in their season from year to year by the space of eight days, from the five and twentieth day of the month Casleu, with mirth and gladness (1 Macc. 4:59).

And it was at Jerusalem the feast of the dedication, and it was winter (Jn 10:22).

The feast of the dedication is known as Hanukkah. Jesus celebrated this feast along with his Jewish brethren. Jesus has no problems with the feast of Hanukkah, as described in 1 Maccabees, being added to the feasts prescribed in the Law of Moses. The fact that Jesus celebrated Hanukkah does not require that 1 Maccabees be Sacred Scripture, but it certainly allows for it.

The Branches that Bear no Fruit

The imperfect branches shall be broken off, their fruit unprofitable, not ripe to eat, yea, meet for nothing (Wis 4:5).

If a man abide not in me, he is cast forth as a branch, and is withered; and men gather them, and cast them into the fire, and they are burned (Jn 15:6).

And if some of the branches be broken off, and thou, being a wild olive tree, wert graffed in among them, and with them partakest of the root and fatness of the olive tree; Boast not against the branches. But if thou boast, thou bearest not the root, but the root thee. Thou wilt say then, The branches were broken off, that I might be graffed in. Well; because of unbelief they were broken off, and thou standest by faith. Be not highminded, but fear: For if God spared not the natural branches, take heed lest he also spare not thee (Rom 11:17-21).

These two are parallel passages. Jesus is clearly using the imagery from the Wisdom of Solomon. In Wisdom, the argument is for virtue over unrighteousness — that the "multiplying brood of the ungodly" will be broken off, so it is better to be virtuous with no children than to be ungodly with a "multiplying brood." Jesus takes the same imagery of branches being children, and advances the agricultural metaphor, declaring Himself to be the true vine, and the branches his children.

The apostle Paul argues that the Jews, the natural children, are the branches which bear no fruit and are cut down and burned up; he also argues that the Gentiles, who are not the natural brethren, are the wild branches who are grafted into the vine.

The Knowledge of the Creator

Surely vain are all men by nature, who are ignorant of God, and could not out of the good things that are seen know him that is: neither by considering the works did they acknowledge the workmaster; But deemed either fire, or wind, or the swift air, or the circle of the stars, or the violent water, or the lights of heaven, to be the gods which govern the world. With whose beauty if they being delighted took them to be gods; let them know how much better the Lord of them is: for the first author of beauty hath created them. But if they were astonished at their power and virtue, let them understand by them, how much mightier he is that made them. For by the greatness and beauty of the creatures proportionably the maker of them is seen. But yet for this they are the less to be blamed: for they peradventure err, seeking God, and desirous to find him. For being conversant in his works they search him diligently, and believe their sight: because the things are beautiful that are seen. Howbeit neither are they to be pardoned. For if they were able to know so much, that they could aim at the world; how did they not sooner find out the Lord thereof? But miserable are they, and in dead things is their hope, who call them gods, which are the works of men's hands, gold and silver, to shew art in, and resemblances of beasts, or a stone good for nothing, the work of an ancient hand (Wisdom 13:1-10).

For the wrath of God is revealed from heaven against all ungodliness and unrighteousness of men, who hold the truth in unrighteousness; Because that which may be known of God is manifest in them; for God hath shewed it unto them. For the invisible things of him from the creation of the world are clearly seen, being understood by the things that are made, even his eternal power and Godhead; so that they are without excuse: Because that, when they knew God, they glorified him not as God, neither were thankful; but became vain in their imaginations, and their foolish heart was darkened. Professing themselves to be wise, they became fools, And changed the glory of the uncorruptible God into an image made like to corruptible man, and to birds, and fourfooted beasts, and creeping things. Wherefore God also gave them up to uncleanness through the lusts of their own hearts, to dishonour their own bodies between themselves: Who changed the truth of God into a lie, and worshipped and served the creature more than the Creator, who is blessed for ever. Amen (Rom 1:18-25).

The first chapter of Romans is heavily indebted to Wisdom chapter 13. We have already discussed Paul's usage of the phrase "silver and gold" during his sermon on Mars Hill, which is an admittedly minor turn of phrase. In the first chapter of Romans, Paul begins his discourse on the subject of general revelation. He argues that God has revealed enough of Himself in His creation that men are without excuse. Paul derives his argument from the Wisdom of Solomon. The argument in Wisdom is that the existence of God is demonstrated not by the existence of things in and of themselves, but rather their beauty. The fact that things are beautiful in and of themselves, and that we seem to exist to recognize and share in that beauty tells us that there must be a point to all this.

In the book of Romans, Paul condenses this argument by saying: "that which may be known of God is manifest in them [the ungodly]"; that is to say, in their knowledge of God through His creation of and operations within the material world (Rom 1:19). Note that Paul does *not* say that God may be known through His creation — which is to say, known in His essence. Instead, Paul speaks of "*that which may be known of God,*" which is an entirely different thing. To use the terminology of the Eastern Church, Paul is speaking of the difference between God's essence and God's energies; between the fullness of God and God as revealed through His actions. Using this idea, both General and Special Revelation together constitute God's energies — God's actions within and on behalf of this world, his divine economy. God in His essence, in His essential self, remains altogether beyond our grasp.

Idolatry and Perversions

For the devising of idols was the beginning of spiritual fornication, and the invention of them the corruption of life. ... They kept neither lives nor marriages any longer undefiled: but either one slew another traiterously, or grieved him by adultery. So that there reigned in all men without exception blood, manslaughter, theft, and dissimulation, corruption, unfaithfulness, tumults, perjury, Disquieting of good men, forgetfulness of good turns, defiling of souls, changing of kind, disorder in marriages, adultery, and shameless uncleanness. For the worshipping of idols not to be named is the beginning, the cause, and the end, of all evil (Wisdom 14:12, 24-27).

Wherefore God also gave them up to uncleanness through the lusts of their own hearts, to dishonour their own bodies between themselves: Who changed the truth of God into a lie, and worshipped and served the creature more than the Creator, who is blessed for ever. Amen. For this cause God gave them up unto vile affections: for even their women did change the natural use into that which is against nature: And likewise also the men, leaving the natural use of the woman, burned in their lust one toward another; men with men working that which is unseemly, and receiving in themselves that recompence of their error which was meet. And even as they did not like to retain God in their knowledge, God gave them over to a reprobate mind, to do those things which are not convenient; Being filled with all unrighteousness, fornication, wickedness, covetousness, maliciousness; full of envy, murder, debate, deceit, malignity; whisperers, Backbiters, haters of God, despiteful, proud, boasters, inventors of evil things, disobedient to parents, Without understanding, covenantbreakers, without natural affection, implacable, unmerciful: Who knowing the judgment of God, that they which commit such things are worthy of death, not only do the same, but have pleasure in them that do them (Rom 1:24-32).

The apostle Paul begins with a description of idolatry (Rom 1:21-23), and the immorality arising from it. In this Paul is saying nothing new, but is simply repeating the ideas found in Wisdom. Paul is copying his thematic material from Wisdom and is more graphic in his depiction.

- In Wisdom, we read that idolatry is the beginning of spiritual fornication; in Romans, we read that after becoming idolaters, God "gave them up" to immorality.
- In Wisdom, we read that idolatry is the source of defiled marriages; in Romans, we read that because men worshipped the "creature more than the Creator," they dishonored their bodies.
- In Wisdom, we see idolatry as the source of murders, manslaughter, theft, dishonesty, corruption, unfaithfulness, tumults, perjury, and more. In Romans, Paul describes idolaters as filled with all unrighteousness, fornication, wickedness, covetousness, maliciousness; full of envy, murder, debate, deceit, malignity; whisperers, etc.
- In Wisdom, we read of "disorder in marriages, adultery, and shameless uncleanness; in Romans, we read of fornication and "vile affections," which Paul goes on to explain as male and female homosexual acts — which is an explication of Wisdom's "shameless uncleanness."[545]

---

[545] I do not intend to get into the culture wars over the acceptance of homosexuality, except to say this. The one side fails to

Everything we see the section of Romans under consideration, we first read in the book of Wisdom, which was Paul's source material — his Bible, if you will.

Death Entered into the World

Nevertheless through envy of the devil came death into the world: and they that do hold of his side do find it (Wisdom 2:24).

Wherefore, as by one man sin entered into the world, and death by sin; and so death passed upon all men, for that all have sinned (Rom 5:12).

Paul is seemingly commenting on Wisdom 2:24 when he describes how sin and death came into the world. Paul is making a Christological point; he focuses on the first Adam (the man by who sin came into the world), and the last Adam (the Christ, by whom life was given to those dead in sin).

---

differentiate between the person who is loved by God and the homosexual acts that person commits, or the homosexual impulses endemic to that person. The other side states that homosexuality is not a choice, which may be true. After all, no one chooses as a young child a sexual orientation that puts them at odds with society at large. And since (they say) homosexuality is not a choice, then (they say) it is a valid expression of human sexuality. I simply state that we must deal with the homosexual as a person loved by God, while recognizing that the scriptures class homosexuality as "vile affections" and "shameless uncleanness." We must also recognize that in vilifying the homosexual (while allowing other sins such as gluttony), we drive them away from the Gospel.

The Potter and the Clay

For the potter, tempering soft earth, fashioneth every vessel with much labour for our service: yea, of the same clay he maketh both the vessels that serve for clean uses, and likewise also all such as serve to the contrary: but what is the use of either sort, the potter himself is the judge (Wis 15:7).

Hath not the potter power over the clay, of the same lump to make one vessel unto honour, and another unto dishonour (Rom 9:21)?

The apostle Paul is clearly using the imagery from Wisdom and is using it in much the same way. There is a clear corollary between the clean/unclean imagery in Wisdom and the honor/dishonor imagery in Romans. The correlation makes it clear that Paul is not talking about double predestination after the manner of the Calvinists. The idea of clean/unclean has to do with ceremonial purity, not intrinsic or imputed righteousness. Clean/Unclean, being ceremonial terms, meant that things that were ceremonially clean (such as the lamb without blemish) could become sacred through connection with sacred things whereas unclean things profaned the sacred. This temple imagery permeates the New Testament. Ignorance of Old Testament worship leads to a misinterpretation of important New Testament passages, such as Paul's description of the potter and the clay.

Then I went down to the potter's house, and, behold, he wrought a work on the wheels. And the vessel that he made of clay was marred in the hand of the potter: so he made it again another vessel, as seemed good to the potter to make it (Jer 18:3-4).

It should be clear that Paul is using Wisdom as his source rather than Jeremiah; the passage in Jeremiah has nothing to do with a potter making one vessel to be ceremonially clean, and another to be ceremonially unclean. Rather, the passage from Jeremiah has to do with a potter's vessel that was damaged while being turned on the wheel, so the potter took that clay and reworked it into something useful.

Confession with the Mouth

If ye turn to him with your whole heart, and with your whole mind, and deal uprightly before him, then will he turn unto you, and will not hide his face from you. Therefore see what he will do with you, and **confess him with your whole mouth**, *and praise the Lord of might, and extol the everlasting King. In the land of my captivity do I praise him, and declare his might and majesty to a sinful nation. O ye sinners, turn and do justice before him: who can tell if he will accept you, and have mercy on you [emphasis added] (Tobit 13:6)?*

But what saith it? The word is nigh thee, even in thy mouth, and in thy heart: that is, the word of faith, which we preach; That if thou shalt **confess with thy mouth** *the Lord Jesus, and shalt believe in thine heart that God hath raised him from the dead, thou shalt be saved. For with the heart man believeth unto righteousness; and with the mouth confession is made unto salvation [emphasis added] (Rom 10:8-10).*

The entire Pauline understanding of the salvific consequences of the confession with the mouth comes from Tobit. Both refer to the confession with the mouth as being not merely verbal, but something that encompasses the whole person. Tobit refers to the heart, the mind, and the mouth; Paul refers to the heart and the mouth.

It is important to note that the ancient's understanding of the mind and the heart are much different than ours. We think of the heart as the seat of emotions, but for the ancients, the intellect and the emotions had the same source: the mind. The heart was something much different. Metropolitan Jonah Pauffhausen makes the following statement: "The human person was created with two centers of consciousness: the rational, and the heart. The rational mind, which includes the emotions; and the heart, which is otherwise known in Greek terminology as the *nous* [νουσ, pronounced as noose]."⁵⁴⁶ Although there is no good, single-word English translation for *nous*, we can think of it as our spiritual consciousness. When Tobit refers to the mind, he refers to our intellect and our emotions. Likewise, when both Paul and Tobit refer to the heart, they refer to the spiritual consciousness. When the spiritual consciousness is darkened, it is manifested through the mouth. Likewise, when the spiritual consciousness is enlightened, the mouth both confesses and praises God.

Many Gods, One Lord

Surely vain are all men by nature, who are ignorant of God, and could not out of the good things that are seen know him that is: neither by considering the works did they acknowledge the workmaster; But deemed either fire, or wind, or the swift air, or the circle of the stars, or the violent water, or the lights of heaven, to be the gods which govern the world. With whose beauty if they being delighted took them to be gods; let them know how much better the Lord of them is: for the first author of beauty hath created them (Wisdom 13:1-3).

For though there be that are called gods, whether in heaven or in earth, (as there be gods many, and lords many,) But to us there is but one God, the Father, of whom are all things, and we in him; and one Lord Jesus Christ, by whom are all things, and we by him (1 Cor 8:5-6).

Paul acknowledges many are called "gods," but there is only one Lord. This thought, which is similar to Paul's treatise in the first few chapters of Romans, is also derived from the Wisdom of Solomon. Paul takes the idea further into the political realm when he mentions the political leaders who are also called gods. Christians were persecuted for refusing to acknowledge Caesar as God, thereby undermining the legitimacy of the Roman government. Thus, to the Romans, Christians were enemies of the state.

---

⁵⁴⁶ (Pauffhausen 2005)

Sword of the Spirit

He shall take to him his jealousy for complete armour, and make the creature his weapon for the revenge of his enemies. He shall put on righteousness as a breastplate, and true judgment instead of an helmet. He shall take holiness for an invincible shield. His severe wrath shall he sharpen for a sword, and the world shall fight with him against the unwise (Wis 5:17-20).

This passage (and the following passage from Wisdom 18) is the source for the metaphor used by the apostle's Paul and John, and the anonymous author of Hebrews — that of putting on the armor of God, and arming oneself with God's weaponry.

Thine Almighty word leaped down from heaven out of thy royal throne, as a fierce man of war into the midst of a land of destruction, And brought thine unfeigned commandment as a sharp sword, and standing up filled all things with death; and it touched the heaven, but it stood upon the earth (Wis 18:15-16).

The connection between the New Testament and Wisdom is clear. The sword, in this case, is the "unfeigned commandment," which is another way of saying the law of the Lord (Ps 119:1). There is a connection between the sword of the "unfeigned commandment," the "word of God" as sharper than any two-edged sword, and the sword of the Spirit is clear. In John's Revelation, Christ has a two-edged sword coming out of his mouth — the same metaphor used for the word of God in the book of Hebrews.

The sword in Wisdom 18 is the "unfeigned commandment," which is another way of saying the law of the Lord (Ps 119:1). The connection between the sword of the "unfeigned commandment," the "word of God" as sharper than any two-edged sword is clear.

For the word of God is quick, and powerful, and sharper than any twoedged sword, piercing even to the dividing asunder of soul and spirit, and of the joints and marrow, and is a discerner of the thoughts and intents of the heart (Heb 4:12).

The apostle Paul borrows this metaphor in his famous passage regarding putting on the "whole armor of God." The martial metaphor borrowed from Wisdom is often taken to represent the Christian life. However, Paul provides additional detail. His call to "withstand in the evil day" is an apocalyptic statement. In other words, Paul is not primarily talking about the daily life of the Christian, although that is part of it. But the putting on of the "whole armor of God," which includes being armed with the "sword of the Spirit," is something we do every day so that we may be ready for the day of the Lord, the day of judgment.

Wherefore take unto you the whole armour of God, that ye may be able to withstand in the evil day, and having done all, to stand. Stand therefore, having your loins girt about with truth, and having on the breastplate of righteousness; And your feet shod with the preparation of the gospel of peace; Above all, taking the shield of faith, wherewith ye shall be able to quench all the fiery darts of the wicked. And take the helmet of salvation, and the sword of the Spirit, which is the word of God (Eph 6:13-17).

And out of his mouth goeth a sharp sword, that with it he should smite the nations: and he shall rule them with a rod of iron: and he treadeth the winepress of the fierceness and wrath of Almighty God (Re 19:15).

The passages from Wisdom link to the passages from Ephesians and especially John's Revelation, where the author describes Christ as having a two-edged sword coming out of His mouth — the same metaphor used for the word of God in the book of Hebrews.

Reconciliation for the Dead

And when he had made a gathering throughout the company to the sum of two thousand drachms of silver, he sent it to

Jerusalem to offer a sin offering, doing therein very well and honestly, in that he was mindful of the resurrection: For if he had not hoped that they that were slain should have risen again, it had been superfluous and vain to pray for the dead. And also in that he perceived that there was great favour laid up for those that died godly, it was an holy and good thought. Whereupon he made a reconciliation for the dead, that they might be delivered from sin (2 Macc. 12:43-45).

Else what shall they do which are baptized for the dead, if the dead rise not at all? why are they then baptized for the dead (1 Cor 15:29)?

I have no intention of entering into an extended discussion of the baptism of the dead and its meaning. I merely point out the connection between Judas Maccabee taking up a collection and having sin offerings performed on behalf of the dead, and the apostle Paul's mention of baptism for the dead. In both cases, the resurrection is in view; it is the hope of the resurrection that is the focus of both passages. In other words, we pray for the dead because we believe in the resurrection and because we believe that while their bodies sleep in the ground, their souls are kept by the power of God, awaiting the general resurrection from the dead.

The Crown of Righteousness

*But the righteous live for evermore; their reward also is with the Lord, and the care of them is with the most High. Therefore shall they receive a glorious kingdom, and a **beautiful crown** from the Lord's hand: for with his right hand shall he cover them, and with his arm shall he protect them [emphasis added] (Wis 5:15-16).*

*I have fought a good fight, I have finished my course, I have kept the faith: Henceforth there is laid up for me a **crown of righteousness**, which the Lord, the righteous judge, shall give me at that day: and not to me only, but unto all them also that love his appearing [emphasis added] (2 Tim 4:8).*

No matter what you think this crown of righteousness is, it should be clear that Paul is alluding to the "beautiful crown" offered to the righteous in the passage from the Wisdom of Solomon. The metaphor of the extended passage — which describes the spiritual warfare of the righteous — is used in numerous places in the New Testament, as we have previously discussed.

Enoch and the Roll Call of Faith

One of the more well-known passages in the book of Hebrews is the "Roll Call of Faith" in chapter 11. This passage lists some of the heroes of the faith. The chapter begins as such:

Now faith is the substance of things hoped for, the evidence of things not seen. For by it the elders obtained a good report. Through faith we understand that the worlds were framed by the word of God, so that things which are seen were not made of things which do appear (Heb 11:1-3).

The chapter then lists a variety of people who are notable for their great faith, by which they "attained a good report." Fascinatingly enough, the passage of Hebrews is nothing more than a more succinct version of Ecclesiasticus [Sirach] 44-50. Due to the length of the source material, we will not reproduce it here. However, the passage discussing Enoch as an example of faith is notable in that it is almost a direct quotation from Ecclesiasticus.

By faith Enoch was translated that he should not see death; and was not found, because God had translated him: for before his translation he had this testimony, that he pleased God (Heb 11:5).

Enoch pleased the Lord, and was translated, being an example of repentance to all generations (Ecclus 44:16).

Compare the two passages, and it is immediately apparent that the author of Hebrews is using Ecclesiasticus as source material. Moreover, it is reasonable to assume that the author of Hebrews was not plagiarizing Ecclesiasticus, but is intending his audience to recognize his repurposing of the source material and reflect upon the relationship between the two works.

The individuals mentioned by name in both Hebrews and Ecclesiasticus are Enoch, Noah, Abraham, Isaac, Jacob, Moses, and David. The author also mentions other prophets listed in Ecclesiasticus not by name, but by how they died. The unknown author of Hebrews writes: "And what shall I more say? for the time would fail me to tell of Gideon, and of Barak, and of Samson, and of Jephthah; of David also, and Samuel, and of the prophets" (Heb 11:32). The author condenses the six chapters of Ecclesiasticus down to a single chapter. Nevertheless, it is clear the author is not only condensing the material from Ecclesiasticus but is referring to the longer and more encompassing passage.

The Seven Holy Maccabee Martyrs

It came to pass also, that seven brethren with their mother were taken, and compelled by the king against the law to taste swine's flesh, and were tormented with scourges and whips. But one of them that spake first said thus, What wouldest thou ask or learn of us? we are ready to die, rather than to transgress the laws of our fathers. ...But the mother was marvellous above all, and worthy of honourable memory: for when she saw her seven sons slain within the space of one day, she bare it with a good courage, because of the hope that she had in the Lord. Yea, she exhorted every one of them in her own language, filled with courageous spirits; and stirring up her womanish thoughts with a manly stomach, she said unto them, I cannot tell how ye came into my womb: for I neither gave you breath nor life, neither was it I that formed the members of every one of you; But doubtless the Creator of the world, who formed the generation of man, and found out the beginning of all things, will also of his own mercy give you breath and life again, as ye now regard not your own selves for his laws' sake. ...Last of all after the sons the mother died (2 Macc 7:1-2; 20-23; 41).

Women received their dead raised to life again: and others were tortured, not accepting deliverance; that they might obtain a better resurrection (Heb 11:35).

From 2 Maccabees comes the story of the death of an entire family — seven sons and their mother — who were tortured to death rather than profane the covenant of God. This story was part of the cultural memory of the Hebrew people, and thus the author need only to have mentioned those who were tortured and not accepting deliverance for his audience to have understood who he was talking about. The fact that we need this to be explained to us is perhaps evidence of our ignorance of the world of which the Bible speaks.

The mother's speech as recorded in 2 Maccabees is evidence that Judaism encompassed a belief in the resurrection. When Antiochus asked the mother to counsel her seventh son to save his life by defiling the covenant, the mother instead spoke these powerful words:

I beseech thee, my son, look upon the heaven and the earth, and all that is therein, and consider that God made them of things that were not; and so was mankind made likewise. Fear not this tormentor, but, being worthy of thy brethren, take thy death that I may receive thee again in mercy with thy brethren (2 Macc 7:28-29).

Judaism in Jesus' day was quite fluid, with many doctrinal and canonical questions unsettled. Interestingly, when the Sadducees challenged Jesus concerning the resurrection of the dead, Jesus did not base his reply upon the passage from 2 Maccabees. The Sadducees (it is generally believed) held that only the five books of Moses were canonical.[547] This view was prevalent among some of the church fathers, but modern scholars think the fathers were conflating the

---

[547] (Ross 2006)

Samaritans and the Sadducees.[548] If the latest scholarship is correct, the canon for both the Sadducees and Pharisees could include the Apocrypha.

The primary difference between the Pharisees and the Sadducees was not the canon itself, but the use to which they put the canon. The Sadducees were strict literalists, meaning that it if couldn't be found in scripture, they didn't accept it as part of Judaism. By contrast, the Pharisees had a body of tradition which served to enhance or interpret scripture; some of these regulations were extra-scriptural, in that they could not be traced back to scriptural texts. For this reason, the Sadducees rejected the traditions and regulations of the Pharisees.[549] It is perhaps for this reason that Jesus' answer to the Pharisees was based on the Pentateuch, rather than referencing 1 Maccabees.

The Meekness of Wisdom

My son, go on with thy business in meekness; so shalt thou be beloved of him that is approved. The greater thou art, the more humble thyself, and thou shalt find favour before the Lord. Many are in high place, and of renown: but mysteries are revealed unto the meek. For the power of the Lord is great, and he is honoured of the lowly (Sir 3:17-20).

Who is a wise man and endued with knowledge among you? let him shew out of a good conversation his works with meekness of wisdom (James 3:13).

While this allusion is obscure, the connection is clear. James is interested in the way the heart of man is revealed by what the words of his mouth. Meanwhile, Sirach connects humility and gentleness as characteristics that bring one favor before the Lord. The person who conducts his or her business with

---

[548] The Samaritans held that only the five books of Moses were scripture, although their version of the first five books of Moses were slightly different. (S. Davidson 1877)

[549] (Skarsaune 2002, 109-111)

the gentleness of heart will show this through good conversation. This meekness and lowliness is a characteristic of Christ the King, and therefore the person who is meek and lowly finds favor "of Him that is approved," who is Christ the King.

Your Gold and Silver are Rusted

Lose thy money for thy brother and thy friend, and let it not rust under a stone to be lost. Lay up thy treasure according to the commandments of the most High, and it shall bring thee more profit than gold (Sir 29:10-11).

Go to now, ye rich men, weep and howl for your miseries that shall come upon you. Your riches are corrupted, and your garments are motheaten. Your gold and silver is cankered; and the rust of them shall be a witness against you, and shall eat your flesh as it were fire. Ye have heaped treasure together for the last days (James 5:1-3).

We have already discussed this passage from Sirach and how Jesus alluded to it when He warned people not to lay up treasures on earth where "moth and rust doth corrupt" (Matt 6:19).[550] Sirach says not to let your money "rust under stone"; James says your "gold and silver is cankered." James alludes to the Sermon on the Mount *and* the underlying passage in Sirach. For the connection between the giving of alms (losing your money for your brother and friend) and laying up treasure in heaven, see the section entitled "Treasures in Heaven" above.

The Oppression of the Righteous

Let us oppress the poor righteous man, let us not spare the widow, nor reverence the ancient gray hairs of the aged. Let

---

[550] Rust is the oxidation of iron. Metaphorically, rust is the oxidation of metals in general. Silver tarnish is oxidation, and falls under the general metaphor. While gold is generally held to be a stable metal, there are six different gold oxides. Technically, gold can also rust.

our strength be the law of justice: for that which is feeble is found to be nothing worth. Therefore let us lie in wait for the righteous; because he is not for our turn, and he is clean contrary to our doings: he upbraideth us with our offending the law, and objecteth to our infamy the transgressings of our education. He professeth to have the knowledge of God: and he calleth himself the child of the Lord. He was made to reprove our thoughts. He is grievous unto us even to behold: for his life is not like other men's, his ways are of another fashion. We are esteemed of him as counterfeits: he abstaineth from our ways as from filthiness: he pronounceth the end of the just to be blessed, and maketh his boast that God is his father. Let us see if his words be true: and let us prove what shall happen in the end of him. For if the just man be the son of God, he will help him, and deliver him from the hand of his enemies. Let us examine him with despitefulness and torture, that we may know his meekness, and prove his patience. **Let us condemn him with a shameful death:** *for by his own saying he shall be respected [emphasis added]* (Wis 2:10-20).

Ye have condemned and killed the just; and he doth not resist you [emphasis added] (James 5:6).

The context of the passage in James has to do with the condemnation of the rich man who oppresses people who are poor and just. The extended passage from Sirach is more generic, speaking not of the rich in particular, but the general oppression of and lying in wait for the righteous. The very existence of the righteous is an offense to those who live ungodly lives. Therefore, the ungodly rejoice in the condemnation and death of the just, saying that if they are truly beloved of God, God will save them.

God does save the just. It happened for the three holy youths, who were saved from the fiery furnace; it happened at Capernaum when the crowd sought to throw Jesus over a cliff and he walked through them unmolested. But it is also true that God does not always save the just. James tells us that the righteous dies at the hands of evil men,[551] but James is also speaking specifically of Jesus Christ, the One who alone is Just. Jesus died at the hands of the wealthy Jewish leaders, who said that if God was truly His Father, then God would save Him. What they failed to understand is that the death of Christ was necessary for there to be a general resurrection from the dead. As if to prove the point, James the Just was killed by the Jews.

Trial by Fire

And having been a little chastised, they shall be greatly rewarded: for God proved them, and found them worthy for himself. **As gold in the furnace hath he tried them**, *and received them as a burnt offering [emphasis added] (Wis 3:5-6).*

For **gold is tried in the fire**, *and acceptable men in the furnace of adversity [emphasis added] (Sir 2:5).*

Wherein ye greatly rejoice, though now for a season, if need be, ye are in heaviness through manifold temptations: That the trial of your faith, being much **more precious than of gold that perisheth, though it be tried with fire**, *might be found unto praise and honour and glory at the appearing of Jesus Christ [emphasis added] (1 Pet 1:6-7).*

It is clear that Peter is simply rephrasing the passage from the Wisdom of Solomon, combining it with some of the wording from Sirach. Peter is exhorting his hearers using words they would already have been familiar with, thereby applying the Old Testament Scriptures to their current situation. Peter acknowledges the trials they were all going through, describing them as temptations; yet the connection with Wisdom and Sirach also brings in the ideas of chastening and sacrifice. This last connects the ideas presented by Peter with those of Paul when he writes:

---

[551] James became known as James the Just, and in his old age was himself martyred by the Jews.

"present your bodies a living sacrifice, holy, acceptable unto God, which is your reasonable service" (Rom 12:1).

The Delivery of the Righteous Man

When the ungodly perished, **she delivered the righteous man**, who fled from the fire which fell down upon the five cities. Of whose wickedness even to this day the waste land that smoketh is a testimony, and plants bearing fruit that never come to ripeness: and a standing pillar of salt is a monument of an unbelieving soul [emphasis added] (Wisdom 10:6-7).

And turning the cities of Sodom and Gomorrha into ashes condemned them with an overthrow, making them an ensample unto those that after should live ungodly; **And delivered just Lot**, vexed with the filthy conversation of the wicked [emphasis added] (2 Pet 2:6-7).

The extended passage from Wisdom and the passage from 2 Peter are both discussing the same event, using much the same language. It is clear that Peter expected his hearer to connect his discussion of this event with the extended discussion from Wisdom.

Peter discusses God's preservation of the righteous and his punishment of the wicked, using the fallen angels, the preservation of Noah, and the rescue of righteous Lot from the judgment levied upon Sodom and Gomorrah. The author of Wisdom makes much the same case, using the salvation of Adam, the condemnation of Cain, the preservation of Noah, the rescue of righteous Lot, the protection of Jacob, the liberation of Joseph, and the deliverance of Israel at the Red Sea. Peter intends us to understand that the rescue of righteous Lot stands in for all these other examples as well. Thus, Peter intends us to see things with our spiritual eyes, to look forward to the eschaton and the end of all things — when the ultimate rewards and judgments will be handed out.

The Seven Spirits of God

I am Raphael, one of the seven holy angels who present the prayers of the saints and enter into the presence of the glory of the Holy One (Tobit 12:15).

*Grace be unto you, and peace, from him which is, and which was, and which is to come; and **from the seven Spirits which are before his throne** [emphasis added] (Revelation 1:4).*

*And I saw **the seven angels which stood before God**; and to them were given seven trumpets. And another angel came and stood at the altar with a golden censer; and he was given much incense to mingle with the prayers of all the saints upon the golden altar before the throne; and the smoke of the incense rose with the prayers of the saints from the hand of the angel before God [emphasis added] (Revelation 8:2-4).*

*And I saw another mighty angel come down from heaven, clothed with a cloud: and a rainbow was upon his head, and his face was as it were the sun, and his feet as pillars of fire: And he had in his hand a little book open: and he set his right foot upon the sea, and his left foot on the earth, And cried with a loud voice, as when a lion roareth: and **when he had cried, seven thunders uttered their voices**. And when the seven thunders had uttered their voices, I was about to write: and I heard a voice from heaven saying unto me, Seal up those things which the seven thunders uttered, and write them not [emphasis added] (Re 10:1-4).*

*And I saw another sign in heaven, great and marvellous, **seven angels having the seven last plagues**; for in them is filled up the wrath of God. ...And after that I looked, and, behold, the temple of the tabernacle of the testimony in heaven was opened: And **the seven angels came out of the temple, having the seven plagues**, clothed in pure and white linen, and having their breasts girded with golden girdles. And one of the four beasts gave unto the seven angels seven golden vials full of the wrath of God, who liveth for ever and ever. And the temple was filled with smoke from the glory of God, and from his power; and **no man was able to enter into the temple,*** *till the seven plagues of the seven angels were fulfilled. And I heard a great voice out of the temple saying to the seven angels, Go your ways, and pour out the vials of the wrath of God upon the earth [emphasis added] (Re 15:1, 5-8; Re 16:1)*

The passage from Tobit regarding the seven angels "who present the prayers of the saints and enter into the presence of the glory of the Holy One" is referenced numerous times in The Revelation of St. John. We first see them connected with the appearance of the resurrected Christ, Who refers to the seven spirits which enter into the presence of God. While the Lamb of God is connected to the opening of the seven seals, the seven holy angels are connected with the judgments of the seven trumpets and the seven bowls. There is a cryptic reference to the seven thunders, of which John is forbidden to write; it is reasonable to assume these seven thunders are associated with the seven holy angels.

The Gates of Hell

For it was neither herb, nor mollifying plaister, that restored them to health: but **thy word, O Lord**, which healeth all things. For thou hast power of life and death: **thou leadest to the** *gates of hell, and bringest up again [emphasis added] (Wis 16:12-13).*

I am he that liveth, and was dead; and, behold, I am alive for evermore, Amen; and have the **keys of hell and of death** *[emphasis added] (Re 1:18).*

And I say also unto thee, That thou art Peter, and upon this rock I will build my church; and **the gates of hell** *shall not prevail against it [emphasis added] (Matt 16:18).*

Who has the power of life and death? Who can release someone from the gates of hell? According to Wis 16:12, it is the Word of the Lord, the Logos, the Son of God who trampled down death by death, descended into Hades, and led captivity captive. Our Lord, by his death and resurrection, has the keys of hell and death, and therefore, the gates of hell cannot prevail against His church.

The Two-Edged Sword

Thine Almighty word leaped down from heaven out of thy royal throne, as a fierce man of war into the midst of a land of destruction, And brought **thine unfeigned commandment as a sharp sword**, and standing up filled all things with death; and it touched the heaven, but it stood upon the earth [emphasis added] (Wis 18:16).

And to the angel of the church in Pergamos write; These things saith he which hath **the sharp sword with two edges** [emphasis added] (Re 2:12).

The Revelation of St. John is an apocalypse, a literary form popular in Second Temple Judaism. While Wisdom is not an apocalypse, the passage where the "unfeigned commandment" is described as a "sharp sword" is apocalyptic. The Almighty Word leaping from heaven to earth and bringing death to the Egyptians looks back to the exodus from Egypt and forward to a future deliverance.

Paul and John borrow the metaphor of the "sharp sword" from Wisdom, along with its apocalyptic context. The apocalyptic is not only a description of the end of days but gives us comfort in our afflictions. Paul uses imagery from apocalyptic literature so that we know that there is a purpose, that God is in control, and that evil will not have its way forever.

The Prayers of the Saints

Now therefore, when thou didst pray, and Sara thy daughter in law, **I did bring the remembrance of your prayers before the Holy One**: and when thou didst bury the dead, I was with thee likewise. ... I am Raphael, **one of the seven holy angels, which present the prayers of the saints**, and which go in and out before the glory of the Holy One [emphasis added] (Tobit 12:12,15).

*And another angel came and stood at the altar, having a golden censer; and there was given unto him much incense, that he should offer it with **the prayers of all saints** upon the golden altar which was before the throne. And the smoke of the incense, which came with **the prayers of the saints**, ascended up before God out of the angel's hand [emphasis added] (Re 8:3-4).*

The idea that the angels present the prayers of the saints before the throne of the Holy One comes from the book of Tobit. John's Apocalypse adds additional details — such as the incense offered twice daily upon the Altar of Incense before the veil of the temple, and the smoke from the daily sacrifices ascending from the altar. These images, derived from the liturgical life of the Old Testament church,[552] were declared by the author of Hebrews to be "the example and shadow of heavenly things" (Heb 8:5).

Rain of Hail and Fire

*But snow and ice endured the fire, and melted not, that they might know that **fire burning in the hail**, and sparkling in the rain, did destroy the fruits of the enemies [emphasis added] (Wis 16:22).*

*Fire, and hail, and famine, and death, all these **were created for vengeance** [emphasis added] (Sir 39:29).*

*The first angel sounded, and there followed **hail and fire mingled with blood**, and they were cast upon the earth: and the third part of trees was burnt up, and all green grass was burnt up [emphasis added] (Re 8:7).*

John's Apocalypse follows a particular Jewish pattern. The events that prefigured the exodus, the ten plagues and the like, are given an eschatological dimension in the Second

---

[552] The Old Testament liturgy was carried on in the early church. The apostles worshipped in the Temple, then taught on the temple mount in an area called Solomon's Porch. (Acts 5:12-42).

Temple literature. The apostle John uses the elements from the Old Testament as viewed through the prism of Wisdom and Sirach to create the image of hail and fire mingled with blood. What this means is unknown, but John left clues behind in his source material. From Sirach, we know these are tools of vengeance; from Wisdom, we know these tools of vengeance have been tempered with mercy. We see both in Revelation, for the destruction takes only a third, giving the rest a space to repent.

Rain of Locusts

*For them **the bitings of grasshoppers** [locusts] and flies killed, neither was there found any remedy for their life: for they were worthy to be punished by such. But thy sons not the very teeth of venomous dragons overcame: for thy mercy was ever by them, and healed them [emphasis added] (Wisdom 16:9-10).*

*And **there came out of the smoke locusts** upon the earth: and unto them was given power, as the scorpions of the earth have power. And it was commanded them that they should not hurt the grass of the earth, neither any green thing, neither any tree; but only those men which have not the seal of God in their foreheads [emphasis added] (Re 9:2-3).*

Even in judgment, we see evidence of God's mercy. In the times of the Exodus, the grasshoppers and flies did not kill the sons of Israel.[553] In John's Apocalypse, the locusts have no power over the green things of earth, nor over those people who have been sealed by the Lord. Judgment mingled with mercy is a theme carried forward from the stories of the Exodus and used by the writers during the Second Temple period. St. John used these themes as he developed his

---

[553] In general, the threat of locusts is not in their bite. They are unlikely to bite humans; since they are not venomous, their bite would not kill you. A plague of locusts is frightening because they eat every green plant in their path, causing widespread starvation.

apocalypse; the destruction is never total, and humanity is given great space to repent. Of those sealed by God, some are saved out of the judgment, and some are martyred on behalf of the judgment. But our God is a God of second chances, not willing that any should perish, but that all should come to repentance; mercy is ready to be granted, even unto the very end.

The Ark of the Covenant

It is also found in the records, that Jeremy the prophet commanded them that were carried away to take of the fire, as it hath been signified: And how that the prophet, having given them the law, charged them not to forget the commandments of the Lord, and that they should not err in their minds, when they see images of silver and gold, with their ornaments. And with other such speeches exhorted he them, that the law should not depart from their hearts. It was also contained in the same writing, that the prophet, being warned of God, commanded the tabernacle and the ark to go with him, as he went forth into the mountain, where Moses climbed up, and saw the heritage of God. **And when Jeremy came thither, he found an hollow cave, wherein he laid the tabernacle, and the ark, and the altar of incense, and so stopped the door.** *And some of those that followed him came to mark the way, but they could not find it. Which when Jeremy perceived, he blamed them, saying,* **As for that place, it shall be unknown until the time that God gather his people again together, and receive them unto mercy.** *Then shall the Lord shew them these things, and the glory of the Lord shall appear, and the cloud also, as it was shewed under Moses, and as when Solomon desired that the place might be honourably sanctified* [emphasis added] (2 Mac 1-8).

And the temple of God was opened in heaven, and **there was seen in his temple the ark of his testament**: and there were lightnings, and voices, and thunderings, and an earthquake, and great hail. **And there appeared a great wonder in heaven; a woman clothed with the sun, and the moon** *under her feet, and upon her head a crown of twelve stars: And she being with child cried, travailing in birth, and pained to be delivered.* And there appeared another wonder in heaven; and behold a great red dragon, having seven heads and ten horns, and seven crowns upon his heads. And his tail drew the third part of the stars of heaven, and did cast them to the earth: and the dragon stood before the woman which was ready to be delivered, for to devour her child as soon as it was born. And she brought forth a man child, who was to rule all nations with a rod of iron: and her child was caught up unto God, and to his throne *[emphasis added] (Re 11:19-12:5).*

This book is not the place for an extended discussion of the Virgin Mary as the new Ark. There is much more that could be said, as the church fathers wrote extensively on the subject. The original Ark of the Covenant, if you recall, was the only artifact found in the Holy of Holies (Ex 40:3), and remained perpetually shrouded (overshadowed, Luke 1:35) in thick darkness (1 Kings 8:12). The Ark itself contained Aaron's rod, a pot of manna, and the stone tablets upon which the law was inscribed (Heb 9:1-5). This is typologically significant: the manna is fulfilled in Jesus as the bread of life (Jn 6:35); Aaron's rod that budded is fulfilled by Jesus, the rod out of the stem of Jesse (Isa 11:1); and the law is fulfilled in Jesus (Matt 5:17), whose own body and blood is the new covenant (I Cor 11:23-26). The New Testament argues that the entire sacrificial system is a pattern, example, or type of heavenly realities (Heb 8:5; 10:1). Therefore, we can say that the Ark of the Covenant is nothing less than a type and a prefiguring of the Virgin Mary. She is the fulfillment of the Old Testament type, for within her womb the Blessed Virgin contained the source of the law of Moses, the incarnate Word of God.[554]

---

[554] Symbols are polysemic (have multiple meanings and applications). The Virgin Mary is not the mercy seat upon which Christ offered His own blood. That is a different sense and application.

The author of 2 Maccabees does not identify the writing that was the source for its account of the hiding of the temple treasures, but it bears a family resemblance to the hidden treasures described in the Copper Scroll found among the Dead Sea Scrolls. This copper scroll is a curious find from cave three at Qumran, and is, according to Geza Vermes, the "only non-religious composition recovered from Qumran."[555] Robert Mock writes: "[A]mong the passages of the Copper Scroll was an inventory of the Holy Treasures that appeared to have been hidden by the Prophet Jeremiah and the Temple Guardians before the destruction of Solomon's Temple by the Babylonians."[556] A direct connection between the "Holy Treasures" hidden by Jeremiah before the Babylonian captivity and the Copper Scroll is a fantasy, as the Copper Scroll appears to describe temple treasures hidden before the Roman destruction of Jerusalem, an event that occurred several centuries after the Babylonian captivity. But the idea that the temple guardians would have hidden away the holy things is not so far-fetched. Thus, the existence of the Copper Scroll, while having no direct connection to the account of 2 Maccabees, nevertheless indicates the 2 Maccabees account is reasonable.

But for our purposes, we are not so concerned with the physical ark, which is merely the type; we are more concerned with its antitype, which John's Revelation identifies as the Virgin Mary.[557] The prophecy from 2 Maccabees says that the ark, along with the temple treasures, would remain hidden until the regathering of the Lord's people. When the ark would be recovered, the glory of the

---

[555] (Vermes, The Copper Scroll 2002)

[556] (Mock 2002)

[557] The identification of the woman with child from Revelations 12 is a problem for some Protestants. Dispensationalists usually posit this woman as Israel. (Pentecost 1958, 215) Most Protestants would identify the woman as the Church. (Brighton 1999, 318-319) But if the woman is indeed the Church, then why do they resist the idea of the Church's role in the creation, identification, and transmission of the Bible?

Lord would be revealed. We see this mentioned twice in the Gospels: first, when the Holy Spirit "overshadowed" the Virgin Mary; and second, at the transfiguration of our Lord.

Hallelujah and the Marriage of the Lamb

For Jerusalem shall be built up with sapphires and emeralds, and precious stone: thy walls and towers and battlements with pure gold. And the streets of Jerusalem shall be paved with beryl and carbuncle and stones of Ophir. **And all her streets shall say, Alleluia;** *and they shall praise him, saying, Blessed be God, which hath extolled it for ever [emphasis added] (Tobit 13:16-18).*

And after these things I heard **a great voice of much people in heaven, saying, Alleluia;** *Salvation, and glory, and honour, and power, unto the Lord our God. And I heard as it were the voice of a great multitude, and as the voice of many waters, and as the voice of mighty thunderings, saying, Alleluia: for the Lord God omnipotent reigneth. Let us be glad and rejoice, and give honour to him: for the marriage of the Lamb is come, and his wife hath made herself ready [emphasis added] (Re 19:1, 6-7).*

The word Hosanna, which was the cry of the people when Jesus rode into Jerusalem (Matt 21:9), is not originally a cry of praise, but rather a request for divine favor. Hallelujah, on the other hand, means "God be praised," or "Praise God." Hosanna is the cry of those in need of deliverance; Hallelujah is the cry of those whose desire is to glorify God.

In heaven, we see the multitudes crying "Hallelujah," praising God, and falling before the throne. John's apocalypse takes its cue from Tobit's prayer of rejoicing, wherein he describes Jerusalem as it will be at the end of days. In particular, we see the streets (a metaphor for the assembled peoples) crying Alleluia; in John's apocalypse, we see the voices of the peoples in heaven crying out "Alleluia; Salvation, and glory, and honour, and power, unto the Lord our God." No longer are the people of God crying out for

Salvation but are praising God and thanking Him for their salvation, to the glory and honor of God.

The Lord's Appears on a White Horse

Nevertheless Heliodorus executed that which was decreed. Now as he was there present himself with his guard about the treasury, the Lord of spirits, and the Prince of all power, caused a great apparition, so that all that presumed to come in with him were astonished at the power of God, and fainted, and were sore afraid. **For there appeared unto them an horse with a terrible rider upon him,** *and adorned with a very fair covering, and he ran fiercely, and smote at Heliodorus with his forefeet, and it seemed that he that sat upon the horse had complete harness of gold. Moreover two other young men appeared before him, notable in strength, excellent in beauty, and comely in apparel, who stood by him on either side; and scourged him continually, and gave him many sore stripes. And Heliodorus fell suddenly unto the ground, and was compassed with great darkness: but they that were with him took him up, and put him into a litter. Thus him, that lately came with a great train and with all his guard into the said treasury, they carried out, being unable to help himself with his weapons: and manifestly they acknowledged the power of God. For he by the hand of God was cast down, and lay speechless without all hope of life [emphasis added] (2 Macc 3:23-29).*

And I saw heaven opened, and behold a white horse; and he that sat upon him was called Faithful and True, and in righteousness he doth judge and make war [emphasis added] (Re 19:11).

In 2 Maccabees we see the Lord appearing on a white horse, accompanied by two men in white. From the New Testament accounts, we know these two men to be angels, the same angels that announced our Lord's resurrection and ascension. (See "Two Men in Bright Array" above). Therefore, what we see in 2 Maccabees is a theophany, an appearance of Christ in the Old Testament, one of the many appearances of Christ before the Incarnation, and a foreshadowing of that which was to come. It is no mistake that John uses the theophany from 2 Maccabees as a description of Christ as King of Kings and Lord of Lords.

The New Jerusalem

For Jerusalem shall be built up with sapphires and emeralds, and precious stone: thy walls and towers and battlements with pure gold. And the streets of Jerusalem shall be paved with beryl and carbuncle and stones of Ophir (Tobit 13:16-17).

And the building of the wall of it was of jasper: and the city was pure gold, like unto clear glass. And the foundations of the wall of the city were garnished with all manner of precious stones. The first foundation was jasper; the second, sapphire; the third, a chalcedony; the fourth, an emerald; The fifth, sardonyx; the sixth, sardius; the seventh, chrysolite; the eighth, beryl; the ninth, a topaz; the tenth, a chrysoprasus;[558] *the eleventh, a jacinth; the twelfth, an amethyst. And the twelve gates were twelve pearls; every several gate was of one pearl: and the street of the city was pure gold, as it were transparent glass (Re 21:18-21).*

The description of the New Jerusalem as a city filled with gold and precious jewels is lifted directly from Tobit's prayer of rejoicing. Many have described the typological significance of these descriptions. The author is not describing a literal place, nor giving a purely factual description. The glories of the New Jerusalem are veiled in human language. For example, St. Andrew of Cesarea (c. 563– 637), in his

---

[558] Chrysoprase, chrysophrase or chrysoprasus is a gemstone variety of chalcedony that contains small quantities of nickel. Its color is normally apple-green, but varies to deep green. The darker varieties of chrysoprase are also referred to as prase. (Wikipedia 2018)

commentary on Revelation,⁵⁵⁹ indicates the 12 stones are related to the twelve stones worn by the High Priest of the Old Covenant, and as the foundation stones represent the twelve apostles, he is describing a connection between the Old Covenant and the New.⁵⁶⁰

Balanced Parallelism

There is a connection between the New Testament allusions to the Old Testament and Hebrew poetry. Hebrew poetry consists not of rhyme and meter, as in Western poetry, but rather in Balanced Parallelism.⁵⁶¹ Thus, in the Psalms, we see the same thoughts repeated in parallel forms. Sometimes the thought is repeated using different words, called Synonymous Parallelism. In other cases, the thought is expanded upon in subsequent lines, which is called Synthetic Parallelism. Finally, the thought may be expressed in contrasting thoughts, called Antithetical Parallelism.

In the New Testament, we will sometimes see a statement that forms a balanced parallel when compared with a passage from the Old Testament. The ease with which these balanced parallels exist between the Protestant Old Testament and the Apocrypha seems intentional.

The Golden Rule

Do that to no man which thou hatest (Tobit 4:15a).

---

⁵⁵⁹ St Andrew's commentary was the earliest accepted Greek commentary on Revelation. It was preceded by a commentary by Oikoumenios, although as the theology was not orthodox, his commentary was not accepted as authoritative.

⁵⁶⁰ (Constantinou, Andrew of Caesarea and the Apocalypse 2008, Part 2, 219-227)

⁵⁶¹ These parallels may be repeated in two lines, which are called "bicolon" or "dystich". In some cases there may be three lines, which are called "tricolon" or "tristich".

Therefore all things whatsoever ye would that men should do to you, do ye even so to them: for this is the law and the prophets (Matt 7:12).

In the Sermon on the Mount, Jesus offers what has (in shortened form) become known as The Golden Rule: "Do unto others as they would have you do unto you." The converse statement is found in Tobit: "Do that to no man which thou hatest." Together, the two statements are a form of Hebrew poetry, which consists of a balanced repetition of a phrase or thought.

In this instance, Jesus would have expected His hearers to know the statement from Tobit and to understand His statement as poetry. The specific form of this poetry is called *antithetical parallelism*, which consists of pairs (or sometimes triplets) of statements that contrast with each other. Thus, this couplet, when placed together, form a balanced and antithetical repetition of the primary thought.

Do that to no man which thou hatest.

Whatsoever ye would that men should do to you, do ye even so to them;

Jesus expands upon the context. In Tobit, the statement "Do that to no man which thou hatest" comes in the midst of a father's moral and ethical prescriptions for his son. In the Sermon on the Mount, the Golden Rule comes at the end of a larger passage on prayer. This passage is known by its three key words: Ask, Seek, Knock. Often the statement "Ask, and it shall be given you" is interpreted as a promise that God will give us whatever we ask of Him. But that is not what the context tells us. The context of the asking, seeking, and knocking is The Golden Rule, which is an ethical precept that teaches us how to treat our neighbor. This is very much in line with its context in the book of Tobit. Thus, in prayer, we should be interceding with God on behalf of others, asking God for the things they need, seeking for that which our neighbor has lost, and knocking on heaven's door on their behalf. In other words, just as we desire others to pray for the health of our soul and body, we should pray for the soul and body of our neighbor. If we seek wisdom for ourselves, that must be the content of our prayers for others. If we desire heaven, we must intercede on behalf of others.

Known by their Fruits

The fruit declareth if the tree have been dressed [pruned]; so is the utterance of a conceit in the heart of man (Sir 27:6).

Wherefore by their fruits ye shall know them (Matt 7:20).

This passage from Sirach is alluded to by Jesus when he states: "By their fruits ye shall know them" (Matt 7:20). The allusion may not be clear from this one verse but is increasingly clear when reading the entire passage from the Sermon on the Mount. Jesus is warning against false prophets; a good tree brings forth good fruit, Jesus argues, and a corrupt tree brings forth corrupt fruit. Therefore, false prophets are those who bring forth corrupt fruit.

In the Gospel of Luke, we read the Parable of the Barren Fig Tree, a tree which has not borne fruit for three years. (Luke 13:6-9) The dresser tells the master he will pay special attention to this tree over the following year; he will dig around it and fertilize the soil with manure. A tree that has been properly pruned and fertilized is one that should bear good rather than corrupt fruit.

What does the relationship between dressing a tree and human beings? This is made clear in other passages such as Hebrews 12:6-7, where we read how the Lord chastens those whom he loves. In other words, the Lord prunes us, shapes us, and does uncomfortable things to us, so that we might bring forth fruit more abundantly.

As the passage from Sirach makes clear (through antithetical parallelism), the heart of man needs much pruning as it is the source of evil. In the Sermon on the Mount, Jesus is saying that the heart of the false prophets has not been pruned and that evil flourishes within them. While they may be able to hide it for a time, they will not be able to hide it forever. Eventually, their corrupt fruit will be made manifest, and their sins will be found out (Num 32:23).

47: Doctrinal Sources and Explanations

Doctrinal issues and explanations have been important to the church as far back as we have written records. Since these written records extend into the post-apostolic era, we can safely presume these doctrines to have the apostolic imprimatur. Some these doctrines have been abandoned by the Protestant churches along with the books which provide the scriptural basis for them. There are also those passages of scripture that are difficult to understand without reference to the so-called Apocryphal books. Moreover, there are doctrines and theological problems which are explained more clearly in the so-called Apocrypha than in the Protestant Scriptures.

The Existence of Suffering and Evil

The problem of the existence of evil and death, given the power and goodness of God, is summed up by the theological term theodicy. Theodicy is a profoundly difficult question and one we all struggle with. Even young children sometimes ask questions about whether God created evil and, if He did not, how and why He allows evil to exist. This question has been wrestled with by both young and old, by both the simple and the educated, by both saint and sinner alike.

And yet there is another more profound question: why God is silent in the face of the suffering of His people? Metropolitan Nahum of Strumica makes mention of the Divine silence in connection with Christ's suffering and death.[562] We read in the Scriptures. "He was led as a sheep to the slaughter; and like a lamb dumb before his shearer, so opened he not his mouth" (Isa 53:7; Acts 8:32). Christ himself was silent in the face of this great evil being done to him. He did not object, he did not present a defense, he did not protest his innocence — all of which made the act of the Jewish and Roman leaders even more monstrous.

---

[562] (Metropolitan Nahum of Strumica 2013, Kindle Locations 383-388)

The Divine Silence of Jesus Christ in the face of the evil perpetrated upon Him is clear. In the Nicene Creed, we read that the Incarnation was "for us and for our salvation" and the crucifixion was "for our sake." The incarnation is not why *we* suffer; nor is it why God seems to be silent in the face of our suffering. However, we know from both Scripture and experience that Christ is most present with us during times of suffering. He suffers with us; we suffer with Him. In Mark thirteen Jesus says when we are called to give an account of our faith we are to give no thought as to what we will speak; the Holy Spirit will speak through us. Given this, perhaps God speaks to us through and with the voice the martyrs. If this is true, then the voice of the martyrs speaks not truth *to* power, but rather speaks truth *with* power; God is not silent but speaks through His suffering servants.

Before we can understand the meaning of the suffering of God's people, we must come to an understanding of holiness. In nearly every case the word "Holy" is used of God, God's law, and the Sacred Scriptures. However, in Paul's writings, we begin to see the idea of God's people becoming Holy through their connection with Christ. In Paul's letter to the Romans, he builds upon Christ's metaphor of the vine and the branches: "For if the firstfruit be holy, the lump is also holy: and if the root be holy, so are the branches" (Ro 11:16). God wants us to be a holy people (Lev 11:45; 1Pe 1:16).

Paul indicates that holiness is to be the normative state of the Christian life: "I beseech you therefore, brethren, by the mercies of God, that ye present your bodies a living sacrifice, holy, acceptable unto God, which is your reasonable service" (Ro 12:1). Paul tells us the point of Christ's crucifixion was so He could present us to God as holy (Col 1:22). Writing to the Corinthians, Paul first states that the "temple of God is holy" and then that we are the "temple of the Holy Ghost" (1 Cor 3:17; 6:19). Paul describes the church as a holy temple, holy and without blemish (Eph 2:21; 5:27). In his moral and ethical prescriptions that typically end the writings of Paul, he describes holiness as the goal of the Christian life.

If holiness is the goal, why do God's people suffer? In the second book of Maccabees, we read that suffering comes into the life of God's people not as punishment, but as a corrective tool. Suffering is presented as a sign of God's mercy in that he doesn't leave us to our sins but rather guides us away from them. The point of our present sufferings is for us to avoid the judgment of God. The prophet writes:

Now I beseech those that read this book, that they be not discouraged for these calamities, but that they judge those punishments not to be for destruction, but for a chastening of our nation. For it is a token of his great goodness, when wicked doers are not suffered any long time, but forthwith punished. For not as with other nations, whom the Lord patiently forbeareth to punish, till they be come to the fulness of their sins, so dealeth he with us, lest that, being come to the height of sin, afterwards he should take vengeance of us. And therefore he never withdraweth his mercy from us: and though he punish with adversity, yet doth he never forsake his people. But let this that we have spoken be for a warning unto us (2 Macc 6:12-17).

The apostle Peter writes how it is better to "suffer for well doing, than for evil doing" (1Pe 3:17). He then describes "the longsuffering of God," how "God waited in the days of Noah, while the ark was a preparing, wherein few, that is, eight souls were saved by water" (1Pe 3:20). In this passage the sufferings of the few are seen as God's mercy; the sufferings are also seen as nothing when compared to the judgment of the world, a theme Peter appears to have taken from the 2 Maccabees passage.

The Old Testament speaks of the suffering of righteous Job. The Bible provides no reason for Job's suffering. Despite this, Job speaks of the insignificance of his suffering in light of eternity:

For I know that my redeemer liveth, and that he shall stand at the latter day upon the earth: And though after my skin worms destroy this body, yet in my flesh shall I see God: Whom I shall see for myself, and mine eyes shall behold, and not another; though my reins be consumed within me (Job 19:25-27).

The psalmist cries out with us against the evil of this world: "Truly God is good to Israel, even to such as are of a clean heart. But as for me, my feet were almost gone; my steps had well-nigh slipped. For I was envious at the foolish, when I saw the prosperity of the wicked" (Ps 73:1-3). The passage from Psalms 73 is the clearest expression of the problem of theodicy; theodicy becomes a problem when we take our eyes off of God and focus on our neighbor's continuing good fortune in the face of their sin. When we cease repenting of our sins and focus on the sin of our brother, the goodness of God seems far away. The psalmist continues his protest against God until something changes. "When I thought to know this, it was too painful for me; Until I went into the sanctuary of God" (Ps 73:16-17).

When reading this, we cannot help but think of the disciple Peter disciple walking on water; he was fine until he took his eyes off of Jesus and focused on his immediate circumstances. When he begins to sink he cries out to Jesus; Jesus then pulls him from the water and places him back in the boat. The boat, of course, reminds us of Noah's Ark, which is itself a type of the church.

I have no definitive answers to the problem of evil, but I trust in the mercies of God, which are renewed every morning (La 3:22-23). I only hope that when my time comes, that the Holy Spirit speaks through me as powerfully as He speaks through one of the new martyrs of Syria: "I am a Christian, and if you want to kill me for this, I do not object to it."[563]

Free Will

One of the most interesting disagreements among Protestants is in the area of Free Will. To put it another way, Protestants differ as to the effects of the fall of man (hereafter

---

[563] (Nofal 2013)

Doctrinal Sources and Explanations

referred to as the fall). John Calvin declared the fall was total, and that humanity is totally depraved. Moreover, as God is sovereign over His creation, we have no choice as to whether to believe or not. We have no Free Will; instead, God chooses some of us to be saved and others to be damned. May God be ever glorified.

Luther is less hardcore, claiming that humanity is free in lower things but passive in higher things; any movement toward God is the result of the Holy Spirit's working in us. To put it another way, we are free to turn to the left or the right, but we are unable to make an independent choice between heaven and hell. Luther was not a believer in total depravity, as he allowed for civic righteousness, for the ability of humanity to behave with justice and show compassion. These acts of civic righteousness, however, do not open the door to heaven.

Besides these views, there are some Protestants who fall into the heresy of Pelagianism. Pelagius taught that human will is not damaged by original sin and that human beings are still able to choose between good and evil. Evangelicals typically do not fall into this heresy, but there are some other Protestants who do. (A milder form of this some Protestants call semi-Pelagianism, in which free will is unable to choose God on its own unless aided by divine grace).

The initial (or magisterial) reformers denied the existence of free will (a.k.a. free moral agency.) Of course, Protestants were not the first to encounter this problem. The question of free will was debated amongst the Jews as well. Dr. Carol A. Newsome, Professor of Old Testament at Emory University, describes three basic positions: 1) Moral Agency is affirmed; 2) Moral agency is internally impaired, but the impairment is not total, and humans are still responsible for their actions; 3) Moral agency is denied, which may reflect upon the creator.[564]

---

[564] (Newsom 2012, 15)

Jesus Ben Sira, the author of Sirach (a.k.a. Ecclesiasticus), rails against those who deny the existence of free moral agency and blame God for the existence of evil.

Say not thou, It is through the Lord that I fell away: for thou oughtest not to do the things that he hateth.

Say not thou, He hath caused me to err: for he hath no need of the sinful man (Sir 15:11-12).

Dr. Carol A. Newsom says Jesus ben Sira is arguing against the position of 4 Ezra, also known as 2 Esdras.

In some ways the position sounds closes to the moral anthropology articulated three hundred years later in the book of 4 Ezra. There Ezra sharply questions the model of free human agency and attributes the moral failure of the vast majority of persons to the "evil heart" with which humans were created, and which god did not act to remove or correct.[565]

Ezra says "For the first Adam bearing a wicked heart transgressed, and was overcome; and so be all they that are born of him" (2 Esdras 3:21). Ezra also complains that although God gave the law, He did not take away the wickedness that prevented humans from obeying the law.

And thy glory went through four gates, of fire, and of earthquake, and of wind, and of cold; that thou mightest give the law unto the seed of Jacob, and diligence unto the generation of Israel. And yet tookest thou not away from them a wicked heart, that thy law might bring forth fruit in them (2 Esdras 3: 19-20).

The angel Uriel comes to him and confirms Ezra's view of humanity's moral agency, and God's complicity in the existence of evil. The angel Uriel says he will explain to Ezra

---

[565] (Ibid, 5)

Doctrinal Sources and Explanations

"from whence the wicked heart cometh" (2 Esdras 4:4). He then says: "For the grain of evil seed hath been sown in the heart of Adam from the beginning" (2 Esdras 4:30).[566]

Jesus Ben Sira disagrees with this. He affirms Free Will and insists that God is not the source of evil.

The Lord hateth all abomination; and they that fear God love it not. He himself made man from the beginning, and left him in the hand of his counsel; If thou wilt, to keep the commandments, and to perform acceptable faithfulness. He hath set fire and water before thee: stretch forth thy hand unto whether thou wilt. Before man is life and death; and whether him liketh shall be given him. For the wisdom of the Lord is great, and he is mighty in power, and beholdeth all things: And his eyes are upon them that fear him, and he knoweth every work of man. He hath commanded no man to do wickedly, neither hath he given any man licence to sin (Sir 15:13-20).

In Sirach, we read that God created man with Free Will, and that man still can choose. Sirach is not claiming man is not affected by Adam's sin. Rather, he is claiming that man still has a choice and is therefore morally responsible for his actions.

The Harrowing of Hell

For Christ also hath once suffered for sins, the just for the unjust, that he might bring us to God, being put to death in the flesh, but quickened by the Spirit: By which also he went and preached unto the spirits in prison; Which sometime were disobedient, when once the longsuffering of God waited in the days of Noah, while the ark was a preparing, wherein few, that is, eight souls were saved by water. The like figure whereunto even baptism doth also now save us (not the putting away of

---

[566] It is possible to read 4 Ezra in a thoroughly orthodox way. It is never stated that God is the one who sowed evil in the heart of man; the most that can be said is that God has not yet acted to take away man's wicked heart.

the filth of the flesh, but the answer of a good conscience toward God,) by the resurrection of Jesus Christ: Who is gone into heaven, and is on the right hand of God; angels and authorities and powers being made subject unto him (1 Pet 3:18-22).

For Protestants, this is a difficult and most troubling passage, a passage whose meaning is unclear and therefore subject to all sorts of interpretations. What does the phrase "spirits in prison" mean? Why did Jesus preach to them, and what was the content of His sermon?[567] When I was in High School, I remember a sermon on this passage in which the preacher claimed the "spirits in prison" were the fallen angels, and Jesus message was: "I have beaten you!" While it made for a powerful sermon, this interpretation cannot be supported by the text — although, in the absence of other evidence, it is certainly no worse than any of the other interpretations I had heard.

And yet, none of the Protestant interpretations of this passage relate to the interpretation given by the early church which was derived from the book of Tobit and various Old Testament passages, as illumined by the life of Christ. In the book of Tobit, we read his prayer of thanksgiving. In it, Tobit refers to what most Christians call the Harrowing of Hell; the descent of Christ into Hell, where he led captivity captive — that is, from where he delivered the Old Testament saints from their bondage of sin, death, and the devil.

Then Tobit wrote a prayer of rejoicing, and said, Blessed be God that liveth for ever, and blessed be his kingdom. For he doth scourge, and hath mercy: he leadeth down to hell [Hades], and bringeth up again: neither is there any that can avoid his hand (Tobit 13:1-2).

It is important to note that the verses above are from the King James Version which tends to conflate the terms for Hell

---

[567] Later we will briefly discuss the problematic phrase: "even baptism doth also now save us".

Doctrinal Sources and Explanations

and Hades, translating them both as Hell. However, the word used here is not the Greek word for Hell, but the word for Hades [ᾅδην], the place for disembodied spirits; in the Old Testament this equates to the Hebrew word Sheol [שְׁאוֹל], being the grave, the abode of the dead. While in the New Testament Hades is reserved for the wicked awaiting judgment, in the Old Testament (before Christ's Descent into Hades), Hades/Sheol held both the righteous and the damned.

We find one of the most important Old Testament passages concerning Christ's descent into Hades in Psalms 24. This passage comes in two parts; the first declares that all of the creation is the LORD'S, and states that only the pure in heart will stand in the holy place of God.

The earth is the LORD'S, and the fulness thereof; the world, and they that dwell therein. For he hath founded it upon the seas, and established it upon the floods. Who shall ascend into the hill of the LORD? or who shall stand in his holy place? He that hath clean hands, and a pure heart; who hath not lifted up his soul unto vanity, nor sworn deceitfully. He shall receive the blessing from the LORD, and righteousness from the God of his salvation. This is the generation of them that seek him, that seek thy face, O Jacob. Selah (Ps 24:1-6).

After this passage comes the word Selah, which is a musical and liturgical term, giving one time to pause and reflect on what has come before. Reflecting on the fact that only the pure in heart will see God (Mt 5:8), we must ask: who, then, is pure? And who is without sin (Jn 8:7)? The answer is He who was tempted like us, yet without sin (Heb 4:15); He who was offered for and on behalf of our sins, and was raised again without sin (Heb 9:28). In the remainder of Psalm 24, we see Christ, the King of glory, as being the one able to conquer the hold death had on humanity, and who has opened for us the gates of paradise.

Lift up your heads, O ye gates; and be ye lift up, ye everlasting doors; and the King of glory shall come in. Who is this King of glory? The LORD strong and mighty, the LORD mighty in battle. Lift up your heads, O ye gates; even lift them up, ye everlasting doors; and the King of glory shall come in. Who is this King of glory? The LORD of hosts, he is the King of glory. Selah (Ps 24:7-10).

These last verses from Psalm 24 are part of the Paschal liturgy of the Eastern Church. After reciting (and acting out) this passage, the doors of the church are flung open, and the people enter, after which the peope sing the Easter Troparion: "Christ is risen from the dead, trampling down death by death, and upon those in the tomb bestowing life." This refrain, dating as early as the 2nd century,[568] refers to the Harrowing of Hell. Death could not hold Him. In defeating death, Christ led captivity captive (Ps 68:18; Eph 4:8), meaning He led the souls of the departed righteous out of their resting place, and they are now kept by the power of God through faith unto salvation (1 Pet 1:5).

We should note that this doctrine is not some medieval invention of the Roman Catholic Church, but is, in fact, the universal witness of the Church all the way back to the apostolic age. We know this from a variety of sources; the New Testament itself, the apocryphal writings of the New Testament period, Christian poetry, and fathers of the early church.

New Testament sources include Jesus' discussion of His impending three-day burial: "For as Jonas was three days and three nights in the whale's belly; so shall the Son of man be three days and three nights in the heart of the earth" (Matt 12:40); Christian tradition holds this to be a foretelling of Christ's descent into Hell.[569] Other incidental passages include Peter's sermon at Pentecost (Acts 2:22-32) and Paul's sermon in the synagogue of Antioch (Acts 13:34-37). Bishop Hilarion Alfayev writes: "St Paul's words that speak of how Christ 'descended into the lower parts of the earth' [Eph 4:9]

---

[568] (Alfeyev, Christ the Conqueror of Hell 2009, 34)

[569] (Ibid, 17)

and of his victory over death and hell' [1 Cor 15:54-57; Rom 10:7; Col 2:14-15]."[570] Perhaps the most important passage, which became a prototype for other writings of the post-apostolic period, is the passage from 1 Peter which opens this discourse.

Archbishop Hilarion Alfeyev notes the Harrowing of Hell is much more prominent in the Christian Apocalypses than in the canonical texts. Among these texts, which were "indirectly" used by the early church are the Christian interpolations into the *Ascension of Isaiah* and *The Testament of Asher*, along with the "Christian adaptation" of *The Testament of the Twelve Patriarchs*. Other texts include *The Gospel of Peter, The Epistle of the Apostles, The Shepherd of Hermas, The Sibylline Oracles, The Teachings of Silvanus, The Gospel of Bartholomew*, and *The Gospel of Nicodemus*. This last book "exerted decisive influence on the formation of church doctrine on the subject."[571]

Besides the previously mentioned Easter Troparion, we should mention the poem "On Pascha" by St Melito of Sardis (mid-2nd Century), a portion of which is quoted below.

66. When this one came from heaven to earth for the sake of the one who suffers, and had clothed himself with that very one through the womb of a virgin, and having come forth as man, he accepted the sufferings of the sufferer through his body which was capable of suffering. And he destroyed those human sufferings by his spirit which was incapable of dying. He killed death which had put man to death.

68. This is the one who covered death with shame and who plunged the devil into mourning as Moses did Pharaoh. This is the one who smote lawlessness and deprived injustice of its offspring, as Moses deprived Egypt. This is the one who delivered us from slavery into freedom, from darkness into light, from death into life, from tyranny into an eternal

---

[570] (Ibid, 19)

[571] (Ibid, 20-29)

kingdom, and who made us a new priesthood, and a special people forever.

70. This is the one who became human in a virgin, who was hanged on the tree, who was buried in the earth, who was resurrected from among the dead, and who raised mankind up out of the grave below to the heights of heaven.

71. This is the lamb that was slain. This is the lamb that was silent. This is the one who was born of Mary, that beautiful ewe-lamb. This is the one who was taken from the flock, and was dragged to sacrifice, and was killed in the evening, and was buried at night; the one who was not broken while on the tree, who did not see dissolution while in the earth, who rose up from the dead, raising up mankind below. [572]

St Melito of Sardis does not place the saving work of Christ into different categories and treating each atomistically (as is done in western theology.) Instead, St Melito of Sardis connects it all into one seamless narrative flowing from the pre-existence of the Son of God, His clothing of himself of the flesh of the Virgin Mary, His life, death, burial, and His raising of mankind from the grave by virtue of His own resurrection. This same method is repeated elsewhere in his "On Pascha," to similar effect.

Another interesting bit of poetry comes to us by way of the *Odes of Solomon*, a work most scholars believe first appeared in Syria in the mid-second century. About their origin, Rutherford Hayes Platt states: "one of the most plausible explanations is that they are songs of newly baptized Christians of the First Century."[573] With this in mind, it is interesting to note that these Odes contain significant references to and descriptions of Christ's descent into Hades.[574] Ode 42 is particularly interesting, in that it

---

[572] (St Melito of Sardis 1989, 20-23; 32-34)
[573] (Platt 2007, 205)
[574] See Odes 17, 22, 24, and 42.

Doctrinal Sources and Explanations

describes both the "spirits in prison" and the content of Christ's preaching.

ODE 42.

The Odes of Solomon, the Son of David, are ended with the following exquisite verses.

1   I stretched out my hands and approached my Lord:
2   For the stretching of my hands is His sign:
3   My expansion is the outspread tree which was set up on the way of the Righteous One.
4   And I became of no account to those who did not take hold of me; and I shall be with those who love me.
5   All my persecutors are dead; and they sought after me who hoped in me, because I was alive:
6   And I rose up and am with them; and I will speak by their mouths.
7   For they have despised those who persecuted them;
8   And I lifted up over them the yoke of my love;
9   Like the arm of the bridegroom over the bride,
    So was my yoke over those that know me:
    And as the couch that is spread in the house of the bridegroom and bride,
12 So is my love over those that believe in me.
13 And I was not rejected though I was reckoned to be so.
14 I did not perish, though they devised it against me.
15 Sheol saw me and was made miserable:
    Death cast me up, and many along with me.
17 I had gall and bitterness, and I went down with him to the utmost of his depth:
18 And the feet and the head he let go, for they were not able to endure my face:
19 And I made a congregation of living men amongst his dead men, and I spake with them by living lips:
20 Because my word shall not be void:
21 And those who had died ran towards me: and they cried and said, Son of God, have pity on us, and do with us according to thy kindness,

22 *And bring us out from the bonds of darkness: and open to us the door by which we shall come out to thee.*
23 *For we see that our death has not touched thee.*
24 *Let us also be redeemed with thee: for thou art our Redeemer.*
25 *And I heard their voice; and my name I sealed upon their heads:*
26 *For they are free men and they are mine. Hallelujah.*

While Ode 42 compares with Psalm 22 as a description of the crucifixion, the latter half describes Christ's descent into Hell. Verse 26 in particular sums up the soteriological [salvific] theology contained within the description of Christ's Harrowing of Hell. We were all in bondage to sin, death, and the devil; Christ has broken our chains, destroyed the gates of hell, and declares to all concerned: "They are free men and they are mine. Hallelujah."

An interesting patristic passage (one of many) comes to us by way of Eusebius, in "The Story Concerning the King of Edessa." King Agbar of Edessa[575] was ill with some form of wasting disease. Hearing of Jesus, the King requested Jesus come and heal him. Jesus sent King Agbar a letter saying one of his disciples would come and heal his sicknesses and bring salvation to his people. After the resurrection of Christ, Thomas sent Thaddeus (one of the seventy) to Edessa. Thaddeus healed King Agbar and a great many others. He also preached the following Gospel to them, which included a description of Christ's descent into Hades:

Because I have been sent to preach the word of God, assemble me tomorrow all the people of thy city, and I will preach before them, and sow amongst them the word of life; and will tell them about the coming of Christ, how it took place; and about His

---

[575] Edessa was the capital city of Osreone, which was part of the Syriac empire. The country of Osreone is roughly located in the border area of Turkey and Syria; the city of Edessa is located in modern-day Turkey, and known as Şanlıurfa (or colloquially as Urfa).

mission, for what purpose he was sent by His Father; and about His power and His deeds, and about the mysteries which He spake in the world, and by what power He wrought these things, and about His new preaching, and about His abasement and His humiliation, and how He humbled and emptied and abased Himself, and was crucified, and descended to Hades, and broke through the enclosure which had never been broken through before, and raised up the dead, and descended alone, and ascended with a great multitude to His Father.[576]

The fact that the Harrowing of Hell featured prominently in the Apocryphal texts, Christian poetry, and patristic sources testifies to the early origins of this Christian doctrine. And the fact that this doctrine is supported from the Old Testament, including both canonical and so-called Apocryphal texts, suggests the loss of something vital to the Gospel when the Apocrypha were separated from the rest of the Old Testament.

Prayer for the Dead

The default Protestant position is that that prayer to the saints and angels is worse than useless — that it is not found in scripture and is an example of paganism infecting the church. For some Protestants, the examples of prayer for the dead in the Apocrypha are evidence that they should not be part of Sacred Scripture. One hopes this is their *prima facie* position — a position accepted as true until contradicted by evidence. With that hope in mind, let us examine the evidence.

In 2 Maccabees we see the aftermath of a great victory. Having routed the troops of Gorgias, Judas (the governor of Idumea)[577] had his men gather up the bodies of the fallen for burial. When they found that some of the fallen were wearing Jamnian idols, Judas took a collection and offered it as a sin offering on their behalf.

---

[576] (Schaff, ANF08 2005, 1098)

[577] King Herod was an Idumean.

And when he had made a gathering throughout the company to the sum of two thousand drachms of silver, he sent it to Jerusalem to offer a sin offering, doing therein very well and honestly, in that he was mindful of the resurrection: for if he had not hoped that they that were slain should have risen again, it had been superfluous and vain to pray for the dead. And also in that he perceived that there was great favor laid up for those that died godly, it was an holy and good thought. Whereupon he made a reconciliation for the dead, that they might be delivered from sin (2 Maccabees 12:43-45).

The passage connects the belief in the resurrection with sacrifices and prayers for the dead, to "set them free from their transgression." The apostle Paul alludes to this passage when he discusses the baptism of the dead.

Otherwise, what do people mean by being baptized on behalf of the dead? If the dead are not raised at all, why are people baptized on their behalf (1 Corinthians 15:29)?

To demonstrate the connection between resurrection, prayer for the dead, and baptism, we must allow St. John Chrysostom to have his say. In Homily XL [40] on 1 Corinthians, Chrysostom begins by providing the explanation of baptism given to the recently baptized Christians. In baptism, we are buried with Christ in His death and resurrected with Christ unto new life. This resurrection is not symbolic; the words are performative words: they do what they say.

"I believe in the resurrection of the dead," and upon this faith we are baptized. For after we have confessed this together with the rest, then at last are we let down into the fountain of those sacred streams. This therefore Paul recalling to their minds said, "if there be no resurrection, why art thou then baptized for the dead?" i.e., the dead bodies. For in fact with a view to this art thou baptized, the resurrection of thy dead body, believing that it no longer remains dead. And thou indeed in the words makest mention of a resurrection of the dead; but the priest, as in a kind of image, signifies to thee by very deed

Doctrinal Sources and Explanations

the things which thou hast believed and confessed in words. When without a sign thou believest, then he gives thee the sign also; when thou hast done thine own part, then also doth God fully assure thee. How and in what manner? By the water. For the being baptized and immersed and then emerging, is a symbol of the descent into Hades and return thence. Wherefore also Paul calls baptism a burial, saying, "Therefore we are buried with Him by baptism into death" (Rom. 4:4).[578]

Paul says if the dead are not raised, then why are we baptized? If baptism does not affect the resurrection of the body, then what is the point? On this subject, we shall let Chrysostom speak.

Yet again, because the term Resurrection is not sufficient to indicate the whole: for many after rising have again departed, as those in the Old Testament, as Lazarus, as they at the time of the crucifixion: one is bid to say, "and the life everlasting," that none may any longer have a notion of death after that resurrection. These words therefore Paul recalling to their minds, saith, "What shall they do which are baptized for the dead?" "For if there be no resurrection," saith he, "these words are but scenery. If there be no resurrection, how persuade we them to believe things which we do not bestow? ...This then he here saith of those who are baptized also. "What shall they do which are baptized," saith he, "having subscribed to the resurrection of dead bodies, and not receiving it, but suffering fraud? And what need was there at all of this confession, if the fact did not follow?[579]

One of the more interesting passages on this subject comes from the book of 2 Esdras, referred to by scholars as 4 Ezra (chap 3-14), 5 Ezra (chap 1-2), & 6 Ezra (chap 14-15).

Remember thy children that sleep, for I shall bring them out of the sides of the earth, and shew mercy unto them: for I am

---

[578] (Schaff, NPNF1-12 2002, 379-380)

[579] (Ibid, 380-381)

merciful, saith the Lord Almighty. Embrace thy children until I come and shew mercy unto them: for my wells run over, and my grace shall not fail (2 Esd 2:31-32).

This passage comes at the end of a section describing the moral and ethical responsibilities of the people of God. Scholars refer to the first two chapters of 2 Esdras as 5 Ezra. 5 Ezra is thought to be a Christian interpolation as it contains numerous references to the New Testament; thus, 2 Esd 2:31-32 is evidence of the Christian practice of praying for the dead.[580]

Is prayer for the dead efficacious? Does it do anything? Does it affect any change in the eternal status of those who have departed this life? Of this, the 5 Ezra tells us that God will show mercy. We cannot draw back the curtain any further; we cannot peer beneath the veil. And yet we cannot deny that the believing Jews of the Old Testament period had this belief and practice, a practice continued by the early Church.

---

[580] (Davila 2007) He writes:

The book of 5 Ezra also quotes from or alludes to a number of earlier works. 5 Ezra 2:2-5a alludes to Baruch 4:8-23. (The book of Baruch seems to have been written by 70 CE). Of greater interest are the allusions to the New Testament. 5 Ezra 1:30 seems to be dependent on Matthew 27:37//Luke 13:34 and is closest to Matthew's version, although we cannot rule out direct dependence on Q (on which both Gospel passages arguably rely). This implies that 5 Ezra existed by sometime in the second half of the first century CE. Likewise, there is possibly a connection between 5 Ezra 1:32 and Matthew 23:34-35//Luke 11:49-50 (or on the Q passage behind them), although this contributes nothing more to the question the dating of the work. Also, 5 Ezra 2:42 has some connection with Revelation 7:9. Likewise, 5 Ezra 2:42-43 seems to be dependent on Shepherd of Hermas 83:1 (9.6.1), which involves a crowd with a tall man who is later (89:7-8) identified with the "Son of God"). (Davila 2007)

The Intercessory Prayer of Saints and Angels

In 2 Maccabees the departed Onías speaks of the prophet Jeremiah and his fervent prayer for the people of God.

And this was his vision: That Onías, who had been high priest, a virtuous and a good man, revered in conversation, gentle in condition, well spoken also, and exercised from a child in all points of virtue, holding up his hands prayed for the whole body of the Jews. This done, in like manner there appeared a man with gray hairs, and exceeding glorious, who was of a wonderful and excellent majesty. Then Onías answered, saying, This is a lover of the brethren, who prayeth much for the people, and for the holy city, to wit, Jeremiah the prophet of God. Whereupon Jeremiah holding forth his right hand gave to Judas a sword of gold, and in giving it spake thus, Take this holy sword, a gift from God, with the which thou shalt wound the adversaries (2 Maccabees 15:12-16).

In this passage, we see the vision of Judas Maccabaeus of an angel appearing to Onías, "who had been high priest" while Onías was praying for the Jews. The departed Onías states this angel "is a lover of the brethren, who prayeth much for the people." Thus, we are led to understand that the departed are aware of us and pray for us, just as the angels pray for us. Therefore, those who have "fallen asleep," those who are "kept by the power of God," those whose God is "the God of the living, and not the dead," and those who are "like the angels," can hear our prayers and intercede for us, just as our brothers and sisters among the living can intercede for us.

Prayer and worship are the two primary activities described in heaven. In the book of Revelation, the point of view shifts between the events taking place on the earth and the liturgical worship taking place in heaven, primarily consisting of prayers of praise and intercession. That the book of 2 Maccabees informs us the angels pray for us should not be at all surprising, given the Christian concept of the Guardian Angel.[581]

Surprisingly, the passage from 2 Maccabees is mentioned in the Apology to the Lutheran Confessions (Ap) as possibly showing that the saints in heaven pray for us. However, the Apology also states that there is no command, promise, or example of prayer to the saints in Scripture. The Reformation took this as their default position.

Even if the saints do pray fervently for the church, it does not follow that they should be invoked. But our Confession affirms only this much, that Scripture does not teach us to invoke the saints or to ask their help. Neither a command nor a promise nor an example can be shown from Scripture for the invocation of the saints; from this it follows that consciences cannot be sure about such invocation.[582]

The Apology does reference the prophet Zechariah where we see an example of an angel praying to God for us.[583] In context, we see the prophet speaking with an angel. The angel then speaks directly to the Angel of the Lord (being a theophany, an appearance of Christ in the Old Testament), who Himself cries out to the Lord of hosts (who is God the Father), and finally, the prophet receives an answer (Zec 1:8-17).[584]

There are passages in John's Revelation informing us that the departed are aware of what is happening on the earth. For example, in the four and twenty elders around the throne of God are aware of what has transpired upon the earth, and pray to God about it.

---

[581] The existence of Guardian Angels is derived from Job 33:23-6, Daniel 10:13, Matthew 18:10, and Hebrews 1:14. The early Christian belief in the Guardian Angel is found in Acts 12:12-15.

[582] (Tappert, et al. 1959, Ap XXI, 10)

[583] (Ibid, Ap XXI, 8)

[584] This provides an example of the way intercessory prayer functions; the intercessor is a mediator between the person in need and God.

And the four and twenty elders, which sat before God on their seats, fell upon their faces, and worshipped God, Saying, We give thee thanks, O Lord God Almighty, which art, and wast, and art to come; because thou hast taken to thee thy great power, and hast reigned. And the nations were angry, and thy wrath is come, and the time of the dead, that they should be judged, and that thou shouldest give reward unto thy servants the prophets, and to the saints, and them that fear thy name, small and great; and shouldest destroy them which destroy the earth (Re 11: 16-18).

Then, at the judgment of the great whore of Babylon the saints rejoice.

And after these things I heard a great voice of much people in heaven, saying, Alleluia; Salvation, and glory, and honour, and power, unto the Lord our God: For true and righteous are his judgments: for he hath judged the great whore, which did corrupt the earth with her fornication, and hath avenged the blood of his servants at her hand (Re 19:1-2).

We see that the argument against the invocation of saints is weak. Not only do we see an example from the so-called Apocrypha of the departed prophet Jeremiah praying for the people of God, but we see Zechariah questioning an angel, who intercedes with the Angel of the Lord, who Himself calls upon God the Father. We see in John's revelation the witness of the four and twenty elders and the saints in heaven. Thus, the argument that there is no scriptural referent for prayer to the saints and angels is questionable at best, as it is found in both the so-called Apocrypha, in the Hebrew Scriptures, and the book of Revelation.

The best argument, from the standpoint of non-Protestant Christians, is that the Christian Church is one. The saints in heaven are just as much a part of the Christian Church as we the living are, and perhaps more so. If we ask our brothers and sisters to pray for us, what does it matter if some of them are alive and some have fallen asleep in the Lord?

Wisdom and the Incarnation

Hear, Israel, the commandments of life: give ear to understand wisdom. ...Thou hast forsaken the fountain of wisdom. For if thou hadst walked in the way of God, thou shouldest have dwelled in peace for ever. ...O Israel, how great is the house of God! and how large is the place of his possession! Great, and hath none end; high, and unmeasurable. ...Who hath gone up into heaven, and taken her, and brought her down from the clouds? ...This is our God, and there shall none other be accounted of in comparison of him. He hath found out all the way of knowledge, and hath given it unto Jacob his servant, and to Israel his beloved. Afterward did he show himself upon earth, and conversed with men (Baruch 3:9, 12-13, 24-25, 29, 35-37).

Baruch prophesies the Incarnation of our Lord when he writes: "Who hath gone up into heaven, and taken her, and brought her down from the clouds? ...This is our God, and there shall none other be accounted of in comparison of him." Baruch is doing something unusual here by connecting Wisdom with the Incarnation. Of course, we can only read that back into Baruch in light of the Christ event, which is how Christians read the entire Old Testament. Looking back after the Incarnation, we see it foretold in Baruch, something that would not have been clear at all before Christ's coming. The reference to the Incarnation may be why the Jews eventually decided to leave Baruch out of their canon of scripture.

Supersessionism

Supersessionism is also known as Replacement Theology or Fulfillment Theology. Supersessionism is the idea that the people of the New Covenant have replaced the people of the Old Covenant. Supersessionism is a theological concept developed by western academics in the 19th century and only gained widespread use in the late 20th century. Some Protestants deride Supersessionism as because it does not

Doctrinal Sources and Explanations

give a continued place of prominence to Israel in the plan of God. The use of the term Supersessionism is prominent among dispensationalists and messianic Jews whose theology depends upon God having one plan for the Jewish people, and another plan for the Gentiles. Those accused of being Supersessionist rarely hold the specific views ascribed to them — their views are more nuanced. For example, while Protestants may criticize the Eastern Orthodox for their Supersessionist views, the Orthodox do not believe the New Covenant supplanted (replaced) the Old Covenant, but merely fulfilled the Old. Moreover, the idea that the Church is spiritual Israel does not deny Paul's statement that God may yet have a plan for Israel (see Romans 9-11).

In 2 Esdras chapter 1 we read of Israel's continued faithlessness toward God, culminating in the following: "Thus saith the Almighty Lord, Your house is desolate, I will cast you out as the wind doth stubble" (2 Esd 1:33). As the first two chapters of 2 Esdras are a Christian interpolation written sometime in the 2nd century, we know this to be the position of the early Church. We also know this passage is quoting Christ (Mt 23:28; Lk 13:35). In the Old Testament, we often read of the land being left desolate due to Israel's unfaithfulness, but never the house of Israel. In 2 Esdras we read of the house of Israel being given to the Gentiles.

Thus saith the Almighty Lord, Your house is desolate, I will cast you out as the wind doth stubble. And your children shall not be fruitful; for they have despised my commandment, and done the thing that is an evil before me. Your houses will I give to a people that shall come; which not having heard of me yet shall believe me; to whom I have shewed no signs, yet they shall do that I have commanded them. They have seen no prophets, yet they shall call their sins to remembrance, and acknowledge them. I take to witness the grace of the people to come, whose little ones rejoice in gladness: and though they have not seen me with bodily eyes, yet in spirit they believe the thing that I say (2 Esd 1:33-37).

2 Esdras refers to the Christian Church, the Gentile Bride of Christ. This is not the whole story. Luke quotes Jesus as follows: "Behold, your house is left unto you desolate: and verily I say unto you, **Ye shall not see me, until the time come when ye shall say, Blessed is he that cometh in the name of the Lord**" [emphasis added] (Lu 13:35). The implication is that while Israel has been set aside, this may not be a permanent condition. While most people who are called Supersessionist believe that the Church replaced Israel, yet they often also believe that God may yet have a plan for the household of Israel.

Conclusion

Was Martin Luther correct in his decision to alter the canon? The apostle Peter says that "holy men of God spake as they were moved by the Holy Ghost" (2 Pet 1:21). Holy men of God wrote the Scriptures. Likewise, holy men of God throughout history have interpreted scripture and decided these canonical issues. I am not a holy man (far from it). Rather than being filled with the Spirit, I quench the Spirit every day. As a result, I question my qualifications to interpret scripture.

Likewise, I question my qualifications to write on theological matters, and would not have done so had I ever found a book aimed at answering the questions inquiring Protestants may have. If you are a person such as this, find the holiest person you know and question them. Often they are not your pastor, your parents, or your peers, but instead someone who is dismissed as odd by your friends and fellow church members. Let me explain.

When I was in high school, there were two elderly men in my church whose prayers were one scripture verse after another. They often made me uncomfortable. They asked probing questions and raised uncomfortable issues, yet talking with them encouraged me and gave me peace of spirit. These are the people you want to speak with about things such as these, not the ideologues among your friends and family. Talk with holy people about holy things; do not cast your pearls before swine.

It is my prayer that the information presented in this book will be useful to you in your spiritual journey.

The Lord bless you and keep you;
The Lord make his face to shine upon you and be gracious to you;
The Lord lift up His countenance upon you and give you peace.

Appendix A: Arguments Against the Apocrypha

1: Johann Gerhard and the Apocrypha

Johann Gerhard is the premier Lutheran theologian and is often considered to be the Lutheran Thomas Aquinas. In his 17th century book, *On the Nature of Theology and Scripture*, Gerhard writes of the distinction between books in the "codex of the Old Testament" that the "papists" consider canonical and those the Lutherans consider apocryphal.

The apocryphal books of the Old Testament are all the rest contained in the codex of the Old Testament **besides the canonical books**. *We can arrange them in two classes. First, some are apocryphal by confession of the papists themselves,* **though they are contained in the Greek or Latin Codex of the Bible.** *...Second, some are considered canonical by the papists, though they are in fact apocryphal.*[585] *[Emphasis added.]*

Gerhard argues against the Latins regard for any Apocryphal book as canonical. Moreover, he provides the various reason why some books are considered apocryphal: first, "books whose origin is hidden"; second, "books that contain myths, errors, and lies"; third, because "every canonical book of the Old Testament is written in the Prophetic language, namely, Hebrew."[586] Unfortunately, Gerhard's arguments are flawed.

The Apocrypha are not Inspired

Rather than provide extensive quotes from Gerhard, I reproduce his arguments in the form of syllogisms. He refers to syllogisms in his arguments by using terms like the major and minor premise, so I am not inventing anything Gerhard did not intend.

Gerhard's first argument is that the Apocrypha are not inspired, and therefore not canonical.

---

[585] (Gerhard 2006, 91)

[586] (Ibid, 91)

- Every canonical book of the Old Testament was written by a prophet by impulse and inspiration of the Holy Spirit.
- The Apocrypha were not written by prophets (and by extension, under the impulse and inspiration of the Holy Spirit).
- Therefore, the Apocrypha are not canonical.[587]

As we all likely agree to the first (and major) premise, we need not explore that further. The second (or minor) premise is problematic. Gerhard argues that the last Old Testament prophet was Malachi, and therefore concludes that since the Apocrypha were produced after the prophet Malachi, they were not written by prophets.

Those books we listed were written after the time of Malachi, the last prophet of the Old Testament. From Malachi until John the Baptist one can point out no prophet among the people of Israel; therefore he concludes the prophetic writing of the Old Testament.[588]

Gerhard is following a line of argument similar to that used by Flavius Josephus (as discussed in chapter 8, *Flavius Josephus and the Canon*). Merrill F. Unger, writing in his book, *Unger's Bible Dictionary*, defines the Apocrypha as those books written after the canon of the Old Testament was closed.[589] Echoing Unger's reasoning, the Baptist teacher Bob Connolly makes the following statement:

Between the last writings of the Old Testament (Malachi being one of the last Old Testament books written) and the birth of Christ, there was a 400-year 'period of silence' in which no inspired writings were added to the canon.[590]

---

[587] (Ibid, 92)
[588] (Ibid, 92)
[589] (Unger 1966, 70)
[590] (Connolly n.d.)

Appendix A: Arguments Against the Apocrypha

This is circular reasoning, the argument being that the Apocrypha are not inspired because the O.T. canon was closed, and the O.T. canon was closed because the Apocrypha are not inspired.

From my youth, I remember hearing the argument that the line of the prophets ended with the prophet Malachi, after which came the intertestamental period. Besides the circular reasoning, the evidence given for this point of view was typological. The Scriptures describe the period before the prophet Samuel as follows: "And the word of the LORD was precious in those days; there was no open vision." (1 Sam 3:1) Thus, the period before Samuel is the type of which the period before John the Baptist is the fulfillment.[591] But this is an argument from two ostensibly analogous conditions rather than from evidence. Gerhard provides an additional argument, which is that Malachi is the seal of the Old Testament, for it was Malachi who prophesied of John the Baptist.[592] This is a tenuous interpretation at best.

It is said that Jesus provides support for the idea that Malachi was the last Old Testament prophet. Jesus says:

Wherefore, behold, I send unto you prophets, and wise men, and scribes: and some of them ye shall kill and crucify; and some of them shall ye scourge in your synagogues, and persecute them from city to city: That upon you may come all the righteous blood shed upon the earth, from the blood of righteous Abel unto the blood of Zacharias son of Barachias, whom ye slew between the temple and the altar. (Mt 23:34-35)

Supposedly, the Zechariah mentioned by Jesus was the last prophet whose death was recorded in 2 Chron 24:20-22. The argument went that Jesus was making the connection between the first prophet and the last, and therefore anything written after Zechariah is not inspired. Even if this

---

[591] This argument does not appear to be widespread among Protestants; at least I can find no independent verification of it.

[592] (Gerhard 2006, 92)

were true, this is a feeble argument. There is a problem with the identification of the Zechariah Jesus mentioned. The Zechariah mentioned in 2 Chronicles was not the son of Barachiah.[593] There is an argument from Church history that this was Zechariah, son of Barachias and father of John the Baptist. One church tradition says that after Jesus birth, Zechariah brought the Virgin Mary to the Temple and had her stand in the place reserved for virgins, for which offense he was killed.[594] Another church tradition says that at the slaughter of the innocents, Herod also intended to kill the infant John, whom Elizabeth had hidden. While Zechariah was serving as a priest in Jerusalem, Herod's soldiers demanded that he tell them where the infant John was. When he refused, he was killed between the altar and the temple.[595] If Jesus is referring to the Zechariah who is the father of John the Baptist, then the entire argument regarding the cessation of prophecy falls apart.

Gerhard offers no good evidence for his position. He claims Malachi was the last prophet before John the Baptist. This claim is not based on Scripture Alone but upon an extra-biblical Protestant tradition. Therefore, we cannot accept Gerhard's minor premise that the Apocrypha were not written by prophets, and must reject Gerhard's first argument as logically unsound (which does not make it untrue; it merely means that the argument as constructed is incorrect).

In addition to the above problems, R. H. Charles notes that prophecy was actively suppressed in post-exilic Judaism. The primacy of the law was thought of as "the final and supreme revelation of God." If God had spoken through the Law, there was no need for a prophet to represent God, except to adjudicate the Law. R. H. Charles writes:

---

[593] Some scholars think Barachiah is another name for Jehoida; if so, the Zechariah mentioned by Jesus would be the one written of in 2 Chron 24:20-22. This argument appears to be wishful thinking.

[594] (Blessed Theophylact 1992, 202)

[595] (Baker n.d.)

From the time of Ezra and Nehemiah «the Law has not only assumed the functions of the ancient pre-Exilic prophets, but it has also, so far as it lay in its power, made the revival of such prophecy an impossibility.» The prophet who issued a prophecy under his own name after the time of Ezra and Nehemiah could not expect a hearing unless his prophecy had the imprimatur of the Law.[596]

While R. H. Charles ignores the Christological implications, it is clear that Jesus posed a profound challenge to post-exilic Jewish orthodoxy. He spoke in his own name, and as one having authority (Mt 7:29). Jesus claimed that John the Baptist was a prophet, and the greatest of those born of women. He then states: "all the prophets and the law prophesied until John" (Mt 11:11-13), which suggests there had been no end to the prophetic role. If the prophetic rule had not ended, the ruling class was illegitimate, a claim that contributed to Jesus' death (Jn 11:49-53).

The Apocrypha are not written in Hebrew

Gerhard's second argument is based on the language of the Old Testament.
- Every canonical book of the Old Testament is written in the prophetic language, namely, Hebrew.
- Those controversial books were not written in Hebrew.
- Ergo. [The controversial books are not canonical.][597]

The Jews considered Hebrew to be a sacred language; Johann Gerhard considered Hebrew to be the prophetic language and is, therefore, using a Jewish argument. Gerhard's argument that Hebrew is the "prophetic language" is a problem because the New Testament was primarily written in Greek (with the probable exception of Matthew). Gerhard is not completely honest, for he surely knew that portions of

---

[596] (Charles, The Apocrypha and Pseudepigrapha of the Old Testament in English Vol 2 1913, viii)

[597] (Gerhard 2006, 93)

the Old Testament are written in Aramaic, the language of Babylon. There are four passages written in Aramaic:
- Genesis 31:47, where a Hebrew place name is translated into Aramaic.
- Jeremiah 10:11, where a single sentence is in Aramaic instead of Hebrew.
- Daniel 2:4b–7:28, including the complete text of Nebuchadnezzar's pronouncement of the Hebrew God as the true God.
- Ezra 4:8–6:18 and 7:12–26.

If Hebrew is the prophetic language, then are the Aramaic portions prophetic and inspired? Yes, because God's native tongue is not Hebrew, nor Aramaic, nor Greek. Nor, for that matter, is God's native tongue the Jacobean English of the King James Version.

As for his second premise, Gerhard wrote in the seventeenth century, well before the discovery of the Dead Sea Scrolls. It is unfair to find fault with his assumption that the Apocrypha were not written in Hebrew (although how someone could continue to make that claim in the late 20th and early 21st century escapes me). Regarding the Apocrypha found among the Dead Sea Scrolls, Michael E. Stone writes of those written in Aramaic and Hebrew, the languages of the Old Testament:

Among the Dead Sea Scrolls were a number of manuscripts of the Apocrypha and Pseudepigrapha, including ten manuscripts of the Book of Enoch in the original Aramaic (until then copies were extant only in an Ethiopic translation of a Greek translation of a Semitic original), which were vital to answering many questions about its origins. Dating of the manuscripts by their script shows that certain parts of Enoch are at least as old as the third century BCE. Fragments of Ben Sira in Hebrew, Tobit in Aramaic, the Epistle of Jeremiah in Greek, and others were also found at Qumran.[598]

---

[598] (Stone, The Apocrypha and Pseudepigrapha 2001)

Gerhard notes that Jerome translated Tobit and Judith from Chaldaic into Latin, but did not consider them to be Canonical. However, Jerome is an anomaly among the fathers of the early church, in that he preferred the Hebrew text over the Septuagint. Jerome's position does not square with Jewish practice in the time of Christ, for the diaspora typically used the Septuagint in their synagogues. Alfred Edersheim notes that after the Babylonian captivity, the Hebrew language was no longer the common language of the people, and was only used by students and in the Synagogue. "Even there a *Methurgeman*, or interpreter, had to be employed to translate into the vernacular the portions of Scripture read in the public services, and the addresses delivered by the Rabbis."[599] As we mentioned previously, the Hasmonean dynasty implemented Hebrew using the Babylonian square script, but Aramaic may have continued as the language of the lower classes. Moreover, the need for an interpreter in the synagogue is what led to the creation of the Septuagint.

The Apocrypha are not about Christ

Gerhard's third argument regards the subject matter of the Apocrypha, which he claims is different than that of the Protestant Old Testament.
- Every canonical book of the Old Testament contains prophecies about Christ, promised in the Old Testament but revealed in the New.
- Those controversial books do not contain prophecies about Christ.
- Ergo. [The controversial books are not canonical.][600]

With all due respect to Johann Gerhard, this claim is nonsense. The following list is a compilation of prophecies about Christ, as well as passages from the Apocrypha used by Christ and by the evangelists.

---

[599] (Edersheim 1993, 7-8)

[600] (Gerhard 2006, 94)

- Mt 2:16 - Herod's decree of slaying innocent children was prophesied in Wis. 11:7 – "slaying the holy innocents."
- Mt 6:19-20 - Jesus' statement about laying up for yourselves treasure in heaven follows Sirach 29:11 – "lay up your treasure."
- Mt 7:12 - Jesus' golden rule "do unto others" is the converse of Tobit 4:15 – "what you hate, do not do to others."
- Mt 7:16, 20 - Jesus' statement "you will know them by their fruits" follows Sirach 27:6 - "the fruit discloses the cultivation."
- Mt 9:36 - the people were "like sheep without a shepherd" is same as Judith 11:19 – "sheep without a shepherd."
- Mt 11:25 - Jesus' description "Lord of heaven and earth" is the same as Tobit 7:18 – "Lord of heaven and earth."
- Mt 12:42 - Jesus refers to the wisdom of Solomon which was recorded and made part of the so-called deuterocanonical or apocryphal books.
- Mt 16:18 - Jesus' reference to the "power of death" and "gates of Hades" references Wisdom 16:13.
- Mt 22:25; Mk 12:20; Lk 20:29 - Gospel writers refer to the canonicity of Tobit 3:8 and 7:11 regarding the seven brothers.
- Mt 24:15 - the "desolating sacrilege" Jesus refers to is also taken from 1 Macc. 1:54 and 2 Macc. 8:17.
- Mt 24:16 - let those "flee to the mountains" is taken from 1 Macc. 2:28.
- Mt 27:43 - if He is God's Son, let God deliver him from His adversaries follows Wisdom 2:18.
- Mk 4:5, 16-17 - Jesus' description of seeds falling on rocky ground and having no root follows Sirach 40:15.
- Mk 9:48 - description of hell where their worm does not die and the fire is not quenched references Judith 16:17.
- Lk 1:42 - Elizabeth's declaration of Mary's blessedness above all women follows Uzziah's declaration in Judith 13:18.

- Lk 1:52 - Mary's Magnificat addressing the mighty falling from their thrones and replaced by lowly follows Sirach 10:14.
- Lk 2:29 - Simeon's declaration that he is ready to die after seeing the Child Jesus follows Tobit 11:9.
- Lk 13:29 - the Lord's description of men coming from east and west to rejoice in God follows Baruch 4:37.
- Lk 21:24 - Jesus' usage of "fall by the edge of the sword" follows Sirach 28:18.
- Lk 24:4 and Acts 1:10 - Luke's description of the two men in dazzling apparel reminds us of 2 Macc. 3:26.
- Jn 1:3 - all things were made through Him, the Word, follows Wisdom 9:1.
- Jn 3:13 - who has ascended into heaven but He who descended from heaven references Baruch 3:29.
- Jn 4:48; Acts 5:12; 15:12; 2 Cor. 12:12 - Jesus', Luke's and Paul's usage of "signs and wonders" follows Wisdom 8:8.
- Jn 5:18 - Jesus claiming that God is His Father follows Wisdom 2:16.
- Jn 6:35-59 - Jesus' Eucharistic discourse is foreshadowed in Sirach 24:21.
- Jn 10:22 - the identification of the feast of the dedication is taken from 1 Macc. 4:59.
- Jn 15:6 - branches that don't bear fruit and are cut down follows Wis. 4:5 where branches are broken off.[601]

Gerhard's minor premise that the Apocrypha contain no prophecies about Jesus Christ is clearly false. I content the number of fulfilled prophecies found in the Apocrypha are a powerful argument for their canonicity.

The Apocrypha are not accepted by Jews

Gerhard's fourth argument is that the Apocryphal books do not have the witness of the Israelitic Church (by which he means the Jewish people).
- The canonical books of the Old Testament have the witness of the Israelitic church.

---

[601] (Salza 2007)

- Those controversial books lack the witness of the Israelitic Church.
- Ergo. [The controversial books are not canonical].[602]

We have already demonstrated that notion is incorrect, as there were multiple canons in existence at the time of Christ. Also, the canon of the Ethiopian Jews (a.k.a. Beta Israel) contains several of the so-called Apocryphal books such as Sirach, Judith, 1 and 2 Esdras, and a variety of other biblical and non-biblical books. Gerhard goes on to provide a variety of proofs for his position, all of which are meaningless in the face of what we now know to be true about the Jewish faith during the time of Christ.

The Apocrypha were not accepted by the primitive Church

Gerhard's fifth argument is that the Apocrypha are not supported as Scripture by the primitive Christian Church.
- Books that are truly canonical have the supporting testimony of the primitive Christian Church.
- Those controversial books lack the unanimous witness of the primitive church.
- Therefore, they are not canonical.[603]

It is perhaps unfair to pile on this way, but when a luminary such as Gerhard makes such a bold and unsupported statement, it needs to be refuted. Henceforth, a list of statements regarding the Apocrypha from the Primitive Church through the Post-Nicene era.[604]

---

[602] (Gerhard 2006, 95)

[603] (Ibid, 98)

[604] (Anonymous, Old Testament: Dead Sea Scrolls 2014) This list is an expanded version of that originally found at

http://www.catholic.com/tracts/the-old-testament-canon

Appendix A: Arguments Against the Apocrypha

References to the Apocrypha from the Fathers

The Didache (ca. 50-70 AD)

Do not be someone who stretches out his hands to receive but withdraws them when it comes to giving (Sir. 4:31).

The Sirach passage is more or less quoted in the Didache.

You should not be someone who opens his hands when it comes to receiving, but then keeps them shut when it comes to giving (Didache 4:5).

The Didache (ca. 50-70 AD)

When thou wilt do good know to whom thou doest it; so shalt thou be thanked for thy benefits (Sirach 12:1).

This passage is thought by scholars to be the source of the following passage.[605]

But remember it has also been said that 'you should let your gift sweat in your hands until you know to whom to give it' (Didache 1:6).

The Epistle of Barnabas (ca. 74 AD)[606]

Therefore let us lie in wait for the righteous; because he is not for our turn, and he is clean contrary to our doings: he upbraideth us with our offending the law, and objecteth to our infamy the transgressions of our education (Wis. 2:12).

This passage is summarized in the following passage.

Since, therefore, He was about to be manifested and to suffer in the flesh, His suffering was foreshown. For the prophet speaks against Israel, "Woe to their soul, because they have counselled an evil counsel against themselves, saying, Let us

---

[605] (Varner, The Didache's Use of the Old and New Testaments 2005, 137-138)

[606] The *Epistle of Barnabas* is attached at the end of the New Testament in the Codex Sinaiticus. It is traditionally ascribed to the Barnabas mentioned in the Acts of the Apostles.

bind the just one, because he is displeasing to us." (Letter of Barnabas 6:7).[607]

Clement of Rome (ca. 80 AD)

For who shall say, What hast thou done? or who shall withstand thy judgment?[608] *or who shall accuse thee for the nations that perish, whom thou made? or who shall come to stand against thee, to be revenged for the unrighteous men? (Wis. 12:12).*

This passage is quoted by Clement in the following passage.

By the word of his might [God] established all things, and by his word he can overthrow them. 'Who shall say to him, "What have you done?" or who shall resist the power of his strength?' (Letter to the Corinthians 27:5).

---

[607] This passage quotes both Isaiah and the Wisdom of Solomon as Scripture. (Schaff, ANF01 1884, 214)

[608] "The Hebrew word 'judgment' (or 'justice') can mean 'salvation.' In the same way, the verb 'judge' often means 'save.' When David is in trouble, he cries out, 'Judge me, 0 God....' (Psalm 43:1). The judges of the Old Testament were saviors or deliverers of the people, and not judges in the modern sense of the word. God is called 'the Judge' (Judges 11:27; Isaiah 33:22), or 'the Judge of all the earth' (Genesis 18:25; Psalm 94:2). 'Righteousness and judgment' are the foundation of His throne (Psalm 89:14). Over and over, the Prophet Isaiah uses 'judgment' as a synonym for 'salvation'": 'Therefore judgment is far from us; and righteousness does not reach us...We look for judgment, but there is none; for salvation, but it is far from us... Judgment is turned back; and righteousness stands at a distance' " (Isaiah 59:9,11,14).

Polycarp of Smyrna (ca. 135 AD)

Because that alms do deliver from death, and suffereth not to come into darkness. ...For alms doth deliver from death, and shall purge away all sin. Those that exercise alms and righteousness shall be filled with life: (Tob. 4:10, 12:9).

Polycarp, a disciple of the apostle John, quotes Tobit in the following passage.

"Stand fast, therefore, in these things, and follow the example of the Lord, being firm and unchangeable in the faith, loving the brotherhood. ...When you can do good, defer it not, because 'alms delivers from death'. Be all of you subject to one another, having your conduct blameless among the Gentiles, and the Lord may not be blasphemed through you. But woe to him by whom the name of the Lord is blasphemed!" (Letter to the Philadelphians 10).[609]

Irenaeus (ca. 189 AD)

So he put him aside, and commanded to bring the other, and said unto him, O thou seed of Chanaan, and not of Juda, beauty hath deceived thee, and lust hath perverted thine heart. (Susanna 56; in the Septuagint, Susanna prefixes the Masoretic text of Daniel).

The bolded text below shows where Irenaeus quotes Susanna.

"Those ... who are believed to be presbyters by many, but serve their own lusts and do not place the fear of God supreme in their hearts, but conduct themselves with contempt toward others and are puffed up with the pride of holding the chief seat and work evil deeds in secret, saying 'No man sees us,' shall be convicted by the Word, who does not judge after outward appearance, nor looks upon the countenance, but the heart; ***and they shall hear those words to be found in Daniel the prophet: 'O you seed of Canaan and not of Judah, beauty***

---

[609] (Schaff, ANF01 1884, 61-62)

has deceived you and lust perverted your heart'." [emphasis added] (Against Heresies 4:26:3).⁶¹⁰

Irenaeus (yet again)

O Jerusalem, look about thee toward the east, and behold the joy that cometh unto thee from God. Lo, thy sons come, whom thou sentest away, they come gathered together from the east to the west by the word of the Holy One, rejoicing in the glory of God. (Bar. 4:36,37; Baruch is part of Jeremiah in the Septuagint).

For God shall lead Israel with joy in the light of his glory with the mercy and righteousness that cometh from him. (Bar. 5:9).

In the passage below, Irenaeus quotes the two passages above.

"And **Jeremiah the prophet** has pointed out that as many believers as God has prepared for this purpose, to multiply those left on the earth, should both be under the rule of the saints and to minister to this [new] Jerusalem and that [his] kingdom shall be in it, saying, **'Look around Jerusalem toward the east and behold the joy which comes to you from God himself. Behold, your sons whom you have sent forth shall come: They shall come in a band from the east to the west. . . . God shall go before with you in the light of his splendor, with the mercy and righteousness which proceed from him'** [emphasis added] (Against Heresies 5:35:1).⁶¹¹

---

⁶¹⁰ (Schaff, ANF01 1884, 832) The same passage cites the New Testament, the Old Testament, and refers to citation from Susanna as being from Daniel the prophet.

⁶¹¹ (Ibid, 951)

Appendix A: Arguments Against the Apocrypha

Hippolytus (ca. 204 AD)

Hippolytus does not quote without attribution but actually cites Susannah as his source.

What is narrated here [in the story of Susannah] happened at a later time, although it is placed at the front of the book [of Daniel], for it was a custom with the writers to narrate many things in an inverted order in their writings. . . . [W]e ought to give heed, beloved, fearing lest anyone be overtaken in any transgression and risk the loss of his soul, knowing as we do that God is the judge of all and the Word himself is the eye which nothing that is done in the world escapes. Therefore, always watchful in heart and pure in life, let us imitate Susannah (Commentary on Daniel).[612]

Cyprian of Carthage (ca. 248, 253 AD)

Was not Abraham found faithful in temptation, and it was imputed unto him for righteousness? (1 Macc 2:52; see also Jas. 2:21–23).

For though they be punished in the sight of men, yet is their hope full of immortality. (Wis. 3:4).

Cyprian of Carthage does not merely quote the apocrypha but cites them by name.

In Genesis [it says], 'And God tested Abraham and said to him, "Take your only son whom you love, Isaac, and go to the high land and offer him there as a burnt offering"' ...Of this same thing in the Wisdom of Solomon [it says], 'Although in the sight of men they suffered torments, their hope is full of immortality...'. Of this same thing in the Maccabees [it says], 'Was not Abraham found faithful when tested, and it was reckoned to him for righteousness'[613] (1 Macc. 2:52; see Jas. 2:21–23).

Cyprian of Carthage (yet again)

---

[612] (Schaff, ANF05 2004, 341,345)

[613] (Ibid, 949)

And the king worshipped it and went daily to adore it: but Daniel worshipped his own God. And the king said unto him, Why dost not thou worship Bel? Who answered and said, Because I may not worship idols made with hands, but the living God, who hath created the heaven and the earth, and hath sovereignty over all flesh. (Bel and the Dragon 4-5; in the Septuagint, Bel and the Dragon is part of the book of Daniel).

Yet another direct citation.

"So Daniel, too, when he was required to worship the idol Bel, which the people and the king then worshipped, in asserting the honor of his God, broke forth with full faith and freedom, saying, 'I worship nothing but the Lord my God, who created the heaven and the earth'" (Epistle LV, To the People of Thibaris, Exhorting to Martyrdom. 5).[614]

The Apostolic Constitutions (ca. 375 - 380 AD)

The *Apostolic Constitutions* belong to a type of writing called "Church Orders." As such they serve as a manual of worship. These are functionally oriented, describing the manner in which the services were to be conducted. In later years, and especially following the legalization of Christianity, these church orders grew in size and complexity and contained more explanatory material.

Now women also prophesied. Of old, Miriam the sister of Moses and Aaron [Ex. 15:20], and after her, Deborah [Judges. 4:4], and after these Huldah [2 Kgs. 22:14] and Judith [Jdt 8], the former under Josiah, the latter under Darius (Apostolic Constitutions 8:2).[615]

Augustine (ca. 397, 421 AD)

We read in the books of the Maccabees [2 Macc. 12:43] that sacrifice was offered for the dead. But even if it were found nowhere in the Old Testament writings, the authority of the

---

[614] (Ibid, 618)

[615] (Schaff, ANF07 2004, 720)

Catholic Church which is clear on this point is of no small weight, where in the prayers of the priest poured forth to the Lord God at his altar the commendation of the dead has its place (The Care to be Had for the Dead 1:3).[616]

Jerome (ca. 401 AD)

What sin have I committed in following the judgment of the churches? But when I repeat what the Jews say against the Story of Susanna and the Hymn of the Three Children, and the fables of Bel and the Dragon, which are not contained in the Hebrew Bible, the man who makes this a charge against me proves himself to be a fool and a slanderer; for I explained not what I thought but what they commonly say against us. I did not reply to their opinion in the Preface, because I was studying brevity, and feared that I should seem to be writing not a Preface but a book. I said therefore, 'As to which this is not the time to enter into discussion.' (Against Rufinius II:33).[617]

Canonical Lists

Besides the above allusions, quotations, and citations, we must also take into account the substantial number of canonical lists which included the apocrypha. These are admittedly late since the early church was not concerned with defining the limits of the canon. These lists to indicate that the issue was unsettled and that the Apocrypha were nearly always included in the Old Testament.

Council of Rome (ca. 382 AD)

The Bishop of Rome (Pope Damascus) called a regional council and afterward issued what has come to be known as the Damasine List.

---

[616] (Schaff, NPNF1-03 1890, 692)

[617] (Ibid, 894) This passage suggests that while Jerome may have preferred the Hebrew text for translation purposes, he was content to leave the matter of canonicity to the judgment of the Church.

Now indeed we must treat of the divine Scriptures, what the universal Catholic Church accepts and what she ought to shun. The order of the Old Testament begins here: Genesis, one book; Exodus, one book; Leviticus, one book; Numbers, one book; Deuteronomy, one book; Joshua [Son of] Nave, one book; Judges, one book; Ruth, one book; Kings, four books [that is, 1 and 2 Samuel and 1 and 2 Kings]; Paralipomenon [Chronicles], two books; Psalms, one book; Solomon, three books: Proverbs, one book, Ecclesiastes, one book, [and] Canticle of Canticles [Song of Songs], one book; likewise Wisdom, one book; Ecclesiasticus [Sirach], one book.... Likewise the order of the historical [books]: Job, one book; Tobit, one book; Esdras, two books [Ezra and Nehemiah]; Esther, one book; Judith, one book; Maccabees, two books (Decree of Pope Damasus).[618]

Council of Hippo (ca. 393 AD)

One of the several North African regional councils compiled the following list.

Besides the canonical Scriptures, nothing shall be read, in the church, under the title of "divine writings." The canonical books are :—Genesis, Exodus, Leviticus, Numbers, Deuteronomy, Joshua, Judges, Ruth, the four books of Kings, the two books of Paraleipomena (Chronicles), Job, the Psalms of David, the five books of Solomon, the twelve books of the (Minor) Prophets, Isaiah, Jeremiah, Daniel, Ezekiel, Tobias, Judith, Esther, two books of Esdras, two books of the Maccabees. The books of the New Testament are:—the four Gospels, the Acts of the Apostles, thirteen Epistles of S. Paul, one Epistle of S. Paul to the Hebrews, two Epistles of S. Peter, three Epistles of S. John, the Epistle of S. James, the Epistle of S. Jude, the Revelation of S. John. Concerning the confirmation of this canon, the transmarine Church shall be consulted. On the

---

[618] (Anonymous, The Companion to the Catechism of the Catholic Church 2002, 35)

anniversaries of martyrs, their acts shall also be read. (Canon 36).[619]

Council of Carthage III (ca. 397 AD)

Protestants cite the Council of Carthage as establishing the canon of the New Testament; Protestant commentators conveniently ignore the decree concerning what constitutes the Old Testament.

It was also determined that besides the Canonical Scriptures nothing be read in the Church under the title of divine Scriptures. The Canonical Scriptures are these: Genesis, Exodus, Leviticus, Numbers, Deuteronomy, Joshua the son of Nun, Judges, Ruth, four books of Kings, two books of Paraleipomena, Job, the Psalter, five books of Solomon, the books of the twelve prophets, Isaiah, Jeremiah, Ezechiel, Daniel, Tobit, Judith, Esther, two books of Esdras, two books of the Maccabees. Of the New Testament: four books of the Gospels, one book of the Acts of the Apostles, thirteen Epistles of the Apostle Paul, one epistle of the same [writer] to the Hebrews, two Epistles of the Apostle Peter, three of John, one of James, one of Jude, one book of the Apocalypse of John.[620]

St. Augustine (ca. 397, 421 AD)

St. Augustine was the Bishop of Hippo, an important Roman city in North Africa. It was destroyed by Muslim Jihadists in 698 AD and rebuilt nearby. Today the city is known Annaba and located in Algeria.

Now the whole canon of Scripture on which we say this judgment is to be exercised, is contained in the following books: — Five books of Moses...; one book of Joshua the son of Nun; one of Judges; one short book called Ruth, which seems rather to belong to the beginning of Kings; next, four books of Kings, and two of Chronicles. There are other books ...such as Job, and

---

[619] (Hefele 1876, 400)

[620] (Marlowe, Third Council of Carthage (A.D. 397) n.d., Canon 47)

Tobias, and Esther, and Judith, and the two books of Maccabees, and the two of Ezra, which last look more like a sequel to the continuous regular history which terminates with the books of Kings and Chronicles. Next are the Prophets, in which there is one book of the Psalms of David; and three books of Solomon, viz., Proverbs, Song of Songs, and Ecclesiastes. For two books, one called Wisdom and the other Ecclesiasticus, are ascribed to Solomon from a certain resemblance of style, but the most likely opinion is that they were written by Jesus the son of Sirach. Still they are to be reckoned among the prophetical books, since they have attained recognition as being authoritative. The remainder are the books which are strictly called the Prophets: twelve separate books of the prophets which are connected with one another, and having never been disjoined, are reckoned as one book; the names of these prophets are as follows:—Hosea, Joel, Amos, Obadiah, Jonah, Micah, Nahum, Habakkuk, Zephaniah, Haggai, Zechariah, Malachi; then there are the four greater prophets, Isaiah, Jeremiah, Daniel, Ezekiel. The authority of the Old Testament is contained within the limits of these forty-four books.[621]

---

[621] (Schaff, NPNF1-02 1890, On Christian Doctrine 2:8:13)

Pope Innocent I (ca. 405 A.D).

A short annotation shows what books are to be accepted as canonical. As you wished to be informed specifically, they are as follows: The five books of Moses, that is, Genesis, Exodus, Leviticus, Numbers, Deuteronomy; and Jesus Nave [Joshua], one of Judges, four of Kingdoms [1 & s Samuel, 1 & 2 Kings], and also Ruth, sixteen books of Prophets, five books of Solomon [Proverbs, Ecclesiastes, Song of Songs, Wisdom of Solomon, and Ecclesiasticus], the Psalter. Likewise, of histories, one book of Job, one book of Tobias [Tobit], one of Esther, one of Judith, two of Maccabees, two of Esdras [Ezra, Nehemiah], two books of Paralipomenon [Chronicles]. (Letter of Pope Innocent I to Exsuperius, Bishop of Toulouse.)[622]

A Final Word

I don't want to pile onto Johann Gerhard, as he was arguing from the knowledge that was available at that time and in support of a Lutheran argument created in opposition to Rome. Still, Gerhard's discredited arguments are in use today. Evangelical Bible scholars, with all the evidence of the Dead Sea Scrolls right in front of them, behave like the policeman standing between crowd and carnage and announcing: "Move along folks. Nothing to see here."

What does this all mean? The Dead Sea Scrolls have exposed the fact that the Hebrew Scriptures changed over time, thus calling into question the 20th-century theological innovation known as "verbal, plenary inspiration." In turn, this has led to more and more convoluted definitions of inspiration, such as "verbal, plenary inspiration of the Scriptures, inerrant in the original manuscripts." Since the Dead Sea Scrolls are examples of the Septuagint textual tradition, they raise questions involving the translations

---

[622] (Jurgens 1979, 180)

based upon the Masoretic text.[623] Perhaps this is why conservative evangelical scholars will still tell you that the Dead Sea Scrolls were not needed; to admit otherwise would call into question their entire theological paradigm.

---

[623] I do not say that the Masoretic text is not Scripture; merely that it is not the best available text of scripture. A text need not be perfect to be inspired. Inspiration, as testified to by Sacred Scripture, is profitable for doctrine, for reproof, for instruction in righteousness. Clearly the Masoretic text meets that benchmark.

2: Merrill Unger and the Apocrypha

The late Merrill F. Unger, former professor of Old Testament studies at Dallas Theological Seminary, provides a series of arguments for the Protestant's shorter canon. Although I once accepted these arguments without question, they now seem quite odd.

They abound in historical and geographical inaccuracies and anachronisms.[624]

This is a most curious argument, given that the Sacred Scriptures are full of seeming inconsistencies, contradictions, pre-scientific descriptions, anthropomorphisms, and even what some might claim to be actual errors of fact. If the arguments for inerrancy apply to the Protestant canon, why would they not apply to the Apocrypha? But as we discussed in Part II, the existence of supposed errors is not an argument against inspiration, for the Bible never claims to be inerrant.

Let us examine, for a moment, the historical and geographical inaccuracies and anachronisms in one of the acceptable books, the book of Revelation. Six times the book of Revelation mentions the fall of Babylon as being a cataclysmic event and an event yet to happen. At the time Revelation was written, Babylon was no longer a major political center, yet it continued as an inhabited city well into the 7th century. Given this, the ancient capital of the Chaldeans and the Medo-Persian Empire cannot be in view. Moreover, Revelation describes Babylon as being "drunken with the blood of the saints, and with the blood of the martyrs of Jesus" (Re 17:6). The Babylon of history was not in power during the Christian era, and could not have been "drunken with the blood of the saints." This is a historical inaccuracy, and saying that Babylon stands in for Rome is to depart from

---

[624] (Unger 1966, 70)

the literal meaning of the text.[625] In another instance, John uses coded language when describing a person known as "the Beast." "Let him that hath understanding count the number of the beast: for it is the number of a man; and his number is Six hundred threescore and six" (Re 13:18). Since Arabic numerals did not exist, both Hebrew and Greek used letters to represent numbers. John is using a rather simple Gematria[626] code in which letters are used to represent numbers.

Table 5: The Number of the Beast

The Hebrew for "Neron Caesar" is NRWN QSR.
N = 50
R = 200
W = 6
N = 50
Q = 100
S = 60
R = 200
The number of the beast is = 666[627]

We know that the Bible often uses one thing to stand in for another. Thus, the number 666 stands in for Nero. The problem with this is that by the time Revelation was written, Nero had been dead for several years. Yet another of John's supposed historical inaccuracies. The natural explanation is

---

[625] It does no good to use modern terminology like the "figurative literal interpretation" of Scripture. The literal interpretation of Scripture is one thing, and the figurative another.

[626] The use of Gematria in the apostle John's Revelation has its roots in Jewish techniques of scriptural interpretations. (Froehlich 1984, Kindle Location 94)

[627] Some ancient manuscripts give the number of the beast as "616," which could stand for "Caesar God" in Greek, for which the Gematria equivalent is 616.

Appendix A: Arguments Against the Apocrypha

that John was using 666 to stand in for Nero, and using Nero to stand in for all the Roman emperors.[628]

They teach doctrines which are false and foster practices which are at variance with inspired Scripture.[629]

The argument here is that of Martin Luther who tried to exclude from the canon any books that disagreed with his theology. Once Luther had created his doctrinal system, that system was used to determine the canon. This reasoning is similar to that of the early church which determined the catalog of acceptable books based in large measure on their concordance with the *regula fidei*, the rule of faith. The difference is that while Martin Luther was attempting to reason his way towards the apostolic deposit, the early church was operating from within the apostolic deposit. The New Testament books and the Septuagint were consistent with the rule of faith. Apostolic succession is a testimony to and guarantee of the continuity of the apostolic deposit, of which the laying on of hands serves as a sign, symbol, and witness.

Unger's argument is curious, as it assumes two things. First, that the Apocrypha are not Scripture; second, that it contains doctrines not found in the inspired writings. Unger's argument is the argument of the Jews against the New Testament. The New Testament differs from the Hebrew Scriptures in significant ways. For example, the doctrine of

---

[628] If we accept that one thing can stand in for another, such as Babylon for Rome, or 666 for Rome's rulers, why would it be so difficult in the case of the Apocrypha? For example, take Judith 1:1 "In the twelfth year of the reign of Nabuchodonosor, who reigned in Nineve, the great city; in the days of Arphaxad, which reigned over the Medes in Ecbatane." But Nebuchadnezzar reigned over the Chaldeans, not the Medo-Persians, and ruled from Babylon, not Nineveh. Could this be an attempt to use Nebuchadnezzar not as a historical figure, but as a typological representation of the rulers of this world?

[629] (Unger 1966, 70)

the Trinity cannot be found in the Hebrew Scriptures. Only by reading the New Testament back into the Old can the Trinity be seen (as in Abraham's three angelic visitors, which Christians understand both as a type of the Trinity and a Theophany of our Lord Jesus Christ). The idea of a crucified Messiah scandalizes the Jews to this day; they don't find it in their Hebrew Scriptures; the suffering servant concept is metaphorically applied to the Jewish people.

The New Testament adds to the Old Testament, fills in the gaps, supplies what is missing, and provides a Christological perspective. If we apply Unger's argument globally, we will end up with only the five books of Moses. Everything else is suspect, as it teaches things not found in the Pentateuch. This is easily Unger's worst argument.

They resort to literary types and display an artificiality of subject matter and styling out of keeping with inspired Scripture.[630]

Unger's statement is curious, given that the bulk of the New Testament consists of letters, Gospels, an apocalypse (Revelation), and a theological treatise (Hebrews) — literary types not found in the Old Testament Scriptures. The only historical book of the New Testament is Acts; the only wisdom literature is the book of James. The Old Testament does not contain an apocalypse, a style of writing that was common in Second Temple literature, but absent from the Old Testament (whether listed with or without the Apocrypha).[631] Nearly all of the New Testament is made up of "literary types" and contains "subject matter and styling out of keeping with inspired Scripture" — at least depending on your point of view.

---

[630] (Ibid, 70)

[631] Even though the New Testament contains an apocalypse, many in the ancient church rejected the Revelation of St. John precisely because of its mysterious symbolism and apocalyptic character — something the heretics were able to twist to their advantage.

Appendix A: Arguments Against the Apocrypha

Table 6: Literary Types

Literary Types	Hebrew Scriptures	Apocrypha
Historical accounts	Judges, Ruth, I & II Samuel, I & II Kings, I & II Chronicles, Ezra, Nehemiah, Esther	Tobit, Judith, I, II, & III Maccabees,
Psalter	Psalms	Psalm 151
Wisdom Literature	Job, Proverbs, Ecclesiastes, Song of Solomon	Wisdom of Solomon, Wisdom of Sirach (a.k.a. Sirach or Ecclesiasticus)
Prophets	Isaiah, Jeremiah, Lamentations, Ezekiel, Daniel, Hosea, Joel, Amos, Obadiah, Jonah, Micah, Nahum, Habakkuk, Zephaniah, Haggai, Zechariah, Malachi	Baruch, Lamentations of Jeremiah, Epistle of Jeremiah

All the literary types found in the Apocrypha have their counterpart in the literary types of the Hebrew Scriptures. This cannot be said of the Christian New Testament. Lester L. Grabbe writes the following concerning the Apocrypha:

This collection is the result of historical accident. There is nothing special or mysterious about these books [the Apocrypha]. They are made up of a variety of literary genres: epistle, history, tale, wisdom. They are as early as some of the books of the Hebrew Bible, and there is nothing to set them apart from the canonical books.[632]

Given the obvious parallel between the literary genres of the Old Testament and the Apocrypha, it is clear that Dr. Unger's contention is unsupported by the evidence.

---

[632] (Grabbe 2010, Kindle Location 474-481)

They lack the distinctive elements which give genuine Scripture their divine character, such as prophetic power and poetic and religious feeling.[633]

This argument is not only completely subjective but utter nonsense as well. Let us examine Unger's critique that the Apocrypha lack prophetic power. In his book, *The Life and Times of Jesus the Messiah*, Alfred Edersheim points to the almost hypostatic conception of the Logos in the Apocrypha.

Similarly, we can perceive, how the Apocrypha — especially the book of Wisdom — following up on the Old Testament typical truth concerning 'Wisdom' (as specially set forth in the Book of Proverbs,) almost arrived so far as to present 'Wisdom' as a special 'Subsistence' (hypostatising it.)[634]

The book of Barach takes this even further, going so far as to hint at the Incarnation of the Logos (something we mentioned in Part V).

Hear, Israel, the commandments of life: give ear to understand wisdom. ...Thou hast forsaken the fountain of wisdom. For if thou hadst walked in the way of God, thou shouldest have dwelled in peace for ever. ...O Israel, how great is the house of God! and how large is the place of his possession! Great, and hath none end; high, and unmeasurable. ...Who hath gone up into heaven, and taken her, and brought her down from the clouds? ...This is our God, and there shall none other be accounted of in comparison of him. He hath found out all the way of knowledge, and hath given it unto Jacob his servant, and to Israel his beloved. Afterward did he show himself upon

---

[633] (Unger 1966, 70) I do not wish to be too hard on Mr. Unger, whose book was written before the implications of the Dead Sea Scrolls were widely known. Still, he lived until 1980 and never updated this portion of his Bible Dictionary.

[634] (Edersheim 1993, 32)

Appendix A: Arguments Against the Apocrypha

earth, and conversed with men (Baruch 3:9, 12-13, 24-25, 29, 35-37).

As for "poetic and religious feeling" let us read the supplicatory prayer of Judith, a prayer which holds up to anything in the Hebrew Scriptures.

For, behold, the Assyrians are multiplied in their power; they are exalted with horse and man; they glory in the strength of their footmen; they trust in shield, and spear, and bow, and sling; and know not that thou art the Lord that breakest the battles: the Lord is thy name. Throw down their strength in thy power, and bring down their force in thy wrath: for they have purposed to defile thy sanctuary, and to pollute the tabernacle where thy glorious name resteth, and to cast down with sword the horn of thy altar (Jdt 9:7-8).

And again, this, from Judith's song of rejoicing:

I will sing unto the Lord a new song: O Lord, thou art great and glorious, wonderful in strength, and invincible. Let all creatures serve thee: for thou spakest, and they were made, thou didst send forth thy spirit, and it created them, and there is none that can resist thy voice. For the mountains shall be moved from their foundations with the waters, the rocks shall melt as wax at thy presence: yet thou art merciful to them that fear thee. For all sacrifice is too little for a sweet savor unto thee, and all the fat is not sufficient for thy burnt offering: but he that feareth the Lord is great at all times (Jdt 16:13-16).

As we can see, none of Merrill F. Unger's reasonings stand up to scrutiny. Therefore, it would appear that his opposition to the Apocrypha being in the canon is ultimately subjective, based on unstated and perhaps unwarranted assumptions.

Appendix B: Second Temple Writings and the Bible

1: The Apocrypha and Other Second Temple Writings

One of the key features of biblical hermeneutics is the insistence on reading the Bible in context. The context of the verse is the passage; the context of the passage is the chapter; the context of the chapter is the book; the context of the book is the entirety of the Bible. You could also say the context of a verse or passage is all the passages discussing that subject. There is yet another way of looking at the context of a passage — examining it in light of the intended audience and their cultural understandings. For the authors of the New Testament, the turmoil of the Second Temple period was the spirit of their age, a turmoil resulting in the wealth of Second Temple literature. David Bentley Hart writes of the influence of 1 Enoch:

It is difficult to exaggerate how influential the intertestamental "Noachic" literature was for the Jews and then Christians of the first century. On the whole, too many New Testament scholars over the years have neglected properly to assess not only the three centuries of Hellenistic culture in which Jewish culture had been steeping by the time of Christ and the apostolic church, but also the profound importance for the early church (quite explicit at numerous places in the New Testament) of the angelology, demonology, cosmology, and eschatology of texts like 1 Enoch and Jubilees. Too often in the past, the first-century Judaism of pious New Testament and early church studies has been a fantastic abstraction, decocted from equal parts the biblical prophets and later rabbinic Judaism, while the pervasive Greek and Persian and apocalyptic and other influences of that remarkably and gloriously culturally promiscuous age have been ignored or treated as extraneous minor features of late antique Judaism, as well as (of course) corruptions.[635]

---

[635] (Hart, The Vale of Abraham 2018)

The New Testament authors had some surprising literary influences from the Second Temple period. The texts of the four Gospels, as well as the books of Jude, 1 & 2 Peter, and Revelation, make liberal use of Second Temple literature. Biblical scholar Margaret Barker notes:

A great deal of what was important in early Christianity may not be spelt out in the New Testament because it was already accepted. Much of the theology developed by the early Churches may have been no more than unpacking what was already there from the start. Thus we owe it to ourselves to make some sort of effort to understand this curious book [Enoch], and the others like it.[636]

Robert Henry Charles describes two strains of Jewish literature — the Apocalyptic and the Legalistic, created by two broad strains of Judaism.[637]

APOCALYPTIC Judaism and legalistic Judaism were not in pre-Christian times essentially antagonistic. Fundamentally their origin was the same. Both started with the unreserved recognition of the supremacy of the Law. This is to be expected in regard to legalistic Pharisaism, which was therein only adopting the teaching of the priesthood. But it is enforced also in apocalyptic Pharisaism. Thus the most universalistic and ethical of all the apocalyptic writings, i.e. the Testaments of the XII Patriarchs, declares that this Law is 'the light that lighteth

---

[636] (Barker, The Lost Prophet 2005, 17)

[637] We are talking broadly and in one dimension about different strains of Judaism. There are other ways of looking at the Judaism of this period, other dimensionalities to explore. Margaret Barker, for example, draws a distinction between first temple and second temple Judaism. Distinctions are often drawn between the Judaism of the diaspora and the Judaism of Jerusalem; between the Pharisees and the Sadducees; between the Essenes and the Hasmonean priesthood; between the Samaritans and the Hebrews. These different dimensionalities are based on different presumptions and reveal different things about the state of Judaism.

every man'. To all Jewish apocalyptic writers the Law was of eternal validity, but they also clung fast to the validity of the prophetic teaching as the source of new truth and the right of apocalyptic as its successor in this respect. We have early evidence of this conjunction of legalism and apocalyptic in the Book of Joel. The Law is there recognized as authoritative, its ritual as of the highest import, while at the same time the impending advent of the kingdom of God is depicted in highly apocalyptic colouring.[638]

The New Testament is a product of both apocalyptic and legalistic Judaism but leans more heavily towards the Apocalyptic, this being a consistent strain in the Gospels.[639] The Jews did not accept an apocalypse into their Hebrew Scriptures, but the New Testament contains one — the book of Revelation.[640] We see the apocalyptic in the teachings of Jesus and also in the way Jesus consistently refers to himself as the "Son of Man." Jesus does this around eighty times, emphasizing the significance of this title. Many of the theological discussions of this title say Jesus is identifying himself as Representative Man.[641] However, that is *not* how

---

[638] (Charles, The Apocrypha and Pseudepigrapha of the Old Testament in English Vol 2 1913, vii)

[639] The division of Apocalyptic and Legalistic Judaism should not be applied too formally. The Judaism of the time was essentially apocalyptic. (Heyler 2002, 119) What differed was the emphasis placed upon the apocalyptic among the different strains of Judaism.

[640] The (so-called) Apocrypha of the Old contains one Apocalypse, known as 2 Esdras. This is listed in the Latin Vulgate as 4 Esdras. The Slavonic Bible includes it as 3 Esdras, but it is not part of the wider Orthodox canon.

[641] For example, Merrill F. Unger writes regarding the term 'Son of Man': "It portrays Him as the Representative Man. It designates Him as the 'last Adam' in distinction to the "first man Adam" (1 Cor. 15:45). It sets Him forth as "the Second Man...the Lord from heaven" as over against "the first man...of the earth" (I Cor. 15:47). "The Son of Man" is thus our Lord's racial name, as the "Son of David" is distinctly his Jewish name and "the Son of God" His Divine Name." (Unger 1966, 1038)

the Jews would have understood it, which is clear from a reading of the Second Temple literature. "Son of Man" is a Messianic term, implying divine origins; the 'Son of Man' is given a kingly throne in heaven from which he will judge the nations. Based on the grammatical-historical hermeneutic claimed by many Protestants, we should be interpreting this term as Jesus knew His audience would understand it, not in a manner consistent with western theological norms.

Some of the arguments for accepting the so-called Apocrypha could be applied to the books of 1 and 2 Enoch, as well as other Second Temple literature. We previously discussed Merrill F. Unger's arguments why the Apocrypha are not scripture, and we will not rehash those arguments here. However, it would be dishonest not to point out certain similarities between those books the post-Nicene church accepted as scripture and those books they did not. In this context, two of Merrill F. Unger's arguments are worth a brief mention.

They resort to literary types and display an artificiality of subject matter and styling out of keeping with inspired Scripture.

As you may recall, our original argument is that the literary types, subject matter, and styling of the New Testament are quite different from that of the Old Testament, which demonstrates the hollowness of Unger's argument. By contrast, the books of 1 and 2 Enoch, along with Jubilees, have much in common with the Old Testament. While these Second Temple writings fall into the apocalyptic genre, there are several sections in the prophets which are apocalyptic. 1 and 2 Enoch, along with Jubilees, expand upon the Old Testament historical books and provide background information for some troubling passages.

They lack the distinctive elements which give genuine Scripture their divine character, such as prophetic power and poetic and religious feeling.

Appendix B: Second Temple Writings and the Bible

We previously discussed how the so-called Apocrypha meet these criteria. For example, we showed some prophetic passages which apply to Jesus Christ, and we provided examples of passages rich in poetic and religious feeling. We demonstrated that Johann Gerhard's arguments against the so-called Apocrypha were badly flawed and that the Apocrypha did not meet his criteria for excluding them from the Old Testament. The same could be said for the books of 1 and 2 Enoch, as well as Jubilees.

One of Gerhard's arguments was: *The Apocrypha are not about Christ.* We previously showed that the Apocrypha contained messianic prophecies that were fulfilled by Jesus Christ. Likewise, there are prophetic passages in 1 Enoch that the Ante-Nicene church accepted as being about Christ — this, despite 1 Enoch not being accepted into the canon. There are reasons why 1 Enoch lost favor with the Church, but without 1 Enoch we have lost an important source for a good deal of New Testament content, misunderstand the theological motifs, and have difficulty with the interpretation of that content.

Another of Gerhard's arguments was: *The Apocrypha are not accepted by Jews.* We demonstrated that this was a flawed argument because the Jewish people had not settled the question of what books constituted the Hebrew Scriptures. The inclusion of some of this Second Temple literature in the Dead Sea Scrolls demonstrates the possibility that these books were at least considered valuable for instruction and were possibly read from in the Synagogues.

These books were written by Jews, for Jews, and touched upon themes and motifs of Jewish thought extant in the time of Christ — some of which did not pass on into Talmudic Judaism. Theologian and Professor Margaret Barker writes:

Until recently, all that we knew of Enoch was in Genesis 5.18-24. He was the son of Jared and the father of Methuselah; he walked with God and he was not, for God took him. ...That is all the Old Testament tells us about him, yet books and visions in his name had once been widely known and very influential.

It is clear that there was more to the figure than appeared in Genesis, and a considerable cult of Enoch did undoubtedly exist, even though the biblical writers gave no place to it.[642]

Jude cites 1 Enoch, and it is either quoted from or alluded to by the apostles Peter and John. Amy Richter notes that Matthew uses motifs from Enochian literature.[643] To understand these passages, we have to understand the Enochian literature, even if we (like the Jews) do not accept that literature as scripture.

Also, Johann Gerhard stated: *The Apocrypha was not accepted by the primitive Church.* We have previously shown that the early church accepted the Apocrypha. They also accepted some Second Temple literature. Since some early church authors either quoted from or alluded to 1 Enoch, we can argue that while the status of 1 Enoch was unclear, there were some in the early church who considered it to be an important and valuable book. Moreover, 2 Enoch was an important source for the book of Hebrews, and in particular the description of Jesus Christ being a priest after the order of Melchizedek.[644]

Given all this, why have we spent so much time discussing the likelihood that the so-called Apocrypha are Scripture, only to exclude other books which potentially meet the same criteria? Our argument has not been that the Apocrypha are scripture because they meet some scholastic criteria. Instead, we accept the Apocrypha as Scripture because the Church, operating under the guidance of the Holy Spirit, determined the content of Sacred Scripture. The same Church defined the contents of both the New and the Old Testament, and we cannot reject the one without

---

[642] (Barker, The Lost Prophet 2005, 5)

[643] (Richter 2010, 22)

[644] Since the Hasmoneans justified their takeover of the Aaronic priesthood by saying they were priests after the order of Melchizedek, the author of Hebrews is providing a none-to-subtle rebuke of the Hasmonean high priests.

rejecting the other. It was the Church that decided that 1 and 2 Enoch, along with Jubilees, were not Scripture, despite being important source material for the New Testament.

2: The Apocalypse and Second Temple Judaism

The Old Testament prophetic books occasionally have apocalyptic sections that reflect the times before and during the Babylonian captivity. It was the turmoil of Second Temple Judaism that gave rise to the apocalypse as a Jewish literary genre — a genre that contrasted the troubles of this life with descriptions of the world to come. F. Crawford Burkitt describes these Apocalypses as follows:

They are the most characteristic survival of what I will venture to call, with all its narrowness and its incoherence, the heroic age of Jewish history, the age when the nation attempted to realize in action the part of the peculiar people of God. ...We study the Apocalypses to learn how our spiritual ancestors hoped again that God would make all right in the end; and that we, their children, are here to-day studying them is an indication that their hope was not wholly unfounded. [645]

The apocalypse functions as an unveiling of God's plan for the ages. It confesses a belief that history has a purpose: evil will eventually be punished, and good will eventually triumph. The apocalypse purports to give the reader a glimpse behind the veil. But the apocalyptic is not merely about the end times or the end of me. As Amy Richter points out, the apocalyptic is about a transcendent reality encompassing past, present, and future.[646] The Books of 1 & 2 Enoch, along with Jubilees, embodies all these characteristics.

Second Temple Judaism builds upon Biblical characters and themes but uses them for its own ends. Take the mention of the 'Son of Man' in one of the apocalyptic sections of Daniel. The 'one like the Son of man' in Daniel 7 is given 'dominion, and glory, and a kingdom,' yet also seems to be

---

[645] (Burkitt 1914, 15-16)

[646] (Richter 2010, 13)

identified with 'the saints of the most High' who had suffered under the four beasts. This identification does *not* make this 'Son of Man' a mere symbol [647] but links the 'Son of Man' in Daniel to suffering — particularly to suffering as one of us.[648] Darrell L. Bock notes: "The *Parables of Enoch* takes a symbol [a symbolic character] from Daniel 7 and turns it into a full character."[649] Second Temple Judaism borrowed the celestial origins of the 'Son of Man,' together with the character's being granted dominion, and glory, and a kingdom, and used the character of the 'Son of Man' as a political and theological springboard.

Judaism in the time of Christ was quite diverse; multiple groups took different approaches, yet all of them dependent upon (or, in the case of the Essenes, related to) the temple cult. As we have mentioned before, one way to distinguish between these parties is the emphasis they give to the Law and the Prophets; to legalism vs. the apocalyptic. Christians embraced the apocalyptic strain of Judaism, whereas after the destruction of the temple the Jews virtually abandoned the apocalyptic, becoming purely about the Law. Robert Henry Charles writes:

The affinity then between Jewish apocalyptic and legalism is essential, since the Law was for both valid eternally, but when apocalyptic passed over into Christianity and therein naturally abandoned this view of the Law, it became in a measure anti-legalistic. Even before the Christian era each of these two sides of Pharisaism necessarily tended to lay more and more emphasis on the chief factor in its belief and study to the almost complete exclusion of the other, and thus legalistic Pharisaism in time drove out almost wholly the apocalyptic element as an active factor (though it accepted some of its developments) and became the parent of Talmudic Judaism, whereas apocalyptic Judaism developed more and more the apocalyptic, i.e.

---

[647] (Owen 2013, 115)

[648] (Dunn 2013, 24)

[649] (Bock 2013, 99)

prophetic, element, and in the process came to recognize, as in 4 Ezra, the inadequacy of the Law for salvation. From this it follows that the Judaism that survived the destruction of the Temple, being almost wholly bereft of the apocalyptic wing which had passed over into Christianity, was not the same as the Judaism of an earlier date. Before A. D. 70 Judaism was a Church with many parties: after A.D. 70 the legalistic party succeeded in suppressing its rivals, and so Judaism became in its essentials a Sect.[650]

Let us accept as a given that Christianity adopted the apocalyptic strain of Judaism, reinterpreting and repurposing it in light of the Christ event. With that in mind, it behooves us to examine the primary texts which influenced the New Testament authors, as well as the subject of the Gospels — our Lord Jesus Christ.

---

[650] (Charles, The Apocrypha and Pseudepigrapha of the Old Testament in English Vol 1 1913, vii)

3: The Place of Enoch within Judaism

We have already mentioned Margaret Barker's contention that Enoch played a much larger part in Judaism than suggested by the biblical literature. This interest in Enoch passed over into the early church. Given the hostility of Judaism to the Christians, it should not be surprising to find that Enoch fell out of favor among the Jews. Margaret Barker notes: "In the early Christian centuries Jewish writers had condemned him [Enoch], perhaps because he was so important for the newly emerging Christians."[651]

The scholar Martin Hengel discusses some of Tertullian's arguments for considering Enoch as a Christian document. He then writes:

According to Tertullian, the epistle of Jude cites «1 Enoch.» The Jews, by contrast, later rejected the work precisely because it deals with Christ. 'It is no wonder that they did not accept a few documents that speak of him since they did not recognize him himself, when he spoke to them in person.' Naturally, the decisive weakness in Tertullian's argument is that he cites no evidence that «Enoch» was ever part of a Jewish 'canon' from which it could have been removed.[652]

While Martin Hengel says Tertullian's argument is weak in that that Enoch was never part of a Jewish canon, his own argument is weak, in that Second Temple Judaism had no defined canon. As we have shown previously, there multiple competing Judaisms at the time of Christ, each having an idea of which books were acceptable for use in the synagogues. However, there were no formal lists (apart from the Tanakh or Pentateuch), merely categories such as the law and the prophets. The idea of a list of approved Scriptures was a Christian concept that was later adopted by Jews. Even so, western Christianity did not formally define a list of approved Scriptures until the 15th century, a list that was

---

[651] (Barker, The Lost Prophet 2005, 5)

[652] (Hengel, The Septuagint as Christian Scripture 2002, 54)

endorsed by the 16th century Council of Trent. More to the point, the concept of 'canon' as a list rather than a guide began as a secular concept in the 19th century and was applied to Christianity in the late 19th century.

History does not record that Enoch was every read in the synagogues, nor that its use was forbidden. The character of Enoch and the writings about him were important in Second Temple Judaism, but the book later fell out of favor. For example, the 1906 version of the Jewish Encyclopedia describes a less exalted view of Enoch held by Jews engaged in disputes with Christians after the destruction of the Temple.

According to Targ. Pseudo-Jonathan (Gen. v. 24) Enoch was a pious worshiper of the true God, and was removed from among the dwellers on earth to heaven, receiving the names (and offices) of Metatron and "Safra Rabba" (Great Scribe). This view represents one and (after the complete separation of Christianity from Judaism) the prevailing rabbinical idea of Enoch's character and exaltation. Another, not quite so favorable, appears in the polemics carried on by Abbahu and others with Christian disputants (Friedländer, "Patristische und Talmudische Studien," p. 99; "R. E. J." v. 3). Enoch is held to have been inconsistent in his piety and therefore to have been removed by God before his time in order to forestall further lapses. The miraculous character of his translation is denied, his death being attributed to the plague (Gen. R. v. 24; Yalk., Gen. v. 24; Rashi and Ibn Ezra on the verse; comp. Wisdom iv. 10-14; Frankel, "Ueber den Einfluss der Palästinischen Exegese," etc., pp. 44, 45; Ecclus. [Sirach] xliv. 16; Zohar to Gen. v. 24; but see also Philo, "De Abrahamo," § 3). But withal Enoch is one of those that passed into Gan Eden without tasting the pangs of death (Yalk., Gen. v. 24).[653]

There are three important questions: first, whether Enoch was important in early Judaism; second, why Enoch

---

[653] (Hirsch and Schechter 1901-1906)

was so important to Second Temple Judaism; and third, why Enoch fell out of favor in Talmudic Judaism.[654] As to the first, we cannot confirm that scribal literature concerning Enoch existed in the distant past. Time has destroyed the scribal libraries, and nearly all of the manuscripts have succumbed to the ravages of age. However, scholars believe 1 Enoch, at the very least, is comprised of multiple documents composed by different authors at different times.[655] For example, the 1st section, known as *The Book of the Watchers*, is a compilation of different source material.[656] The mention of Enochian literature among ancient writers indicates there was a wealth of written Enochian material.[657] Given that cultural transmission in pre-Hellenic times was primarily oral, it is reasonable to assume there was an oral Enochian tradition coexisting side-by-side with priestly Judaism and was represented in scribal libraries (else it would not have survived.)

During the Second Temple period, and under the influence of Hellenism, writers developed and promoted their ideas. They used Enoch as the authority for their apocalyptic speculations, as well as their arguments for a solar rather than a lunar calendar.[658] It seems unlikely that the wealth of Enochian literature would have no antecedent.

---

[654] A corollary question is why Talmudic Judaism developed a view of Enoch that is at odds with the Torah.

[655] (Charles, The Apocrypha and Pseudepigrapha of the Old Testament in English Vol 1 1913, 7)

[656] (Barker, The Lost Prophet 2005, 22)

[657] Ibid., 21

[658] During the second temple period, writers often attributed authorship to various biblical figures from the distant past. (Stone, Jewish Writings of the Second Temple Period 1984, XXI) This is a characteristic of second temple literature, and not — as some claim — the result of a "crisis of authority." (Heyler 2002, 117) Vincente Dubroruka notes that instead of being "mere fraud or a stylistic device," the author may mystically identify himself with the author, considering himself to be a channel of revelation. (Dobroruka 2013, 1, 8) Thus, the pseudonymous authorship.

Instead, it is likely that the surviving Enochian literature was an extension of works which had come before, just as the Wisdom of Solomon depends upon the existence of previous Wisdom literature. It is possible that the brief mention of Enoch in Genesis 5:18-24 was intriguing enough to spark speculation. As presented in Genesis, the person of Enoch is a blank slate which a creative author might use for his purposes. This reasoning, however, is nothing more than idle speculation.

The Jewish loss of interest in the character of Enoch seems to have had two causes. First was the destruction of the temple in 70 AD, something that struck deep into the hearts of the Jewish people. They went from being a temple cult to a people of the book; as the apocalyptic books did not seem to mention the temple's destruction, it would have been easy for the Jewish people to have rejected the Enochian literature, just as they rejected the priestly sects. Also, the importance of Enoch to early Christians seems to have led to a less exalted view of Enoch among the Jews.

Among the early Church, the writings about Enoch were held in high regard. As we will demonstrate, some interesting problems are resolved by an acquaintance with Enochian literature. The references to Enoch and the uses of subjects explained in the Enochian literature are found in the four Gospels, as well as the books of Jude, 1st & 2nd Peter, and Revelations. However, the post-Nicene Church lost faith in the books of Enoch. St. Augustine of Hippo mentions it unfavorably, and the Apostolic Constitutions condemn Enoch, linking it to the books written by the heretics. In a paragraph entitled "Concerning Books with False Inscriptions," these books are called "poisonous books," being "pernicious and repugnant to the truth."[659]

1 Enoch survived as part of the canon of the Ethiopian Coptic Church. The internal evidence suggests there are

---

[659] (Schaff, ANF07 2004, Apostolic Constitutions, Book VI, § III, para XVI, p. 680)

multiple sections and multiple authors of this material. Therefore, 1 Enoch may be just a sample of the Enochian literature, something demonstrated by the Enochian material contained in the Dead Sea Scrolls.[660] In particular, *The Book of Giants* was part of the version of 1 Enoch among the Manicheans. Margaret Barker writes:

There are ancient texts which quote 'Enoch', but not any Enoch text that we know. The Testament of Simeon says Enoch predicted war between the Sons of Simeon and the sons of Levi. The Testament of Levi knew a passage in which Enoch predicted the future corruption of the Levitical priesthood. The testament of Judah knew a prophecy that Judah would be evil. The Testament of Benjamin and the Testament of Naphtali predicted, on the basis of Enoch, that their descendants would fall into evil ways. We cannot place any of these in known Enochic texts, and we can only assume that there must have been far more Enochic literature than we now know.[661]

When we discuss the Book of Enoch, we must discuss three different books with the same name. The first is the Ethiopian Book of Enoch which appears to have influenced the New Testament authors. 1 Enoch is likely a product of the 2nd century BC, and could not have been written any earlier than 250BC (due to mentioning countries that did not exist before that date). 2 Enoch is the Slavonic Book of Enoch (aka The Secrets of Enoch), containing a variety of omissions and insertions. These show the extant copy of 2 Enoch to be a 7th century AD recension of a Second Temple manuscript. Despite the revisions, there is much to be gleaned from 2 Enoch. Finally, we have 3 Enoch, known as the Hebrew book of Enoch. 3 Enoch claims to be a product of the 2nd century AD, but no manuscript evidence exists before the 4th century

---

[660] The Prayer of Enosh and Enoch (4Q369); The Book of Enoch (4Q201-2, 204-12); The Book of Giants (1Q23-4, 2Q26, 4Q203, 530-33, 6Q8); the Book of Noah (1Q19, 1Q19 *bis*, 4 Q534-6, 6Q8, 19) (Vermes, The Complete Dead Sea Scrolls in English 2004)

[661] (Barker, The Lost Prophet 2005, 8)

AD. This third version is not part of the Second Temple literary output, but instead reflects rabbinic changes to Judaism following the destruction of the temple in 70 AD. Therefore, we will limit ourselves to the first two books of Enoch.

The Ethiopian Book of Enoch (1 Enoch)

The book of 1 Enoch, or the Ethiopian Book of Enoch, was once important to both Jews and Christians. Enoch is the only non-canonical book cited by name in the New Testament. Despite its early importance, the book was lost, surviving mainly due to its inclusion in the canon of the Ethiopian Coptic Church.

As 1 Enoch is a compilation of multiple texts, each likely composed at different times, it might be more appropriate to think of this as the Books of Enoch.[662] Margaret Barker writes:

The book we call 1 Enoch is a collection of five Enochic works extant in Ethiopic, and brought to light by Bruce in the early nineteenth century. The five parts are: The Book of Watchers (BW), the Similitudes (SS), the Astronomical Book (AB), the Book of Dreams (BD) which includes the Animal Apocalypse (AA), and the Epistle of Enoch (EE) which incorporates the Apocalypse of Weeks (AW).[663]

The Astronomical Book is noteworthy for its use of a solar calendar instead of a lunar calendar. The weakness of the lunar calendar was apparent, and the issue of the calendar was a matter of some discussion during the Second Temple period. Aside from the apocalyptic nature of this section, it could also be viewed as an attempt to persuade the Jews to adopt its version of the solar calendar.

Regarding the Hebrew calendar, Joseph Lumpkin writes:

---

[662] (Charles, The Book of Enoch 1917, xv)

[663] (Barker, The Older Testament 2005, 8)

The Hebrew calendar is a lunar-based system. In this system Passover occurs after sundown on the 15th day of the month Nisan. Passover is celebrated for seven days. The first Passover was in the springtime and many thought it should be keep [sic] in that period of the year. Since the calendar is based in lunar movements the Hebrew calendar is offset to the solar calendar by about 11 days a year. This meant that Passover would drift from spring, to winter, to autumn, and back again.[664]

The book of Enoch proposes a solar calendar that eliminates the annoying drift of the Passover, ensuring that it would occur at approximately the same time each year. Joseph Lumpkin writes:

During the time period Enoch was written, the Jewish community was torn regarding which type of calendar to use. Enoch seems to [tout] a solar-based calendar that is 364 days long with a week added as needed to make up for the missing a day and a quarter (1.25). Compare 365.25 days to 364 days. The Enochian calendar began each year on a Sunday. The starting point for the calendar was the spring equinox, which occurs around March 21st or 22nd. Since the year always begins on the same day of the week, and only a full week is added when needed, the calendar is considered to be a calendar of weeks.[665]

The early church began to address the issue of the calendar by separating their celebration of Pascha from that of the Jewish Passover. The Christian Church eventually adopted the Julian calendar, a solar calendar with a 365-day year divided into 12 months. Because of the way the Julian calendar calculates the leap year, the Julian calendar has drifted from the solar year. Recognizing the problem, the Western Church adopted the Gregorian calendar which, by changing the leap year calculations, stays true to the solar year. However, because Pope Gregory imposed the Gregorian

---

[664] (Lumpkin, The Books of Enoch 2011, 19)

[665] (Ibid, 18)

calendar by papal decree, most Christian Churches in the East continue to use a Julian liturgical calendar. The Second Temple disputes over calendar issues, therefore, have their Christian counterpart.

The Slavonic Book of Enoch (2 Enoch)

The book we call 2 Enoch is also known as *"Slavonic Enoch or Book of the Secrets of Enoch."*[666] Originally written in Greek, the book now exists only in several Slavic translations. The longer versions show evidence of Christian interpolations, but the shorter and earlier versions were products of Second Temple Judaism.[667]

2 Enoch differs from 1 Enoch. It appears to come from a different strain of Judaism than that of 1 Enoch, although the particulars have been lost. Michael E. Stone divides the book into three parts.

2 Enoch deals with three chief subjects. First, Enoch ascends through the heavens, achieves a vision of God, is transfigured into an angel, and receives God's revelation of the secrets of the process of creation (chaps. 1-34). Next he descends upon earth, reveals the heavenly mysteries to his children and gives them his moral instruction (chaps 35-68). From this point until the end of the book, the story of the antediluvian priesthood is found. This narrative commences with Adam and reaches its climax in the narrative of the miraculous birth of Melchizedek who is Noah's nephew by his apocryphal brother Nir. Melchizedek is eventually assumed to heaven where he is guarded safely until after the Flood.[668]

We must not underestimate the importance of the Melchizedek story; the book of Hebrews presumes familiarity with the apocalyptic material. While the author

---

[666] (Stone, Jewish Writings of the Second Temple Period 1984, 406)
[667] (Ibid, 406-407)
[668] (Ibid, 407)

does not quote from 2 Enoch, he certainly makes use of the Jewish interest in the person of Melchizedek.

The connection between 2 Enoch and Hebrews led some scholars to assume this was a Christian interpolation; the internal evidence suggests otherwise. The story of Melchizedek in 2 Enoch contains no Christian elements. For example, 2 Enoch provides an origin story for Melchizedek; Hebrews argues from the lack of an origin story, using that as a similarity between Melchizedek and Jesus Christ.[669]

The Dead Sea Scrolls demonstrate the Jewish interest in Melchizedek. Taken from Qumran Cave 11 are a set of manuscript fragments designated 11Q13 (aka 11QMelchizedek). These fragments are an apocalypse whose main character, Melchizedek, is portrayed as a "Heavenly Prince." Geza Vermes describes the contents for us.

It takes the form of an eschatological midrash in which the proclamation of liberty to the captives at the end of days (Isa. lxi, 1) is understood as being part of the general restoration of property during the year of Jubilee (Lev. xxv, 13), seen in the Bible (Deut. xv, 2) as a remission of debts.

The Heavenly deliverer is Melchizedek. Identical with the archangel Michael, he is the head of the 'sons of Heaven' or 'gods of Justice' and is referred to as «elohim» and «el.» ...Here Melchizedek is portrayed as presiding over the final Judgement and condemnation of his demonic counterpart, Belial/Satan, the Prince of Darkness.[670]

---

[669] For this Melchisedec, king of Salem, priest of the most high God, who met Abraham returning from the slaughter of the kings, and blessed him; To whom also Abraham gave a tenth part of all; first being by interpretation King of righteousness, and after that also King of Salem, which is, King of peace; Without father, without mother, without descent, having neither beginning of days, nor end of life; but made like unto the Son of God; abideth a priest continually (Heb 7:1-3).

[670] (Vermes, The Complete Dead Sea Scrolls in English 2004, 532)

Here, instead of a human origin story as in 2 Enoch, the person of Melchizedek is identified as the Archangel Michael. While these two stories disagree, they do provide evidence that the apocalyptic character of Melchizedek was present within the Judaism of the time of Christ.

2 Enoch vs. Ecclesiasticus

While 2 Enoch contains a great deal of information about Melchizedek, we cannot say the same about Ecclesiasticus (a.k.a. Sirach). The author of Hebrews used Ecclesiasticus 44-50 as source material for Hebrews chapter 11, as we discussed in chapter 45. What is especially interesting about Ecclesiasticus is the focus on Aaron as the first High Priest and the father of the Aaronic line of High Priests. We see the first mention of Aaron in chapter 45 in connection with Moses. The passage discussing Aaron is much larger and more detailed than that given to Moses, indicating the author's interested in the Aaronic priesthood. Then we read the following:

Moses consecrated him, and anointed him with holy oil: this was appointed unto him by an everlasting covenant, and to his seed, so long as the heavens should remain, that they should minister unto him, and execute the office of the priesthood, and bless the people in his name. (Ecclus 45:15)

The passage from Enoch is similar in tone to Exodus.

And they shall be upon Aaron, and upon his sons, when they come in unto the tabernacle of the congregation, or when they come near unto the altar to minister in the holy place; that they bear not iniquity, and die: it shall be a statute for ever unto him and his seed after him. (Ex 28:43)

The Aaronic passage in Ecclesiasticus 45 strengthens the language found in Exodus. Whereas Exodus states this "shall be a statute for ever unto him and his seed after him," Ben Sirach goes further by calling it an "everlasting covenant," one which lasts "so long as the heavens should remain."

Ecclesiasticus Chapter 50 completes the "roll call of faith" by returning to the person of Aaron, and pays special attention to the role of the Aaronic priesthood both in pronouncing the blessing of the Lord and the reception of that blessing by the people of Israel. Jesus ben Sirach begins and ends this "roll call of faith" with a description of the Aaronic priesthood. By describing the call of Aaron as an everlasting covenant, and by picturing the role of the Aaronic priesthood in distributing the blessings of God to the people, Jesus ben Sirach is rebuking the Hasmonean priesthood. The refusal to mention Melchizedek is a rejection of the Hasmonean claim that they were priests of the "order of Melchizedek." The author of Hebrews is less subtle; by claiming the Lord Jesus Christ is a "priest for ever after the order of Melchisedek" (He 5:6), the author is explicitly rejecting the Hasmonean claim. He might as well have called the Hasmonean dynasty usurpers of the Aaronic priesthood. As you may remember, the Essenes made the same argument upon rejecting the Temple cult.

Once again, we see evidence that Judaism in the time of Christ was highly fluid. There was no consensus among the Jews then, just as there is no consensus today. Apart from ethnicity, there has never been a generally accepted definition of what it means to be a Jew.

The Hebrew Book of Enoch (3 Enoch)

There is not much to say about 3 Enoch. It purports to have been written in the 2nd century AD by Rabbi Ishmael (d. 132 AD) but appears to have been constructed in the 5th or 6th century AD.[671] Philip Alexander notes that 3 Enoch shows signs of careful editing of materials. "The overall structure of the work is reasonably coherent, and thematically related materials have been grouped together."[672] It is apparent the author or editor pulled together some independent works

---

[671] (Charlesworth, The Old Testament Pseudepigrapha Volume One 1983, 225-226)

[672] (Ibid, 223)

that existed before 3 Enoch. This work is significant for its preservation of pre-exilic materials that survived in Jewish Merkabah mysticism during the Middle Ages. 3 Enoch is one of the Merkabah texts,[673] and as such is of little interest for New Testament studies.

---

[673] (Barker, The Older Testament 2005, 8) The Merkabah texts were secret teachings that were not for public consumption. Some scholars see a connection between Merkabah Mysticism and Gnosticism. (Charlesworth, The Old Testament Pseudepigrapha Volume One 1983, 236-238)

4: Enoch and the Book of Revelation

The Old Testament used by most Christians does not contain an apocalypse. Yes, there are portions of some Major and Minor Prophets that are apocalyptic, but no single book is apocalyptic in its entirety.[674] Despite this, the New Testament contains the Revelation of St. John, a book steeped in Second Temple apocalyptic imagery and its thematic material.

The primary difference between the Revelation of St. John and Second Temple apocalypses is Christology. Whereas the Second Temple imagery looks forward to the coming of the Messiah, the Revelation of St. John describes Jesus Christ as the Messiah who came, was slain, was resurrected, and is coming again to judge the living and the dead. The Book of Revelation borrows the apocalyptic imagery of Enoch in support of its Christology.

In examining this imagery, it is important to note that in the Second Temple, the Holy of Holies was empty; the Ark of the Covenant was missing. The Ark of the Covenant was shrouded in the "thick darkness" of the First Temple's Holy of Holies (I Kings 8:12). Ezekiel had a vision of the glory of God departing from the temple as a consequence for Israel's sin (Ez 8-10). After the Babylonian captivity and the rebuilding of the temple, Ezra makes no mention of the glory of God returning, filling the temple, and overshadowing the Ark. The Roman historian Tacitus tells us that when the Roman General Pompey captured Jerusalem in 63 BC, he entered the Holy of Holies. Tacitus writes:

Roman control of Judaea was first established by Gnaeus Pompey. As victor he claimed the right to enter the Temple, and

---

[674] The Ethiopian Coptic Church has a canon including an Old Testament apocalypse (1 Enoch). Some Slavonic bibles contain 2 Esdras (aka 4 Esdras, or 4, 5, and 6 Ezra) as an appendix to the Old Testament, and the Georgian Orthodox Bible contains 2 Esdras, calling it 3 Ezra.

this incident gave rise to the common impression that it contained no representation of the deity—the sanctuary was empty and the Holy of Holies untenanted.[675]

Interestingly, Josephus leaves this out of his account. He writes:

No small enormities were committed about the temple itself, which, in former ages, had been inaccessible, and see by none; for Pompey went into it, and not a few of those that were with him also, and saw all that which was unlawful for any other men to see, but only for the high priests.[676]

In like fashion, the Jewish Encyclopedia fails to mention that Pompey found the Holy of Holies empty.[677] The missing ark should be no surprise; while the temple liturgies carried on in the Second Temple, the glory of the Lord was missing. Since the Ark of the Covenant was missing, there was no Mercy Seat, and therefore no atonement for sin. The ancient men of Judah, those who had seen the first temple, wept over their loss when viewing the Second Temple. "But many of the priests and Levites and chief of the fathers, who were ancient men, that had seen the first house, when the foundation of this house was laid before their eyes, wept with a loud voice" (Ezra 3:12).

The sense of loss, the sense that God was no longer among them, is quite likely the source of much of the Second Temple literature. The apocalypses, in particular, supply us with vivid images of a heavenly temple full of angels serving God, a temple filled with the glory of God, and a temple where God sits upon His throne within the heavenly Holy of Holies. This heavenly temple, unlike the earthly Second Temple, was a place where God was present.

The calling of Enoch is similar to that of the apostle John. Enoch "was blessing the Lord of majesty and the King of the

---

[675] (Tacitus 2015)

[676] (Josephus 1987, The Antiquities of the Jews, 14.4.69ff, p. 370)

[677] (Gottheil and Krauss 1906)

ages" when the watcher called out to him (Enoch 12:3): John was "in the spirit on the Lord's Day," and was called up to heaven (Re 1:10; 4:1). Both of them were called into the heavenlies, where they both alike had visions of the Son of Man (Enoch 46:1-8; Re 1:13-18; 5:5-9; 19:11-16). Both alike witness the angels serving God, both witnessed the heavenly liturgies, and both were called into the presence of God, the fully-furnished Holy of Holies.[678]

The similarities between the thematic material of Enoch and Revelation are striking, so much so that it is clear that Revelation is a product of the Second Temple literary tradition. Despite it's similarities to Jewish apocalyptic material, John's Apocalypse is clearly Christian. For example, the Revelation begins by claiming the Son of Man had come, had died, and now liveth for evermore (Re 1:18). The scandal of the cross is entirely missing from Second Temple literature, yet is ever present within John's Revelation. Whatever debt the apostle John owed to Second Temple literature in general, and the Book of Enoch in particular, his apocalypse is clearly of Christian origin.

---

[678] (Barker, Temple Theology: An Introduction 2004, 21)

5: The Place of Enoch in the New Testament

We should by no means read Enoch as giving us an accurate cosmology, nor should consider it to be inspired or authoritative. It is nonetheless instructive to read it as background material for the New Testament, as it reflects the Second Temple context of the gospel writers. Of the influence of Enoch, Professor Norman Gold writes: "The Aramaic «Book of Enoch» ...very considerably influenced the idiom of the New Testament and patristic literature, more so in fact than any other writing of the Apocrypha and Pseudepigrapha."[679]

F. Crawford Burkitt, English academic and theologian, makes the point that without understanding Enoch's rationale for the existence of evil, we will miss some of the nuances of the New Testament texts.

Nevertheless it is an attempt to see the world steadily and to see it whole, to unify the physical world, the moral world, and the political world, the world, that is, of the national destiny of God's chosen People. It contains a serious attempt to account for the presence of Evil in human history, and this attempt claims our attention, because it is in essentials the view presupposed in the Gospels, especially the Synoptic Gospels. It is when you study Matthew, Mark and Luke against the background of the Books of Enoch that you see them in their true perspective.[680]

F. Crawford Burkitt tells us that many of the sayings of Jesus can be regarded as *"Midrash* upon the words and concepts taken from Enoch." Burkitt claims a failure to understand the cultural context causes us to assume these are new teachings instead of references to what is "presupposed and

---

[679] (Golb 2012, Kindle Locations 8048-8050)

[680] (Burkitt 1914, 21)

assumed."[681] Most tellingly, we see this in the Sermon on the Mount. Joseph B. Lumpkin provides an interesting side-by-side comparison of these New Testament passages. [682]

Table 7: 1 Enoch and the Gospels

The Gospels	1 Enoch
Blessed are they which are persecuted for righteousness' sake: for theirs is the kingdom of heaven. Blessed are ye, when men shall revile you, and persecute you, and shall say all manner of evil against you falsely, for my sake. Rejoice, and be exceeding glad: for great is your reward in heaven: for so persecuted they the prophets which were before you. (Mt 5:10-12) But woe to you who are rich, for you have already received your comfort. Woe to you who are well fed now, for you will go hungry. Woe to you who laugh now, for you will mourn and weep. Woe to you when all men speak well of you, for that is how their fathers treated the false prophets. (Lk 6:24-26)	Woe to you, sinners, for you persecute the righteous; for you shall be delivered up and persecuted because of injustice, and your yoke shall be heavy on you. (1En 95:7)

---

[681] (Ibid, 21) As an Orthodox Christian, I give more weight to the interpretive history of a passage than to the cultural background.

[682] All citations from Enoch come from Joseph Lumpkin's translation. Lumpkin supplied other references as inter-textual notes; these have been added to the list. (Lumpkin, The Books of Enoch 2011, passim)

The Gospels	1 Enoch
The Son of man shall send forth his angels, and they shall gather out of his kingdom all things that offend, and them which do iniquity. (Mt 13: 41)	And this Son of Man whom you have seen shall raise up the kings and the mighty from their seats, and the strong from their thrones and shall loosen the reins of the strong, and break the teeth of the sinners. And he shall put down the kings from their thrones and kingdoms because they do not exalt and praise Him, nor humbly acknowledge who bestowed their kingdom on them. (1En 46:4-5)
And Jesus said unto them, Verily I say unto you, That ye which have followed me, in the regeneration when the Son of Man shall sit in the throne of his glory, ye also shall sit upon twelve thrones, judging the twelve tribes of Israel. (Mt 19: 28)	And I will bring out in shining light those who have loved My holy name, and I will seat each on the throne of his honor. (1En 108:12)
When the Son of Man shall come in His glory, and all the holy angels with Him, then shall He sit upon the throne of His glory: (Mt 25: 31)	And one portion of them shall look at the other, and they shall be terrified, and they shall look downcast, and pain shall seize them, when they see that Son of Man sitting on the throne of His glory. (1En 62:5)

Appendix B: Second Temple Writings and the Bible

The Gospels	1 Enoch
Woe unto that man through whom the Son of man is betrayed! It had been good for that man if he had not been born. (Mt 26: 24)	Where will there be the dwelling for sinners, and where the will there be a resting-place for those who have denied the Lord of spirits? It had been good for them if they had not been born. (1En 38: 2)
When the Son of man shall come in his glory, and all the holy angels with him, then shall he sit upon the throne of his glory. (Mt 25:31) And his raiment became shining, exceeding white as snow; so as no fuller on earth can white them. (Mk 9:3)	And He who is Great in Glory sat on the throne, and His raiment shone more brightly than the sun and was whiter than any snow. (1En 14:20)
Now the brother shall betray the brother to death, and the father the son; and children shall rise up against their parents, and shall cause them to be put to death. (Mk 13: 12)	And in those days in one place the fathers together with their sons shall kill one another and brothers shall fall in death together until the streams flow with their blood. For a man shall not withhold his hand from killing his sons and his sons' sons, and the sinner shall not withhold his hand from his honored brother, from dawn until sunset they shall kill one another. (1En 100:1-2)

The Gospels	1 Enoch
"Woe unto you that are rich! for ye have received your consolation. (Lk 6: 24)	Woe to you, you rich, for you have trusted in your riches, and from your riches shall you depart, because you have not remembered the Most High in the days of your riches. (1En 94: 8)
...between us and you there is a great gulf fixed. (Lk 16: 26)	Then I asked, regarding all the hollow places (chasm): 'Why is one separated from the other?' And he answered me and said to me: 'These three have been made that the spirits of the dead might be separated. (1En 22: 8-9)
And Jesus answering said unto them, The children of this world marry, and are given in marriage: But they which shall be accounted worthy to obtain that world, and the resurrection from the dead, neither marry, nor are given in marriage: Neither can they die any more: for they are equal unto the angels; and are the children of God, being the children of the resurrection. (Lk 20:34-36)	Go and say to the Watchers of heaven... Therefore I have not appointed wives for you; you are spiritual beings of heaven, and in heaven was your dwelling place. (1En 15:2, 7)

Appendix B: Second Temple Writings and the Bible

The Gospels	1 Enoch
In the beginning was the Word, and the Word was with God, and the Word was God. The same was in the beginning with God. All things were made by him; and without him was not any thing made that was made. In him was life; and the life was the light of men. And the light shineth in darkness; and the darkness comprehended it not. (Jn 1: 1-5)	And when the Righteous One shall appear before the eyes of the elect righteous ones, whose works are weighed by the Lord of spirits, light shall appear to the righteous and the elect who dwell on the earth. (1En 38:2)
...the water that I shall give him shall be in him a well of water springing up into everlasting life. (Jn 4: 14)	And in that place I saw the spring of righteousness which was inexhaustible. And around it were many springs of wisdom. And all the thirsty drank of them, and were filled with wisdom, and their dwellings were with the righteous and holy and elect. (1En 48: 1)
The Father judgeth no man, but hath committed all judgment unto the son. (Jn 5: 22)	And he sat on the throne of his glory, and the sum of judgment was given to the Son of Man. (1En 69:27).
...that ye may be called the children of light (Jn 12: 36)	And now I will summon the spirits of the good who belong to the generation of light... (1En 108: 11)

The Gospels	1 Enoch
In my Father's house are many mansions: if it were not so, I would have told you. I go to prepare a place for you. 3 And if I go and prepare a place for you, I will come again, and receive you unto myself; that where I am, there ye may be also. (Jn 14: 2-3)	And there I saw the mansions of the elect and the mansions of the holy. (1En 41:2)

The apostles Peter John, Paul, and Jude, together with the writer of Hebrews, were influenced by the Enochian material. John's Apocalypse, as demonstrated below, was especially influenced by 1 Enoch.

Table 8: 1 Enoch and the Apostolic Writings

Apostolic Writings	1 Enoch
To them who by patient continuance in well doing seek for glory and honour and immortality, eternal life: But unto them that are contentious, and do not obey the truth, but obey unrighteousness, indignation and wrath, Tribulation and anguish, upon every soul of man that doeth evil, of the Jew first, and also of the Gentile; But glory, honour, and peace, to every man that worketh good, to the Jew first, and also to the Gentile: For there is no respect of persons with God. (Rom 2: 7-11)	In the day of our suffering and tribulation He does not save and we find no respite for confession that our Lord is true in all His works, and in His judgments and His justice, and His judgments have no respect of persons. (1En 63:8)

Appendix B: Second Temple Writings and the Bible

Apostolic Writings	1 Enoch
I say then, Have they stumbled that they should fall? God forbid: but rather through their fall salvation is come unto the Gentiles, for to provoke them to jealousy. Now if the fall of them be the riches of the world, and the diminishing of them the riches of the Gentiles; how much more their fulness? (Rom 11:11-12)	He shall be a staff to the righteous and they shall steady themselves and not fall. And he shall be the light of the Gentiles, and the hope of those who are troubled of heart. (1En 48:4)
For it is written, As I live, saith the Lord, every knee shall bow to me, and every tongue shall confess to God. So then every one of us shall give account of himself to God. (Rom 14: 11-12)	In those days shall the mighty and the kings who possess the earth beg Him to grant them a little respite from His angels of punishment to whom they were delivered, that they might fall down and worship before the Lord of spirits, and confess their sins before Him. (1En 63:1)
But we all, with open face beholding as in a glass the glory of the Lord, are changed into the same image from glory to glory, even as by the Spirit of the Lord. (2Co 3: 18)	And they shall not be able to look at the face of the holy ones, because the Lord of spirits has caused His light to appear on the face of the holy, righteous, and elect. (1En 38:4)

Apostolic Writings	1 Enoch
The Spirit clearly says that in later times some will abandon the faith and follow deceiving spirits and things taught by demons. (1Ti 4: 1) The rest of mankind that were not killed by these plagues still did not repent of the work of their hands; they did not stop worshiping demons, and idols of gold, silver, bronze, stone and wood— idols that cannot see or hear or walk. Nor did they repent of their murders, their magic arts, their sexual immorality or their thefts. (Rev 9:20-21)	And Uriel said to me: 'The angels who have had sex with women shall stand here, and their spirits, having assumed many different forms, are defiling mankind and shall lead them astray into sacrificing to demons as gods, here shall they stand, until the day of the great judgment in which they shall be judged and are made an end of. (1En 19:1)
And to you who are troubled rest with us, when the Lord Jesus shall be revealed from heaven with his mighty angels, In flaming fire taking vengeance on them that know not God, and that obey not the gospel of our Lord Jesus Christ: Who shall be punished with everlasting destruction from the presence of the Lord, and from the glory of his power? (2Th 1: 7-9)	Woe to you, you sinners, on account of the words of your mouth, and on account of the deeds of your hands which your godlessness has caused, in blazing flames burning worse than fire shall you burn. (1En 100:9)

Appendix B: Second Temple Writings and the Bible

Apostolic Writings	1 Enoch
Let no man deceive you by any means: for that day shall not come, except there come a falling away first, and that man of sin be revealed, the son of perdition. (2Th 2: 3)	And when sin and unrighteousness and blasphemy and violence in all kinds of deeds increase, and apostasy and transgression and uncleanness increase; a great chastisement shall come from heaven on all these, and the holy Lord will come out with wrath and chastisement to execute judgment on earth. (1En 91:7) And after that in the seventh week shall an apostate generation arise, and many shall be its deeds, and all its deeds shall be apostate. (1En 93:9)
Which in his times he shall shew, who is the blessed and only Potentate, the King of kings, and Lord of lords; Who only hath immortality, dwelling in the light which no man can approach unto; whom no man hath seen, nor can see: to whom be honour and power everlasting. Amen. (1Ti 6: 15-16)	And they said to the Lord of the ages: 'Lord of lords, God of gods, King of kings, and God of the ages, the throne of your glory endures through all the generations of the ages, and your name holy and glorious and blessed to all the ages! (1En 9:4) And I looked and saw a throne set on high, its appearance was like crystal, and its wheels were like a shining sun, and there was the vision of cherubim. And from underneath the throne came rivers of fire so that I could not look at it. (1En 14:18-19)

Apostolic Writings	1 Enoch
For we which have believed do enter into rest, as he said, As I have sworn in my wrath, if they shall enter into my rest: although the works were finished from the foundation of the world. (Heb 4: 3)	And so there shall be length of days with the Son of Man, and the righteous shall have peace and an upright way in the name of the Lord of spirits forever and ever.' (1En 71:17)
For here have we no continuing city, but we seek one to come. (Heb 13: 14)	And I stood up to see until they folded up that old house ...And I saw until the Lord of the sheep brought a new house greater and loftier than that first, and set it up in the place of the first which had been folded up. (1En 90: 28a-29a)
But let him ask in faith, nothing wavering. For he that wavereth is like a wave of the sea driven with the wind and tossed. For let not that man think that he shall receive any thing of the Lord. A double-minded man is unstable in all his ways. (Jas 1: 6-8)	Love righteousness and walk in it, and draw near to righteousness without a double heart, and do not associate with those of a double heart, but walk in righteousness, my sons. And it shall guide you on good paths. And righteousness shall be your companion. (1En 91:4)
By the same word the present heavens and earth are reserved for fire, being kept for the day of judgment and destruction of ungodly men. (2Pe 3: 7)	Here their spirits shall be set apart in this great pain until the great day of judgment and punishment and torment of those who curse forever and retribution for their spirits. (1En 22:11)

Appendix B: Second Temple Writings and the Bible

Apostolic Writings	1 Enoch
For all that is in the world, the lust of the flesh, and the lust of the eyes, and the pride of life, is not of the Father, but is of the world. And the world passeth away, and the lust thereof: but he that doeth the will of God abideth for ever. (1Jo 2:16-17)	For the judgment shall come on them, because they believe in the lust of their body and deny the Spirit of the Lord. (1En 67:10)
And the angels which kept not their first estate, but left their own habitation, he hath reserved in everlasting chains under darkness unto the judgment of the great day. (Jude 1: 6)	I heard the voice of the angel saying: 'These are the angels who descended to the earth, and revealed what was hidden to the children of men and seduced the children of men into committing sin.' (1En 64:2)
And Enoch also, the seventh from Adam, prophesied of these, saying, Behold, the Lord cometh with ten thousands of his saints, To execute judgment upon all, and to convince all that are ungodly among them of all their ungodly deeds which they have ungodly committed, and of all their hard speeches which ungodly sinners have spoken against him. (Jude 1:14-15)	And behold! He comes with ten thousand of His holy ones (saints) to execute judgment on all, and to destroy all the ungodly (wicked); and to convict all flesh of all the works of their ungodliness which they have ungodly committed, and of all the hard things which ungodly sinners have spoken against Him. (1En 1:9)

Apostolic Writings	1 Enoch
And the kings of the earth, and the great men, and the rich men, and the chief captains, and the mighty men, and every bondman, and every free man, hid themselves in the dens and in the rocks of the mountains; And said to the mountains and rocks, Fall on us, and hide us from the face of him that sitteth on the throne, and from the wrath of the Lamb: For the great day of his wrath is come; and who shall be able to stand? (Re 6: 15-17)	And I looked and turned to another part of the earth, and saw there a deep valley with burning fire. And they brought the kings and the powerful, and began to cast them into this deep valley. (1En 54:1-2)
And the winepress was trodden without the city, and blood came out of the winepress, even unto the horse bridles, by the space of a thousand and six hundred furlongs. (Re 14: 20)	And the horse shall walk up to the breast in the blood of sinners, and the chariot shall be submerged to its height. (1En 100:3)
And the beast was taken, and with him the false prophet that wrought miracles before him, with which he deceived them that had received the mark of the beast, and them that worshipped his image. These both were cast alive into a lake of fire burning with brimstone. (Re 19:20)	And on the day of the great judgment he shall be hurled into the fire. (1En 10:6)

Appendix B: Second Temple Writings and the Bible

Apostolic Writings	1 Enoch
And I saw an angel come down from heaven, having the key of the bottomless pit and a great chain in his hand. And he laid hold of the dragon, that old serpent, which is the Devil, and Satan, and bound him a thousand years, And cast him into the bottomless pit, and shut him up, and set a seal upon him, that he should deceive the nations no more, till the thousand years should be fulfilled: and after that he must be loosed for a little season. (Re 20: 1-3)	And again the Lord said to Raphael: 'Bind Azazel hand and foot, and cast him into the darkness and split open the desert, which is in Dudael, and cast him in. 5 And fill the hole by covering him with rough and jagged rocks, and cover him with darkness, and let him live there forever, and cover his face that he may not see the light. (1En 10:4-5)
And I saw the dead, small and great, stand before God; and the books were opened: and another book was opened, which is the Book of Life: and the dead were judged out of those things which were written in the books, according to their works. And the sea gave up the dead which were in it; and death and hell delivered up the dead which were in them: and they were judged every man according to their works. And death and hell were cast into the lake of fire. This is the second death. And whosoever was not found written in the Book of Life was cast into the lake of fire. (Re 20: 12-15)	And in those days shall the earth also give back that which has been entrusted to it, and Sheol (the grave) also shall give back that which it has received, and hell shall give back that which it owes. For in those days the Elect One shall arise, And he shall choose the righteous and holy from among them. For the day has drawn near that they should be saved. (1En 51:1-2)

Apostolic Writings	1 Enoch
And he carried me away in the spirit to a great and high mountain, and shewed me that great city, the holy Jerusalem, descending out of heaven from God, Having the glory of God: and her light was like unto a stone most precious, even like a jasper stone, clear as crystal. (Re 21: 10-11)	And he translated (carried) my spirit into heaven of heavens, and I saw there as it were built of crystals, and between those crystals tongues of living fire. (1En 71:5)
And he shewed me a pure river of water of life, clear as crystal, proceeding out of the throne of God and of the Lamb. In the midst of the street of it, and on either side of the river, was there the tree of life, which bare twelve manner of fruits, and yielded her fruit every month: and the leaves of the tree were for the healing of the nations. And there shall be no more curses: but the throne of God and of the Lamb shall be in it; and his servants shall serve him. (Re 22: 1-3)	And as for this fragrant tree, no mortal is permitted to touch it until the great judgment, when He shall take vengeance on all and bring everything to its completion forever. It shall then be given to the righteous and holy. Its fruit shall be for food to the Elect: it shall be transplanted to the holy place, to the temple of the Lord, the Eternal King. (1En 25:4-5)

It is possible to explain away a number of these references and to argue that they don't derive from Enoch specifically. Some of the comparisons between Enoch and Revelations could have been made to other apocalyptic literature, or perhaps were informed by motifs present in Enochic and related Second Temple literature (making up the zeitgeist, the spirit of the age).⁶⁸³ Despite these arguments, it is difficult to argue against the entire list of Enochian references. Many of them are too specific, and some are word-for-word quotations. It is clear that the New Testament authors were heavily influenced by 1 Enoch, which makes the book an important resource for understanding the New Testament.

Despite the importance of 1 Enoch, it is not scripture because the things ascribed to Enoch are the prerogatives of Jesus Christ. Enoch is said to have ascended to heaven and then descended to teach heavenly secrets to the elect. James H. Charlesworth notes the Gospel of John makes it clear that only Jesus Christ has descended to bring knowledge and eternal life to mankind. He writes:

With these insights, one may perceive a polemic against the claim in the Parables of Enoch that Enoch is the revealer, the one who ascended into heaven and then descended as "the son of Man." Note this passage attributed to Jesus by the Fourth evangelist (italics mine):

《*No one has ascended into heaven except*》 *the one who descended from heaven,* 《*the Son of Man.*》 *And just as Moses lifted up the serpent in the wilderness, so must* 《*the Son of Man*》 *be lifted up, that* 《*whoever believes in him may have eternal life.*》 *(Jn 3:13-15 [NRSV])*⁶⁸⁴

This passage makes it clear that Jesus Christ knew the Enoch traditions, and that He used them as a means of explaining who He was. The fact that Enoch is portrayed as doing that

---

⁶⁸³ James H. Charlesworth, writing in his introduction to the *History of the Rechabites*, notes any relationship between it and 2 Baruch "is apparently not the result of literary dependence in either direction; it can be explained by a shared mileu or body of traditions, perhaps by a shared tradition, and possibly by independent influence from a lost apocryphon." (Charlesworth, The Old Testament Pseudepigrapha Volume Two 1983, 446)

⁶⁸⁴ (Charlesworth, Did Jesus Know the Traditions in the Parables of Enoch 2013, 176)

which belongs to Christ alone is enough reason for it to have been left out of the canon. However, despite its being non-canonical, it is still useful.

Knowledge of Enochic material adds depth to our understanding of the New Testament. In her doctoral thesis, Amy Richter makes the case that the first two chapters of Matthew use motifs from Enochian tradition to demonstrate that "Jesus completes what Enoch does not."[685] In Enochic tradition, the Watchers were a particular class of fallen angels who introduced illicit knowledge to mankind. These Watchers are based on the passage from Genesis 6, and are identical to the "sons of God" who married the "daughters of men."

In the Book of Enoch there are three accounts of the Watcher's activities, and three types of illicit or forbidden knowledge they brought to mankind. In her article on Genesis 6: 5-6, Dr. Miryam T. Brand explains the

In one account, the angel Asael descends to earth and teaches forbidden knowledge to women concerning female adornment, which facilitates lust. He also teaches men how to create weapons, which enables war. ...In another thread woven into the story of the Watchers in Enoch, humans are taught magic and other forbidden knowledge. ...The predominant tradition and main thread in the Book of Watchers, into which the other traditions are interwoven, focuses on the desire of the angels, led by Shemihaza, to mate with human women.

The result of this union is unnatural, as could be expected: the women bear violent giants. The giants' violence and voracious hunger cause humans tremendous distress, as well as setting off a "domino effect" of violence among all creatures of the world. The final result of all this illicit angelic intervention is the Flood, either to rid the world of contamination or to end the humans' sin.

---

[685] (Richter 2010, 3)

In this third version of the story, the giants themselves are killed. Their spirits, however, deriving from immortal heavenly beings (the angels), cannot be destroyed completely, but also cannot return to heaven. They remain connected to earth as evil spirits, wreaking havoc among humankind and causing both physical evil (such as disease) and moral evil (sin).[686]

---

[686] (Brand 2016)

6: Enoch and the Ancient Church

Enoch was an important and influential document in the early church before rapidly falling out of favor. Some considered 1 Enoch to be scripture, while others did not. For example, the Epistle of Barnabas quotes Enoch and Daniel together, implying the inspiration of both.

It therefore behooves us, who inquire much concerning events at hand, to search diligently into those things which are able to save us. Let us then utterly flee from all the works of iniquity, lest these should take hold of us; and let us hate the error of the present time, that we may set our love on the world to come: let us not give loose reins to our soul, that it should have power to run with sinners and the wicked, lest we become like them. The final stumbling-block (or source of danger) approaches, concerning which it is written, as Enoch says, "For this end the Lord has cut short the times and the days, that His Beloved may hasten; and He will come to the inheritance." And the prophet also speaks thus: "Ten kingdoms shall reign upon the earth, and a little king shall rise up after them, who shall subdue under one three of the kings."[687]

In Book IV of his work, *Against Heresies*, Irenaeus uses Enochian material to demonstrate that righteousness comes not from circumcision or other legal ceremonies. He compares the scriptural accounts of Abraham, Lot, and Noah with the accounts of Enoch that come not from Genesis, but from the Enochian writings. Specifically, he describes Enoch's role as "legate to the angels," a role not found in holy writ.

And that man was not justified by these things, but that they were given as a sign to the people, this fact shows, — that Abraham himself, without circumcision and without observance of Sabbaths, "believed God, and it was imputed

---

[687] (Schaff, ANF01 1884, 213)

unto him for righteousness; and he was called the friend of God." Then, again, Lot, without circumcision, was brought out from Sodom, receiving salvation from God. So also did Noah, pleasing God, although he was uncircumcised, receive the dimensions [of the ark], of the world of the second race [of men]. Enoch, too, pleasing God, without circumcision, discharged the office of God's legate to the angels although he was a man, and was translated, and is preserved until now as a witness of the just judgment of God, because the angels when they had transgressed fell to the earth for judgment, but the man who pleased [God] was translated for salvation.[688]

The founder of Latin Christianity, Tertullian, is considered by the Western Church to be one of the church fathers.[689] Tertullian believed 1 Enoch to be scripture. In his work "On Idolatry" he writes:

Enoch had preceded, predicting that "the demons, and the spirits of the angelic apostates, would turn into idolatry all the elements, all the garniture of the universe, all things contained in the heaven, in the sea, in the earth, that they might be consecrated as God, in opposition to God." All things, therefore, does human error worship, except the Founder of all Himself. The images of those things are idols; the consecration of the images is idolatry. Whatever guilt idolatry incurs, must necessarily be imputed to every artificer of every idol. In short, the same Enoch fore-condemns in general menace both idol-worshippers and idol-makers together. [690]

And again:

For we ought to be sure if there are any whose notice it escapes through ignorance of this world's literature, that there are

---

[688] (Ibid, 803)

[689] Because he joined the heretical sect of the Montanists before he died, the Eastern Church does not consider Tertullian to be a church father.

[690] (Schaff and Menzies, ANF03 2006, 92)

among the Romans even gods of entrances; Cardea (Hinge-goddess), called after hinges, and Forculus (Door-god) after doors, and Limentinus (Threshold-god) after the threshold, and Janus himself (Gate-god) after the gate: and of course we know that, though names be empty and feigned, yet, when they are drawn down into superstition, demons and every unclean spirit seize them for themselves, through the bond of consecration. Otherwise demons have no name individually, but they there find a name where they find also a token. Among the Greeks likewise we read of Apollo Thyræus, i.e. of the door, and the Antelii, or Anthelii, demons, as presiders over entrances. These things, therefore, the Holy Spirit foreseeing from the beginning, fore-chanted, through the most ancient prophet Enoch, that even entrances would come into superstitious use.[691]

In Tertullian's work "On the Apparel of Women," the argument in the second chapter is that female ornamentation can be traced back to the fallen angels — the Watchers who left their first estate and lusted after women. In 1 Enoch, the Watchers took human wives for themselves and taught men and women a great many things for which humanity was not ready.

And the angels taught them charms and spells, and the cutting of roots, and made them acquainted with plants. ...And Azazel taught men to make swords, and knives, and shields, and breastplates, and taught them about metals of the earth and the art of working them, and bracelets, and ornaments, and the use of antimony, and the beautifying of the eyelids, and all kinds of precious stones, and all coloring and dyes. And there was great impiety; they turned away from God, and committed fornication, and they were led astray, and became corrupt in all their ways. (1En 7:2; 8:1-2)[692]

---

[691] (Schaff and Menzies, ANF03 2006, 106)
[692] (Lumpkin, The Books of Enoch 2011, 28-29)

Tertullian uses this Enochian material to argue against women wearing jewelry, fine apparel, and makeup. He then justifies this in chapter 3 by explicitly calling 1 Enoch scripture.

I am aware that the Scripture of Enoch, which has assigned this order (of action) to angels, is not received by some, because it is not admitted into the Jewish canon either.

And again, he writes:

But since Enoch in the same Scripture has preached likewise concerning the Lord, nothing at all must be rejected by us which pertains to us; and we read that "every Scripture suitable for edification is divinely inspired."[693]

In Chapter 3 of "On First Principles," Origen quotes from the Shephard of Hermas and alludes to much the same material in Enoch to show that while God created all things, nothing in Scripture ever implies the Holy Spirit is part of the created order. How he juxtaposes Hermas, Enoch, and Scripture could imply he is using the former as Scripture.[694]

For even in that little treatise called The Pastor or Angel of Repentance, composed by Hermas, we have the following: "First of all, believe that there is one God who created and arranged all things; who, when nothing formerly existed, caused all things to be; who Himself contains all things, but Himself is contained by none." And in the book of Enoch also we have similar descriptions. But up to the present time we have been able to find no statement in holy Scripture in which the Holy Spirit could be said to be made or created, not even in

---

[693] (Schaff, ANF04 2006, 22-23)

[694] It could also be argued that Origen is juxtaposing useful writings on the one hand, and scripture on the other. If this is the case, Origen's method suggests ways in which those who do not believe the Apocrypha to be scripture could nonetheless use them as an adjunct to scripture.

the way in which we have shown above that the divine wisdom is spoken of by Solomon, or in which those expressions which we have discussed are to be understood of the life, or the word, or the other appellations of the Son of God.[695]

We could continue, but to what end? It is enough to show that the early church held Enoch in high regard, that some considered it to be scripture, and it even made its way not some collections of the New Testament. And yet the Church eventually determined that no matter how useful it was to the authors of the New Testament, 1 Enoch was not Scripture.

---

[695] (Ibid, 444)

7: Jubilees

The Book of Jubilees, also known as The Little Genesis, is "a midrashic retelling of the story of Genesis (and the beginning of Exodus) in the form of a revelation conveyed by angels to Moses."[696] This book was originally written in Hebrew, as evidenced by manuscript evidence from the Dead Sea Scrolls (4Q216-218, 1Q17-18, 2Q19-20, 3Q5, 4Q482(?), and 11Q12). While Geza Vermes categorizes this as a biblically-based apocalyptic document, George W. E. Nickelsburg describes this as a rewriting and expanding of the Bible, where "the largest group of additions to the biblical text are halakhic."[697] Robert Henry Charles would agree, classifying the book as "Primitive History Rewritten from the Standpoint of the Law."[698]

The book of Jubilees contains information important to our understanding of the New Testament and the early Church. First, Jubilees contains a section containing the history of Enoch, including a summary of the apocalyptic material contained in 1 Enoch. Second, Jubilees contains a summary account of the Watchers — their original purpose, how they "left their first estate" (Jude 1:6), and their punishment. Third, and conspicuous by its absence, is any mention of Melchizedek. R. H. Charles demonstrates that the original text contained a reference to Melchizedek, but the "Maccabean high-priests" appropriated the order of Melchizedek as a way to assert the legitimacy of their non-Aaronic priesthood.[699] Removing references to Melchizedek could be seen as a protest against the Maccabean priesthood.

---

[696] (Vermes, The Complete Dead Sea Scrolls in English 2004, 539)

[697] (Stone, Jewish Writings of the Second Temple Period 1984, 89, 97) The term *halakhic* has to do with the *Halakha*, being the collection of Jewish religious law derived from the written and oral Torah. (Vermes, The Complete Dead Sea Scrolls in English 2004, 537)

[698] (Charles, The Apocrypha and Pseudepigrapha of the Old Testament in English Vol 2 1913, v)

[699] (Ibid, 9, 33, 61, 289)

Finally, the author of Jubilees is claiming the legitimacy of a solar calendar of 364 days, so much so that he rewrites Genesis 1:14 to leave off the mention of the moon as a means of measuring time. This is significant due to the early church's adoption of the Julian solar calendar instead of the Jewish lunar calendar.

One of the central elements of Jubilees is the chronology based on the number 7. Joseph Lumpkin writes:

The name "Jubilees" comes from the division of time into eras known as Jubilees. One Jubilee occurs after the equivalent of forty-nine years, or seven Sabbaths or weeks of years has passed. It is the numerical perfection of seven sevens. In a balance and symmetry of years, the Jubilee occurs after seven cycles of seven or forty-nine years have been completed. Thus, the fiftieth year is a Jubilee year. Time is told by referencing the number of Jubilees that have transpired from the time the festival was first kept. For example, Israel entered Canaan at the close of the fiftieth Jubilee, which is about 2450 BCE.[700]

The genealogies in the gospel of Matthew also demonstrate a similar interest in the number seven. "So all the generations from Abraham to David are fourteen generations; and from David until the carrying away into Babylon are fourteen generations; and from the carrying away into Babylon unto Christ are fourteen generations." (Mt 1:17) This doesn't indicate Matthew borrowed the notion from Jubilees, especially given the usage of the number throughout the Old Testament, but it does suggest a shared interest in arranging events using the number seven.

Jubilees, or *The Little Genesis*, was cited approvingly by a number of the early church fathers. Epiphanius of Salamis

---

[700] (Lumpkin, The Book of Jubilees 2006, 9-10) Dispensationalists use the same chronology based on the number seven to deciphers the times and dates expressed in the apocalyptic sections of the Hebrew Scriptures. By their reckoning, Daniel's 40 weeks become 40 periods of 7 years, or 280 years total. And so on.

(ca. 315-403 AD) cites Genesis as scripture, and then adds additional details from The Book of Jubilees. Epiphanius found Jubilees to be authoritative and possibly inspired.[701] In the last verse of this passage, he indicates Genesis is a "reflection" of what is more fully explained in *The Little Genesis*.

But as we find in Jubilees which is also called 'The Little Genesis,' the book even contains the names of both Cain's and Seth's wives, so that the persons who recite myths to the world may be put to shame in every way. For after Adam had sired sons and daughters it became necessary at that time that the boys marry their own sisters. Such a thing was not unlawful, as there was no other human stock. Indeed, in a manner of speaking Adam himself practically married his own daughter who was fashioned from his body and bones and had been formed by God in conjunction with him, and it was not unlawful. And his sons were married, Cain to the older sister, whose name was Saue; and a third son, Seth, who was born after Abel, to his sister named Azura. And Adam had other sons too as the Little Genesis says, nine after these three, so that he had two daughters but twelve sons, one of whom was killed but eleven survived. You have the reflection of them too in the Genesis of the World, the first Book of Moses, which says, 'And Adam lived 930 years, and begat sons and daughters, and died.'[702]

In the *Chronicon* of Hippolytus, the Divisions of Nations among the three sons of Noah is described using the material from Jubilees instead of Genesis.

---

[701] In the *Panarion* of Epiphanius of Salamis (aka *Adversus Haereses*, or Against Heresies), Epiphanius provides a list of the books accepted by the Jews. This list represents the works accepted by the Jews in the 4th century, and should not be used to describe either the Hebrew Scriptures in the time of Christ, or the Christian Old Testament.

[702] (Epiphanius of Salamis 2012, Book 1, Section 3, Part 39, 6:1-6:6)

Hippolytus' «Chronicon» ...contains a large section called "Division of the Earth" (Διαμερισμός τῆς γῆς, §§ 44-239) which, like «Jubilees» 8-9, covers the parceling of the earth among the sons of Noah based on the Table of Nations in Genesis 10 (cf. 1 Chr 1:1-2:2).[703]

James M. Scott concludes:

The foregoing study offers evidence that the Hippolytus' «Diamerismos» [Division of Nations] was indeed based on «Jubilees» 8-9. It seems likely that Hippolytus epitomized and reworked the lost Greek version of Jubilees 8-9 and incorporated it into his «Chronicon.»[704]

Once again, this does not mean that Jubilees is scripture, but it does indicate that early Christians found it useful enough to use as source material for their writings.

---

[703] (Albani, Frey and Lange 1997, 296)

[704] (Ibid, 319)

8: Melchizedek

We have discussed the Second Temple personage of Melchizedek in connection with the book of Hebrews. However, the Dead Sea Scrolls contains text known as the Melchizedek scroll (a.k.a. 11QMelchizedek or 11Q13.) Geza Vermes describes this as "an eschatological midrash," meaning a commentary on death, judgment, and the ultimate destiny of the soul.[705] James A. Sanders notes the particular "midrashic technique" employed by the author is its "weaving of the Old Testament into its own fabric."[706] This technique of midrashic weaving is also used in Mary's Magnificat, which is one Old Testament reference after another, woven into a coherent narrative.

Central to the Melchizedek scroll is the following passage:

The Spirit of the Lord GOD is upon me; because the LORD hath anointed me to preach good tidings unto the meek; he hath sent me to bind up the brokenhearted, to proclaim liberty to the captives, and the opening of the prison to them that are bound; To proclaim the acceptable year of the LORD, and the day of vengeance of our God; to comfort all that mourn. (Isa 61:1-2)

This is the passage Luke records as being the source text for Jesus' first sermon.

And he came to Nazareth, where he had been brought up: and, as his custom was, he went into the synagogue on the sabbath day, and stood up for to read. And there was delivered unto him the book of the prophet Esaias. And when he had opened the book, he found the place where it was written, The Spirit of the Lord is upon me, because he hath anointed me to preach the gospel to the poor; he hath sent me to heal the brokenhearted, to preach deliverance to the captives, and recovering of sight to the blind, to set at liberty them that are

---

[705] (Vermes, The Complete Dead Sea Scrolls in English 2004, 532)
[706] (Sanders, The Old Testament in 11Q Melchizedek 1973, 374)

bruised, To preach the acceptable year of the Lord. And he closed the book, and he gave it again to the minister, and sat down. And the eyes of all them that were in the synagogue were fastened on him. And he began to say unto them, This day is this scripture fulfilled in your ears. (Lu 4:16-21)

To understand the Melchizedek scroll, you must understand its connection with the Year of Jubilee, which involves "canceling debts, freeing bondservants, and returning land to its cultivator-occupants who had lost it through debt foreclosure or economic distress."[707] When Jesus preached "deliverance to the captives," he was proclaiming that their debts had been canceled and they were no longer in bondage. The literal meaning of the text was intended to be applied in the physical realm, but it had a deeper spiritual meaning as well.

The declaration of the Year of Jubilee is a consistent theme of Jesus' ministry. The Lord's Prayer contains the following: "And forgive us our debts, as we forgive our debtors." (Mt 6:12) In this passage, Jesus connects the temporal forgiveness of the debts we owe each other with God's forgiveness of the debts we to Him. This is an explicitly eschatological message, something that would have been clear to Jews who were familiar with Second Temple literature and, in particular, the Melchizedek scroll.

The Hebrew word for liberty (דְּרוֹר, deror,) which is the proclamation of the Year of Jubilee, is found throughout the Melchizedek scroll. Michael Hudson suggests:

The author(s) evidently searched through the Jewish Bible to find all its references to «deror,» and collated them in such a way as to describe the Day of Judgement as a grand release to end all releases. At the End of Time the Lord will return to earth to save his followers and smite those who have digressed from the path of righteousness.[708]

---

[707] (Hudson 2018, 9)

[708] (Hudson 2018, 10)

The message of the Melchizedek scroll is drenched with the Old Testament concept of liberty, which is connected with the forgiveness of bondage to debt. The proclamation of the Year of Jubilee in Isaiah 61:1-3 is repeated several times, and is central to the message of the Melchizedek scroll. The Old Testament cross-references for the Melchizedek scroll are as follows:[709]

- Leviticus 25:13
- Deuteronomy 15:2
- Isaiah 61:1
- Leviticus 25:10
- Leviticus 25:9
- Isaiah 61:2
- Psalms 82:1
- Psalms 7:7-8
- Psalms 82:2
- Isaiah 61:2
- Isaiah 61:3

- Psalms 7:8
- Isaiah 52:7
- Isaiah 52:7
- Isaiah 61:1
- Daniel 9:25
- Isaiah 52:7
- Isaiah 61:2-3
- Isaiah 61:2
- Isaiah 52:7
- Isaiah 8:11
- Leviticus 25:9

The Melchizedek scroll opens and closes with references to the Levitical passages concerning the proclamation of Jubilee, which are also interspersed within the text. Interleaved within the Torah passages are references to Isaiah 61:1-3, the passage Jesus chose as the text for his first sermon.[710]

The Melchizedek scroll is important for our understanding of the ministry of Christ. The author of Hebrews makes a connection between Christ and Melchizedek, and it is important to understand who Melchizedek was historically and who he was in Second Temple literature. The New Testament focuses on Melchizedek a priest who performed a sacrifice for

---

[709] (Sanders, The Old Testament in 11Q Melchizedek 1973, 374-379) Sanders supplies the majority of the cross-references.

[710] This is not completely accurate. Jesus stopped reading in the middle of verse 2, immediately prior to the eschatological references to the year of the LORD and the day of vengeance.

Abraham, and to whom Abraham paid tithes. This means that Melchizedek had a prior claim to the priesthood. The claim made in Hebrews is that Jesus is a priest after the order of Melchizedek. Underpinning Hebrews is the linkage between the historical Melchizedek and the manner in which second temple literature transforms Melchizedek into a messianic and semi-divine figure. The name Melchizedek means "King of Righteousness," which ties in nicely to the messianic title "Righteous One" which we shall discuss in the next chapter.

9: Eschatological & Messianic Titles

The Second Temple literature, and especially the apocryphal genre, contains several messianic titles. Alfred Edersheim lists several: the Woman's Son, the Son of Man, the Elect, the Just One, and the Son of God.[711] There are others, such as Righteous One, Anointed One, and Chosen One. While the title "Righteous One" is not always eschatological, the others nearly always occur in an eschatological context. We will focus on four of these terms: Righteous One, Anointed One, Chose One, and Son of Man.

Righteous One

The Ethiopic text of the Parables uses the title Righteous One four times.[712] Only one time is the title Righteous One used in an eschatological context. The previous verses describe the last judgment when sinners shall be "banished from off the face of His earth, And they shall perish for ever and ever" (1En 53:3). After the final judgment comes the following verse: "And after this the Righteous and Elect One shall cause the house of his congregation to appear: henceforth they shall be no more hindered in the name of the Lord of Spirits" (1En 53:6).

The Greek word δίκαιος (dikaios) is translated both as "Just One" and "Righteous One," and is used in the New Testament as a messianic title.[713] When Peter healed the lame man who was begging before the temple, the people were amazed. As part of his response to them, Peter said: "But ye denied the Holy One and the Just [dikaios], and desired a murderer to be granted unto you" (Acts 3:14). In the protomartyr Stephen's speech before the council, he says:

---

[711] (Edersheim 1993, 122)

[712] (Boccaccini 2007, 125)

[713] There are other places where *dikaios* is not used as a messianic title, such as when the Jews call Cornelius the centurion "just" (Acts 10:22).

"Which of the prophets have not your fathers persecuted? and they have slain them which shewed before of the coming of the Just One [dikaios]; of whom ye have been now the betrayers and murderers" (Acts 7:52). After Saul's (Paul) vision on the Damascus road, Ananias says to him: "And he said, The God of our fathers hath chosen thee, that thou shouldest know his will, and see that Just One [dikaios], and shouldest hear the voice of his mouth (Acts 22:14). In Paul's letter to the Romans he writes: "For scarcely for a righteous man [dikaios] will one die: yet peradventure for a good man some would even dare to die" (Ro 5:7). The apostle John writes: "If ye know that he is righteous [dikaios], ye know that every one that doeth righteousness is born of him (1Jo 2:29).

Anointed One

The term Anointed One is usually a title for the Messiah. Cyrus, the Persian king, was called the LORD's Anointed (Isa 45:1), one of the few times this title is used of someone other than the Messiah. In the book of 1 Enoch, this phrase occurs twice, both in an eschatological context. The first passage describes how the wicked will fall before the Son of Man (1En 48:2) but will be rejected. Andrei A Orlov points out the entire passage is using biblical terminology, in particular, that of Ps 2:2.[714]

And on the day of their affliction there shall be rest on the earth, And before them they shall fall and not rise again: And there shall be no one to take them with his hands and raise them: For they have denied the Lord of Spirits and His Anointed. The name of the Lord of Spirits be blessed (1En 48:10).

Then, in 1 Enoch chapter 52, the patriarch Enoch is taken by a whirlwind and shown the secrets of heaven through images similar to Nebuchadnezzar's vision found in the book of

---

[714] (Boccaccini 2007, 126)

Daniel. Enoch's vision contains a variety of mountains, each made up of different metals. The angel with Enoch tells him: "All these things which thou hast seen shall serve the dominion of His Anointed that he may be potent and mighty on the earth" (1En 52:4).[715]

The correlation between the Righteous One of 1 Enoch chapter 53 and the Anointed One is clear. They have to do with future events, with the final judgment, and with the reconciliation of all things to God. Both titles are messianic.

Chosen One

The title "Chosen One" is often found in the Ethiopian text of Enoch's *Book of Parables*. Like the previous two examples, these have "an eschatological character."[716] Andrei A. Orlov writes:

The Chosen One in the Parables paints a picture of a highly elevated celestial being. This being apparently has his own throne in the celestial realm since one of the passages, 45:3-4, depicts him as the one who has been installed on the throne of glory.[717]

This passage from Enoch is as follows:

*On that day Mine Elect One shall sit on the throne of glory
And shall try their works,
And their places of rest shall be innumerable.
And their souls shall grow strong within them when they see Mine Elect Ones,
And those who have called upon My glorious name:
Then will I cause Mine Elect One to dwell among them.*

---

[715] (Charles, The Book of Enoch 1917)
[716] (Boccaccini 2007, 126)
[717] (Ibid, 126-127)

And I will transform the heaven and make it an eternal blessing and light (1En 45:3-6).[718]

The passage goes on to describe the transformation of the earth and the judgment of evildoers. This messianic figure is now shown to have divine characteristics, to be more than just a man.

The title of The Chosen One, or The Elect One, is found in the account of the Transfiguration in the Gospel of Luke. Most translate this as some form of The Chosen One. The translators of the King James Version chose not to translate this as written but instead attempted to harmonize this passage with similar accounts in Matthew and Mark. Joseph Lumpkin writes:

Other evidence of the early Christians' acceptance of the Book of Enoch was for many years buried under the King James Bible's mistranslation of Luke 9: 35, describing the transfiguration of Christ: "And there came a voice out of the cloud, saying, 'This is my beloved Son. Hear him.'" Apparently the translator here wished to make this verse agree with a similar verse in Matthew and Mark. But Luke's verse in the original Greek reads, "This is my Son, the Elect One (from the Greek «ho eklelegmenos», literally, "the elect one"). Hear him."[719]

Luke, the historian, would certainly have been aware of the meaning of this title in the Second Temple literature and chose for theological reasons to use it in his account of the Transfiguration. As the Chosen One, Jesus was the promised Messiah upon whom the eschatological hopes rested. However, as the Son of God, Jesus was The Chosen One of the father, the one upon whom the plan of salvation relied.

---

[718] (Charles, The Book of Enoch 1917)

[719] (Lumpkin, The Books of Enoch 2011, 13)

Son of Man

Of all the Messianic titles in Second Temple literature, the title "Son of Man" is the most common. Not only that, but the use of the term in the Gospels has perhaps more to do with 1 Enoch than with the Old Testament. James H. Charlesworth writes:

Within second temple Judaism, a theological pinnacle was reached with the son of Man term, concept, and eventually title. In the Parables of Enoch, the son of Man is a construct that designates a heavenly figure who at the end of time will serve as cosmic Judge. This is a massive exegetical and midrashic development beyond the similar expressions in Ezekiel and Daniel.[720]

In the Enochian *Book of Parables*, the "Son of Man" has similar characteristics to the previous three titles: Righteous One, Anointed One, and Chosen one. These four terms apply to the same person. Andrei A. Orlov writes:

The profile of the "Son of Man" is an elevated celestial being recalls the figure of the Chosen One analyzed in the previous section. As with the Chosen One, Son of Man is a character associated with the celestial secrets who also has a throne of glory (62:5; 69:27, 29) from which he will judge sinners.[721]

Andrei A. Orlov goes on to point out the similarities between the treatment of the "Son of Man" in Daniel 7 and Enoch 46. In particular, the phrase "head of days" from Daniel is similar to the phrase "ancient of days" from Enoch. He writes:

The significant feature of the Son of Man's profile in the Parables is that the text understands this character as

---

[720] (Charlesworth, Did Jesus Know the Traditions in the Parables of Enoch 2013, 202)

[721] (Boccaccini 2007, 127)

preexistent, even possibly a divine being who received his name before the time of Creation.[722]

The Son of Man in Hebrew Scripture and Second Temple Literature.

The phrase "son of man" is used over 100 times in the Hebrew Scriptures. Sabino Chialà describes the evolution of the phrase, beginning with its use in Jeremiah, Isaiah, Psalms, Numbers, and Job.

In almost all these texts the expression appears in a sentence composed of two parts: in the first part the subject is "man," or a similar noun, and in the second part the subject is "son of man." "Man" and "son of man" are meant to be synonyms, and when placed in sequence, the second embellishes and accentuates the first.[723]

The use of the phrase "son of man" in Ezekiel is a phrase only God or his angels use and is used only as descriptive of Ezekiel. The use of the phrase "son of man" in apocalyptic literature takes on a wholly different meaning. Sabino Chialà writes:

In this book «ben 'adam» appears almost a hundred times and is the formal address God typically uses in speaking to the prophet. The term does not yet represent a particular function, but it is no longer a simply linguistic device used to emphasize the fragility of human nature.[724]

The book of Daniel varies widely in its use of the phrase "son of man." In some places, it is a synonym for "man." In other places, it is used by an angel when speaking to Daniel. Finally, it is used in connection with eschatological visions. Sabino Chialà writes:

---

[722] (Boccaccini 2007, 128)

[723] (Ibid, 155)

[724] (Ibid, 155)

Appendix B: Second Temple Writings and the Bible

The Aramaic plural «bene 'anasha», which appears twice (Dan 2:38; 5:21), and the Hebrew «bene 'adam», which appears once (10:16), are simple synonyms for "men". ...In 8:17, on the other hand, the Hebrew singular «ben 'adam» recalls the book of Ezekiel: God's messenger, Gabriel, speaks to Daniel the visionary, call him "son of man.[725]

The third meaning of the phrase "son of man" is found in Daniel 7, and is the first use of the phrase to be associated with eschatological visions. This use of the phrase "son of man," and the vision associated with it, were important during the Second Temple period.

I beheld till the thrones were cast down, and the Ancient of days did sit, whose garment was white as snow, and the hair of his head like the pure wool: his throne was like the fiery flame, and his wheels as burning fire.

*I saw in the night visions, and, behold, one like the **Son of man** came with the clouds of heaven, and came to the Ancient of days, and they brought him near before him.*

And there was given him dominion, and glory, and a kingdom, that all people, nations, and languages, should serve him: his dominion is an everlasting dominion, which shall not pass away, and his kingdom that which shall not be destroyed [emphasis added] (Dan 7:9, 13-14).

Of this text, Sabino Chialà writes:

This text provided most of the imagery that was used in later centuries to describe eschatological visions. The two main protagonists are already on the scene: the first one, characterized by his age (he is described as dressed in white and white-haired), is called "Ancient of Days"; in other words, old. The second protagonist, call "son of man," is characterized by his human appearance. The fiery throne on which the

---

[725] (Ibid, 157)

Ancient of Days sits, the heavenly ministers, and the books of judgement — all typical eschatological images — are already present here as well.[726]

It is important to notice that in the Daniel passage, the Ancient of Days confers power upon the Son of Man. Sabino Chialà sums these up as "dominion, glory, and kingdom." When Jesus appropriated the term "Son of Man" for Himself, He was appropriating this imagery. Moreover, when He used the phrase "Kingdom of God" or "Kingdom of Heaven," He was referring to the kingdom conferred upon Him by the Ancient of Days.

Fr. Thomas Hopko, in his podcast entitled "Jesus - Son of Man," describes how Jesus' used Daniel's vision in his defense before the High Priest.

But Jesus is being questioned by the high priest, by Ananias, by Caiaphas, and this is, again, the high priest, says to Jesus in Mark's Gospel [Mk 14:60-64]. He says, "Are you the Christ, the Son of the Blessed?" Jesus said, "I am"—and that is, of course, a powerful expression because "I am" is that divine name, the [Tetragrammaton] that was given to Moses. Then he said, "You will see the Son of Man ...seated at the right hand of power and coming with the clouds of heaven."

Now, do you remember in Daniel, how it spoke about "the one like unto a son of man coming on the clouds"? The clouds are mentioned there. No Jew, knowing Scripture, could hear that sentence without thinking of Daniel: "the son of man coming on the clouds in power," in God's power, in the power of the Ancient of Days, in the power of him who sits upon the throne, to whom is sung, "Holy, holy, holy. Holy God, holy Mighty, holy Immortal, have mercy on us."

So Jesus said, "You will see the Son of Man"—he uses that expression again—"seated at the right hand of power and

---

[726] (Ibid, 157)

coming with the clouds of heaven." And it says in Mark, "The high priest tore his garments and said, 'Why do we need anything more? He blasphemes. He's got to be crucified.'"[727]

Fr. Hopko is correct when he claims the account of Jesus before the High Priest relies heavily on the book of Daniel. But the importance of the title "Son of Man," and in particular its messianic relevance, grew in the second temple literature. It was interpreted, expanded upon, used in different ways and different contexts. Steeped as they were in Second Temple apocalyptic literature, the Jews of Jesus' day clearly understood what Jesus meant when he called himself the "Son of Man." Indeed, this is their rationale for the crucifixion (Mat 26:64-66).

The appropriation of the Old Testament's apocalyptic imagery within Second Temple literature becomes increasingly clear when we examine the Parables of Enoch. Sabino Chialà writes:

In the Book of Parables, what was only a «symbol» or «metaphor» in the book of Daniel — at least in chap. 7 — becomes a «character» to whom precise traits and functions are attributed. The Book of Parables reproduces Daniel's entire iconographic repertoire. In the text, passages of Daniel are cited almost word for Word, but they are used to indicate different realities.[728]

Sabino Chialà then points out that Enoch's *Book of Parables* makes additions to the iconography of Daniel.[729] He writes:

Before the author describes the Son of Man's functions, he tells us about his origins, and here too the Book of Parables is entirely independent from Daniel. By giving the Son of Man certain prerogatives, the text stresses his "messianic" nature,

---

[727] (Hopko 2009)
[728] (Boccaccini 2007, 159)
[729] (Ibid, 159)

an element absent from the book of Daniel. This Son of Man is the support for the righteous ones, the light of the Gentiles, the hope of those who suffer, the Chosen one. The language is clearly that of Isaiah, and is borrowed from those passages of Isaiah that have strongly messianic overtones.[730]

Unfortunately, Sabino Chialà draws an unwarranted connection between the Son of Man and the Messiah. In Second Temple Judaism, these were two different characters with entirely different origins. James H. Charlesworth writes: "In Jewish texts that defined Jesus' Judaism, the son of Man is a celestial and heavenly being and the Messiah is a human anointed by God to serve him on earth."[731] We are correct in linking the two, but we should be clear that the Jews do not (and did not) share our understanding.

The Son of Man in the New Testament

The title "Son of Man" is used over 80 times in the New Testament, and most of the uses are in the Gospels.[732] The phrase is Jesus' favorite way of referring to Himself. Unfortunately, our ignorance of Second Temple literature

---

[730] (Ibid, 161)

[731] (Charlesworth and Bock, Parables of Enoch: A Paradigm Shift 2013, xi) When Caiaphas the High Priest asked Jesus if he was the Christ (the Messiah) and the Son of God, he was asking a loaded question. Since the Judaism of Jesus' day differentiated between the Messiah and the Son of Man, Jesus could not claim to be the one without repudiating His claim upon the other. Instead, Jesus claimed both human and divine origin, something unacceptable to the thoroughly Hellenized Jewish leaders.

[732] In the account of the protomartyr in the Acts of the Apostles, Stephen uses the Son of Man as a title when addressing the Sanhedrin (Acts 7:56). In Revelation we have two mentions of the Son of Man, both used as a Title (Re 1:13; 14:14). Hebrews quotes an OT Psalm in which Son of Man is a term, not a title (He 2:6; cf. Ps 8:4); however, the author expands upon this passage in a manner consistent with the Enoch tradition.

has led to difficulties in understanding Jesus' intention, as well as a misunderstanding of what Jesus' hearers understood Him to mean. For example, Merrill F. Unger says:

It portrays Him as the Representative Man. It designates Him as the "last Adam" in distinction to the "first man Adam: (I Cor 15:45). The "Son of Man" is our Lord's racial name, as the "Son of David" is distinctly his Jewish name and "the Son of God" His Divine Name.[733]

Merrill F. Unger goes on to point out the title's use in Old Testament prophecy, saying it indicates that the "Messiah as the Representative Man[734]" is "chosen, spiritually endowed and designated by God."[735] He ignores the eschatological connections and messianic implications of the title and how the Jews would have understood it. Paul Owen writes:

At the same time that The Parables of Enoch was most likely circulating in Palestine (early first century CE), the historical Jesus was speaking of himself by way of allusion to Dan 7:13 through the "son of man" expression.[736]

Ignorance of the Second Temple context for Jesus use of the phrase 'Son of Man' has theological consequences. Instead of focusing on the title's importance to Jesus' self-identification as divine, Protestants read their satisfaction theory of the atonement into their understanding of the title. By doing so, they distort the Scriptures, making Jesus say things he never

---

[733] (Unger 1966, 1038)

[734] The idea of a "representative man" is sometimes used in a political sense. The idea is that God operates on a federal system. Adam was the first representative man, and when our representative fell, we all became guilty of Adam's sin. Jesus is the last Adam, the final representative man, and by his sinless live, death, and resurrection the penalty for original sin was lifted.

[735] (Ibid, 1038)

[736] (Owen 2013, 120)

intended. Jesus never claimed to be Unger's "representative man"; instead, he claimed to be a celestial, pre-existent being, the Redeemer of his people Israel, and the One predestined for a throne in heaven.

The Son of Man as a Circumlocution

In 1965, Geza A. Vermes set the scholarly world ablaze with his depiction of the phrase 'Son of Man' in Aramaic. In a comprehensive (although admittedly not exhaustive) survey of Aramaic literature, he noted that the Aramaic equivalent was often used as a "circumlocutionary self-reference"[737] *— "that 'Son of Man' was the speaker's particular way to allude to himself in special circumstances."*[738] He writes:

The circumstances requiring evasion or equivocation of this kind are multiple. The motive may be modesty. As the French say, "Le moi est haïssable" ("the 'I is detestable"). To declare, "I have the authority to pardon sins" sounds pretentious and offensive. To say, "the son of man" has this power is more discreet and acceptable.[739]

To demonstrate his thesis, Geza A. Vermes provides the following examples that demonstrate Jesus' use of circumlocutionary self-reference:

---

[737] "Let me make my point as clear as I possibly can. A circumlocutional self-reference is a statement made by a speaker about himself, framed in the third person form with "son of man" as the surrogate. In circumstances of modesty, self-effacement, fear or awe, this speaker uses roundabout talk because he does not want to call a spade a spade. Understood in this meaning, the "son of man" idiom makes full sense and can be applied to all the Gospel passages that display the corresponding Greek phraseology. [Emphasis in the original] (Charlesworth and Bock, Parables of Enoch: A Paradigm Shift 2013, 9)

[738] (Vermes, The Son of Man Debate Revisited 2013, 3)

[739] (Ibid, 9)

Appendix B: Second Temple Writings and the Bible

New Testament "son of man" / "I" parallel sayings[740]
1. Lk 6:22 Blessed are you when men hate you on account of the *son of man*.

Mt 5:11 Blessed are you when men revile you ...on *my* account.

2. Mk 2:10 That you may know that the *son of man* has authority to forgive sins ...*I* say to you take up your pallet and go home.

Lk 5:24 That you may know that the *son of man* has authority on earth to forgive sins ...I say to you, rise, take up your bed and go home.

Mt 9:6 That you may know that the *son of man* has authority on earth to forgive sins – he then said to the paralytic – rise, take up your bed and go home.

3. Mt 16:13 who do men say that the *son of man* is?
Mk 8:27 who do men say that *I* am?
Lk 9:18 who do people say that *I* am?
4. Mk 10:45 The *son of man* came not to be served but to serve.

Mt 20:28 The *son of man* came not to be served but to serve.

Lk 22:27 *I* am among you as one who serves.
[Emphasis in the original]

The main problem with Geza A. Vermes' proposal is that he is closing the door on other interpretations. It is obvious that Jesus Christ is referring to himself when he uses the term 'Son of Man.' However, to state that Jesus' use of "Son of Man" is only a circumlocution is wrong. Jesus has no problem using the first person — the most famous example is the following: "Jesus said unto them, Verily, verily, I say unto you, Before Abraham was, I am" (Jo 8:58). Moreover, He uses both the first person and the phrase 'Son of Man' in the same sentence: "When Jesus came into the coasts of Caesarea Philippi, he asked his disciples, saying, Whom do men say that I the Son of man am?" (Mt 16:13) In another famous

---

[740] (Ibid, 16)

instance, Jesus is obviously referring to Himself as the apocalyptic 'Son of Man,' but in a manner at odds with Jewish tradition, something that troubles the disciples:

And he began to teach them, that the Son of man must suffer many things, and be rejected of the elders, and of the chief priests, and scribes, and be killed, and after three days rise again.

And he spake that saying openly. And Peter took him, and began to rebuke him.

But when he had turned about and looked on his disciples, he rebuked Peter, saying, Get thee behind me, Satan: for thou savourest not the things that be of God, but the things that be of men (Mt 8:31-33).

James D. G. Dunn is a contemporary of Geza A. Vermes but takes a very different approach. Using the Gospel of Mark, he demonstrates that Jesus uses 'Son of Man' as more than a circumlocutionary self-reference. He points out that this term was both a title and a term of authority.[741] Dunn makes the point that dismissing these references as a Semitic reference to Himself as a fellow human being doesn't work:

In Mark's usage the phrase once again has to be understood in a titular sense – "the son of Man." Moreover, if we give the context and central position of the first Passion prediction (Mk 8:31) the significance it seems to deserve, we have to infer that for Mark (and his tradition?) the title "the son of Man" was a more appropriate or effective designation for Jesus than "Messiah" (8:27-33).[742]

Dunn goes on to point out that the 'suffering Son of Man sayings' in Mark have no counterpart in Enoch, but refer to the use of 'Son of Man' in Daniel.

---

[741] (Dunn 2013, 19)

[742] (Ibid, 24)

Here the most striking feature, of course, is that the most obvious root of such "son of Man" reflection in second temple Judaism (Dan 7:13-14) includes a considerable degree of suffering. That is, the interpretation already given to Daniel's vision in Daniel 7 presupposes that the man-like figure ("one like a son of man") symbolizes or represents "the saints of the Most high." For it is "the saints of the Most high" who suffer horrendously (7:7, 19-21, 23-25), and it is "the saints of the Most High" who thereafter receive the dominion and kingship given to the "one like a son of man" (7:13-14, 22, 26-27). If we are to look for a precedent or root for the idea of the son of Man as a representative figure vindicated and exalted after intense suffering, then we hardly need to look beyond Daniel's vision and its interpretation.[743]

When we read the Christ event back into the Old Testament, connections such as this are obvious. But for the disciples, it was less clear. The Son of Man was thought to be a celestial being, and how could celestial beings suffer? This why the disciples reacted so strongly to Jesus' suggestions. They could understand the suffering of a mere mortal, but not of the 'Son of Man.'

Jesus' use of Eschatological Titles

These four titles — Righteous One, Anointed One, Chosen One, and Son of Man — ultimately represent the same person. These are messianic titles, referring to a celestial, preexistent being come to save his people, a being who was then seated upon a heavenly throne and judged the world. When Jesus referred to Himself as the Son of Man, he was using a common eschatological title. The Jews would have understood the eschatological import of what He was saying, for they were living in expectation of their Messiah.

However, we already mentioned that not all the references to the Righteous One are messianic. And we have the case in Enoch 71 where the term "Son of Man" refers to

---

[743] (Ibid, 24)

Enoch. This last is in line with the Old Testament use of the term, where it sometimes refers to an ordinary human, and at other times to a celestial being. And in Second Temple literature the Son of Man and the Messiah were two different characters. We are combining the terms as Jesus did, something that scandalized the Jewish leaders.

10: Second Temple Writings and the Canon

Second Temple literature is important to us as Christians. From it, we gain a better understanding of the expectations of the Jews, expectations which inform our understanding of the Scriptures. Jesus used Second Temple themes and terms in his discourses; understanding Second Temple literature helps us understand Jesus in the way he expected to be understood. We find the thematic material of Second Temple literature throughout the New Testament. The apostle John used the apocalyptic genre and gave its thematic material a Christological twist.

Given all this, why didn't more of this Second Temple literature make it into the canon? Perhaps the best way to answer this is to ask why 1 Enoch, in particular, did not make it into the canon.

The brief, tantalizing mention of Enoch in Genesis was enough to spawn an Enochian apocalyptic sub-genre. This ranges from 1 Enoch, which is relatively sober, to versions seemingly written in answer to a challenge: "Can you top this?" In contrast to 2 Enoch, for example, the Revelation of St. John seems relatively tame. John's Revelation spends more time in describing the heavenly judgments than on his accounts of the heavenly liturgy. 2 Enoch, by way of contrast, begins with an account of Enoch's travel through the various heavens, each more fantastic than the last. 2 Enoch is tied to the ancient cosmology in a way that Revelation is not. 3 Enoch is even wilder and is as much a mystical text as it is an apocalypse.

Perhaps the biggest difference between the Apocrypha and other Second Temple literature lies in their treatment of the heavenly realm. Second Temple literature is preoccupied with describing what heaven is like, whereas the Protestant Apocrypha avoids the subject. Heaven, like God in His essence, is veiled in silence, hidden in shadow, glimpsed but never seen. The Bible speaks more of Hell than of Heaven, and yet we know very little about Hell. Much of Second Temple literature has more in common with Dante's Divine

Comedy than with biblical literature.[744] Sometimes they approach the realm of satire, something similar to Jonathon Swift's 'Gulliver's Travels.' Some Second Temple literature bears a striking resemblance to magic realism. Take, for example, the rather matter-of-fact treatment of Enoch. All this remarkable stuff happens around him, yet Enoch is the only real thing in the book; the rest is all fantastical imagery.

Second Temple apocalyptic writings are aimed at specific issues of the day; they argue against the Hasmonean dynasty, against the suppression of the Aaronic priesthood, and for a solar rather than a lunar calendar. They imply heavenly support for their version of Judaism. Later writings are an expression of an occupied people: of opposition to Rome, of hope for Jewish independence, and the ultimate Jewish hegemony over the Gentile nations.

Another difference between the Apocrypha and other Second Temple literature lies in their treatment of the Torah. Books like Jubilees have no problem with correcting the Torah, whereas the Apocrypha are content to explain it. Take, for example, the way Jubilees altered Genesis to remove its use of the moon as a means of counting time.

Despite superficial similarities, what we have described above and in other places are clear differences between the Apocrypha and other Second Temple literature. These differences are so striking that it is clear why the church accepted the Apocrypha as Scripture, and why the remainder of Second Temple literature was left out. At a two-millennia remove, we are more likely to read our situation into interpretations of this literature, just as the Second Temple authors read their situation back into the Law and the Prophets. We would be wise to use this literature as background material for the New Testament and avoid giving weight to the more speculative elements.

---

[744] The common notion of Satan ruling in Hell comes from Dante, not from the scriptures.

Glossary

Second Temple Judaism: see Second Temple Judaism

Adoptionism: the idea that Jesus was adopted as the Son of God at his baptism, resurrection, or ascension

Ante-Nicene: the period from the Apostolic Age through to the First Council of Nicaea in 325 A.D

Apocrypha: 1) Writings not considered to be inspired, yet considered to be valuable. 2) Writings not part of the accepted Protestant canon of scripture. 3) Writings not considered to be genuine.

Apollinarians: followers of Apollinarius of Laodicea, who proposed that Jesus had a human body and emotions, but a divine mind, thus making Jesus neither fully God, nor fully man

Archimandrite: in Greek usage, an abbot of a large or important monastery; in Slavic usage, a rank given to a celibate priest, ranked just below a bishop

Arianism: the belief that the Father is a superior and distinct being to the Son (there was a time when the Son was not), and the Son is a superior and distinct being to the Holy Spirit

Axiomatic: a statement so self-evident that it goes unquestioned

Baraitha: a Jewish oral tradition not incorporated into the Mishnah; also an independent commentary on the oral law.

Canon: 1) In modern usage, a list of inspired Scriptures. 2) In ancient usage, the term denotes a table, rule, or measuring stick. 3) Canon was another term for *regula fidei*, the rule of faith.

Canonical: 1) In modern usage, belonging to a list of inspired Scriptures. 2) In ancient usage, in accordance with the *regula fidei*, the rule of faith.

Chiasm (chiasmus): a symmetric literary structure whereby a series of ideas or events are presented (A and B), with variant ideas or events (A' and B') being presented in reverse order (A, B, B', A'). Sometimes you might have a central idea (X) around which the other ideas are arranged (A, B, X, B', A').

Christology: a field of study concerned with the nature and person of Jesus Christ

Codex (pl Codices): hand-written sheets, stacked and bound at one edge, although sometimes a long sheet will be folded back and forth concertina style

Consanguineous: sharing the same blood, the same kinship, the same origins.

Conspectus: a brief survey or overview of a subject, often providing an outline.

Diaspora: The dispersion of the Jewish people from Palestine, their land of origin

Deuterocanonical: a term used by Roman Catholics since the 16th century to refer to the texts that are not part of the Hebrew Bible. (Protocanonical books are those books forming the Hebrew Bible).

Ecthesis: the use of a thesis to state a belief

Epistemic Criteria: the standards and rules used to determine the accuracy and validity of propositions claiming to be true; epistemic criteria are used to separate justified knowledge from belief.

Epistemology: a philosophical concept having to do with the foundation, scope, and validity of knowledge. In other words, how do we think, how do we acquire knowledge, and how do we recognize truth from error.

Etymology: the study of the source and historical development of a word.

Evangelical: a designation for Protestant Christians who believe in the authority of the Bible, one's personal conversion by faith in Jesus Christ, one's salvation from sin & hell, and the preaching of these beliefs to others.

Gloss: an interpretation or explanation

Glossa Ordinaria (pl. Glossae Ordinariae): A medieval collection of commentary on the sacred scripture.

Gnostics: believers in secret knowledge and that salvation was a matter of gaining that knowledge. Gnostics were also dualists, believing that matter was evil, and spirit was good; therefore, the human spirit is a divine spark trapped in the body of flesh.

Halakhic: the term *halakhic* has to do with the *Halakha*, being the collection of Jewish religious law derived from the written and oral Torah.

Hebrew Scriptures: the collection of sacred texts acknowledged as Scripture by rabbinic Judaism

Heresy: the denial or deformation of dogma, being something essential to the faith

Hermeneutics: the interpretation of a text; in particular, religious texts

Imprimatur: official approval; an official license to print or publish

Lectionary: the selection of scripture readings appointed for reading in the Divine Liturgy on a particular day of the Church calendar.

Nag Hammadi Library: a collection of twelve surviving papyrus codices found in an earthenware jar in 1945. These contain some 52 mostly Gnostic treatises, including the only complete copy of the Gospel of Thomas.

Nestorians: believed that Mary was the Mother of Christ, but not of God

Passim: used in bibliographical references for material scattered throughout the work in question.

Philologia Sacra: the study of sacred texts and determining their authenticity, their original form, and their meaning

Plenary: Unqualified and absolute

Pluriformity: a diversity or variety of forms

Polysemic; a sign or symbol having multiple meanings, interpretations, or applications

Prima Facie: accepted as true on the first impression; accepted as true until contradicted by evidence

Propositional knowledge: knowledge expressed in declarations or propositions.

Pseudepigrapha: falsely-attributed works. The attribution may be intentionally misleading or may mean the work is following in the tradition of an earlier authority.

Qoheleth: the Hebrew name for the book of Ecclesiastes, which is written as the autobiography of Qoheleth, the "Teacher" or "Preacher."

Recension: an edited version of a text

Second Temple Judaism: Judaism as it existed between the rebuilding of the temple in 551 BCE and the destruction of the temple in 70 CE.

Semeiotic: relating to the study of signs and symbols as elements of communication

Septuagint: The Greek translation of the Hebrew Scriptures. Commonly referred to by the Roman numerals LXX, which stand for the legendary seventy scholars who translated the text. May also refer to its authorization by the Sanhedrin, which was composed of seventy-two members.

Shibboleth: In Judges 12, the pronunciation of the word Shibboleth was used to determine who was an Ephraimite and who was a Gileadite. In modern usage, a shibboleth is a belief or principle used by one group to distinguish them from other groups.

Sine qua non: indispensable, absolutely essential.

Supersessionism: the teaching that the Church fulfills, replaces, or supersedes the nation of Israel. This is sometimes called Fulfillment Theology or Replacement Theology. Some Protestants reject Supersessionism, believing God has one plan for the Jews, another for the Christians.

Typology: the interpretation of the Old Testament in light of the New, where something in the O.T. prefigures something in the N.T. (i.e., Joseph is a type of Christ)

Valentinians: a particular Gnostic sect

Vernacular: The common language of the people, as opposed to liturgical languages such as Latin, Church Slavonic, and Koine Greek.

Bibliography

Abraham, William J. 1998. *Canon and Criterion in Christian Theology.* New York: Oxford University Press.

Achtemeier, Paul J. 1990. "Omne verbum sonat: The New Testament and the Oral Environment of Late Western Antiquity." *Journal of Biblical Literature* 109 (1): 3-27. Accessed October 31, 2016. http://www.jstor.org/stable/3267326?seq=1#page_sca n_tab_contents.

Albani, Matthias, Jörg Frey, and Armin Lange, . 1997. *Studies in the Book of Jubilees.* Tübingen: Mohr Siebeck.

Alfeyev, Hilarion. 2009. *Christ the Conqueror of Hell.* Crestwood: St Vladimir's Seminary Press.

—. 2012. *Orthodox Christianity: Doctrine and Teaching of the Orthodox Church.* Translated by Andrew Smith. Vol. II. Yonkers: St Vladimir's Seminary Press.

Alter, Robert. 2007. *The Book of Psalms: A Translation with Commentary.* New York: W. W. Norton & Company, Inc.

—. 2019. *The Hebrew Bible: A Translation with Commentary.* First Edition. Vol. 1. 3 vols. New York: W. W. Norton & Company.

Althaus, Paul. 1966. *The Theology of Martin Luther.* Translated by Robert C. Schultz. Philadelphia: Augsburg Fortress Press. Accessed 2016. http://www.questia.com/read/117335795/the-theology-of-martin-luther.

Anderson, Jeff S. 2002. *The Internal Diversification of Second Temple Judaism: An Introduction to the Second Temple Period.* Lanham: University Press of America, Inc.

Angel, Hayyim. 2011. "The End of Prophecy: Malachi's Position in the Spiritual Development of Israel." *Institute for Jewish Ideas and Ideals.* February 25.

Accessed January 16, 2014. http://www.jewishideas.org/articles/end-prophecy-malachis-position-spiritual-developmen.

Anonymous. n.d. "28 Bible verses about Killed With The Sword." *knowing-jesus.com*. Accessed May 24, 2014. http://bible.knowing-jesus.com/topics/Killed-With-The-Sword.

—. 2014. "Old Testament: Dead Sea Scrolls." *Institute for Biblical & Scientific Studies*. March 4. Accessed March 4, 2014. http://www.bibleandscience.com/bible/sources/dead seascrolls.htm.

—. 2002. *The Companion to the Catechism of the Catholic Church: A Compendium of Texts Referred to in the Catechism of the Catholic Church*. Kindle Edition. San Francisco: Ignatius Press.

Archer, Gleason L. Jr. 1974. *A Survey of Old Testament Introduction*. Chicago: Moody Press.

Archimandrite Ephrem Lash. 2008. "The Orthodox Study Bible — A Review." *ANASTASIS*. Accessed January 02, 2014. http://www.anastasis.org.uk/bible_review.htm.

Archimandrite Sophrony. 1991. *St Silouan the Athonite*. Translated by Rosemary Edmonds. Crestwood: St Vladimir's Seminary Press.

Archimandrite Zacharias Zacharou. 2015. *Man, the Target of God*. Essex: The Stavropegic Monastery of St John the Baptist.

Armstrong, Dave. 2014. *Bible Conversations: Catholic-Protestant Dialogues on the Bible, Tradition, & Salvation*. Raleigh: Lulu Press, Inc.

Askowith, Dora. 1915. *The Toleration and Persecution of the Jews in the Roman Empire (Part I)*. New York: Columbia University.

Aune, D. E. 1991. "On the Origins of the "Council of Javneh" Myth." *Journal of Biblical Literature* (The Society of Biblical Literature) 110 (3): 491-493. Accessed January 30, 2014. http://www.jstor.org/stable/3267786.

Epstein, Isidore, ed. n.d. "Babylonian Talmud: Tractate Sanhedrin." *Come and Hear*. Accessed January 27, 2015. http://www.come-and-hear.com/sanhedrin/sanhedrin_21.html#PARTb.

Baker, Beth Ann. n.d. "Antiochian Orthodox Christian Archdiocese of North America." *Zacharias the Prophet*. Accessed May 20, 2016. http://www.antiochian.org/zacharias_the_prophet.

Barclay, Joseph. 1878. *The Talmud*. London: John Murray, Albemarle Street.

Barker, Margaret. 2004. *Temple Theology: An Introduction*. London: The Society For Promoting Christian Knowledge.

—. 2005. *The Lost Prophet: the Book of Enoch and its Influence on Christianity*. Sheffield: Sheffield Phoenix Press Ltd.

—. 2012. *The Mother of the Lord, Volume 1*. Kindle Edition. Vol. 1. London: Continuum UK.

—. 2005. *The Older Testament: The Survaval of Themes from the Ancient Royal Cult in Sectarian Judaism and Early Christianity*. Sheffield: Sheffield Phoenix Press.

Barr, James. 1985. "Why the World Was Created In 4004 B.C.: Archbishop Ussher And biblical Chronology." *Bulletin of the John Rylands Library* (Manchester University Press) 67 (2): 575-608.

Barrera, Julio Trebolle. 1998. *The Jewish Bible and the Christian Bible; An Introduction to the History of the Text*. Translated by Wilfred G. E. Watson. Grand Rapids: Wm. B. Eerdmans Publishing Co.

Barth, Karl. 2009. *Church Dogmatics I.1: The Doctrine of the Word of God.* New York: T&T Clark Ltd.

—. 2004. *Church Dogmatics I.2: The Doctrine of the Word of God.* New York: T&T Clark.

Barton, John. 1997. *Holy Writings, Sacred Text: The Canon in Early Christianity.* Louisville: Westminster John Knox Press.

Behr, John. 2001. *Formation of Christian Theology, Volume 1: The Way to Nicea.* Vol. 1. Crestwood: St Vladimir's Seminary Press.

Bennett, William Henry. 1895. *The Book of Jeremiah Chapters XXI – LII.* New York: A. C. Armstrong and Son.

Bivin, David, and Roy Blizzard Jr. 1994. *Understanding the Difficult Words of Jesus: New Insights From a Hebrew Perspective.* Revised Edition. Shippensburg: Destiny Image Publishers.

Blessed Theophylact. 1992. *The Explanation by Blessed Theophylact of the Holy Gospel According to St. Matthew.* Translated by Christopher Stade. House Springs: Chrysostom Press.

Boadt, Lawrence. 1984. *Reading the Old Testament: An Introduction.* New York: Paulist Press.

Board, Executive Committee of the Editorial, George A. Barton, Wilhelm Bacher, and Judah David Eisenstein. 1906. "Rechabites." *Jewish Encyclopedia.* Accessed May 12, 2015. http://www.jewishencyclopedia.com/articles/12616-rechabites.

Bobrinskoy, Boris. 1999. *The Mystery of the Trinity.* Translated by Anthony P. Gythiel. Crestwood: St Vladimir's Seminary Press.

Boccaccini, Gabriele, ed. 2007. *Enoch and the Messiah Son of Man: Revisiting the Book of Parables.* Grand Rapids: William B. Eerdmans Publishing Company.

Bock, Darrell L. 2013. "Dating the Parables of Enoch: A Forschungsbericht." In *Parables of Enoch: A Paradigm Shift*, by James H. Charlesworth and Darrell L. Bock, 58-113. New York: Bloomsbury T & T Clark.

Bowker, John. 1973. *Jesus and the Pharisees*. New York: Cambridge University Press.

Brand, Miryam T. 2016. *The Benei Elohim, the Watchers, and the Origins of Evil*. November 3. Accessed May 14, 2018. https://thetorah.com/the-benei-elohim-the-watchers-and-the-origins-of-evil/.

Breck, John. 2001. *Scripture in Tradition: The Bible and Its Interpretation in the Orthodox Church*. Crestwood: St Vladimir's Seminary Press.

Breed, Brennan. 2015. *Canon: Process, Not Product?* December 16. Accessed February 12, 2019. http://www.ancientjewreview.com/articles/2015/12/16/canon-process-not-product.

Brenton, L.C.L. n.d. "Psalms 13." *Elpenor's Bilingual (Greek / English) Old Testament*. Accessed October 12, 2014. http://www.ellopos.net/elpenor/greek-texts/septuagint/chapter.asp?book=24&page=13.

Brighton, Louis A. 1999. *Revelation*. Saint Louis: Concordia Publishing House.

Bromiley, Geoffrey W. 1988. *The International Standard Bible Encyclopedia, Volume 4*. Vol. 4. Grand Rapids: William B. Eerdmans Publishing Company.

Bruce, F. F. 2008. "The Canon of Scripture." *BiblicalStudies.org.uk*. Edited by Robert I Bradshaw. Religious & Theological Students Fellowship. March. Accessed January 4, 2014. http://www.biblicalstudies.org.uk/pdf/canon_bruce.pdf.

—. 2010. *The Canon of Scripture*. Kindle Edition. Downers Grove: IVP Academic.

Bullinger, E. W. (Ethelbert William). 1909. "The Dispensational Position of the Book of Acts (Appendix 181)." *www.markfoster.net*. Accessed January 9, 2016. http://www.markfoster.net/rn/companion_bible_app endices.pdf.

Burkitt, F. Crawford. 1914. *Jewish and Christian Apocalypses*. London: Oxford University Press. Accessed March 28, 2015. https://archive.org/details/jewishandchristi00burkuo ft.

Calvin, John. 1585. *Commentary on Acts Volume 1*. Translated by Christopher Featherstone. Vol. 1. 2 vols. Grand Rapids: Christian Classics Ethereal Library.

—. 1999. *Commentary on Matthew, Mark, Luke - Volume 3*. Grand Rapids: Christian Classics Ethereal Library.

—. 2005. *The Institutes of the Christian Religion*. Translated by Henry Beveridge. Grand Rapids: Christian Classics Ethereal Library.

Chadwick, Henry. 2001. *The Church in Ancient Society: From Galilee to Gregory the Great*. Oxford: Clarendon Press.

Charles, Robert Henry. 1913. *The Apocrypha and Pseudepigrapha of the Old Testament in English: Volume I, The Apocrypha*. Vol. 1. 2 vols. Oxford: Clarendon Press.

—. 1913. *The Apocrypha and Pseudepigrapha of the Old Testament in English; Volume II, Pseudopedigrapha*. Oxford: Clarendon Press.

—. 1917. *The Book of Enoch*. Translated by R. H. Charles. London: Society for Promoting Christian Knowledge. Accessed March 15, 2015. http://www.sacred-texts.com/bib/boe/boe000.htm.

Charlesworth, James H. 2013. "Did Jesus Know the Traditions in the Parables of Enoch." In *Parables of Enoch: A Paradigm Shift*, by James H. Charlesworth and Darrell L. Bock, 173-217. New York: Bloomsbury T & T Clark.

Charlesworth, James H., ed. 1983. *The Old Testament Pseudepigrapha Volume One: Apocalyptic Literature and Testaments*. Peabody: Hendrickson Publishers.

Charlesworth, James H., ed. 1983. *The Old Testament Pseudepigrapha Volume Two: Expandions of the "Old Testament" and legends, Wisdom and Philosophical Literature, Prayers, Psalms, and Odes, Fragments of Lost Judeo-Hellenistic Works*. Peabody: Hendrickson Publishers.

Charlesworth, James H., and Darrell L. Bock, . 2013. *Parables of Enoch: A Paradigm Shift*. ePDF Edition. New York: Bloomsbury T & T Clark.

Clarke, Adam. 1833. *The Holy Bible: containing the Old and New Testaments, with a commentary and critical notes*. Royal Octavo Stereotype Edition. Vol. I. New York: B. Waugh and T. Maxon.

Committee on Theology and Church Relations (LCMS). 1995. "The Inspiration of Scripture." *Lutheran Church - Missouri Synod*. March. Accessed November 29, 2008. http://www.lcms.org/graphics/assets/media/CTCR/Inspiration_%20Scripture1.pdf.

Connolly, Bob. n.d. "How God Produced the Bible." *Purified By Faith*. Accessed January 17, 2014. http://www.purifiedbyfaith.com/NewFormat/theology/WOG/WOG_How_God_Produced_the_Bible.htm.

Constantinou, Eugenia Scarvelis. 2008. *Andrew of Caesarea and the Apocalypse in the Ancient Church of the East: Studies and Translation*. Translated by Eugenia Scarvelis Contantinou. Laval: Faculté des études supérieures de l'Université Laval. http://www.theses.ulaval.ca/2008/25095/25095.pdf.

—. 2008. "Introduction to the Bible - Lesson 2: Inspiration and inerrancy." *Search the Scriptures.* Ancient Faith Ministries, Jun 14. Accessed July 25, 2014. http://www.ancientfaith.com/podcasts/searchthescriptures/introduction_to_the_bible_lesson_2_inspiration_and_inerrancy.

—. 2008. "Introduction to the Bible - Lesson 9: The Canon part 1." *Search the Scriptures.* Ancient Faith Ministries, August 02. Accessed October 22, 2014. http://www.ancientfaith.com/podcasts/searchthescriptures/introduction_to_the_bible_lesson_9_the_canon_part_1.

Constas, Maximos. 2018. *On Difficulties in Sacred Scripture: The Responses to Thalassios.* Washington, D.C.: Catholic University of America Press.

Cross, Frank Moore. 1998. *From Epic to Canon: History and Literature in Ancient Israel.* Baltimore: The John Hopkin's University Press.

Cunningham, Mary B., trans. 2011. *Wider Than Heaven: Eighth-century Homilies on the Mother of God.* Kindle Edition. Yonkers, New York: St Vladimir's Seminary Press.

Davidson, Brian. 2012. "MT and the "Oldest Text" of Jeremiah." *Academia.edu.* November 13. Accessed March 2, 2014. https://www.academia.edu/2476942/MT_and_the_Oldest_Text_of_Jeremiah.

Davidson, Samuel. 1877. "The Samaritan and Alexandrian Canons." *Christian Bookshelf.org.* Accessed December 25, 2013. http://christianbookshelf.org/davidson/the_canon_of_the_bible/chapter_iii_the_samaritan_and.htm.

Davila, J. R. 2007. "The Book of 5 Ezra." *University of St. Andrew.* February 16. Accessed July 23, 2016.

https://www.st-andrews.ac.uk/divinity/rt/otp/abstracts/5ezra/.

de Ward, Jan. 2003. *A Handbook on Jeremiah.* Winona Lake: Eisenbrauns.

DeConick, April D. 2006. "What is Early Jewish and Christian Mysticism?" *Jewish Roots of Eastern Christian Mysticism.* Accessed August 7, 2017. http://www.marquette.edu/maqom/definition.pdf.

Dobroruka, Vicente. 2013. *Second Temple Pseudepigraphy: A Cross-Cultural Comparison of Apocalyptic Texts and Related Jewish Literature.* Berlin: Walter de Gruyter.

Dunn, James D. G. 2013. "The Son of Man in Mark." In *Parables of Enoch: A Paradigm Shift*, by James H. Charleworth and Darrell L. Bock, 18-34. New York: Bloomsbury T & T Clark.

Edersheim, Alfred. 1993. *The Life and Times of Jesus the Messiah: New Updated Edition.* Peabody: Hendrickson Publishers, Inc.

Edgecomb, Kevin P. 1880. ""Verse" Article, Cyclopaedia of Biblical Literature." *http://www.bombaxo.com/index.html.* Edited by John Kitto. Accessed February 25, 2012. http://www.bombaxo.com/verse.html.

Ehrman, Bart D. 2005. *Misquoting Jesus: The Story Behind Who Changed the Bible and Why.* Kindle Edition. San Francisco: HarperSanFrancisco.

Epiphanius of Salamis. 1935. *Epiphanius' Treatise on Weights and Measures.* Edited by James Elmer Dean. Chicago: University of Chicago Press. Accessed August 28, 2016. https://oi.uchicago.edu/sites/oi.uchicago.edu/files/uploads/shared/docs/saoc11.pdf.

—. 2012. "The Panarion of Epiphanius of Salamis: A Treatise Against Eighty Sects in Three Books." *Masseiana*

Home Page. April 25. Accessed October 22, 2016. http://www.masseiana.org/panarion_bk1.htm.

Faber, Reimer. 1993. "The Apostle and the Poet: Paul and Aratus." *Clarion,* July 2: 291-293. Accessed July 8, 2016. http://www.clarionmagazine.ca/archives/1993/285-304_v42n13.pdf.

Fagerberg, Holsten. 1972. *A New Look at the Lutheran Confessions: 1529-1537.* Translated by Gene J. Lund. St. Louis: Condordia Publishing House.

Fiorenza, Francis Schüssler. 1991. *Systematic Theology: Tasks and Methods.* Vol. 1, in *Systematic Theology: Roman Catholic Perspectives,* by Francis Schüssler Fiorenza and John P. Galvin, 1-88. Minneapolis: Augsburg Fortress Press.

Florensky, Pavel. 2014. *At the Crossroads of Science & Mysticism: On the Cultural-Historical Place and Premises of the Christian World-Understanding.* Kindle Edition. Edited by Boris Jakim. Translated by Boris Jakim. Kettering: Semantron Press.

Florovsky, Georges. 1972. *Bible, Church, Tradition: An Eastern Orthodox View.* Vol. 1. Belmont: Nordland Publishing Company.

Foley, Richard. 2001. *Intellectual Trust in Oneself and Others.* New York: Cambridge University Press.

Fores, Vicent. 1996. "The Majority Text vs. The Critical Text." *Teoria Universitat de València Press.* December 9. Accessed January 25, 2015. http://www.uv.es/~fores/programa/majorityvscritical.html.

Freeman, Stephen. 2014. "Has Your Bible Become a Quran?" *Glory to God for All Things.* October 1. Accessed October 1, 2014. http://blogs.ancientfaith.com/glory2godforallthings/2014/10/01/bible-become-quran/.

—. 2014. "The Church and the Scriptures." *Glory to God for All Things.* October 10. Accessed October 13, 2014. http://blogs.ancientfaith.com/glory2godforallthings/2014/10/10/church-scriptures/.

—. 2014. "There Is No "Bible" in the Bible." *Glory to God for All Things.* September 28. Accessed September 28, 2014. http://blogs.ancientfaith.com/glory2godforallthings/2014/09/28/bible-bible/.

Froehlich, Karlfried. 1984. *Biblical Interpretation in the Early Church.* Kindle Edition. Philadelphia: Fortress Press.

Gafney, Wilda C. 2013. "Jesus' Bible and the History Channel's Bible." *The Rev. Wil Gafney, Ph.D.* March 17. Accessed December 7, 2014. http://www.wilgafney.com/2013/03/17/jesus-bible-and-the-history-channels-bible/.

Geisler, Norman L., and Ralph E. MacKenzie. 1995. *Roman Catholics and Evangelicals: agreements and differences.* Grand Rapids: Baker Books.

General Council of the Assemblies of God. 1976. *The Inerrancy of Scripture.* Springfield: General Council of the Assemblies of God. Accessed February 8, 2015. http://ag.org/top/Beliefs/Position_Papers/pp_downloads/pp_4175_inerrancy.pdf.

Gentry, Peter J. 2014. "The Great Code: Greek Bible and the Humanities." *Midwestern Journal of Theology* (Midwestern Baptist Theological Seminary) 13 (1): 50-80.

Gentry, Peter J. 2009. "The Text of the Old Testament." *Journal of the Evangelical Theological Society* 52 (1): 19-45.

Gerhard, Johann. 2006. *On the Nature of Theology and Scripture.* Translated by Richard J. Dinda. St. Louis: Concordia Publishing House.

Gigot, Frances Ernest Charles. 1900. *General introduction to the study of the Holy Scriptures*. New York: Benziger Brothers.

Gipp, Samuel C. 2016. *What is the Septuagint?* Accessed October 28, 2016. http://samgipp.com/answerbook/?page=09.htm.

Gleason, Joseph. 2012. "Masoretic Text vs. Original Hebrew." *The Orthodox Life*. March 12. Accessed January 8, 2015. https://theorthodoxlife.wordpress.com/2012/03/12/masoretic-text-vs-original-hebrew/.

—. 2014. "The Apostle Paul's Reading of Psalm 14." *On Behalf of All*. October 1. Accessed October 12, 2014. http://blogs.ancientfaith.com/onbehalfofall/apostle-pauls-reading-psalm-14/.

Golb, Norman. 2012. *Who Wrote the Dead Sea Scrolls?* Kindle Edition. Sudbury: eBookIt.com.

Gottheil, Richard, and Samuel Krauss. 1906. "Pompey the Great." *Jewish Encyclopedia*. Accessed May 9, 2015. http://www.jewishencyclopedia.com/articles/12264-pompey-the-great.

Grabbe, Lester L. 2010. *An Introduction to Second Temple Judaism*. Kindle Edition. New York: T&T Clark.

Grass, Tim. 2012. *F. F. Bruce: A Life*. Grand Rapids: Wm. B. Eerdmans Publishing Company.

Gray, James M. 2005. "The Inspiration of the Bible — Definition, Extent and Proof." *The Fundamentals: A Testimony to the Truth*. December 22. Accessed November 20, 2008. http://www.xmission.com/~fidelis/volume2/chapter1/gray.php.

Hagenston, Richard. 2014. "8 Things Your Pastor Will Never Tell You About the Bible." *Patheos.com*. September 29. Accessed October 4, 2014. http://www.patheos.com/blogs/friendlyatheist/2014/0

9/29/8-things-your-pastor-will-never-tell-you-about-the-bible/.

Halnon, Dennis. n.d. "Early Christian History." *The Reality of the Biblical Canon.* Accessed December 23, 2008. http://www.earlychristianhistory.info/canon.html.

Hart, David Bentley. 2015. *Ad Litteram.* January. Accessed May 16, 2018. https://www.firstthings.com/article/2015/01/ad-litteram.

—. 2018. *The Vale of Abraham.* October 11. Accessed October 14, 2018. https://publicorthodoxy.org/2018/10/11/the-vale-of-abraham/.

Hefele, Joseph. 1876. *A History of the Councils of the Church: Volume II. A.D. 326 to A.D. 429.* Translated by Henry Nutcombe Oxenham. Vol. 2. Edinburgh: T&T Clark.

Hengel, Martin. 1989. *The 'Hellenization' of Judea in the First Century after Christ.* Eugene: Wipf and Stock Publishers.

—. 2002. *The Septuagint as Christian Scripture.* Grand Rapids: Baker Academic.

Heyler, Larry R. 2002. *Exploring Jewish Literature of the Second Temple Period: A Guide for New Testament Students.* Grand Rapids: IVP Academic.

Hill, EJ. 2012. "Did Larry Pierce abridge Thayer's Lexicon?" *The Online Bible Forum.* Winterbourne: Online Bible.

Hirsch, Emil G., and Solomon Schechter. 1901-1906. "Enoch." *Jewish Encyclopedia.* Accessed October 14, 2016. http://www.jewishencyclopedia.com/articles/5772-enoch.

Hirschfeld, Yizhar. 2004. *Qumran in Context: Reassessing the Archeological Evidence.* Peabody: Hendrickson Publishers, LLC.

Hitchens, Christopher. 2007. *God is not Great: How Religion Poisons Everything.* Kindle Edition. New York: Twelve.

Hodge, Archibald Alexander, and Benjamin Breckinridge Warfield. 2007. *Inspiration.* Eugene: Wipf and Stock Publishers.

Hopko, Thomas. 2009. "Jesus - Son of Man." *The Names of Jesus: Explaining the significance of each of the names of Christ.* Elwood City: Ancient Faith Ministries, May 30. Accessed August 8, 2016. http://www.ancientfaith.com/podcasts/namesofjesus/jesus_-_son_of_man.

Horton, Michael. 2010. "The Truthfulness of Scripture." *Modern Reformation,* March/April, Inspiration and Inerrancy ed.: 26-29. Accessed March 7, 2015.

Hudson, Michael. 2018. *...and forgive them their debts: Lending, foreclosure and Redemption From Bronze Age Finance to the Jubilee Year.* Dresden: ISLET-Verlag.

Islamic Awareness. n.d. "Canon of the Bible." *Islamic Awareness.* Accessed December 23, 2008. http://www.islamic-awareness.org/Bible/Text/Canon/.

Jahn, Curtis A. 1997. *Exegesis and Sermon Study of Luke 1:46-55 The Magnificat.* Essay, Mequon: Wisconson Lutheran Seminary, 1-15. Accessed October 15, 1008. http://www.wlsessays.net/files/JahnLuke.pdf.

Jamieson, Robert, A.R. Fausset, and David Brown. 1871. *Commentary Critical and Explanatory on the Whole Bible.* PDF Edition. Edited by Andrew Hanson. Grand Rapids: Christian Classics Ethereal Library. Accessed July 8, 2016. http://www.ccel.org/ccel/jamieson/jfb.pdf.

Joosten, Jan. 2008. "To See God: Conflicting Exegetical Tendencies in the Septuagint." *www.academia.edu.* Accessed February 6, 2018.

https://www.academia.edu/35581776/To_See_God._Conflicting_Exegetical_Tendencies_in_the_Septuagint.

Josephus, Flavius. 1987. *The Works of Josephus Complete & Unabridged.* Translated by William Whiston. 1 vols. Peabody: Hendrickson Publishers, Inc.

Jurgens, William. A., ed. 1979. *The Faith of the Early Fathers, Volume 3.* Vol. 3. 3 vols. Collegeville: The Liturgical Press.

Kelly, J. N. D. 1976. *Early Christian Doctrines.* 5th Edition. San Francisco: Harper & Row, Publishers.

Khomyakov, Aleksei Stepanovich. 1977. "On the Western Confessions of Faith." In *Ultimate Questions: An Anthology of Modern Russian Religious Thought,* by Alexander Schmemann, translated by Ashleigh E. Moorhouse, 31-69. Crestwood: St. Vladimir's Seminary Press.

Kirby, Peter. 2014. "Marcion." *Early Christian Writings.* Accessed January 4, 2014. http://www.earlychristianwritings.com/marcion.html.

Klein, Peter D. 2005. "Epistemology." *Routledge Encyclopedia of Philosophy.* Accessed May 3, 2016. https://www.rep.routledge.com/articles/overview/epistemology/v-2/sections/the-normative-answers-foundationalism-and-coherentism.

Krauth, Charles Porterfield. 1875. *The Conservative Reformation and its Theology.* Philadelphia: J. B. Lippincott & Co.

Kruger, Michael J. 2013. "The Gospel Coalition." *Apocrypha and Canon in Early Christianity.* March 13. Accessed July 13, 2014. http://thegospelcoalition.org/article/apocrypha-and-canon-in-early-christianity/.

Kuligin, Victor. 2008. *The Judgment of God and the Rise of 'Inclusivism' in Contemporary American*

Evangelicalism. PhD Thesis, Stellenbosch: Stellenbosch University. Accessed June 5, 2014. https://www.google.com/url?sa=t&rct=j&q=&esrc=s& source=web&cd=3&cad=rja&uact=8&ved=0CCwQFjA C&url=https%3A%2F%2Fscholar.sun.ac.za%2Fbitstr eam%2Fhandle%2F10019.1%2F1420%2Fkuligin_jud gment_2008.pdf%3Fsequence%3D3&ei=aNWRU8z-Is-OqAay14D4Dw&usg=AFQjCNG9OWVmIUQ.

Lakoff, George. 2016. "A Minority President: Why the Polls Failed, And What the Majority Can Do." *George Lakoff.* November 22. Accessed January 19, 2017. https://georgelakoff.com/2016/11/22/a-minority-president-why-the-polls-failed-and-what-the-majority-can-do/.

Lawler, Andrew. 2010. "Who Wrote the Dead Sea Scrolls?" *Smithsonian.com.* January. Accessed December 7, 2013. http://www.smithsonianmag.com/history-archaeology/Who-Wrote-the-Dead-Sea-Scrolls.html.

LCMS. n.d. "Lutheran Confessions." *The Lutheran Church - Missouri Synod.* Accessed November 20, 2008. http://www.lcms.org/pages/internal.asp?NavID=522.

Lehtonen, Hannu. 1999. "On the Verbal Inspiration of Scripture: Some Aspects from the Period of Lutheran Orthodoxy." *For Bibel og Bekjennelse: Hovedside.* September 3. Accessed November 30, 2008. http://web.archive.org/web/20050214020533/http://www.fbb.nu/nela/lehtonen.htm.

Lewis, Clive Staples. 1970. *The Last Battle.* New York: Collier Books.

Lieber, Chavie. 2013. "The Other Torah." *Tablet Magazine.* May 14. Accessed December 27, 2013. http://www.tabletmag.com/jewish-life-and-religion/132004/the-other-torah.

Lieuwen, Daniel F. 1995. "The Emergence of the New Testament Canon." *St Nicholas Russian Orthodox Church, McKinney (Dallas area) Texas.* Accessed

January 15, 2014. http://www.orthodox.net/faq/canon.htm.

Lim, Timothy H. 2012. *The Formation of the Jewish Canon (The Anchor Yale Bible Reference Library)*. Kindle Edition. New Haven: Yale University Press.

Lossky, Vladimir. 1958. *The Mystical Theology of the Eastern Church*. Crestwood: St. Vladimir's Seminary Press.

Louth, Andrew. 2013. *Introducing Eastern Orthodox Theology*. Downers Grove: IVP Academic.

Lumpkin, Joseph B. 2006. *The Book of Jubilees: The Little Genesis, The Apocalypse of Moses*. Kindle Edition. Blountsville: Fifth Estate.

—. 2011. *The Books of Enoch: The Angels, The Watchers and The Nephilim (with Extensive Commentary on the Three Books of Enoch, the Fallen Angels, the Calendar of Enoch, and Daniel's Prophecy)*. 2nd Edition. Blountsville: Fifth Estate Publishers.

Magness, Jodi. 2002. *The Archeology of Qumran and the Dead Sea Scrolls*. Grand Rapids: Wm B. Eerdmans Publishing Co.

Marlowe, Michael D. 2012. "A Brief Introduction to the Canon and Ancient Versions of Scripture." *Bible Research*. Accessed March 1, 2014. http://www.bible-researcher.com/canon1.html.

—. n.d. "Ancient Canon Lists." *Bible Research*. Accessed January 16, 2014. http://www.bible-researcher.com/canon8.html.

—. n.d. "Third Council of Carthage (A.D. 397)." *Bible Research*. Accessed January 15, 2014. http://www.bible-researcher.com/carthage.html.

Martini, Gabe. 2014. *A Book of the People: Judaism and the Canon of Scripture*. March 13. Accessed March 14, 2014. http://onbehalfofall.org/a-book-of-the-people-judaism-and-the-canon-of-scripture/.

Mastrantonis, George. 1982. *Augsburg and Constantinople: The Correspondence between the Tübingen Theologians and Patriarch Jeremiah II of Constantinople on the Augsburg Confession.* Edited by N. M. Vaporis. Brookline: Holy Cross Orthodox Press.

Maxwell, Joseph A. 2013. *Qualitative Research Design: An Interactive Approach.* Third edition. SAGE Publications, Inc;.

McDonald, Lee Martin. 2007. *The Biblical Canon: Its Origin, Transmission, and Authority.* 3rd. Grand Rapids: Baker Academic.

McGinn, Bernard. 1998. *Visions of the End: Apocalyptic Traditions in the Middle Ages.* New York: Columbia University Press.

Mencken, H. L. 1946. *Treatise on the Gods.* Second Edition. New York: Alfred A. Knopf, Inc.

Metropolitan Hiertheos of Nafpaktos. 2015. *I Know a Man in Christ: Elder Sophrony the Hesychast and Theologian.* First. Edited by Effie Mavromichali. Translated by Sister Palgia Selfie. Levadia: Birth of the Theotokos Monastery.

Metropolitan Nahum of Strumica. 2013. *Neither Will I Tell You.* Kindle Edition. Strumica: Monastery of the Entry of the Most Holy Theotokos Eleusa.

Metzger, Bruce M. 2001. *The Bible in Translation.* Kindle Edition. Grand Rapids: Baker Publishing Group.

Mihai, Vasile. 2014. *Orthodox Canon Law Reference Book.* Brookline: Holy Cross Orthodox Press.

Milavec, Aaron. 2003. *The Didache: Faith, Hope, & Life of the Earliest Christian Communities, 50-70 C.E.* New York: Newman Press.

—. 2003. *The Didache: Text, Translation, Analysis, and Commentary.* Kindle Edition. Collegeville: Liturgical Press.

Miller, Joel J. 2012. "The Real Crisis in Christianity." *Patheos.com.* April 4. Accessed November 3, 2012. http://www.patheos.com/blogs/joeljmiller/2012/04/andrew-sullivan-and-the-real-crisis-in-christianity/.

Mizzi, Dennis. 2017. "Qumran at Seventy: Reflections on Seventy Years of Scholarship on the Archaeology." *Strata: Bulletin of the Anglo-Israel Archeological Society* 35: 9-45. Accessed March 17, 2018. https://www.academia.edu/36090740/Qumran_at_Seventy_Reflections_on_Seventy_Years_of_Scholarship_on_the_Archaeology_of_Qumran_and_the_Dead_Sea_Scrolls.

Mock, Robert. 2002. "The Prophet Jeremiah and the Five Guardians of Solomon's Temple Treasures." *Biblesearchers.com.* November. Accessed September 19, 2014. http://www.biblesearchers.com/temples/jeremiah1.shtml.

Mohler, R. Albert. 2012. "Transcript: Nearing the End – A Conversation with Theologian Stanley Hauerwas." *AlbertMohler.com.* April 21. Accessed May 6, 2014. http://www.albertmohler.com/?p=31352.

Montgomery, John Warwick. n.d. "Lessons from Luther on the Inerrancy of Holy Writ." *Issues, Etc. Article Archive.* Accessed December 28, 2008. http://www.mtio.com/articles/bissar37.htm.

Morgan, Donald. n.d. "Bible Inconsistencies: Bible Contradictions?" *The Secular Web.* Accessed November 19, 2008. http://www.infidels.org/library/modern/donald_morgan/inconsistencies.html.

Multnomah University. n.d. "Doctrinal Statement." *Multnomah University | Bible College and Bible Seminary.* Accessed November 19, 2008. http://www.multnomah.edu/College/PagesProspectiveStudents/AboutCollege/DoctrinalStatement.asp.

Munhall, L. W. 2005. "Inspiration." *The Fundamentals: A Testimony to the Truth.* December 23. Accessed November 20, 2008. http://www.xmission.com/~fidelis/volume2/chapter2/munhall.php.

Murray, Scott. 2001. "Law and Gospel and the Doctrine of God: Missouri in the 1960s and 1970s." *Concordia Theological Quarterly* (Concordia Theological Seminary) 65 (2): 127-156.

Nafziger, Samuel. 1994. "An Introduction to The Lutheran Church—Missouri Synod." *Lutheran Church - Missouris Synod.* Accessed November 30, 2008. http://www.lcms.org/graphics/assets/media/LCMS/introlcms.pdf.

Neusner, Jacob. 1993. *A Rabbi talks with Jesus: an intermillennial, interfaith exchange.* New York: Doubleday.

Newsom, Carol A. 2012. "Models of the Moral Self: Hebrew Bible and Second Temple Judaism." *Journal of Biblical Literature* (Society of Biblical Literature) 131 (1): 5-25. Accessed January 19, 2016. http://www.jstore.org/stable/23488209.

Nichols, Aiden. 1991. *The Shape of Catholic Theology: An Introduction to Its Sources, Principles, and History.* Collegeville: Liturgical Press.

Nofal, Fares. 2013. "One of those killed in Ma'loula: "I am a Christian, and if you want to kill me for this, I do not object to it"." *Orthodox Christianity / OrthoChristian.Com .* September 18. Accessed September 30, 2013. http://www.pravoslavie.ru/english/64403.htm.

Örsy, Ladislas. 1987. "Foundations and Context of the Magisterium." *Wijngaards Instutute for Catholic Research.* Accessed December 26, 2016. http://www.churchauthority.org/resources1/lorsy_1.asp#teaching.

Osborn, Eric. 1997. *Tertullian, First Theologian of the West.* New York: Cambridge University Press.

Osburn, Carroll. 2013. *The Greek Lectionaries of the New Testament: Essays on the Status Quaestionis.* Vol. 42, in *The Text of the New Testament in Contemporary Research,* by Boston, edited by Bart D. Ehrman and Eldon J. Epp, 93-113. Brill.

Owen, Paul. 2013. "Aramaic and Greek Representations of the "Son of Man" and the Importance of the Parables of Enoch." In *Parables of Enoch: A Paradigm Shift,* by James H. Charlesworth and Darrell L. Bock, 114-123. New York: Bloomsbury T & T Clark.

Palmer, William. 1895. *Russia and the English Church During the Last Fifty Years.* Edited by W. J. Birkbeck. Vol. I. London: Rivington, Percival & Co.

Palphrey, Brendan. 2013. *The Secret Seminary: Prayer and the Study of Theology.* Shreveport: Spring Deer Studio.

Parker, David C. 2012. *Textual Scholarship and the Making of the New Testament.* First Edition. Oxford: Oxford University Press.

Pauffhausen, Jonah. 2005. *A Teaching: From Psychology to Spirituality.* 1. Compact Disc.

Peckham, John C. 2011. "Intrinsic Canonicity and the Inadequacy of the Community Approach to Canon-Determination." *Themelios* 36 (2): 203-215.

Pelikan, Jaroslav. 2005. *Whose Bible Is It: A Short History of the Scriptures.* Kindle Edition. New York: Penguin Group US.

Pensicola Christian College. n.d. "Articles of Faith." *Pensicola Christian College.* Accessed November 20, 2008. http://www.pcci.edu/GeneralInfo/ArticlesofFaith.html.

Pentecost, J. Dwight. 1958. *Things to Come: A Study in Biblical Eschatology.* Grand Rapids: Academic Books.

Pieper, Francis. 1950. *Christian Dogmatics*. Edited by Theodore Engelder. Translated by Theodore Engelder, Walter W. F. Albrecht, Dr. Fred E. Mayer and Lorenz F. Blankenbuehler. Vol. 1. 3 vols. St. Louis: Concordia Publishing House.

Piepkorn, Arthur Carl. 2007. *The Significance of the Lutheran Symbols for Today*. Vol. 2, in *The Sacred Scriptures and the Lutheran Confessions: Selected Writings of Arthur Carl Piepkorn, Volume 2*, by Arthur Carl Piepkorn, edited by Philip J. Secker, 78-101. Manafield: CEC Press.

Piepkorn, Arthur Carl. 2007. *What Does "Innerancy" Mean?* Vol. 2, in *The Sacred Scriptures and the Lutheran Confessions: Selected Writings of Arthur Carl Piepkorn, Volume Two*, by Arthur Carl Piepkorn, edited by Phillip J Secke, 25-55. Mansfield: CEC Press.

Pierce, Larry. 2014. ""email conversation"." *Online Bible Tech Support*. Winterbourne: Online Bible, May 5.

Platt, Rutherford H. 2007. *The Forgotten Books of Eden*. Sioux Falls: NuVision Publications, LLC.

Polanyi, Michael. 1966. *The Tacit Dimension*. New York: Doubleday & Company, Inc.

Pope Paul VI. 1964. "Lumen Gentium." *The Holy See*. November 21. Accessed December 26, 2016. http://www.vatican.va/archive/hist_councils/ii_vatican_council/documents/vat-ii_const_19641121_lumen-gentium_en.html.

Portier, William L. 1994. *Tradition and Incarnation: Foundations of Christian Theology*. New York: Paulist Press.

Preus, Robert. 1957. *The Inspiration of Scripture: A Study of the Theology of the 17th-Century Lutheran Dogmaticians*. St. Louis: Concordia Publishing House.

Pseudo-Dionysius, the Areopagite. 1987. *Pseudo-Dionysius: The Complete Works.* Translated by Colm Luibheid. New York: Paulist Press.

Puhalo, Vladika Lazar. 2014. "Question from a Facebook User." *Facebook.* February 9. Accessed January 9, 2015. https://www.facebook.com/vladika.lazar.puhalo.3.

Reformed Internet Ministries. n.d. "Truth Unchanged, Texts Unchanging? The Text of the Bible and the Text of the Quran: A Brief History." *Reformed Internet Ministries.* Accessed November 20, 2008. http://www.rim.org/muslim/texts.htm.

Richter, Amy Elizabeth. 2010. *The Enochic Watchers' Template and the Gospel of Matthew.* Milwaukee: Marquette University. Accessed May 13, 2018. http://epublications.marquette.edu/dissertations_mu/45.

Rogers, Jack B., and Donald K. McKim. 1979. *The Authority and Interpretation of the Bible: An Historical Approach.* San Francisco: Harper & Row, Publishers.

Rogers, John, and Miles Coverdale. 1537. "1537 Matthew's Bible." *Bibles-Online.net.* Accessed September 1, 2014. http://www.bibles-online.net/1537/.

Rollston, Chris A. 2010. *Writing and Literacy in the World of Ancient Israel.* Williston: Society of Biblical Literature.

Rorem, Paul, and John C. Lamoreaux. 1998. *John of Scythopolis and the Dionysian Corpus: Annotating the Areopagite.* Oxford: Clarendon Press.

Ross, Allen. 2006. "The Sadducees." Accessed December 7, 2013. https://bible.org/seriespage/sadducees.

Rudd, Steve. n.d. *Criteria used by apostolic fathers to determine canon.* Accessed September 6, 2014. http://www.bible.ca/b-canon-criteria-of-apostolic-fathers.htm.

Salza, John. 2007. "Deuterocanonical Books In the New Testament." *John Salza Apologetics.* Accessed January 30, 2014. http://www.scripturecatholic.com/deuterocanon.html.

Samworth, Herbert. n.d. "What is the Textus Receptus?" *Sola Scriptura.* Accessed January 25, 2015. http://www.solagroup.org/articles/faqs/faq_0032.html.

Sanders, James A. n.d. "English Translation of the Psalms Scroll (Tehillim) 11QPs." *ibiblio.org.* Accessed January 02, 2014. http://www.ibiblio.org/expo/deadsea.scrolls.exhibit/Library/psalms.html.

Sanders, James A. 1973. "The Old Testament in 11Q Melchizedek." *Journal of the Ancient Near Eastern Society* (Columbia University) 373-382. Accessed February 21, 2019. https://janes.scholasticahq.com/article/2168.pdf.

Scaer, David P. 2003. "Baptism as Church Foundation." *Concordia Theological Quarterly* 67 (2): 109-129. Accessed September 13, 2014. http://www.ctsfw.net/media/pdfs/scaerpbaptismchurchfoundation.pdf.

—. 2004. *Discourse in Matthew: Jesus Teaches the Church.* St. Louis: Concordia Publishing House.

—. 2000. *The Sermon on the Mount: The Church's First Statement of the Gospel.* St. Louis: Concordia Publishing House.

Schaeffer, Frank. 2014. "Author Talk: Frank Schaeffer." *Vimeo.com.* Colorado Springs: PPLD TV, November 20. Accessed November 22, 2014. https://vimeo.com/112396778.

Schaff, Philip. 1884. *ANF01. The Apostolic Fathers with Justin Martyr and Irenaeus.* Edited by Alexander Roberts and James Donaldson. Vol. 1. 10 vols. Grand Rapids: Wm. B. Eerdmans Publishing Company.

—. 2004. *ANF02 Fathers of the Second Century: Hermas, Tatian, Athenagoras, Theophilus, and Clement of Alexandria (Entire)*. Edited by Phillip Schaff. Vol. 2. 10 vols. Grand Rapids: Christian Classics Ethereal Library.

—. 2006. *ANF04 Fathers of the Third Century: Tertullian, Part Fourth; Minucius Felix; Commodian; Origen, Parts First and Second.* Vol. 4. 10 vols. Grand Rapids: Christian Classics Ethereal Library.

—. 2004. *ANF05. Fathers of the Third Century: Hippolytus, Cyprian, Caius, Novatian, Appendix*. Edited by Alexander Roberts, James Donaldson and A. Cleveland Coxe. Translated by S. D. F. Salmond. Vol. 5. 10 vols. Grand Rapids: Wm. B. Eerdmans Publishing Company.

—. 2004. *ANF07. Fathers of the Third and Fourth Centuries: Lactantius, Venantius, Asterius, Victorinus, Dionysius, Apostolic Teaching and Constitutions, Homily, and Liturgies*. Edited by Philip Schaff. Vol. 7. 10 vols. Grand Rapids: Christian Classics Ethereal Library.

—. 2005. *ANF08. The Twelve Patriarchs, Excerpts and Epistles, The Clementia, Apocrypha, Decretals, Memoirs of Edessa and Syriac Documents, Remains of the First Age.* Grand Rapids: Christian Classics Ethereal Library.

—. 1876. *Creeds of Christendom, with a History and Critical Notes. Volume 1. The History of Creeds.* Vol. 1. 3 vols. Grand Rapids: Christian Classics Ethereal Library.

—. 1890. *NPNF1-02. St. Augustin's City of God and Christian Doctrine.* Vol. 2. 14 vols. Grand Rapics: Christian Classics Ethereal Library.

—. 1890. *NPNF1-03. On the Holy Trinity; Doctrinal Treatises; Moral Treatises*. Vol. 3. 14 vols. Grand Rapids: Christian Classics Ethereal Library.

—. 2002. *NPNF1-11. Saint Chrysostom: Homilies on the Acts of the Apostles and the Epistle to the Romans*. Grand Rapids: Christian Classics Ethereal Library.

—. 2002. *NPNF1-12. Saint Chrysostom: Homilies on the Epistles of Paul to the Corinthians*. Grand Rapids: Christian Classics Ethereal Library.

—. 1890. *NPNF2-01. Eusebius Pamphilius: Church History, Life of Constantine, Oration in Praise of Constantine*. Edited by Philip Schaff and Henry Wace. Translated by Arthur C. McGiffert and Ernest C. Richardson. Vol. 1. 14 vols. Grand Rapids: Wm. B. Eerdmans Publishing Company.

—. 1892. *NPNF2-03. Theodoret, Jerome, Gennadius, & Rufinus: Historical Writings*. Vol. 3. 14 vols. New York: Christian Literature Publishing Co.

—. 1892. *NPNF2-04. Athanasius: Select Works and Letters*. Edited by Philip Schaff. Vol. 4. 14 vols. Grand Rapids: Copyright Christian Classics Ethereal Library. http://www.ccel.org/ccel/schaff/npnf204.html.

—. 2005. *NPNF2-14 The Seven Ecumenical Councils*. Vol. 14. 14 vols. Grand Rapids: Christian Classics Ethereal Library.

Schaff, Philip, and Allan Menzies. 2006. *ANF03 Latin Christianity: Its Founder, Tertullian*. Vol. 3. 10 vols. Grand Rapids: Christian Classics Ethereal Library. http://www.ccel.org/ccel/schaff/anf03.

Schlink, Edmund. 1961. *Theology of the Lutheran Confessions*. Translated by Paul F Koehneke and Herbert J.A. Bouman. St. Louis: Condordia Publishing House.

Schmid, Heinrich. 1875. *The Doctrinal Theology or the Evangelical Lutheran Church*. 4th. Translated by

Charles A. Hay and Henry E. Jacobs. Philedelphia: Lutheran Publication Society.

Schürer, Emil. 1890. *A History of the Jewish People in the Time of Christ*. Translated by Sophia Taylor and Peter Christie. Vols. Second Division, Volume 1. 3 vols. Edinburgh: T & T Clark.

—. 1890. *A History of the Jewish People in the Time of Christ*. Translated by John Macpherson. Vols. First Division, Volume 1. 2 vols. Edinburgh: T & T Clark.

Shanks, Hershel. 2007. "The Dead Sea Scrolls—Discovery and Meaning." *Biblical Archaeology Society*. Biblical Archeological Society. Accessed January 30, 2014. http://www.biblicalarchaeology.org/free-ebooks/the-dead-sea-scrolls-discovery-and-meaning/.

Siamakis, Constantine. 1997. *Transmission of the Test of the Holy Bible*. Edited by Asterios Gerostergios. Translated by Andrew Hendry. Belmont: Institute for Byzantine and Modern Greek Studies.

Skarsaune, Oskar. 2002. *In the Shadow of the Temple: Jewish Influences on Early Christianity*. Downers Grove: IVP Academic.

Slick, Matt. 2014. "Apocrypha." *CARM*. November 1. Accessed June 23, 2016. http://carm.org/early-church-fathers-apocrypha.

Spence-Jones, Henry Donald Maurice, and Joseph S. Exell. 1897. *Commentary on 1 Corinthians 10*. Edited by Henry Donald Maurice Spence-Jones and Joseph S. Exell. London: Funk & Wagnalls Company. Accessed July 9, 2016. www.studylight.org/commentaries/tpc/1-corinthians-10.html.

Spitz, Sr., Lewis W. 1960. "Luther's Sola Scriptura." *Concordia Theological Monthly* XXXI (12): 740 - 745.

St Cyril of Jerusalem. 2013. *The Catechetical Lectures of St. Cyril of Jerusalem*. Kindle Edition. Translated by Edwin Hamilton Gifford.

St John Chrysostom. 1999. *Homilies on Genesis 1-17*. Translated by Robert C. Hill. Vol. 74. Washington DC: The Catholic University of America Press.

St Melito of Sardis. 1989. "On Pascha." Edited by Jr. James T. Dennison. *KERUX: A Journal of Biblical-Theological Preaching* (Kerux, Inc.) 4 (1): 5-35. Accessed June 13, 2014. http://www.kerux.com/doc/0401A1.asp.

Stark, Rodney. 1996. *The Rise of Christianity*. New York: HarperCollins Publishers.

Stone, Michael E., ed. 1984. *Jewish Writings of the Second Temple Period: Apocrypha, Pseudepigrapha, Qumran Secratian Writings, Philo, Josephus*. Philadelphia: Fortress Press.

—. 2001. "The Apocrypha and Pseudepigrapha." *Jewish Virtual Library*. June. Accessed May 7, 2014. https://www.jewishvirtuallibrary.org/jsource/Judaism/apocrypha.html.

Swan, James. 2011. "Why Luther Removed 2 Maccabees from the Bible." *Beggars All: Reformation & Apologetics*. June 7. Accessed March 4, 2017. http://beggarsallreformation.blogspot.com/2011/06/why-luther-removed-2-maccabees-from.html.

Tacitus. 2015. *The Histories, Book V "The Jews"*. Edited by P Atkinson. Accessed May 9, 2015. http://www.ourcivilisation.com/smartboard/shop/tacitusc/histries/chap18.htm.

Tappert, Theodore G., Jaroslav Pelikan, Robert H. Fischer, and Arthur C. Piepkorn, . 1959. *The Book of Concord: The Confessions of the Evangelical Lutheran Church*. Philadelphia: Fortress Press.

Tenney, Merrill C. 1963. "The Old Testament and the Fourth Gospel." *Bibliotheca Sacra* (Dallas Theological Seminary) (120): 300-308.

Thayer, Gerald Handerson, and Abbott Handerson Thayer. 1907. *Concealing-coloration in the animal kingdom; an exposition of the laws of disguise through color and pattern: being a summary of Abbott H. Thayer's discoveries.* New York: The Macmillan Co.

The Gale Group. 2008. "Hebrew: History of the Aleph-Bet." *Jewish Virtual Library.* Accessed January 27, 2015. http://www.jewishvirtuallibrary.org/jsource/Judaism/hebrewhistory.html.

Tigchelaar, Eiber. 2009. "How did the Qumran Scrolls Transform our Views of the Canonical Process?" *Lirias: Home Lirias.* Accessed January 02, 2014. https://lirias.kuleuven.be/bitstream/123456789/253557/3/tigchelaar-canon.doc .

Tov, Emmanuel. 2008. "The Septuagint as a Source for the Literary Analysis of Hebrew Scripture." In *Exploring the Origins of the Bible*, by Craig A. Evans, edited by Emanuel Tov, Craig Evans and Lee McDonald, Kindle Locations 445-1006. Ada: Baker Publishing Group.

Trenham, Josiah. 2015. *Rock and Sand: An Orthodox Appraisal of the Protestant Reformers and Their Teachings.* Columbia: Newrome Press LLC.

Truss, Lynne. 2006. *Eats, Shoots & Leaves: The Zero Tolerance Approach to Punctuation.* New York: Gotham Books.

Unger, Merrill F. 1966. *Unger's Bible Dictionary.* Third Edition. Chicago: Moody Press.

Van der Toorn, Karel. 2007. *Scribal Culture and the Making of the Hebrew Bible.* Cambridge: Harvard University Press.

Varner, William. 2005. "The Didache's Use of the Old and New Testaments." *The Master's Seminary Journal* (The Master's Seminary) 16 (1): 127-151. Accessed December 12, 2015. https://www.tms.edu/m/tmsj16f.pdf.

—. 2008. "What is the importance of the Dead Sea Scrolls?" *BiblicalArcheology.org.* May 21. Accessed January 02, 2014. http://www.biblearchaeology.org/post/2008/05/21/What-is-the-importance-of-the-Dead-Sea-Scrolls.aspx#Article.

Vermes, Geza A., ed. 2004. *The Complete Dead Sea Scrolls in English.* Revised Edition. Translated by Geza Vermes. London: Penguin Books.

—. 2002. "The Copper Scroll." *The Dead Sea Scrolls in English.* Accessed September 19, 2014. http://www.bibliotecapleyades.net/scrolls_deadsea/deadseascrolls_english/11.htm.

Vermes, Geza A. 2013. "The Son of Man Debate Revisited." In *Parables of Enoch: A Paradigm Shift,* by James H. Charlesworth and Darrell L. Bock, 3-17. New York: Bloomsbury T & T Clark.

Vincent, Marvin R. 1899. *A History of the Textual Criticism of the New Testament.* Edited by Shailer Matthews. New York: The MacMillan Company. Accessed January 12, 2014. https://archive.org/details/historyoftextual00vinc.

Voorwinde, Stephen. 1995. "The Formation of the New Testament Canon." *Reformed Theological College.* Edited by Faculty of Reformed Theological College. Accessed September 6, 2014. http://www.rtc.edu.au/site/DefaultSite/filesystem/documents/The%20Formation%20of%20the%20NT%20Canon%20(SV)%2060-1995.pdf.

Wace, Henry. 1811. *Holy Bible According to the Authorized Version (A.D. 1611)*. Edited by Henry Wace. Vol. 1. 2 vols. London: John Murray.

Walton, John H, and D. Brent Sandy. 2013. *The Lost World of Scripture: Ancient Literary Culture and Biblical Authority*. Downers Grove: InterVarsity Press.

Ward, H. Clifton. n.d. "Marcion and His Critics." *Academia.edu*. Accessed January 7, 2019. https://www.academia.edu/38072080/Marcion_and_His_Critics_for_Oxford_Handbook_on_Early_Christian_Biblical_Interpretation_eds._Blowers_and_Martens_.

Warfield, Benjamin Breckenridge. 1882. "The Canonicity of Second Peter." *The Southern Presbyterian Review* 33 (1): 45-75. http://www.bible-researcher.com/warfield2peter.pdf.

Wasserstein, Abraham, and David J. Wasserstein. 2006. *The Legend of the Septuagint: From Classical Angiquity to Today*. Kindle Edition. New York: Cambridge University Press.

Webster, William. n.d. "The Old Testament Canon and the Apocrypha Part 3: From Jerome to the Reformation." *Christian Resources*. Accessed March 4, 2017. http://www.christiantruth.com/articles/Apocrypha3.html.

Westar Institute. n.d. "The Jesus Seminar." *Westar Institute*. Accessed June 15, 2016. https://www.westarinstitute.org/projects/the-jesus-seminar/.

Wheaton College. n.d. "Mission." *Wheaton College*. Accessed November 19, 2008. http://www.wheaton.edu/welcome/aboutus_mission.html.

Wikipedia. 2019. "11Q13." *Wikipedia*. February 13. Accessed February 21, 2019. https://en.wikipedia.org/wiki/11Q13.

—. 2018. *Chrysoprase.* September 27. Accessed February 17, 2019. https://en.wikipedia.org/wiki/Chrysoprase.

Wimsatt, William Kurtz, and Monroe C. Beardsley. 1953. *The Verbal Icon: Studies in the Meaning of Poetry.* Kindle Edition. The University Press of Kentucky.

Wycliffe, John. 2008. "John Wycliffe's Translation." *Wesley Center Online.* January 14. Accessed September 1, 2015. http://wesley.nnu.edu/fileadmin/imported_site/wycliffe/wycbible-all.pdf.

Index

1 Enoch. 89, 408, 409, 417, 418, 419, 421, 430, 431, 432, 433, 434, 435, 436, 437, 438, 439, 440, 441, 442, 443, 452, 476
1 Esdras 19, 20, 60
1 Maccabees 20, 60, 274, 295, 312, 327
1 Peter 100, 273, 295, 357
2 Baruch 444
2 Enoch 407, 409, 418, 421, 422, 476
2 Esdras 19, 20, 41, 352, 353, 363, 364, 383
2 Maccabees 20, 293, 310, 326, 339, 341, 349, 361, 362, 365, 366
3 Enoch 418
4 Ezra 363
5 Ezra 363, 364
6 Ezra 363
Abraham, William J. 108, 129, 130, 131
Acts 25, 26, 39, 76, 100, 112, 121, 122, 127, 137, 139, 144, 148, 149, 170, 235, 255, 265, 287, 310, 335, 347, 356, 366, 382, 384, 391, 392, 399
Ad fontes 216, 248
Alfeyev, Hilarion 169, 357
Alter, Robert 244
Althaus, Paul 113
Amanuensis 91, 94, 147
Ancient Hebrew 238, 241
Anderson, Jeff S. 11
Andrae, Jacob 220, 221
Angel, Hayyim 150
Ante-Nicene Fathers 14, 205
Antiochus IV Epiphanes 236, 274
Apostle John 103, 111, 141, 245, 310, 336, 386, 397, 427, 428, 476
Apostle Paul . 23, 36, 47, 76, 98, 139, 163, 165, 170, 176, 177, 185, 198, 286, 295, 296, 313, 316, 318, 322, 323, 362, 392
Apostle Peter. 98, 121, 125, 139, 168, 170, 176, 217, 221, 349, 371, 392
Apostol .... See Apostolos
Apostolic Constitutions 389, 417
Apostolos 53, 95

Index

Aquila the Proselyte 61
Aquinas, Thomas 130, 131, 132, 169, 374
Aramaic 39, 44, 45, 61, 208, 235, 236, 379, 466
Archangel Michael 423
Archangel Raphael 271
Archer, Gleason 59
Archer, Gleason L. Jr. 233
Arianism 99, 245, 478
Ark (of the Covenant) 338
Ark of the Covenant 337, 338, 426, 427
Armenian Church 3
Armstrong, Dave 115
Artexerxes 59, 293
Asaph 260
Assemblies of God 186
Atheists, New 191
Atonement 427, 470
Augsburg Confession 33
Authoritative text 50, 55, 215, 216, 241, 248
Authorship 196
Autographs 181, 194, 197, 198, 205, 210, 215, 216, 217
Babylon 39, 45, 90, 93, 247, 284, 367, 379, 396, 398
Babylonian captivity 89, 339, 380, 411, 426
Babylonians 259, 339
Barker, Margaret 13, 234, 405, 408, 414, 418
Barrera, Julio Trebolle 10, 125, 232, 235, 238
Barth, Karl 3, 152, 204
Barton, John 14
Baruch 19, 20, 94, 144, 147, 255, 283, 284, 285, 291, 368, 382, 387, 400, 402
Basil the Great 102
Beatitudes 300
Behr, John 25, 35, 98, 131, 158, 190
Ben Sira 64, 86, 87, 235, 272, 278, 352, 353, 379
ben Zakkai, Yohanan 256
Bennett, William Henry 94
Blessed Theophylact 269
Blivin, David 208

Blizzard, Roy Jr. 208
Boadt, Lawrence 247, 248
Bobrinskoy, Boris..31
Breck, John 35
Bruce, F.F. 2, 6, 7, 16, 17, 21, 30, 62, 64, 66, 101, 141, 148, 254, 256, 264
Bullinger, E.W. 122
Burkitt, F. Crawford 411
Byzantine Majority...56
Calendar, Gregorian 420, 421
Calendar, Julian...420
Calendar, Lunar 416, 419, 477
Calendar, Solar 419, 420, 453
Calvin, John 116, 117, 119, 120, 122, 172, 173, 174, 175, 176, 184, 241, 242, 351
Canon of scripture ....viii, ix, 3, 134, 217, 368, 478
Chadwick, Henry 266, 272
Chaldaic..380
Charles, Robert Henry 2, 405, 412, 452
Charlesworth, James H. 444, 464, 469
Chialà, Sabino 465, 466, 467, 468, 469
Christology 32, 96, 123, 225, 226, 291, 297, 317, 399, 426, 476, 479
Chronicles 51, 139, 149, 391, 392, 394, 400
Church of England..17
Church, invisible..133, 164
Clarke, Adam...50, 240
Clement of Alexandria..183, 186
Codex 29, 53, 374
Codex Alexandrius 140
Codex Sinaiticus 195, 384
Codex Sinaticus 2
Codex Vaticanus..195
codices ....*See* Codex
Colossians 78, 149
Community-Canon..... 109, 118, 119, 127, 129, 133, 135, 158, 161, 168, 169, 178
Congar, Yves Marie Joseph Cardinal......................................130
Connolly, Bob...375

Index

Constantine the Great 101, 135
Constantinou, Eugenia 96, 97, 102, 117
Continental Congress 20, 21
Corinthians 76, 131, 150, 164, 265, 290, 291, 348, 362, 385
Council of Carthage III 392
Council of Chalcedon 26
Council of Ephesus 26
Council of Hippo 391
Council of Jamnia 256
Council of Nicea 205
Council of Rome 390
Council of Trent 105, 119, 133
Council of Trullo
   Quinisext Council 102
Critical Text 56
Dallas Theological Seminary 264, 396
Damasine List 138, 390
Daniel .. 51, 53, 54, 60, 139, 141, 142, 143, 273, 285, 306, 366, 379, 386, 387, 388, 389, 391, 392, 393, 400, 462, 464, 465, 466, 467, 468
Dawkins, Richard 191
de Vaux, Roland 5
Dead Sea Scrolls ix, xii, 5, 15, 33, 43, 47, 60, 61, 92, 208, 216, 231, 232, 233, 234, 235, 236, 237, 240, 241, 245, 247, 248, 249, 250, 251, 252, 253, 254, 339, 374, 379, 394, 401, 408, 418, 422, 452
Demiurge 110
Deuterocanonical 14, 43, 260, 261, 381, 479
Deuteronomy 17, 90, 139, 391, 392, 394
Diaspora, Jewish 6, 251, 254
Diatesseron 99, 100
Didache 16, 98, 167, 384
Diodore of Tarsus 185
Dispensationalist 284
Divina pagina 130
Eastern Orthodox 2, 15, 21, 95, 136, 169, 220
Ebionites 207
Ecclesiastes 10, 51, 60, 139, 391, 393, 394, 400, 482
Ecclesiasticus . 19, 20, 139, 272, 304, 324, 325, 352, 391, 393, 394, 400, 423

Ecumenical Council 96, 135
  Ecumenical Council, First 205
  Ecumenical Council, Fourth 25
Edersheim, Alfred 39, 60, 61, 233, 380, 401, 460
Egyptians 72, 334
Ehrman, Bart 75, 77, 78, 79, 80, 81, 195, 196, 210, 219
Enlightenment, The 24, 130
Enoch 2, 86, 87, 89, 140, 150, 166, 235, 266, 267, 293, 324, 325, 379,
  405, 407, 408, 409, 410, 411, 414, 415, 416, 417, 418, 419, 420, 421,
  422, 423, 426, 427, 428, 429, 430, 440, 443, 452, 461, 462, 463, 464,
  468, 475, 476, 477
  Epistemic Normativity ....See Epistemology
  Epistemological Criteria ....See Epistemology
  Epistemological Primacy ....See Epistemology
Epistemology 109, 127, 129, 130, 480
  Epistemic Normativity 109
  Epistemological Criteria 171
  Epistemological Criterion 129
  Epistemological Primacy 127, 129
Eritrean Orthodox 267
Essenes 5, 61, 250, 251, 252, 253, 254, 405
Esther 20, 51, 61, 139, 149, 235, 254, 302, 391, 392, 393, 394, 400
Ethiopian Jews 383
Ethiopian Orthodox 2, 267
Ethiopian Orthodox Church 2
Eusebius 54, 99, 101, 102, 138, 165, 166, 205, 206, 234, 308, 360
Eusibius 205
Evangelical 7, 62, 180, 182, 185, 228, 229, 264, 351, 394, 480
Evangélion 95
Ezekiel 139, 392
Ezra 45, 51, 64, 90, 234, 251, 293, 352, 353, 379, 391, 393, 394, 400,
  413, 415, 426, 427
Festal letter of Athanasius 102
Figurative literal interpretation 397
Florovsky, Georges 32, 34, 35, 152, 153, 156, 162
Forma 183, 187, 188, 200, 202, 204, 212, 214, 215, 226
Freeman, Stephen 27, 30, 53
Froehlich, Karlfried 4, 5, 73, 89

Fundamentalist 180, 182, 183, 185, 193, 198, 210, 220, 223, 228
Gafney, Wil 2
Gafney, Will 20
Galatians 170, 198, 296
Galileans 250
Gelasian Decree 131, 138
Gematria 397
Geneva Bible 20
Gentry, Peter J. 51, 64
Gerhard, Johann. 117, 151, 221, 222, 224, 374, 379, 380, 394, 408, 409
Gleason, Joseph 47, 239
Gnostic 33, 73, 110, 132, 133, 480, 481, 483
God-Fearers 42
Golb, Norman 252
Gospel of John 141, 166, 202, 444
Gospel of Luke 99, 142, 165, 299, 345, 463
Gospel of Mark 195, 216
Gospel of Matthew 98, 141, 167, 187, 205, 206, 207, 278, 300, 303, 304
Gospel-Reductionism 224
Grabb, Lester L. 9
Graetz, Heinrich 256
Grammatical-historical hermeneutic 407
Gray, James M. 183
Great Apostasy 133, 135
Great Schism 96
Greco-Roman 6
Greek Orthodox Church 3
Habakkuk 129, 259, 393, 400
Hagenston, Richard 218, 219
Hanukkah 312
Harris, Sam 191
Harris, William 76
Harrowing of Hell 273, 353, 354, 356, 357, 360, 361
Hebrew canon 13, 63, 255
Hebrew Scriptures.viii, ix, 3, 6, 7, 10, 12, 14, 15, 43, 44, 50, 56, 59, 61,
    66, 71, 81, 91, 92, 144, 177, 233, 237, 239, 240, 241, 243, 250, 251,
    256, 275, 284, 293, 297, 308, 367, 394, 398, 400, 402, 406, 408, 465,
    480, 482

Hegesippus ... 250
Heliodorus ... 309, 310, 341
Hellenic ... *See* Hellenism
Hellenism ... 23, 61, 78, 84, 195, 233, 235, 250, 416
Hemerobaptists ... 250
Hengel, Martin ... 11, 12, 18, 25, 29, 37, 46, 54, 55, 67, 68, 69, 208, 414
Hermeneutics ... 404
Hexapla ... 54, 55, 248
Hill, Robert C. ... 157
Hirschfeld, Yizhar ... 253
Hitchens, Christopher ... 191
Hodge, A. A. ... 180, 181, 182
Hollaz, David ... 222
Holy Ghost ... *See Holy Spirit*
Holy of Holies ... 89, 338, 426, 427, 428
Holy Scripture ... 16
Holy Spirit ... x, 4, 30, 35, 103, 110, 111, 112, 113, 114, 115, 116, 117, 119, 120, 122, 124, 127, 128, 129, 130, 135, 145, 146, 152, 159, 160, 161, 162, 168, 172, 173, 174, 175, 176, 177, 178, 186, 189, 194, 203, 213, 216, 221, 228, 269, 340, 348, 350, 351, 375, 409, 478
    Holy Ghost ... 111, 121, 125, 176, 177, 212, 217, 275, 348, 371
    The Comforter ... 30, 111, 112, 119, 177
Holy Tradition ... 27, 34, 35
Horton, Michael ... 180
Humanist ... 248
Ignatius of Antioch ... 97
II Peter ... 140, 148, 166, 267
Illiteracy ... 75, 83
Incarnation ... 123, 202, 203, 255, 342, 348, 368, 401
Inerrancy ... xii, 179, 180, 181, 182, 183, 184, 185, 186, 187, 188, 189, 193, 194, 195, 197, 198, 199, 200, 201, 203, 205, 210, 211, 212, 213, 214, 215, 217, 219, 220, 223, 224, 226, 228, 229, 231, 232, 396
    Verbal ... viii, 180, 183, 185, 188, 189, 194, 197, 198, 199, 200, 210, 214, 217, 220, 221, 222
    Plenary ... 53, 192, 193, 200, 215, 216, 248, 394
Inerrant ... 180, 183, 191, 194, 197, 198, 199, 201, 203, 205, 209, 210, 212, 213, 215, 216, 217, 220, 226, 227, 394, 396

Inspiration ... viii, ix, xii, 3, 4, 24, 26, 100, 108, 117, 118, 121, 127, 129, 130, 135, 145, 146, 147, 148, 160, 161, 168, 171, 172, 173, 174, 176, 179, 180, 183, 184, 185, 186, 187, 188, 189, 190, 191, 194, 197, 198, 199, 200, 208, 209, 210, 211, 212, 213, 214, 215, 217, 219, 220, 221, 224, 226, 227, 228, 229, 375, 394, 395, 396

Interpretation, Literal 213, 219, 284, 397
Intrinsic-Canon 118, 145, 146, 147, 148, 152, 158, 169, 178
Ipsissima verba 187, 197
Isaiah 51, 53, 139, 141, 174, 213, 247, 357, 385, 391, 392, 393, 400, 465, 469
Islamic Awareness 3
Jacobean English 379
James ..... ii, 2, 17, 20, 22, 46, 56, 100, 125, 139, 140, 183, 194, 195, 234, 241, 294, 295, 296, 304, 327, 328, 329, 330, 354, 379, 391, 392, 399, 444, 463
Jamnia .... See Council of Jamnia
Jehoakim 147
Jehudi 94
Jeremiah .. 19, 33, 34, 92, 93, 94, 139, 147, 184, 188, 234, 247, 259, 285, 303, 318, 339, 365, 367, 379, 387, 391, 392, 393, 400, 465
Jeremiah II, Ecumenical Patriarch 34
Jericho 252, 254
Jerusalem .. 6, 7, 9, 13, 43, 61, 65, 66, 100, 138, 207, 218, 226, 236, 249, 250, 253, 254, 256, 270, 274, 275, 283, 284, 285, 306, 312, 323, 339, 340, 342, 362, 377, 387, 405, 426, 443
Jesus 338
Jesus Christ . 29, 33, 65, 89, 111, 141, 157, 163, 171, 177, 182, 187, 194, 201, 202, 203, 206, 212, 227, 228, 237, 249, 257, 273, 275, 278, 292, 298, 310, 320, 330, 348, 354, 382, 399, 408, 409, 413, 422, 426, 437, 470, 474, 479, 480
Jesus of Nazareth .... See Jesus Christ
Jesus Seminar 217
Jesus son of Sirach .... *See* Ben Sira
Jewish diaspora 6, 63
Jewish liturgical cycle .... *See* Liturgy
Job 17, 51, 92, 139, 193, 258, 260, 285, 349, 350, 366, 391, 392, 394, 400, 465
John the Baptist 151, 202, 271, 375, 376, 377

Joseph 47, 96, 130, 239, 241, 242, 258, 331, 419, 430, 463, 483
Josephus 16, 59, 61, 62, 150, 253, 375, 427
Joshua ben Sira.. *See* Ben Sira
Jot and Tittle.. 187
Jubilees 2, 89, 235, 407, 408, 410, 411, 452, 477
Judaism.. 5, 9, 11, 12, 14, 39, 40, 42, 43, 61, 63, 65, 66, 71, 85, 206, 234, 237, 249, 250, 254, 305, 326, 327, 334, 405, 406, 408, 411, 412, 413, 414, 415, 419, 421, 423, 477, 478, 480, 482
Judas Maccabaeus 65, 236, 365
Jude 100, 139, 140, 150, 166, 177, 225, 266, 267, 391, 392, 409, 417, 452
Judith 19, 20, 139, 270, 278, 279, 307, 308, 380, 381, 383, 389, 391, 392, 393, 394, 398, 400, 402
Justin Martyr.........................13, 14, 66, 78, 164, 183, 186, 241, 249, 256
Kelly, J.N.D. 42
Kerusso.. 127, 148
Kerygma 127, 147
Khomiakoff, Alexis Stepanovich 30
King James Bible ....*See* King James Version
King James Version ii, 2, 17, 20, 22, 40, 46, 56, 194, 241, 354, 379, 463
Kingdom of God 123, 124, 283, 284, 345, 467
Koran 71
    Quran 71, 199, 203
Krauth, Charles Porterfield 27
Kuligin, Victor.. 201, 203
Lamentations 51, 400
Laodiceans..19, 78, 149
Lash, Ephram... 245
Lectionary... 22, 481
Lectionary, Anglican.. 22
Lehtonen, Hannu... 214
Levi the tax collector 299
Leviticus... 139, 289, 391, 392, 394
Lewis, C.S. 157
Lim, Timothy H. 86, 87
Literacy 72, 75, 76, 77, 272
liturgical items... *See* Liturgy
Liturgy 21

Index

Logos 111, 188, 201, 202, 203, 225, 333, 401
Lossky, Vladimir .... x, 112, 113
Louth, Andrew 54, 55, 131
Lumpkin, Joseph 96, 419, 430, 463
Luther, Martin .... ix, 2, 20, 104, 113, 115, 183, 184, 220, 371, 398
Lutheran Church-Missouri Synod 212, 226
Lutheran Confessions 220, 224, 366
Lutheran Orthodoxy 220
Lutheran Scholastics 220
Lutherans 21, 33, 220
LXX .... *See* Septuagint
Magness, Jodi 253
Magnificat 279, 382
Majority Text 56
Malachi 59, 150, 151, 375, 376, 377, 393, 400
Manicheans 418
Marcion 32, 99, 117, 132, 133, 165, 217
Marlow, Michael 264, 267
Marlowe, Michael D. 139
Martini, Gabe 65
Masbothæans 250
Masoretes 50, 196, 233, 239, 240, 242, 249, 250
Masoretic Text viii, 46, 47, 56, 58, 92, 95, 194, 216, 232, 233, 237, 238, 239, 241, 242, 244, 245, 247, 248, 249, 251, 254, 386, 395
Materia 183, 187, 188, 200, 202, 212, 214, 215, 226
Matthew-Tyndale Bible 20
Maximal statement 201, 203
McDonald, Lee 15, 27, 98, 189
McGee, J. Vernon 308
Melchizedek 409, 421, 422, 423, 452
Mencken, H. L. 191
Metzger, Bruce 50, 51, 54, 92
Michael Polanyi
  Polanyi, Michael 155
Midrash 422, 452
Mihai, Vasile 23
Milik, Jozef 5
Mishnah 66, 478

Montanist heresy 73, 100, 101
Montgomery, John Warwick 183
Moody Bible Institute 210, 229
Moses .. 4, 5, 46, 59, 87, 91, 166, 187, 225, 226, 233, 241, 251, 290, 291, 305, 312, 325, 326, 327, 337, 338, 357, 389, 392, 394, 399, 452
Multnomah University 193
Munhall, L. W. 183
Muratorian Fragment 15, 138
Muslim 199, 392
Muslims 3, 71, 199
Nafziger, Samuel 227
Nag Hammadi Library 15, 481
Nahum of Strumica 347
Nazarenes 206, 207
Nebuchadnezzar 142, 379, 398
Nehemiah 51, 64, 65, 139, 151, 391, 394, 400
Neusner, Jacob 85, 87, 187
New Testament ...... viii, xii, 2, 7, 8, 10, 14, 16, 17, 18, 19, 24, 29, 30, 35, 40, 47, 51, 53, 56, 64, 71, 91, 95, 96, 98, 99, 100, 102, 103, 121, 125, 131, 132, 135, 137, 138, 139, 140, 147, 149, 150, 158, 159, 163, 166, 167, 170, 171, 185, 205, 207, 208, 209, 211, 236, 237, 264, 265, 266, 268, 275, 287, 293, 297, 303, 318, 321, 324, 338, 341, 343, 355, 356, 378, 384, 387, 391, 392, 398, 399, 400, 404, 405, 406, 407, 408, 410, 413, 418, 419, 426, 430, 452, 469, 476, 477
Nicea 96, 131, 158
Nicene Creed 99, 348
Nickelsburg, George W. E. 452
Nicodemus 178, 285, 357
Nunc dimittis 309
Old Testament .. viii, 2, 4, 5, 6, 7, 9, 14, 16, 17, 18, 19, 30, 32, 34, 35, 43, 47, 53, 55, 56, 58, 59, 61, 64, 66, 82, 91, 95, 96, 97, 131, 132, 139, 141, 145, 148, 149, 150, 151, 159, 170, 171, 176, 186, 207, 216, 226, 233, 237, 247, 248, 249, 251, 264, 266, 267, 289, 292, 293, 297, 302, 318, 330, 335, 336, 338, 341, 343, 349, 354, 355, 361, 363, 364, 366, 368, 374, 375, 376, 378, 379, 380, 382, 385, 387, 389, 390, 391, 392, 393, 396, 399, 400, 401, 407, 408, 409, 411, 426, 470, 475, 483
Oral culture 73
Oral tradition 66, 238, 239, 416, 478

Oral traditions 5, 240
Origen 54, 138, 183, 206, 248, 253, 308
Original text .. 43, 147, 181, 182, 215, 216, 217, 241, 242, 244, 268, 452
Orlov, Andrei A. 84, 86, 87, 462, 464
Orthodox Church .... iii, 21, 34, 95, 161, 211
Osborn, Eric iv
Paleo-Hebrew 44, 45
Pamphilus 54, 207
Papias, Bishop of Hierapolis 205
Parable of the Good Samaritan 300
Parable of the Unforgiving Debtor 269
Parallelism 273, 289, 343, 344, 345
Parker, David C. 21, 28
Patriarch Dositheos 161
Pauffhausen, Jonah 319
Peckham, John C. 109, 118, 127, 132, 137, 145, 146, 161, 168, 176
Peleg, Yuval 252
Pelikan, Jaroslav 9, 39, 238
Pentateuch 5, 15, 46, 166, 247, 251, 254, 327, 399
Pentecost 30, 40, 112, 122, 124, 125, 356
Pharisee 250, 412
Pharisees .4, 5, 12, 88, 187, 202, 250, 251, 254, 255, 299, 300, 305, 327, 405
Pieper, Franz August Otto 223, 224
Piepkorn, Arthur Carl 180, 193, 201
Pierce, Larry 20
Pliny the Elder 253
Pompey, Gnaeus (General) 426, 427
Pope Gelasius 131
Pope Innocent I. 394
Post-Nicene 206, 383
Preus, Robert 188
Prophesy 32, 301
Prophetic language 378, 379
Prophetologion 53, 95
Protestant Reformation 20, 105
Proverbs 51, 139, 289, 298, 391, 393, 394, 400, 401

Psalms. 51, 53, 89, 90, 158, 185, 202, 244, 247, 343, 355, 391, 393, 400, 465

Psalter 53, 139, 392, 394, 400

Pseudepigraphic 4

Pseudo-canonical viii

Puhalo, Vladika Lazar 218

Qumran 4, 5, 6, 92, 232, 233, 235, 252, 253, 339, 379, 422

Rabbi Akiba 13

Reformation 14, 17, 19, 24, 26, 27, 56, 96, 105, 118, 132, 133, 135, 158, 161, 169, 175, 220, 241, 366

Reformed 21, 24

Regula Fidei 23, 27, 35, 103, 117, 163, 171, 398, 479

Renaissance 216, 241, 248

Reu, J. Michael 183

Rogers, John 20

Rollston, Chris 77

Roman Catholic .. viii, 2, 3, 14, 33, 95, 96, 104, 105, 108, 115, 119, 122, 124, 135, 161, 170, 174, 220, 296, 301, 356, 479

Roman Empire 39

Ruach Elohim .... *See* Holy Spirit

Rule of faith 10, 23, 24, 26, 27, 29, 33, 103, 105, 117, 163, 164, 171, 398, 479

Sacred Scripture .... ix, 2, 7, 16, 21, 30, 33, 66, 71, 74, 90, 108, 113, 117, 119, 130, 135, 139, 157, 158, 160, 161, 166, 168, 171, 175, 183, 184, 185, 187, 188, 190, 191, 193, 194, 201, 202, 203, 204, 205, 209, 210, 211, 212, 213, 214, 215, 217, 218, 220, 221, 222, 224, 225, 226, 227, 228, 265, 303, 312, 348, 395, 396, 409

Sadducees 4, 5, 12, 250, 251, 254, 305, 326, 327, 405

Samaritan 5, 251, 254, 303

Samaritans 3, 12, 60, 250, 251, 254, 327, 405

Samuel .... x, 90, 139, 149, 151, 325, 376, 391, 394, 400

Sandy, D. Brent 72

Scaer, David 117, 268

Schaeffer, Frank 156

Schürer, Emil 11, 87

Scofield Reference Bible 195, 244

Scribe ... 12, 64, 65, 76, 77, 79, 80, 82, 83, 84, 85, 86, 87, 88, 89, 91, 147, 196, 247

Index

Scribes..See Scribe
Scriptures, Self-Authenticating 108, 110, 111, 113, 116, 117, 140, 171, 176
Second Temple........9, 11, 86, 87, 234, 306, 334, 336, 399, 403, 404, 405, 407, 408, 409, 411, 416, 418, 419, 421, 426, 427, 428, 460, 463, 464, 465, 466, 468, 469, 470, 476, 477, 478, 482
Semitic 10, 23, 44, 307, 379
Seneca 81
Septuagint..viii, 4, 5, 6, 29, 37, 39, 42, 43, 46, 50, 51, 53, 54, 55, 56, 58, 60, 61, 66, 68, 69, 71, 92, 93, 95, 208, 233, 244, 245, 247, 248, 249, 251, 254, 257, 266, 380, 386, 387, 389, 394, 482
Sermon on the Mount 268, 304, 328, 344, 345
Shanks, Hershel 4, 249
Siamakis, Constantine...55, 198
Simon the Pharisee.. 299
Sirach 19, 86, 139, 143, 144, 268, 269, 272, 273, 279, 281, 283, 284, 285, 286, 287, 289, 294, 295, 296, 304, 306, 307, 311, 327, 328, 329, 330, 335, 336, 345, 352, 353, 381, 382, 383, 384, 391, 393, 400, 415
Slick, Matt 18
Son of God.....30, 122, 202, 277, 278, 301, 333, 358, 359, 406, 422, 460, 463, 470, 478
Son of Man..226, 406, 428, 431, 434, 439, 460, 461, 464, 465, 467, 468, 469, 470, 474
Song of Solomon........................... 3, 10, 60, 139, 391, 393, 394, 400
Sophrony, Archimandrite .... x, 211
Spirit of God .... See Holy Spirit
Square Script...44
St. Augustine 138, 183, 389, 392, 417
St. Clement of Rome 385
St. Cyprian of Carthage 388
St. Cyril of Jerusalem 207
St. Epiphanius Epiphanius of Salamis 206, 207
St. Gregory Nazianzus... 138, 186, 187
St. Gregory of Nyssa 112
St. Hippolytus 388
St. Irenaeus 113, 133, 183, 206, 386, 387
St. Jerome 17, 140, 207, 390
St. John Chrysostom 28, 157, 362

St. John of Damascus 138, 157
St. Pantaenus the Philosopher 205
St. Paul .... 113, *See* Apostle Paul
St. Polycarp of Smyrna 386
Staniloae, Dumitru 34
Stark, Rodney 42
Stone, Michael E. 379, 421
Sumerians 72
Susanna 386, 387, 390
Sword of the Spirit 321
Syriac Church 3, 100, 267
Tacitus 426
Talmud 3, 65, 408, 412, 416
  Babylonian Talmud 45, 66, 245
  Jerusalem Talmud 12, 250
Tanakh 238
Tarazi, Paul Nadim 34
Tatian the Assyrian 99, 100
Tenney, Merrill C. 264, 266, 267
Tertullian 39, 73, 101, 165
Textual criticism 190, 199, 210, 215, 216, 232
Textus Receptus 56, 194
The Apostolic Constitutions 98, 389
The Comforter .... *See* Holy Spirit
The communication of attributes 123
The Epistle of Barnabas 140, 384
The Parable of the Sower 306
The Reformers 17, 119, 161, 188
The Shepherd of Hermas 98, 99, 140, 167, 242, 357
The Thirty-Nine Articles 133
The two natures in Christ 123
Theodicy 347, 350
Theodotion 43, 54
Theophany 399
Thessalonians 78, 163
Third Council of Carthage 102, 138, 139
Tobit 19, 20, 139, 271, 304, 305, 308, 309, 319, 320, 332, 333, 334, 335,
  340, 342, 343, 344, 354, 379, 380, 381, 382, 386, 391, 392, 394, 400

Torah 17, 40, 45, 85, 187, 251, 452, 477, 480
   Mosaic Law 87, 90, 305
Torah: 416
Tov, Emanual 189
Transfiguration 125
Truss, Lynn 243, 244
Typology 338
   type 338
Unger, Merrill F. 375, 396, 402, 406, 407, 470
University of North Carolina 195
Ur of the Chaldees 218
van der Toorn, Karel 78, 82, 84, 235
Varner, Will 232, 233
Verbal Icon 152, 155
Vermes, Geza A. 339, 422, 452, 471, 472
Vincent, Marvin R. 197
Virgin Mary 116, 338, 339, 358, 377
Voorwinde, Stephen 24
Vowel points 238, 239, 240, 242, 247
Wace, Henry 17, 22
Walton, John H. 72
Warfield, B. B. 170, 180, 181, 182
Wheaton College 194, 210
Wisdom of Solomon 19, 20, 139, 265, 275, 278, 292, 297, 302, 303, 310, 312, 314, 320, 324, 330, 385, 388, 394, 400
Word of God ... 20, 71, 108, 110, 152, 153, 188, 191, 200, 201, 202, 203, 212, 213, 214, 221, 222, 223, 224, 225, 226, 228, 240, 310
Wycliffe, John 19
Zechariah 42, 184, 366, 367, 376, 377, 393, 400

www.ingramcontent.com/pod-product-compliance
Lightning Source LLC
Chambersburg PA
CBHW021136160426
43194CB00007B/610